Spotsylvania County Virginia

DEED BOOKS

1734–1751

Abstracted and Edited by
Mary Marshall Brewer

HERITAGE BOOKS
2024

HERITAGE BOOKS

AN IMPRINT OF HERITAGE BOOKS, INC.

Books, CDs, and more—Worldwide

For our listing of thousands of titles see our website
at
www.HeritageBooks.com

Published 2024 by
HERITAGE BOOKS, INC.
Publishing Division
5810 Ruatan Street
Berwyn Heights, MD 20740

International Standard Book Number
Paperbound: 978-1-68034-617-6

CONTENTS

Introduction v

Abbreviations and terms vi

Deed Book C, 1734-1742 1

Deed Book D, 1742-1751 110

Index 193

iii

INTRODUCTION

Spotsylvania County was formed from Essex, King and Queen, and King William counties in 1721. In 1734/5 Orange County was formed from the western portion of the county.

Earlier Works:

Marriage Records of the City of Fredericksburg and of Orange, Spotsylvania and Stafford Counties, Virginia, 1722-1850, by Therese A. Fisher. Heritage Books (1990).

Spotsylvania County Order Books, 1724-1751, by Sam and Ruth Sparacio. Antient Press. 14 volumes.

Spotsylvania County Deed Books, 1722-1731, by Sam and Ruth Sparacio. Antient Press. 5 volumes.

F. Edward Wright
Lewes, Delaware
2007

ABBREVIATIONS and TERMS

Some of the abbreviations are those made by the original clerk and others are by the abstractor.

adj. - adjoining
afsd - aforesaid
agt - against
atty - attorney
co. - county
complt(s) - complainant(s)
dau. - daughter
decd - deceased
def - defendant
DShf. - Deputy Sheriff
entrd - entered
esqr - esquire
in account with - estate was administered by
gent. - gentleman
pd - pounds
pg - page
plt(s) - plaintiff(s)
pn - pennies
pt/o - part of
Quarter - usually a slave quarter at a different location than the home plantation
Returned - submitted to the authority (York Co. Court)
sl - shillings
wit - witness or witnesses

SPOTSYLVANIA COUNTY, VIRGINIA
DEED BOOK C
1734-1742

8 Mar 1733. Deed of Lease. David MacMurrin of St. Marks Parish,
Spotsylvania Co for 5 shillings leased to Francis Thornton Junr of St. George
Parish, co afsd a 400 a. parcel of land in St. Marks Parish in the Goard Vine
Fork it being a tr of land the sd David MacMurrin took up & held by a pattent
dated 21 Jul 1732 bounded by a br of Cannons River ... during the term of one
year paying the rent of one ear of Indian corn if demanded ... . Wit: W.
Russell, Robert Green, Frans Slaughter, Robt Slaughter, Augt Smith. Proved 2
Apr 1734 & admitted to record. Attest: John Waller clk. (Pg 1)

9 Mar 1733. Deed of Release. David Mackmurrin of St. Marks Parish,
Spotsylvania Co for 5,000 lbs of good tobacco sold & released to Francis
Thornton Junr of St. George Parish, co afsd ... [same as above] ... . Wit: W.
Russell, Robert Green, Fran Slaughter, Robt Slaughter, Augt Smith. Proved 2
Apr 1734 & admitted to record. Attest: John Waller clk. (Pg 1)

2 Apr 1734. Deed of Lease. Thomas Chew of Spotsylvania Co for 5 shillings
farm letten unto Hugh Gwyn of Glocester Co an 800 a. tr of land being pt/o a
pattent granted to Martha Chew dated 28 Sep 1728 in St. Marks Parish bounded
by Henry Berry, Purvise's line & the Poyson Field ... during the term of one
year paying the yearly rent of one grain of Indian corn on the last day of the sd
year if demanded ... . Wit: W. Bledsoe, W. Johnston, R. Curtis Junr. Ackn 3
Apr 1734 by Thomas Chew gent & Martha his wife & at the motion of Wm
Johnston gent in behalf of the sd Gwyn is admitted to record. Attest: John
Waller clk. (Pg 3)

3 Apr 1734. Deed of Release. Thomas Chew of Spotsylvania Co for £48 sold &
released to Hugh Gwyn of Glocester Co an 800 a. tr of land ... [same as above]
... . Wit: Wm Bledsoe, W. Johnston, R. Curtis Junr. Ackn 3 Apr 1734 by
Thomas Chew gent & Martha his wife & at the motion of William Johnston gent
in behalf of the sd Gwyn is admitted to record. Attest: John Waller clk. (Pg 3)

3 Apr 1734. Bond. I Thomas Chew of Spotsylvania Co am firmly bound unto
Hugh Gwyn of Glocester Co in the sum of £96 ... the condition of this
obligation is such that if the afsd Thomas Chew shall well & truly observe,
perform, fulfill, accomplish & keep all the covenants, grants, articles, clauses,
conditions & agreements whatsoever mentioned in one pair of indentures of
lease & release [see above] then this obligation to be void ... . Wit: Wm
Bledsoe, W. Johnston, R. Curtis Junr. Ackn 3 Apr 1734 by Thomas Chew gent

& at the motion of William Johnston gent in behalf of the sd Gwyn is admitted to record. (Pg 5)

2 Apr 1734. Deed of Lease. David Williams of Saint Marks Parish, Spotsylvania Co planter for 5 shillings leased to William Callaway of same place planter a 200 a. tr of land being pt/o a patent for 1,000 a. granted to George Pen XXVIII Sep MDCCXXVIII & by the sd George Pen sold to the afsd David Williams lying in the parish afsd near the Great Mountains bounded by the Octuna Land … to have & to hold in as full free & ample manner as is granted by patent & all deeds & writings of the same free & acquit from dowry's & other claims & incumbrances whatsoever & the sd David Williams doth hereby covenant to & with the sd William Callaway in the sum of £100 to make any further & better conveyance & assurance in the law to him as shall be reasonably required & to ackn this deed in the Court of Spotsylvania Co when he shall be required … . Wit: Zach Taylor, Wm Conner, John Waller. Ackn 3 Apr 1734 by David Williams & Mary the w/o the sd David's power of atty to John Waller gent being proved the sd Waller ackn her right of dower in the sd land & at the motion of Zachary Taylor in behalf of the sd William is admitted to record. Attest: John Waller clk. (Pg 5)

28 Mar 1734. Power of Attorney. I Mary Williams w/o David Williams of St. Marks Parish, Spotsylvania Co have made & constituted my trusty & loving friend John Waller Senr of sd co my atty to ackn, make over & convey all my right of dower in two trs of land being by my husband David sold to Thomas Callaway & William Callaway [see above], the one 100 a. & the other 200 a. of land … . Wit: Wm Login, Larkin Chew, Thos Chew. Proved 3 Apr 1734 & admitted to record. Attest: John Waller clk. (Pg 6)

6 May MDCCXXXIV. Deed of Lease. Thomas Hubbard of St. George Parish, Spotsylvania Co for 5 shillings leased to John Talbert of same place a messuage & 100 a. tr of land bounded by Robt Stubblefield, John Smith & William Pruet (Pruett) … during the term of one year paying the yearly rent of one peper corn at the feast of St. Michael the Arch Angel if demanded … . Wit: Wm Waller, Robt Turner, Wm Phillips. Ackn 7 May 1734 & admitted to record. Attest: John Waller clk. (Pg 7)

7 May MDCCXXXIV. Deed of Release. Thomas Hubbard of St. George Parish, Spotsylvania Co for 500 lbs of tobacco sold & released to John Talbert of same place a 100 a. tr of land, which tr of land is pt/o a pattent granted to Henry Haines for a greater quantity of land dated XXVIII Sep MDCCXXXI & 200 a. pt/o the sd pattent was conveyed to the sd Thomas Hubbard by the sd Henry Haines by deeds of lease & release ackn in the Spotsylvania Co Court 6 Jul MDCCXXXI … [same as above] … . Wit: Wm Waller, Robt Turner, Wm

Phillips. Ackn 7 May 1734 by Thomas Hubbard & Christian the w/o the sd
Thomas ackn her right of dower & is admitted to record. Attest: John Waller
clk. (Pg 7)

29 Jan 1733. Deed of Lease. Isaac Norman of Spotsylvania Co planter for 5
shillings leased to Nathaniel Hillin of same co planter a 100 a. tr of land in St.
George Parish being pt/o the tr he now liveth on ... during the term of one year
paying the rent of one ear of Indian corne on the day of the Nativity of our
blessed Saviour Christ if demanded ... . Wit: Augt Smith, Joseph Stapp, Joseph
Henderson. Ackn 7 May 1734 & admitted to record. Attest: John Waller clk.
(Pg 9)

30 Jan 1733. Deed of Release. Isaac Norman of Spotsylvania Co planter for
£20 sold & released to Nathaniel Hillin of same co planter a 100 a. tr of land ...
[*same as above*] ... . Wit: Augt Smith, Joseph Stapp, Joseph Henderson. Ackn
7 May 1734 & admitted to record. Attest: John Waller clk. (Pg 9)

30 Jan 1733. Deed of Gift. Isaac Norman of Spotsylvania Co planter for
naturall love & affection & £50 have given to my son in law James Turner
planter & Kerehappuck Turner my dau of the sd co a 100 a. tr of land being pt/o
a patent whereon the sd Isaac Norman now liveth adj Flat Run & John Read ... .
Wit: Augt Smith, Joseph Stapp, Joseph Henderson. Ackn 7 May 1734 &
admitted to record. Attest: John Waller clk. (Pg 11)

30 Apr 1734. Deed of Lease. William Beverley of St. Ann Parish, Essex Co
gent for & in consideration of the rents & covenants hereafter mentioned hath
farm lett to John Burk of St. Mark Parish, Spotsylvania Co planter a 100 a. tr of
land on Elkwood in St. Mark Parish it being the plantation whereon the sd John
now dwelleth bounded by Col Carter ... during the term of the natural lives of
the sd John, Mary his wife & Richard his son & the longest liver of them paying
yearly on the 1st day of Dec the quitrents & 430 lbs of top leaf tobacco in cask &
delivering the same in one hogshead at a lawfull warehouse or rolling house in
Falmouth or Fredericksburg also yearly on the 1st of Dec four fatt hens, capons
or pullets & delivering the same at the sd Williams' chief house or quarter on
Elkwood ... . Wit: W. Russell, Anthony Scott, John Sexton, Edmd Pagett.
Ackn 7 May 1734 & admitted to record. Attest: John Waller clk. (Pg 11)

11 Mar 1733. Deed of Gift. I William Crawford of St. Marks Parish,
Spotsylvania Co planter do hereby give & make over to Benjamin Coward &
Elizabeth his wife a 100 a. parcel of land adj Thomas Jackson, William
Crawford Junr & Thomas Crawford ... during the term & space of the sd
Benjamin Coward's natural life & to the sd Elisabeth his wife ... . Wit: D.
Bryne, George Anderson, William Crafard Junr. Proved 7 May 1734 & at the

motion of George Anderson in behalf of the sd Coward the same is admitted to record. Attest: John Waller clk. (Pg 13)

6 May 1734. Deed of Lease. Benjamin Rush of King George Co, VA for 5 shillings leased to Antho Strother of Spotsylvania Co a 387 a. tr of land in St. Marks Parish in the fork of Rappahanock River on the s side the Robinson River the sd land being formerly granted to the sd Benja Rush by pattent dated 11 May 1726 bounded by a survey made for Wm Rush ... during the term of one year paying the yearly rent of one ear of Indian corn if demanded .... Wit: Frans Thornton Junr, Robt Biscoe, Peter Daniell. Ackn 7 May 1734 & admitted to record. Attest: John Waller clk. (Pg 13)

7 May 1734. Deed of Release. Benja Rush of King George Co, VA for £40 sold & released to Anthony Strother of Spotsylvania Co a 387 a. tr of land ... [*same as above*] .... Wit: Frans Thornton Junr, Robt Biscoe, Peter Daniell. Ackn 7 May 1734 by Benjamin Rush & Amey the w/o the sd Benjamin ackn her right of dower & is admitted to record. Attest: John Waller clk. (Pg 14)

6 May 1734. Deed of Lease. John Foster of Spotsylvania Co for 5 shillings farm letten unto Thomas Benson of same co a 200 a. parcel of land pt/o a pattent granted to John Foster dated 17 Aug 1733 bounded by Capt William Johnston & the Nassaponnax ... during the term of one year paying the yearly rent of one grain of Indian corn on the last day of the sd year if demanded .... Wit: Edwd Herndon Junr, John Asken, R. Eastham. Ackn 7 May 1734 & admitted to record. Attest: John Waller clk. (Pg 16)

7 May 1734. Deed of Release. John Foster of Spotsylvania Co for £16 sold & released to Thomas Benson of same co a 200 a. tr of land ... [*same as above*] ... . Wit: Edwd Herndon Junr, John Ashen, R. Eastham. Ackn 7 May 1734 & admitted to record. Attest: John Waller clk. (Pg 16)

3 Jun MDCCXXXIV. Deed of Lease. Richard Phillips of St. George Parish, Spotsylvania Co for 5 shillings leased to James Edwards of St. John Parish, King William Co, VA a 400 a. tr of land on the n side the Northanna bounded by Gambrill's corner ... during the term of one year paying the yearly rent of one pepper corn at the feast of St. Michael the Arch Angel if demanded .... Wit: Wm Waller, Roger Quarles, Thos Waller. Ackn 4 Jun 1734 & admitted to record. Attest: John Waller clk. (Pg 18)

4 Jun MDCCXXXIV. Deed of Release. Richard Phillips of St. George Parish, Spotsylvania Co for 2,500 lbs of tobacco & cask & £18 sold & released to James Edwards of St. John Parish, King William Co a 400 a. tr of land, which sd tr of land was granted to Dannitt Abney Junr by pattent dated 30 Jun MDCCXXVI &

by the sd Dannitt Abney Junr sold to the sd Richard Phillips & conveyed by deeds of lease & release ackn in the sd co court of Spotsylvania 2 Oct MDCCXXXIII ... [*same as above*] ... . Wit: Wm Waller, Roger Quarles, Thos Waller. Ackn 4 Jun 1734 by Richard Phillips & Catharine the w/o the sd Richard ackn her right of dower & is admitted to record. Attest: John Waller clk. (Pg 19)

4 Jun MDCCXXXIV. Bond. I Richard Phillips of Spotsylvania Co am firmly bound unto James Edwards of King William Co in the penal sum of 5,000 lbs of tobacco & cask & £36 ... the condition of this obligation is such that if the afsd Richd Phillips shall well & truly observe, perform, fulfill, accomplish & keep all the covenants, grants, articles, clauses, conditions & agreements whatsoever mentioned in one indenture of release for land [*see above*] then this obligation to be void ... . Wit: Wm Waller, Roger Quarles, Thos Waller. Ackn 4 Jun 1734 & admitted to record. Attest: John Waller clk. (Pg 20)

3 Jun 1734. Deed of Lease. William Eddins of St. Mark Parish, Spotsylvania Co planter for 5 shillings leased to William Jordan of Lunenburg Parish, Richmond Co gent a 349 a. tr of land in St. Mark Parish adj the sd William Eddins, William McConnicoe, the Mountain Run & the main run of the sd Eddins' Mill Run ... during the term of one year paying the rent of one ear of Indian corn on the birthday of our Lord God next ensuing if demanded ... . Wit: G. Home, Zack Taylor, Jno Willson. Ackn 4 Jun 1734 & admitted to record. Attest: John Waller clk. (Pg 21)

4 Jun 1734. Deed of Release. William Eddings of St. Mark Parish, Spotsylvania Co planter for £60 sold & released to William Jordan of Lunenburg Parish, Richmond Co gent a 349 a. tr of land, being pt/o two trs of land the one containing 531 a. granted to the sd William Eddins by patent dated 30 Jun 1726 the other containing 80 a. which the sd William Eddins bought of William McConnicoe all which sd two trs the sd William Eddins sold to Duncan Buchanan & again repurchased of the sd Duncan Buchanan by deeds dated 2 Nov 1731 ... [*same as above*] ... . Wit: G. Home, Zack Taylor, Jno Willson. Ackn 4 Jun 1734 by William Eddins & Rebecca the w/o the sd Wm Eddins ackn he right of dower & is admitted to record. Attest: John Waller clk. (Pg 21)

3 Jun 1734. Deed of Lease. John Rucker of St. Marks Parish, Spotsylvania Co for 5 shillings farm lett unto William Rucker of same place a 200 a. parcell of land or woodland ground in St. Marks Parish bounded by William Fall & Micall Holt ... during the term of one year paying the yearly rent of one ear of Indian corn on the feast of St. Michaell if demanded ... . Wit: Thos Chew, Willm Crosthwait, Wm Bartlet. Ackn 4 Jun 1734 & admitted to record. Attest: John Waller clk. (Pg 23)

4 Jun 1734. Deed of Release. John Rucker of St. George Parish, Spotsylvania Co for £20 sold & released to William Rucker of same place a 200 a. tr of land ... [*same as above*] ... . Wit: Thos Chew, Will Crosthwait, Wm Bartlet. Ackn 4 Jun 1734 & admitted to record. Attest: John Waller clk. (Pg 24)

3 Jun 1734. Deed of Lease. Richd Mauldin of St. Marks Parish, Spotsylvania Co for 5 shillings leased to Theophilus Edins (Theofelous Eddins) of same place a 248 a. tr of land lying on both sides the head of the Black Walnut Run adj Edward & Richd Sharp ... during the term of one year paying the rent of one peper corn if demanded ... . Wit: Jno Christopher, Will Mackay, Jno Willson. Ackn 4 Jun 1734 & admitted to record. Attest: John Waller clk. (Pg 25)

4 Jun 1734. Deed of Release. Richd Mauldin of St. Mark Parish, Spotsylvania Co for £15 sold & released to Theophilus Edins (Theofelous Eddins) a 248 a. tr of land, which is the hole of a pattent formerly granted to Wm Edins dated 28 Sep 1728 ... [*same as above*] ... . Wit: Jno Christopher, Will Mackay, Jno Willson. Ackn 4 Jun 1734 by Richard Mauldin & Jane the w/o the sd Richard's power of atty to John Waller gent being proved the sd Waller ackn her right of dower & is admitted to record. Attest: John Waller clk. (Pg 26)

3 Jun 1734. Power of Attorney. I Jane Mauldin the lawfull w/o Richd Mauldin doe appoint Col John Waller my well beloved friend my atty to ackn my right of dower in a 248 a. tr of land unto Theofelous Edins as by deeds of lease & released which my sd husband hath sold [*see above*] ... . Wit: Henry Kendell, John Willson, Sarah Maulden. Proved 4 Jun 1734 & admitted to record. Attest: John Waller clk. (Pg 27)

5 Jun 1734. Deed of Gift. Philemon Cavenaugh of St. Mark Parish, Spotsilvania Co for love & affection & £1 hath given to my dau Elizabeth & John Conner her husband a 400 a. parcel of land in the parish afsd on the brs of Muddy Run in the fork of Rappahannock River bounded by Lewis Davis Yancy & William Beverley, to be divided between the first two sons that the sd Elizabeth & John if any such, if it should happen that the sd Eliza & John shall have but one son then the first dau to have an equal part with the sd son & if it should so happen that they should not have a son then to be divided between their two first daus ... . Wit: Wm Deatherage, R. Eastham, Robt Bayley. Ackn 5 Jun 1734 & admitted to record. Attest: John Waller clk. (Pg 27)

3 Jun 1734. Deed of Lease. Charles Stewart of St. George Parish, Spotsylvania Co for 5 shillings farm lett unto George Home of same place a 400 a. parcel of land or woodland ground in St. Marks Parish bounded by the main br of Fleshmans Run, a patent granted to Alexander Howard, a patent granted to James Horsnell, Francis Micall, John Finlason, Petter Russell, the Main Road as

goes from Germanna to the Mountain Run Bridge & the First Station ... during the term of one year paying the yearly rent of one ear of Indian corn on the feast of St. Michael if demanded .... Wit: David Kinkead, Thomas Holson, William Fields. Proved 5 Jun 1734 5 Jun 1734 & admitted to record. Attest: John Waller clk. (Pg 28)

4 Jun 1734. Deed of Release. Charles Stewart of St. George Parish, Spotsylvania Co for £20 sold & released to George Home of same place a 400 a. tr of land ... [same as above] .... Wit: David Kinkead, Thomas Hobson, William Fields. Proved 5 Jun 1734 & admitted to record. Attest: John Waller clk. (Pg 29)

28 Jun MDCCXXXIV. Deed of Lease. Robert Stubblefeild of St. George Parish, Spotsylvania Co for 5 shillings leased to Ralph Williams of same place a messuage & 200 a. tr of land bounded by Pappaw Run, Benjamin Matthews, the sd Ralph Williams & land formerly Lanford's now Stubblefeild's ... during the term of one year paying the yearly rent of one pepper corn at the feast of St. Michael the Arch Angel if demanded .... Wit: Benjamin Matthews Senr, Benjamin Matthews Junr. Ackn 2 Jul 1734 & admitted to record. Attest: John Waller clk. (Pg 30)

29 Jun MDCCXXXIV. Deed of Release. Robert Stubblefield of St. George Parish, Spotsylvania Co for 2,500 lbs of tobacco sold & released to Ralph Williams of same place a messuage & 200 a. tr of land which was first taken up & surveyed for Nicholas Lanford (Langford) & by him sold to John Collier Junr of King & Queen Co & by the sd Collier conveyed to the sd Robert Stubblefield by deeds ackn in Spotsylvania Co Court 6 Oct 1730 & is pt/o a pattent granted to John Collier Junr for 400 a. dated 30 Jun MDCCXXVI ... [same as above] .... Wit: Benjamin Matthews Senr, Benjamin Matthews Junr. Ackn 2 Jul 1734 by Robert Stubblefield & Anne the w/o the sd Robert ackn her right of dower & is admitted to record. Attest: John Waller clk. (Pg 31)

6 May MDCCXXXIV. Deed of Lease. Robert Stubblefield of St. George Parish, Spotsylvania Co for 5 shillings leased to Benjamin Matthews of same place a messuage & 200 a. tr of land bounded by Pappaw Run, Ralph Williams, the sd Benjamin Matthews & land formerly Langford's now Stubblefield's ... during the term of one year paying the yearly rent of one pepper corn at the feast of St. Michael the Arch Angel if demanded .... Wit: William Rice, Daniel Pruit. Ackn 2 Jul 1734 & admitted to record. Attest: John Waller clk. (Pg 32)

7 May MDCCXXXIV. Deed of Release. Robert Stubblefield of St. George Parish, Spotsylvania Co for 4,090 lbs of tobacco sold & released to Benjamin Matthews of same place a messuage & 200 a. tr of land, the sd land was first

taken up & surveyed for Nicholas Langford & by him sold to John Collier Junr of King & Queen Co & by the sd Collier conveyed to the sd Robert Stubblefield by deeds ackn in Spotsylvania Co Court 6 Oct 1730 & is pt/o a pattent granted to John Collier Junr for 400 a. dated 30 Jun MDCCXXVI ... [*same as above*] ... . Wit: William Rice, Daniel Pruit. Ackn 2 Jul 1734 by Robert Stubblefield & Anne the w/o the sd Robert ackn her right of dower & is admitted to record. Attest: John Waller clk. (Pg 33)

23 Feb 1733. Deed of Exchange. Between Tobias Ingram of Essex County of the one part & Robert Brooke of same co gent of the other part, whereas the sd Tobias Ingram stands seized & possessed in ½ pt/o a 333 a. parcel of land in St. Anns Parish, Essex Co hereafter mentioned & described & whereas the sd Robert Brooke stands seized & possessed in a 400 a. tr of land in St. Marks Parish, Spotsylvania Co hereafter mentioned & described & whereas the sd Tobias Ingram & Robert Brooke are minded & willing to exchange the sd lands one for the other ... now this indenture wit in consideration & in pursuance of the sd exchange & also for 5 shillings to the sd Tobias Ingram paid by the sd Robert Brooke the sd Tobias Ingram hath exchanged & sold unto the sd Robert Brooke all that ½ pt/o the sd 333 a. of land before mentioned being pt/o a 400 a. tr of land formerly sold by William Mosely decd unto Thomas Ingram decd grandfather to the sd Tobias Ingram 17 Aug 1657 & afterwards confirmed to Thomas Ingram father of the sd Tobias Ingram party to these presents by Edward Moseley son & heir of the sd William Moseley by deed dated 12 Feb 1712 which sd ½ pt/o the sd 333 a. of land is bounded by the fork of Little Occupation Cr, sd Robert Brooke, Chesehixson Br, Cabbin Br, a road that leads to Rowzees Neck, Duncan Robinson & Wasnonson Cr ... & this indenture further wit that the sd Robert Brooke in consideration & pursuance of the sd exchange & also for 5 shillings paid by the sd Tobias Ingram hath exchanged & sold unto the sd Tobias Ingram all that afsd 400 a. tr of land before mentioned being granted to the sd Robert Brooke by patent dated 20 Jun 1733 & bounded by Alexander McQueen & Philemon Cavenaugh ... . Wit: B. Vawter, Wm Balware, Henery Motley. Ackn 2 Jul 1734 each to the other & admitted to record. Attest: John Waller clk. (Pg 34)

28 Jun 1734. Deed of Lease. Joseph Delayney of Hammilton Parish, Prince William Co planter for 5 shillings leased to Robert Biscoe of Brunswick Parish, King George Co planter a 97 a. tr of land pattented by the sd Joseph Delayney 28 Sep 1728 in St. Georges Parish bounded by a br of Nussaponock Swamp, Stephen Sharp, Lawrence Smith & Francis Thornton ... during the term of one year paying the rent of one ear of Indian corn at the feast of the Annunciation of the Blessed Virgin if demanded ... . Wit: John Latham, James Roy. Ackn 2 Jul 1734 & admitted to record. Attest: John Waller clk. (Pg 36)

29 Jun 1734. Deed of Release. Joseph Delaney of Hammilton Parish, Prince Wm Co planter for £9 sold & released to Robert Biscoe of Brunswick Parish, King George Co planter a 97 a. tr of land ... [*same as above*] ... . Wit: John Latham, James Roy. Ackn 2 Jul 1734 by Joseph Delaney & Mary the w/o the sd Joseph's power of atty to Peter Daniel being proved & the sd Daniel ackn her right of dower & is admitted to record. Attest: John Waller clk. (Pg 37)

2 Apr 1734. Power of Attorney. I Mary Delayney of Prince Wm Co have appointed my trusty & well beloved friend Peter Daniel of King George Co my atty to ackn my right of dower in the land & premises sold by my husband Joseph Delayney to Robt Biscoe of King George Co by indentures of lease & release [*see above*] ... . Wit: Antho Strother, James Elles. Proved 2 Jul 1734 & admitted to record. Attest: John Waller clk. (Pg 39)

22 Jul 1734. Deed of Lease. Robert Jones of Prince William Co gent for 5 shillings leased to John Mercer of Stafford Co gent a 1,000 a. tr of land in the little fork of Rappahannock River on the s side of the North River bounded by Beverdam Run ... during the term of one year paying the rent of one pepper corn upon the feast of St. Michael the Arch Angel if demanded ... . Wit: Charles Brent, James Porteus, Thos Staines, Robt Turner, Js Mercer. Ackn 6 Aug 1734 & admitted to record. Attest: John Waller clk. (Pg 39)

23 Jul 1734. Deed of Release. Robert Jones of Prince William Co gent for £205 sold & released to John Mercer of Stafford Co gent a 1,000 a. tr of land ... [*same as above*] ... . Wit: Charles Brent, James Porteus, Thos Staines, Robt Turner, Js Mercer. Ackn 6 Aug 1734 & admitted to record. Attest: John Waller clk. (Pg 40)

23 Jul 1724. Bond. I Robert Jones of Prince William Co gent am firmly bound unto John Mercer of Stafford Co gent in the sum of £410 ... the condition of this obligation is such that if the afsd Robert Jones do well & truly observe, perform, fullfill, accomplish & keep all the covenants, grants, articles, clauses, conditions & agreements mentioned in an indenture of release [*see above*] then this obligation to be void ... . Wit: Charles Brent, James Porteus, Thos Staines, Robt Turner, Js Mercer. Ackn 6 Aug 1734 & admitted to record. Attest: John Waller clk. (Pg 41)

5 Aug 1734. Deed of Lease. John Mercer of Stafford Co gent for 5 shillings leased to Charles Carter of King George Co esqr a 1,000 a. tr of land in the little fork of Rappahannock River on the s side of the North River bounded by Beverdam Run ... during the term of one year paying the rent of one pepper corn upon the feast of St. Michael the Arch Angell if demanded ... . Wit: John

Waller, Jas Taliaferro, Z. Lewis, M. Battaley, Wm Waller. Ackn 6 Aug 1734 & admitted to record. Attest: John Waller clk. (Pg 42)

6 Aug 1734. Deed of Release. John Mercer of Stafford Co gent for £200 sold & released to Charles Carter of King George Co esqr a 1,000 a. tr of land ... [*same as above*] ... . Wit: John Waller, Jas Taliaferro, Z. Lewis, M. Battaley, Wm Waller. Ackn 6 Aug 1734 & admitted to record. Attest: John Waller clk. (Pg 43)

6 Aug 1734. Bond. I John Mercer of Stafford Co gent am firmly bound unto Charles Carter of King George Co esqr in the sum of £400 ... the condition of this obligation is such that if the afsd John Mercer do well & truly observe, perform, fullfill, accomplish & keep all the covenants, grants, articles, clauses, conditions & agreements mentioned in deeds of lease & release [*see above*] then this obligation to be void ... . Wit: Jas Taliaferro, Frans Thornton Junr, John Waller. Ackn 6 Aug 1734 & admitted to record. Attest: John Waller clk. (Pg 44)

6 Aug MDCCXXXIV. Quit Claim. Thomas Ballard Smith son & heir of William Smith gent of Spotsylvania Co decd for £20 quit claim unto Richard Phillips of same co in his full & peaceable possession & seisen now being all his right, estate, title, claim, interest & demand whatsoever which he the sd Thomas Ballard Smith as heir to his sd father William Smith decd have or may have of, in or to all that 380 a. tr of land in St. George Parish on the n side of the Northanna River bounded by the n side of the East North East River, which sd tr of land was granted to the sd William Smith decd per pattent dated 31 Oct 1726 & by him sold & made over to the sd Richard Phillips by a deed ... . Wit: Edwin Hickman, Wm Waller, Edward Blockley. Ackn 6 Aug 1734 by Thomas Ballard Smith & at the motion of William Waller in behalf of the sd Phillips is admitted to record. Attest: John Waller clk. (Pg 45)

5 Aug 1734. Deed of Lease. Benjamin Berryman of King George Co gent for 5 shillings farm letten unto Frances Fraizer (Frazer) widdow & James Frazer her son of Fredericksburgh, Spotsylvania Co a lott of land in the sd town of Fredericksburgh described in the platt of the sd town by the figures 50 being on Princess Anne Street & Emelia Street ... during the term of one year paying the yearly rent of one pepper corn at the feast of St. Michael the Arch Angel if demanded ... . Wit: Thomas Hill, James Sleet, Robt Stuart. Proved 6 Aug 1734 & admitted to record. Attest: John Waller clk. (Pg 46)

6 Aug 1734. Deed of Release. Benjamin Berryman of King George Co gent for £6:15 sold & released to Frances Frazer widdow & James Frazer her son of Fredericksburgh, Spotsylvania Co lott numbered 50 in Fredericksburgh, during

the natural life of the sd Frances Frazer & unto the sd James Frazer to the only proper use & behoof of the sd James Frazer forever ... [*same as above*] ... . Wit: Thomas Hill, James Sleet, Robt Stuart. Proved 6 Aug 1734 & admitted to record. Attest: John Waller clk. (Pg 46)

5 Aug 1734. Deed of Lease. John Red (Redd) of St. Mark Parish, Spotsylvania Co for 50 lbs weight of good & lawfull tobacco leased to Lazarus Tilly of St. George Parish, co afsd a 100 a. tr of land in St. Mark Parish being a tr of land which the sd John bought of Thomas Cook & being pt/o a 1,000 a. tr granted by patent to the sd Thomas 28 Sep 1728 bounded by James Fidler & Moore's line ... during the term of 6 months ... . Wit: G. Home, Benja Henslee, David Watts. Ackn 6 Aug 1734 & admitted to record. Attest: John Waller clk. (Pg 48)

6 Aug 1734. Deed of Release. John Redd (Red) of Saint Mark Parish, Spotsylvania Co for 300 lbs of tobacco sold & released to Lazarus Tilly of St. George Parish, co afsd a 100 a. tr of land ... [*same as above*] ... . Wit: G. Home, Benja Henslee, David Watts. Ackn 6 Aug 1734 by John Redd & Mary the w/o the sd John's power of atty unto John Waller gent being first proved the sd Waller ackn her right of dower & is admitted to record. Attest: John Waller clk. (Pg 48)

26 Jul 1734. Power of Attorney. I Mary Read (Red) of St. Marks Parish, Spotsylvania Co do appoint Col John Waller of the sd co my atty to ackn all my right of dower to a sartin tr of land containing 100 a. & by my husband John Read sould unto Lazarus Tilly of this co ... . Wit: Willm Crosthwait, James Molton, Benja Henslee, Henry Downs. Proved 6 Aug 1734 & admitted to record. Attest: John Waller clk. (Pg 50)

XXVII Jul MDCCXXXIV. Deed of Gift. John Smith of St. George Parish, Spotsylvania Co for naturall love & affection have given to my well beloved grandson John Tyre a 100 a. tr of land in the parish afsd bounded by Ralph Williams & Pappaw Run, being pt/o a greater tr of land granted by pattent to me the sd John Smith ... also I have given unto the sd John Tyre one cow & calf ... . Wit: Wm Waller, Henry Haynes, John J. Stubblefield. Ackn 3 Sep 1734 by John Smith & admitted to record. Attest: John Waller clk. (Pg 50)

XVI Jul MDCCXXXIV. Deed of Lease. John Smith of Saint George Parish, Spotsylvania Co for 5 shillings leased to William Dobbs of same place a 100 a. tr of land ... during the term of one year paying the rent of one ear of Indian corn on the feast of St. Michaell the Arch Angel if demanded ... . Wit: Wm Waller, Wm Tyre, William Smith. Ackn 3 Sep 1734 & admitted to record. Attest: John Waller clk. (Pg 51)

17 Jul MDCCXXXIV. Deed of Release. John Smith of St. George Parish, Spotsylvania Co for £10 sold & released to William Dobbs of same place a 100 a. tr of land, the same being pt/o a 400 a. tr granted to the sd John Smith by pattent dated 30 Jun MDCCXX--- ... [*same as above*] ... . Wit: Wm Waller, Wm Tyre, Wm Smith. Ackn 3 Sep 1734 by John Smith & Margaret the w/o the sd John ackn her right of dower & is admitted to record. Attest: John Waller clk. (Pg 52)

5 Jul 1734. Deed of Lease. Richard Bayley of Drysdale Parish, King & Queen Co for 5 shillings leased to James Elliott of St. Margarett Parish, King William Co gent a 720 a. tr of land in St. Marks Parish which was granted the sd Richard by patent dated 28 Sep 1728 bounded by the north fork of the Northanna, the line of Habendum & Captain Clowder's old tr ... during the term of one year paying one pepper corn upon the last day of the sd term if demanded ... . Wit: Mar Todd, Roderick Gordon, Edwin Hickman, Humphrey Hill, Benja Hubbard, Robt Bayley. Proved 3 Sep 1734 & admitted to record. Attest: John Waller clk. (Pg 53)

6 Jul 1734. Deed of Release. Richard Bayley of Drysdale Parish, King & Queen Co for £36 sold & released to James Elliott of Saint Margarett Parish, King William Co gent a 720 a. tr of land ... [*same as above*] ... . Wit: Mar Todd, Roderick Gordon, Edwin Hickman, Humphrey Hill, Benja Hubbard, Robt Bayley. Proved 3 Sep 1734 & admitted to record. Attest: John Waller clk. (Pg 54)

3 Sep 1734. Deed of Gift. Humphrey Hill of King Wm Co, VA for 5 shillings but more especially out of good will & effection have given to my two nieces Susannah & Sarah Hill one Negro man named Hercules & one Negro woman named Hellen them & their increase to be equally divided between them when the oldest of them shall arrive to the age of 21 or on her day of marriage provided that the sd Negroes be & remain in the possession of my bro Thos Hill till the time afsd to his own use the produce & crops of corn & tobo till the time afsd do convert & turn ... . Wit: Roderick Gordon, Thomas Todd, Anthony Rhodes. Ackn 3 Sep 1734 by Humphrey Hill gent unto his two nieces Susannah & Sarah Hill & at the motion of their father Thomas Hill is admitted to record. Attest: John Waller clk. (Pg 55)

5 Aug 1734. Deed of Lease. William Beverly gent & Ann Beverly executors of the will of Robert Beverly esqr decd for 5 shillings leased to Lawrence Battaile gent a plantation & 1,000 a. of land ... during the term of one year paying the yearly rent of one ear of corn at the feast of Saint Michael the Arch Angel if demanded ... . Wit: Eliza Jones, Catherine Beverley, Zach Taylor. Ackn 3 Sep 1734 & admitted to record. Attest: John Waller clk. (Pg 55)

6 Aug 1734. Deed of Release. William Beverly (Beverley) & Ann Beverly (Beverley) executors of the will of Robert Beverly (Beverley) esqr decd of Spotsylvania Co for £110 sold & released to Lawrence Battaile of Caroline Co a plantation & 1,000 a. of land bounded by Warner's pattent ... [same as above] .... Wit: Eliza Jones, Catherine Beverley, Zach Taylor. Ackn 3 Sep 1734 & admitted to record. Attest: John Waller clk. (Pg 56)

3 Sep 1734. Bond. I William Beverly (Beverley) & Ann Beverley execrs of the will of Robert Beverley esqr decd are firmly bound to Lawrence Battaile of Caroline Co in the sum of £400 ... the condition of this obligation is such that if the afsd William Beverley & Ann Beverley & the heirs of the sd Robt Beverley esqr decd shall observe, perform, fulfill, accomplish & keep all the covenants, grants, articles, clauses, conditions & agreements mentioned in one pair of indentures [see above] then this obligation to be void .... Wit: Eliza Jones, Catherine Beverley, Zach Taylor. Ackn 3 Sep 1734 & admitted to record. Attest: John Waller clk. (Pg 57)

30 Sep 1734. Deed of Lease. William Rush of Spotsylvania Co for 5 shillings leased to Peter Weaver of same co a 100 a. tr of land in Saint Marks Parish being pt/o a 400 a. tr granted to the sd Wm Rush by pattent dated 11 May 1726 bounded by an Ivey Point on the Robinson River & Quakers Run ... during the term of one year paying one pepper corn upon the feast of St. Michael the Arch Angel if demanded .... Wit: Robt Turner, Jno Cook, Tho Pulliam. Ackn 1 Oct 1784 & admitted to record. Attest: John Waller clk. (Pg 58)

1 Oct 1734. Deed of Release. William Rush of Spotsylvania Co for £10 sold & released to Peter Weaver of same co a 100 a. tr of land ... [same as above] .... Wit: Robt Turner, Jno Cook, Tho Pulliam. Ackn 1 Oct 1734 by William Rush & Mary the w/o the sd Wm ackn her right of dower & is admitted to record. Attest: John Waller clk. (Pg 59)

Last day of Sep 1734. Deed of Lease. James Coward of St. Marks Parish, Spotsylvania Co planter for 5 shillings farm let to John Zachary of same place planter a 100 a. parcel of land or woodland ground being pt/o a greater tr taken up between William Phillips & Nicholas Christopher in St. Marks Parish adj David Phillips, Wm Phillips & Nicholas Christopher's dividing line ... during the term of one year paying the yearly rent of one ear of Indian corn on the feast of St. Michael the Arch Angel if demanded .... Wit: Robt Slaughter, Zach Taylor, Benja Powell. Ackn 1 Oct 1734 & admitted to record. Attest: John Waller clk. (Pg 60)

1 Oct 1734. Deed of Release. James Coward of St. Marks Parish, Spotsylvania Co planter for £30 sold & released to John Zachary of same place planter a 100

a. tr of land ... [*same as above*] ... . Wit: Robt Slaughter, Zach Taylor, Benja Powell. Ackn 1 Oct 1734 by James Coward & Elizabeth the w/o the sd James' power of atty to John Waller gent being first proved the sd Waller ackn her right of dower & is admitted to record. Attest: John Waller clk. (Pg 61)

1 Oct 1734. Power of Attorney. I Elizabeth Coward w/o James Coward of Spotsylvania Co hereby renounce, acquit & ackn to John Zachary all my right & title of dower to a 100 a. tr of land as by deeds of lease & release [*see above*] made by my sd husband & hereby appoint my beloved friend Col John Waller to ackn the same ... . Wit: Thomas Zachry, David Zachry. Proved 1 Oct 1734 & admitted to record. Attest: John Waller clk. (Pg 62)

27 Sep 1734. Deed of Lease. Anthony Gholston of Spotsylvania Co for 5 shillings lease to William Gaines of King & Queen Co a 442 ½ a. tr of land being pt/o a patent dated 28 Sep 1728 containing 1,000 a. being in St. George Parish bounded by Musick's & Allen's corner, Clowder's path & the Mine Run ... during the term of one year paying one pepper corn upon the feast of St. Michael the Arch Angel if demanded ... . Wit: Joseph Thomas, Chas Stevens, Jno Cook. Ackn 1 Oct 1734 by William Gaines & at the motion of Joseph Thomas gent in behalf of the sd Gaines is admitted to record. Attest: John Waller clk. (Pg 63)

28 Sep 1734. Deed of Release. Anthony Gholston of Spotsylvania Co for £23 sold & released to William Gaines of King & Queen Co a 442 ½ a. tr of land ... [*same as above*] ... . Wit: Joseph Thomas, Chas Stevens, Jno Cook. Ackn 1 Oct 1734 by Anthony Gholston & Jane the w/o the sd Anthony ackn he right of dower & at the motion of Joseph Thomas gent in behalf of the sd Gaines is admitted to record. Attest: John Waller clk. (Pg 64)

27 Sep 1734. Deed of Lease. Anthony Gholston of Spotsilvania Co for 5 shillings leased to Jas Jones of Caroline Co a 442 ½ a. tr of land being pt/o a patent granted unto the sd Anthony Gholston containing 1,000 a. dated 28 Sep 1728 in St. George Parish bounded by the se side of Plentifull, Mr. Cam's line, the Mine Run, Thos Foy & Col Corbin ... during the term of one year paying the rent of one ear of Indian corn on the feast of St. Michael if demanded ... . Wit: Joseph Thomas, Chas Stevens, Jno Cook. Ackn 1 Oct 1734 by Anthony Gholston & at the motion of Joseph Thomas gent in behalf of the sd Jones is admitted to record. Attest: John Waller clk. (Pg 65)

28 Sep 1734. Deed of Release. Anthony Gholston of Spotsylvania Co for £27 sold & released to James Jones of Caroline Co a 442 ½ a. tr of land ... [*same as above*] ... . Wit: Joseph Thomas, Chas Stevens, Jno Cook. Ackn 1 Oct 1734 by Anthony Gholston & Jane the w/o the sd Anthony ackn her right of dower &

at the motion of Joseph Thomas gent in behalf of the sd Jones is admitted to record. Attest: John Waller clk. (Pg 66)

23 Sep 1734. Deed of Lease. Richard Phillips & Thomas Ballard Smith of St. Georges Parish, Spotsylvania Co for 5 shillings leased to George Woodroofe of same place a 300 a. tr of land bounded on the brs of South River in Saint Georges Parish adj the Main Road, William Pruess, John Smith & Robert Baylor ... during the term of 6 months paying at the expiration of the sd term one ear of Indian corn if demanded .... Wit: Wm Waller, Edwd Herndon Junr, William Henderson. Proved 5 Nov 1734 & admitted to record. Attest: John Waller clk. (Pg 67)

23 Sep 1734. Deed of Release. Richard Phillips & Thomas Ballard Smith of St. Georges Parish, Spotsylvania Co for 500 lbs of tobo & 40 shillings sold & released to George Woodroofe of same place a 300 a. tr of land ... [same as above] .... Wit: Wm Waller, Edwd Herndon Junr, William Henderson. Proved 5 Nov 1734 & Elizabeth Smith's power of atty to John Waller gent was proved & the sd Waller ackn her right of dower & is admitted to record. Attest: John Waller clk. (Pg 68)

--- 1734. Power of Attorney. I Elizabeth Smith of St. George Parish, Spotsylvania Co have appointed Col John Waller clerk of the afsd co my atty to ackn my right of a 300 a. tr of land sold to George Woodroofe of sd parish .... Wit: Wm Waller, Edwd Herndon Junr, William Henderson. Proved 5 Nov 1734 & admitted to record. Attest: John Waller clk. (Pg 70)

4 Nov 1734. Deed of Gift. John Madison of Drysdale Parish, King & Queen Co for paternall affection & love have given to my well beloved neice Elizabeth Madison eldest dau of my brother Ambroce Madison lately decd a 1,000 a. tr of land adj Capt John Camm, George Taylor, James Madison & Erasmus Taylor, granted to me by pattent dated 28 Sep 1728 in St. Mark Parish ... upon this consideration that the sd Elizabeth Madison within 18 months after she shall attain the age of 21 or in case of her decease her heirs within the sd 18 months after her decease shall by deeds of lease & release or other firm conveyances in the law make & convey over an estate in fee simple of 200 a. of the afsd land to Francis Williams & his heirs forever according as it is already laid off but in case the sd Elizabeth Madison within the time above limited shall not make or refuse or deny to make such deeds as above express then this deed to be void & of non effect .... Wit: Roger Tandy. Ackn 5 Nov 1734 & admitted to record. Attest: John Waller clk. (Pg 70)

4 Nov 1734. Deed of Gift. Henry Madison of St. Johns Parish, King William Co for paternal affection & love have given to my well beloved neice Frances

Madison youngest dau of my brother Ambroce Madison decd a 1,000 a. tr of land bounded by James Madison, George Penn & Zacharias Taylor, granted to me by patent dated 28 Sep 1728 in St. Mark Parish ... upon this consideration that the sd Frances Madison within 18 months after she shall attain the age of 21 or in case of her decease her heirs within the sd 18 months after her decease shall by deeds of lease & release or other firm conveyances in the law make & convey over an estate in fee simple of 150 a. of the afsd land to Daniel Stodghill & his heirs forever adj David Williams & Abraham Estridge but in case the sd Frances Madison within the time above limited shall not make or refuse or deny to make such deeds as above express then this deed to be void & of non effect .... Wit: Roger Tandy. Ackn 5 Nov 1734& admitted to record. Attest: John Waller clk. (Pg 71)

7 Oct 1734. Deed. Elisha Perkins of Saint Mark Parish, Spotsylvania Co for £46 sold to Thomas Wright Belfeild of Lunenburgh Parish, Richmond Co a 470 a. tr of land where the sd Perkins now lives (which sd land the sd Perkins bought of Francis Kirtley) being in Saint Mark Parish in the great fork of Rappahannock River adj Col Alexander Spotswood & the Meander Run, the sd tr of land being granted to Francis Kirtley by pattent dated 28 Sep 1728 .... Wit: Jno Christopher, Hen Downs, Jno Willson, Jos Morton, Wm Morton. Proved 5 Nov 1734 & Margery the w/o the sd Elisha Perkins' power of atty to Wm Morton being first proved the sd Morton ackn her right of dower & is admitted to record. Attest: John Waller clk. (Pg 72)

7 Oct 1734. Power of Attorney. I Margery Perkins doe appoint my friend William Morton my atty to ackn my right of dower in & to a 470 a. tr of land which my husband Elisha Perkins sold to Thomas Wright Belfeild .... Wit: Hen Downs, Jno Christopher, Joseph Morton, Jno Willson. Proved 5 Nov 1734 & admitted to record. Attest: John Waller clk. (Pg 74)

4 Nov MDCCXXXIV. Deed of Lease. Thomas Smith of Prince William Co, VA gent & Augustine Smith of Spotsylvania Co gent for 5 shillings leased to Francis Thornton Junr of Spotsylvania Co gent a messuage & 400 a. tr of land bounded by Thornton's line, Byram's line, Reeves' line, Fantleroy's line, Royston & Buckner's line ... during the term of one year paying the yearly rent of one pepper corn at the feast of St. Michael the Arch Angel if demanded .... Wit: Jonath Gibson, Thos Slaughter, Charles Taliaferro Junr. Ackn 5 Nov 1734 & admitted to record. Attest: John Waller clk. (Pg 74)

5 Nov MDCCXXXIV. Deed of Release. Thomas Smith of Prince William Co, VA gent & Augustine Smith of Spotsylvania Co gent for £10 & 10,000 lbs of tobacco sold & released to Francis Thornton Junr of Spotsylvania Co a messuage & 400 a. tr of land, which sd messuage & tr of land was by the sd

Augustine Smith (by deed of gift dated 2 Nov MDCCXXXI) given to the sd Thomas Smith with a clause of reservation in the sd deed incerted that the sd Augustine Smith might during his life have the use of the sd land & premises ... [*same as above*] ... . Wit: Jonath Gibson, Thos Slaughter, Charles Taliaferro Junr. Ackn 5 Nov 1734 & admitted to record. Attest: John Waller clk. (Pg 75)

5 Nov MDCCXXXIV. Bond. We Thomas Smith of Prince William Co & Augustine Smith of Spotsylvania Co are firmly bound unto Francis Thornton Junr of Spotsylvania Co gent in the penal sums of £20 & 20,000 lbs of tobacco ... the condition of this obligation is such that if the afsd Thomas Smith & Augustine Smith do well & truly observe, perform, fullfill, accomplish & keep all the covenants, grants, articles, clauses, conditions & agreements mention in an indenture of release [*see above*] then this obligation to be void ... . Wit: Jonath Gibson, Thos Slaughter, Charles Taliaferro Junr. Ackn 5 Nov 1734 & admitted to record. Attest: John Waller clk. (Pg 77)

4 Nov 1734. Deed of Lease. Francis Thornton Junr of St. George Parish, Spotsylvania Co for 5 shillings leased to Keamp Taliaferro of St. Maries Parish, Caroline Co, VA a 400 a. tr of land in St. Mark Parish in the Goard Vine Fork it being a tr of land taken up by David MacMurrin & held by a pattent dated 21 Jul 1732 & is bounded by a br of Cannons River & a mountain ... during the term of one year paying the rent of one ear of Indian corn if demanded ... . Wit: Jonath Gibson, Thos Slaughter, Charles Taliaferro Junr. Ackn 5 Nov 1734 & admitted to record. Attest: John Waller clk. (Pg 78)

5 Nov 1734. Deed of Release. Francis Thornton Junr of St. George Parish, Spotsylvania Co for 5,000 lbs of good tobacco according to law sold & released to Keamp Taliaferro of St. Maries Parish, Caroline Co, VA a 400 a. tr of land ... [*same as above*] ... . Wit: Jonath Gibson, Thos Slaughter, Charles Taliaferro Junr. Ackn 5 Nov 1734 & admitted to record. Attest: John Waller clk. (Pg 79)

3 Nov 1734. Deed of Lease. Henry Haynes of Caroline Co planter for 5 shillings leased to Thomas Dillard of Spotsylvania Co planter a 170 a. tr of land on the brs of the South River of Mattapony & is bounded by Robert Baylor, Robert Stubblefeild, John Smith, Thomas Hubbard & Robert Baylor, the sd land being pt/o a 370 a. tr granted by pattent unto the sd Henry Haynes dated 28 Sep 1728 ... during the term of one year paying the rent of one ear of Indian corn at the feast of St. Michael the Arch Angel if demanded ... . Wit: Roger Quarles, John Stubbelfield, John Dickenson. Ackn 5 Nov 1734 & admitted to record. Attest: John Waller clk. (Pg 80)

4 Nov 1734. Deed of Release. Henry Haynes of Caroline Co planter for £10:8 sold & released to Thomas Dillard of Spotsylvania Co a 170 a. tr of land ...

[*same as above*] .... Wit: Roger Quarles, John Stubbelfield, John Dickenson. Ackn 5 Nov 1734 by Henry Haynes & Mary the w/o the sd Henry's power of atty to John Waller gent being first proved the sd Waller ackn her right of dower & is admitted to record. Attest: John Waller clk. (Pg 80)

4 Nov 1734. Power of Attorney. I Mary Haynes w/o Henry Haynes of St. Margaretts Parish, Caroline Co doe appoint Col John Waller clk of Spotsylvania Court my atty to relinquish all my right of dower in & to 170 a. of land in St. George Parish which my husband lately sold to Thomas Dillard .... Wit: Roger Quarles, John Stubelfield. Proved 5 Nov 1734 & admitted to record. Attest: John Waller clk. (Pg 82)

4 Nov 1734. Deed. Roger Tandy of King & Queen Co gent for £22 sold to John Jones of St. Georges Parish, Spotsylvania Co collier a 420 a. tr of land on the brs of East North East in St. Georges Parish, which sd 420 a. is pt/o 520 a. granted to the sd Roger Tandy by patent dated 13 Oct 1727 .... Wit: Anthony Golstone, William Wombwell Cliffe. Ackn 5 Nov 1734 & admitted to record. Attest: John Waller clk. (Pg 82)

23 Oct 1734. Deed of Lease. Alexander Spotswood esqr for & in consideration of the rents & covenants herein after mentioned have farm lett unto William Wood planter a 110 a. tr of land (except all mines, minerals & quarries whatsoever) being in St. Marks Parish on the s side of the River Rapidanne being pt/o a tr of land of 40,000 a. granted by letters patent to the sd Alexander Spotswood & called the Spotsylvania Tract ... to have & to hold the sd land & premises (except before excepted) to sd William Wood & Isabel his wife for & during the natural lives of the sd William Wood & Isabel his wife or the longest liver of them paying yearly of the first four years on 25 Dec one ear of Indian corn & every year after the expiration of the sd four first years 630 lbs weight of good sound merchantable top tobacco clear of ground leaves & trash according to law together with cask & delivering the same at a convenient landing in the co the first of which tobacco paiments to commence & become due on 25 Dec 1738 .... Wit: John Grame, Tho Sims, William Morton. (Pg 84)

Survey: 110 a. of land surveyed by George Home surveyor of Spotsylvania Co by the order of Alexr Spotswood esqr for William Wood bounded by John Jennings, the Rappidann River & the side of a mountain ... [*drawing not included here*] .... Memorandum that on 31 Oct MDCCXXXIV full quiet & peaceable possession & seizen of all the lands & messuages [*above*] mentioned was deliver to the within named William Wood according to the force & effect of the [*above*] written indenture by the sd Alexander Spotswood. Wit: John Pattey, William Moreton. At a court held 5 Nov 1734 Alexander Spotswood esqr ackn the [*above*] deed & livery & seizin unto William Wood & at the

motion of William Morton in behalf of the sd Wood is admitted to record.
Attest: John Waller clk. (Pg 85)

22 Oct ----. Deed of Lease. Alexander Spotswood esqr for & in consideration
of the rents & covenants hereinafter mentioned hath farm let unto John Marks
planter a 100 a. tr of land (except all mines, minerals & quarries whatsoever)
being in St. Mark Parish on the s side of the River Rappidanne being pt/o a
40,000 a. tr of land granted by pattent to the sd Alexander Spotswood & called
the Spotsylvania Tract which bounds & limits of the 100 a. of land are described
by a plot & survey thereof ... the sd John Marks to have & to hold during the
natural lives of Mary the wife & Mary the dau of the sd John & for & during the
natural lives of the longest liver of them paying the yearly rent of the first four
years on 25 Dec one ear of Indian corn & every year after the expiration of the
sd four first years 600 lbs weight of good sound merchantable top tobacco clear
of ground leaves & trash according to law together with cask & delivering the
same at a convenient landing in the co the first of which tobacco paiments to
commence & become due on 25 Dec 1738 ... . Wit: John Grame, Tho Sims,
William Moreton. (Pg 86)

Survey: 100 a. of land [above] mentioned surveyed by George Home surveyor
of Spotsylvania Co by Alexander Spotswood esqr for John Marks adj John
Ingram ... [drawing not included here] ... . Memorandum that on 31 Oct
MDCCXXXIV full quiet & peaceable possession & seizin of the sd lands &
messuages was delivered to the sd John Marks according to the form & effects
of the indenture [above] mentioned by the sd Alexr Spotswood in his own proper
person. Wit: William Moreton, John Ingram. Ackn 5 Nov 1734 & admitted to
record. Attest: John Waller clk. (Pg 88)

23 Oct 1734. Deed of Lease. Alexander Spotswood for & in consideration of
the rents & covenants herein after mentioned have farm letten unto Thomas
Simms planter a 108 a. tr of land (except all mines, minerals & quarries
whatsoever) being in St. Marks Parish on the s side of the River Rappedanne
being pt/o a 40,000 a. tr of land granted by letters of pattent to the sd Alexander
Spotswood & called the Spotsylvania Tract the bounds & limits of the 108 a. of
land are described by a plot & survey thereof ... during the natural lives of
Rebecca the wife & Thomas the son of the sd Thomas Senr & for & during the
natural lives of the longest liver of them paying the yearly rent of the first four
years on 25 Dec one ear of Indian corn & after the expiration of the sd four first
years 624 lbs weight of good sound merchantable top tobacco clear of ground
leaves & trash according to law together with the cask & delivering the same at
a convenient landing in the co the first of which tobacco payments to commence
& become due on 25 Dec 1738 ... . Wit: John Grame, John Pattey, William
Morton. (Pg 88)

Survey: 108 a. of land [*above*] mentioned surveyed by George Home surveyor of Spotsylvania Co by the order of Alexander Spotswood esqr for Thomas Simms Senr adj Thomas Pattey ... [*drawing not included here*] ... . Memorandum that on 31 Oct MDCCXXXIV full quiet & peaceable possession & seizen of the [*above*] lands & messuages was delivered to Thomas Sims according to the form & effect of the [*above*] written indenture by the sd Alexander Spotswood in his own proper person. Wit: John Pattey, William Moreton. At a court held 5 Nov 1734 Alexander Spotswood ackn his [*above*] deed of lease unto Thomas Simms & is admitted to record. Attest: John Waller clk. (Pg 90)

23 Oct 1734. Deed of Lease. Alexander Spotswood esqr for & in consideration of the rents & covenants herein after mentioned have farm let unto Thomas Jones Senr planter a 200 a. tr of land (except all mines, minerals & quarries whatsoever) being in Saint Mark Parish on the s side of the River Rapadam being pt/o a 40,000 a. tr of land granted by letters pattent to the sd Alexander Spotswood & called the Spotsylvania Tract the bounds & limits of which 200 a. of land are described by a plot & survey thereof ... during the natural lives of Thomas & James Jones of sd Thomas Jones Senr & for & during the natural life & lives of the longest liver of them paying yearly the first four years of the term on 25 Dec one ear of Indian corn after the expiration of the sd four first years 900 lbs weight of good sound merchantable top tobacco clear of ground leaves & trash according to law together with cask & delivering the same at a convenient landing in the co the first of which tobacco paiments to commence & become due on the 25 Dec 1734 ... . Wit: John Grame, Tho Sims, William Morton. (Pg 90)

Survey: 200 a. of land [*above*] mentioned survey'd by George Home surveyor of Spotsylvania Co by the order of Alexander Spotswood esqr for Thomas Jones adj a br of Poplar Swamp ... [*drawing not included here*] ... . Memorandum that on 30 Oct MDCCXXXIV full quiet & peaceable possession & seizin of all the lands & messuages [*above*] mentioned was delivered according to the form & effect of the indenture to the sd Thomas Jones by the sd Alexander Spotswood in his own proper person. Wit: James Chisum, Elias Smith. Alexander Spotswood esqr ackn the [*above*] deed 5 Nov 1734 & at the motion of William Morton in behalf of the sd Jones is admitted to record. Attest: John Waller clk. (Pg 92)

23 Oct 1734. Deed of Lease. Alexander Spotswood for & in consideration of the rents & covenants herein after mentioned farm letten unto William Croucher planter a 100 a. tr of land (except all mines, mineralls & quarries whatsoever) being in St. Mark Parish on the s side of the River Rapidanne being pt/o a 40,000 a. tr of land granted by letters pattent to the sd Alexander Spotswood &

called the Spotsylvania Tract the bounds & limits of which 100 a. are described
by a plot & survey thereof ... to the sd William Croucher during the natural lives
of Anne the wife & Priscilla the dau of the sd Wm Croucher & for & during the
natural lives of the longest liver of them paying yearly at the first four years of
the sd term on 25 Dec one ear of Indian corn & every year after the expiration of
the sd first four years 600 lbs weight of good sound merchantable top tobacco
clear of ground leaves & trash according to law together with cask & delivering
the same at a convenient landing in the co the first of which tobacco paiments to
commence & become due on 25 Dec 1738 .... Wit: John Grame, Tho Sims,
William Morton. (Pg 93)

Survey: 100 a. of land [above] mentioned surveyed by George Home surveyor
of Spotsylvania Co by the order of Alexr Spotswood esqr for William Croucher
adj a ridge of a Little Mountain ... [drawing not included here] ... .
Memorandum that on 30 Oct MDCCXXXIV full quiet & peaceable possession
& seizin of all the lands & messuages was according to the form & effect of the
[above] indenture delivered to the sd William Croucher by the sd Alexander
Spotswood in his own proper person. Wit: William Moreton, Thomas Jones.
Alexander Spotswood esqr ackn the [above] deed 5 Nov 1734 & at the motion of
William Morton in behalf of the sd Croucher is admitted to record. Attest: John
Waller clk. (Pg 94)

23 Oct 1734. Deed of Lease. Alexander Spotswood esqr for & in consideration
of the rents & covenants hereinafter mentioned have farm letten unto Thomas
Petty planter a 100 a. tr of land (except all mines, minerals & quarries
whatsoever) being in St. Mark Parish on the s side of the River Rapidanne being
pt/o a 40,000 a. tr of land granted by letters patent to the sd Alexander
Spotswood & called the Spotsylvania Tract the bounds & limits of which 100 a.
of land are described by a plot & survey thereof ... during the natural lives of
Katharine Pettey the wife & Christopher Petty the son of the afsd Thomas for &
during the natural lives of the longest liver of them paying yearly of the first four
years on 25 Dec one ear of Indian corn & every year after the expiration of the
sd four first years 600 lbs weight of good sound merchantable top tobacco clear
of ground leaves & trash according to law together with cask & delivering the
same at a convenient landing in the co the first of which tobacco paiments to
commence & become due on 25 Dec 1736 ... . Wit: John Grame, Tho Sims,
William Morton. (Pg 95)

Survey: 100 a. of land [above] mentioned surveyed by George Home surveyor
of Spotsylvania Co by the order of Alexr Spotswood esqr for Thomas Petty ...
[drawing not included here] ... . Memorandum that on 31 Oct MDCCXXXIV
full quiet & peaceable possession of all the lands & messuages [above]
mentioned was according to the form & effect of the indenture [above] written

delivered to the sd Thomas Pettey by the sd Alexander Spotswood in his own proper person. Wit: G. Home, John Pattey. Alexander Spotswood ackn the [above] deed 5 Nov 1734 & at the motion of William Morton in behalf of the sd Pettey is admitted to record. Attest: John Waller clk. (Pg 96)

23 Oct 1734. Deed of Lease. Alexander Spotswood for & in consideration of the rents & covenants hereinafter mentioned hath farm let to John Petty planter a 100 a. tr of land (except all mines, minerals & quarries whatsoever) being in St. Mark Parish on the s side of the River Rapidanne being pt/o a 40,000 a. tr of land granted by letters patent to the sd Alexander Spotswood & called the Spotsylvania Tract the bounds & limits of which 100 a. of land are described by a plot & survey thereof ... to the sd John Petty during the natural lives of Rebecca the wife & Thomas the son of the sd John & for & during the natural lives of the longest liver of them paying yearly of the first four years of the sd term on 25 Dec one ear of Indian corn & every year after the expiration of the sd four first years 600 lbs weight of good sound, merchantable top tobacco clear of ground leaves & trash according to law together with cask & delivering the same at a convenient landing in the co first of which tobacco paiments to commence & become due on 25 Dec 1736 ... . Wit: John Grame, Tho Sims, William Morton. (Pg 97)

Survey: 100 a. of land [above] mentioned surveyed by George Home surveyor of Spotsylvania Co by the order of Alexr Spotswood esqr for John Patty adj Thomas Pattey & Thomas Taylor ... . Memorandum that on 31 Oct MDCCXXXIII full quiet & peaceable possession of all the lands & messuage [above] mentioned was according to the form & effect of the [above] indenture delivered to the within named John Pettey by Alexander Spotswood in his own proper person. Wit: William Moreton, Luke Thornton. Alexander Spotswood esqr ackn the [above] deed & at the motion of William Morton in behalf of the sd Pettey was admitted to record. Attest: John Waller clk. (Pg 98)

2 Nov 1734. Deed of Lease. Alexander Spotswood esqr for & in consideration of the rents & covenants herein after mentioned have farm letten unto Robert Allistone planter a100 a. tr of land (except all mines, minerals & quarries whatsoever) being in St. Mark Parish on the n side of the River Rapidanne being pt/o a 28,000 a. tr of land granted by letters patent to the sd Alexander Spotswood & called the Alexandria Tract the bounds & limits of which 100 a. of land are described by a plot & survey thereof ... to the sd Robert Allistone during the natural lives of the sd Robert Allistone & his son Jacob Allistone & for & during the natural life of the longest liver of them paying yearly on 25 Dec one ear of Indian corn & after the expiration of four years 600 lbs weight of good sound merchantable top tobacco clear of ground leaves & trash according to law together with cask & delivering the same at a convenient landing in the co

the first of which tobacco paiments to commence & become due on 25 Dec 1736
.... Wit: Joseph Delaney, William Bunting, Thomas Lewis. (Pg 99)

Survey: 100 a. of land [*above*] mentioned survey'd by George Home surveyor
of Spotsylvania Co by the order of Alexander Spotswood esqr for Robert
Alliston adj Joseph Waugh's br, the Rappahannock River within the Great Fork
& Pye Island ... [*drawing not included here*] .... Memorandum that on 4 Nov
MDCCXXXIV full quiet & peaceable possession of all the lands & messuages
[*above*] mentioned was according to the form & effect of the indenture [*above*]
delivered to the sd Robert Allistone by John Lightfoot atty of the sd Alexander
Spotswood for that purpose constituted. Wit: C. W. Hoomes) (or C.
McHoomes), Anthony Sculthorpe. Alexander Spotswood esqr ackn the [*above*]
deed of lease 5 Nov 1734 & at the motion of William Morton in behalf of the sd
Allistone is admitted to record. Attest: John Waller clk. (Pg 100)

25 Oct 1734. Deed of Lease. Alexander Spotswood esqr for & in consideration
of the rents & covenants hereinafter mentioned have farm let unto Simon Miller
planter a 100 a. tr of land (except all mines, minerals & quarries whatsoever)
being in St. Mark Parish on the n side of the River Rapidanne being pt/o a
28,000 a. tr of land granted by letters patent to the sd Alexander Spotswood &
called the Alexandria Tract the bounds & limits of which 100 a. of land are
described by a plot & survey thereof ... to the sd Simon Miller for & during the
natural lives of the sd Simon Miller & John Alliston son of Robert Alliston & for
& during the natural life of the longest liver of them paying yearly of the first
four years on 25 Dec one ear of Indian corn & every year after the expiration of
the sd four first years 100 lbs weight of good sound merchantable top tobacco
clear of ground leaves & trash according to law together with cask & delivering
the same at a convenient landing in the co the first of which tobacco paiments to
commence & become due on 25 Dec 1734 .... Wit: Thomas Lewis, Simon
Miller, John Blackaby. (Pg 101)

Survey: 100 a. of land [*above*] mentioned survey'd by George Home surveyor
of Spotsylvania Co by the order of Alexander Spotswood esqr for Simon Miller
adj Robert Allistone, Waugh's Br & the River Rappahanock ... [*drawing not
included here*] .... Memorandum that on 4 Nov MDCCXXXIV full quiet &
peaceable possession & seizin of all the lands & messuages [*above*] mentioned
was according to the form & effect of the indenture [*above*] written delivered to
the sd Simon Miller by John Lightfoot atty of the sd Alexander Spotswood for
that purpose constituted. Wit: C. W. Hoomes (or C. McHoomes), Anthony
Sculthorpe. Alexander Spotswood esqr ackn the [*above*] deed 5 Nov 1734 & at
the motion of Wm Morton in behalf of the sd Miller the same is admitted to
record. Attest: John Waller clk. (Pg 102)

23 Oct 1734. Deed of Lease. Alexander Spotswood esqr for & in consideration of the rents & covenants hereinafter mentioned farm let unto William Morton a 200 a. tr of land (except all mines, minerals & quarries whatsoever) being in St. Mark Parish on the s side of the River Rapidanne being pt/o a 40,000 a. tr of land granted by letters patent to the sd Alexander Spotswood & called the Spotsylvania Tract the bounds & limits of which 200 a. of land are described by a plot & survey thereof ... to the sd William Morton for & during the natural lives of Jeremiah Morton & Elijah Morton & for & during the natural life of the longest liver of them paying yearly of the first four years on 25 Dec one ear of Indian corn & every year after the expiration of the sd four first years 900 lbs weight of good sound merchantable top tobacco clear of ground leaves & trash according to law together with cask & deliver the same at a convenient landing in the co the first of which tobacco paiments to commence & become due on 25 Dec 1738 ... . Wit: John Grame, Tho Sims, John Pattey. (Pg 103)

Survey: 200 a. of land [above] mentioned survey'd by George Home surveyor of Spotsylvania Co by order of Alexr Spotswood esqr for William Morton adj on the point of a ridge of a mountain ... [drawing not included here] ... . Memorandum that on 31 Oct MDCCXXXIV full quiet & peaceable possession & seizin of all the lands & messuages [above] mentioned according to the form & effect of the [above] indenture delivered to William Morton by the sd Alexander Spotswood in his own proper person. Wit: Stephen Beckham, William Beckham. Alexander Spotswood ackn his deed of lease [above] 5 Nov 1734 unto William Morton at whose motion it is admitted to record. Attest: John Waller clk. (Pg 104)

28 Oct 1734. Deed of Lease. Alexander Spotswood esqr for & in consideration of the rents & covenants hereinafter mentioned farm let unto Elias Smith planter a 100 a. tr of land (except all mines, minerals & quarries whatsoever) in St. Mark Parish on the s side of the River Rapidanne being pt/o a 40,000 a. tr of land granted by letters patent to the sd Alexander Spotswood & called the Spotsylvania Tract the bounds & limits of which 100 a. of land are described by a plot & survey thereof ... to the sd Elias Smith for & during the term of the naturall lives of Elias Smith Junr & William Smith sons of the sd Elias Smith & for & during the natural life of the longest liver of them paying yearly of the first four years on 25 Dec one ear of Indian corn & every year after the expiration of the sd four first years 600 lbs weight of good sound merchantable top tobacco clear of ground leaves & trash according to law together with cask & delivering the same at a convenient landing in the co the first of which tobacco paiments to commence & become due on 25 Dec 1734 ... . Wit: Elliott Benger, John Blackaby, Thomas Pitcher. (Pg 105)

Survey: 100 a. of land [*above*] mentioned surveyed by George Home surveyor of Spotsylvania Co by the order of Alexr Spotswood esqr for Elias Smith adj Thomas Jones ... [*drawing not included here*] ... . Memorandum that on 30 Oct MDCCXXXIV full quiet & peaceable possession & seizin of all the lands & messuages [*above*] mentioned was according to the form & effect of the [*above*] indenture delivered to the sd Elias Smith by the sd Alexander Spotswood in his own proper person. Wit: James Chissum, Thos Jones. Alexander Spotswood esqr ackn the [*above*] deed 5 Nov 1734 & at the motion of William Morton in behalf of the sd Smith is admitted to record. Attest: John Waller clk. (Pg 106)

2 Dec 1734. Deed of Lease. Augustine Smith of St. Marks Parish, Spotsylvania Co for 5 shillings leased to James Roy of St. George Parish, co afsd a 118 a. tr of land in St. George Parish bounded by Col Augustine Warner, the Matapony, Col Henry Fitzhugh & the br of Nassaponax ... during the term of one year paying the rent of one ear of Indian corn if demanded ... . Wit: Frans Thornton Junr, Anthony Rhodes Junr, Thomas Slaughter, G. Home. Ackn 3 Dec 1734 & admitted to record. Attest: John Waller clk. (Pg 107)

3 Dec 1734. Deed of Release. Augustin Smith of St. Marks Parish, Spotsylvania Co for £10 sold & released to James Roy of St. George Parish, co afsd a 118 a. tr of land ... [*same as above*] ... . Wit: Frans Thornton Junr, Thos Slaughter, G. Home, Anthony Rhodes Junr. Ackn 3 Dec 1734 & admitted to record. Attest: John Waller clk. (Pg 107)

XXIX Nov 1734. Deed of Lease. John Davis of St. Johns Parish, King William Co for 5 shillings leased to William Sandige of St. Margarets Parish, Caroline Co a 150 a. tr of land on the n side the Northanna River, the sd tr of land is pt/o a greater tr &c ... . Wit: Joseph Thomas, Robt Turner, Wm Waller. Proved 3 Dec 1734 & at the motion of Wm Waller in behalf of the sd Sandige is admitted to record. Attest: John Waller clk. (Pg 109)

2 Dec 1734. Deed of Release. John Davis of St. John Parish, King William Co for £35 sold & released to William Sandige of St. Margaretts Parish, Caroline Co a 150 a. tr of land ... [*same as above*] ... . Wit: Joseph Thomas, Robt Turner, Wm Waller. Proved 3 Dec 1734 & at the motion of Wm Waller in behalf of the sd Sandige is admitted to record. Attest: John Waller clk. (Pg 109)

1 Dec 1733. Deed. Abraham Estis of Saint Stephens Parish, King & Queen Co for £10 sold to John Leach of Saint Markes Parish, Spotsylvania Co a 200 a. tr of land in Saint Marks Parish on the brs of James River at the feet of the Great Mountains bounded by the Octuana line ... . Wit: Joseph Thomas, Robt Turner, Alexr Freeman. Proved 3 Dec 1734 & at the motion of Robert Turner in behalf of the sd Leach is admitted to record. Attest: John Waller clk. (Pg 110)

7 Jan 1734. Deed of Lease. Col Henry Willis gent of Spotsylvania Co for 5 shillings farm lett unto John Gordon of same co two lotts of land in the town of Fredricksburgh described in the plot of the sd town by the figures 25 & 26 being the two lotts as were formerly laid off for the used of Thomas Buckner one of the proprietors to whom the town land formerly belonged to before the sd town was erected the sd two lotts lying on Sophia Street, William Street & Caroline Street being set apart for the use of the sd Buckner by the trustees of the sd town … during the term of one year paying the yearly rent of one peper corn at the feast of St. Michael the Arch Angel if demanded … . Wit: John Grame, Larkin Chew, G. Home. Ackn 7 Jan 1734 & admitted to record. Attest: John Waller clk. (Pg 111)

8 Jan 1734. Deed of Release. Col Henry Willis gent of Spotsylvania Co for £11:1:6 sold & released to John Gordon of same co two lotts numbered 25 & 26 in the town of Fredricksburgh … [*same as above*] … . Wit: John Grame, Larkin Chew, G. Home. Ackn 7 Jan 1734 & admitted to record. Attest: John Waller clk. (Pg 112)

4 Jan MDCCXXXIV. Deed. John Waller gent of St. George Parish, Spotsylvania Co for £10:16 sold to John Trustee planter of same place a 108 a. tr of land in parish afsd on the brs of Raccoon Swamp bounded by John Wilkins, which sd 108 a. is pt/o a greater tr … . Wit: Robt Barret, Wm Waller, Pr Waller, Edmd Waller. Ackn 4 Mar 1734/5 by John Waller gent & at the motion of William Waller in behalf of the sd Trustee is admitted to record. Attest: John Waller clk. (Pg 113)

3 Mar 1734. Deed of Lease. John Waller & John Taliaferro gent feoffees & trustees appointed for the town of Fredricksburgh for 5 shillings leased to John Grymes esqr a lott of land being ½ a. of ground in the town of Fredericksburgh being one of the lotts of Princess Anne Street described in the town platt by the No. 61 … during the term of one year paying one pepper corn upon the feast of St. Michael the Arch Angel if demanded … . Wit: Wm Waller. Ackn 4 Mar 1734/5 by the sd trustees & at the motion of Henry Willis gent in behalf of the sd Grymes is admitted to record. Attest: John Waller clk. (Pg 115)

4 Mar 1734. Deed of Release. John Waller & John Taliaferro gent feoffees & trustees appointed for the town of Fredericksburgh for 55 shillings sold & released to John Grymes esqr Lot No. 61 in the town of Fredericksburgh … [*same as above*] … . Wit: Wm Waller. Ackn 4 Mar 1734/5 by the sd trustees & at the motion of Henry Willis gent in behalf of the sd Grymes is admitted to record. Attest: John Waller clk. (Pg 115)

3 Mar 1734. Deed of Lease. John Snell of St. George Parish, Spotsylvania Co for 5 shillings farm lett to Samuell Hencely (Hensley), Martha Hencely (Hensley) & Kathren Hencely (Katharine Hensley) of same place a 100 a. parcel of land or woodland ground in St. Georges Parish bounded by the sd John Snell & Greens Br ... during the term of one year paying the yearly rent of one ear of Indian corn on the feast of St. Michaell if demanded ... . Wit: G. Home, William Henslee. Ackn 4 Mar 1734/5 & admitted to record. Attest: John Waller clk. (Pg 116)

4 Mar 1734. Deed of Release. John Snell of St. Georges Parish, Spotsylvania Co for £50 sold & released to Samuell Hencely (Hensley), Martha Hencely (Hensley) & Kathren Hencely (Katharine Hensley) of same place a 100 a. tr of land ... [same as above] ... . Wit: G. Home, William Henslee. Ackn 4 Mar 1734/5 & admitted to record. Attest: John Waller clk. (Pg 117)

28 Feb 1734. Deed of Lease. Edward Pigg of St. Georges Parish, Spotsylvania Co for 5 shillings leased to Abraham Rogers of same place an 85 a. tr of land being pt/o 1860 a. granted to John Madison, John Rogers, Peter Rogers, Henry Pigg, Edward Pigg & John York by pattent dated 1 Apr 1717 being on the n side of the Middle River or forke of Mattapony bounded by Rogers' Mill ... during the term of 6 months ... . Wit: Jno Rogers, Wm Conner, Charles F. Pigg. Ackn 4 Mar 1734/5 & admitted to record. Attest: John Waller clk. (Pg 118)

1 Mar 1734. Deed of Release. Edward Pigg of Saint Georges Parish, Spotsylvania Co for £10 sold & released to Abraham Rogers of same place an 85 a. tr of land ... [same as above] ... . Wit: Jno Rogers, Wm Conner, Charles F. Pigg. Ackn 4 Mar 1734/5 & admitted to record. Attest: John Waller clk. (Pg 119)

27 Aug 1731. Deed of Mortgage. Between Andrew Harrison of Spotsylvania Co of the one part & Wm Johnson (Johnston) of co afsd of the other part, wit that whereas the sd Andrew Harrison is & stands justly indebted to the sd William Johnson in the sum of £50 part being by one judgment of Spotsylvania Court & the other part due by bill the sd judgment was obtain'd by Jno Fox & put into the sd Johnson's hands as sheriff & the sd Andrew in consideration thereof & for the better & more effectuall security of the sd debt to be paid to the sd William Johnson hath sold unto the sd William Johnson one Negro boy named [?], 3 feather beds & furniture, 1 flock ditto & furniture, 30 head of hoggs, 19 herd of cattle, 7 cows & calfs, 2 stears, 2 heffers & 1 bull, 1 duzen of chears & all my potts & dishes, 2 tables, 2 trunks, 1 large chest & 3 mairs ... upon condition that if the sd Andrew Harrison do well & truly pay unto the sd William Johnson the afsd sum of £50 at or upon 1 Dec next ensuing then this

indenture of sale to be voyd ... . Wit: Antho Foster. Proved 4 Mar 1734/5 & admitted to record. Attest: John Waller clk. (Pg 120)

3 Jun 1735. Deed. Rice Curtis of St. George Parish, Spotsylvania Co for £5 sold to Thomas Merry of same place a 180 a. tr of land or woodland ground in St. George Parish laying on the upper side of Greens Br the sd land being pt/o a pattent granted to Larkin Chew decd dated 4 Jun 1722 & sold by Thos Chew gent son & heir of the afsd Larkin to Rice Curtis by deed of lease & release dated 2 Apr 1733, bounded by corner of John Snell (Snale) decd now corner to Saml Hensley, John Talliaferro, the road that leads from Snales Bridge to Fredricksburgh, Wm Richerson & Jonathan Clark ... . Wit: R. Curtis Junr, Peter Mountague, John Wood. Ackn 3 Jun 1735 & admitted to record. Attest: John Waller clk. (Pg 121)

3 Jun 1735. Deed. Rice Curtis of St. George Parish, Spotsylvania Co for £7 sold to Peter Montague of same place a 228 a. tr of land or woodland ground in St. George Parish laying on the upper side of Greens Br the sd land being pt/o a pattent granted to Larkin Chew decd dated 4 Jun 1722 & sold by Thos Chew gent son & heir of the afsd Larkin to Rice Curtis by deeds of lease & release dated 2 Apr 1733 bounded by Wm Richerson, Jonathan Clark, Warner's line, Robt Hucherson, Greens Br & Thomas Merry ... . Wit: R. Curtis Junr, Thomas Merry, John Wood. Ackn 3 Jun 1735 & admitted to record. Attest: John Waller clk. (Pg 123)

3 Jun 1735. Deed. Rice Curtis of St. George Parish, Spotsylvania Co for £12 sold to John Wood of same place a 100 a. tr of land or woodland ground in St. George Parish laying on the upper side of the road that leads from Snales Bridge to Fredricksburgh being pt/o a pattent granted to Larkin Chew decd dated 4 Jun 1722 & the same being sold by Thomas Chew gent son & heir of the afsd Larkin to Rice Curtis by deeds of lease & release dated 2 Apr 1733 bounded by William Richason (Richerson), John Taliaferro (Tolefferro) & Thomas Merry ... . Wit: R. Curtis Junr, Peter Mountague, Thos Merry. Ackn 3 Jun 1735 & admitted to record. Attest: John Waller clk. (Pg 124)

2 Jun 1735. Deed of Lease. Robert Goodloe of St. George Parish, Spotsylvania Co planter for 5 shillings leased to Joseph Carter of same place planter a 190 a. tr of land it being pt/o a tr granted to the sd Robert Goodloe by patent dated 28 Sep 1728 bounded by Robinsons Br ... during the term of one year paying the rent of one ear of Indian corne if demanded on the feast of all Saints ... . Wit: W. Robinson, Larkin Chew, Wm Waller. Ackn 3 Jun 1735 & admitted to record. Attest: John Waller clk. (Pg 125)

3 Jun 1735. Deed of Release. Robert Goodloe of St. George Parish, Spotsylvania Co planter for £20 sold & released to Joseph Carter of Same place planter a 190 a. tr of land ... [*same as above*] .... Wit: W. Robinson, Larkin Chew, Wm Waller. Ackn 3 Jun 1735 & admitted to record. Attest: John Waller clk. (Pg 126)

28 May 1735. Deed of Lease. John Miller Junr of Saint Marys Parish, Caroline Co, VA for 5 shillings leased to Samuel Long of St. Georges Parish, Spotsilvania Co a 70 a. tr of land being pt/o a pattent granted to John Quarles of Spotsylvania Co dated 30 Sep 1723 being in the parish afsd bounded by Wolf Pit Br out of Nessaponack, a br a little above Jno Miller's plantation, sd Quarles Line & Nessaponack Run ... during the term of one year paying the rent of one peper corn att the feast of St. Michael the Arch Angel if demanded .... Wit: Wm Bartlet, Jno Curtis, John Wood. Ackn 3 Jun 1735 & admitted to record. Attest: John Waller clk. (Pg 128)

28 May 1735. Deed of Release. John Miller Junr of Saint Marys Parish, Caroline Co, VA for 5 shillings sold & released to Samuel Long of St. Georges Parish, Spotsilvania Co a 70 a. tr of land ... [*same as above*] .... Wit: Wm Bartlet, Jno Curtis, John Wood. Ackn 3 Jun 1735 & admitted to record. Attest: John Waller clk. (Pg 128)

2 Jun 1735. Deed of Lease. Henry Goodloe gent of Spotsylvania Co for 5 shillings leased to Mark Whealer (Wheeler) of same co a 100 a. tr of land in St. Georges Parish on one of the brs of the North Fork of the South River adj the sd Goodloe ... during the term of one year paying the rent of one ear of Indian corne on the birthday of our Lord God next ensuing if demanded .... Wit: John Minor, Robt Stubblefield, Robt Goodloe, Geo Goodloe. Proved 3 Jun 1735 & at the motion of John Minor in behalf of the sd Wheeler is admitted to record. Attest: John Waller clk. (Pg 130)

3 Jun 1735. Deed of Release. Henry Goodloe gent of Spotsylvania Co for £10 sold & released to Mark Wheeler of co afsd a 100 a. tr of land ... [*same as above*] .... Wit: John Minor, Robt Stubblefield, Robt Goodloe, Geo Goodloe. Proved 3 Jun 1735 & at the motion of John Minor in behalf of the sd Wheeler is admitted to record. Attest: John Waller clk. (Pg 131)

23 Jun MDCCXXXV. Deed of Gift. John Waller of Spotsylvania Co gent for natural love & affection hath given to William Waller (son of the sd John Waller) a 274 ½ a. tr of land on the ridge between Mattapony & Pamunkey River's bounded by John Trustee, Thomas Sertain, John Sertain & Benjamin Waller, the sd tr of land is pt/o a greater tr .... Wit: Thos Carr Junr, B. Waller,

Edmund Waller, Thomas Robinson. Ackn 1 Jul 1735 & admitted to record. Attest: John Waller clk. (Pg 132)

12 Jun 1735. Deed of Lease. Rowland Thomas of King & Queen Co for 5 shillings leased to Joseph Thomas of Spotsylvania Co a 900 a. tr of land on the n side the Northanna in St. George Parish being pt/o a patent granted unto Rowland Thomas for 1,000 a. dated 16 Jun 1727 bounded by Wolf Swamp, Robert Turner, Christopher Smith & Holladays Swamp ... during the term of one year paying one pepper corn upon the feast of St. Michael the Arch Angel if demanded ... . Wit: Thomas Hill, Robt Turner, Wm Waller. Proved 1 Jul 1735 & admitted to record. Attest: John Waller clk. (Pg 134)

13 Jun 1735. Deed of Release. Rowland Thomas of King & Queen Co for £20 sold & released to Joseph Thomas of Spotsylvania Co a 900 a. tr of land ... [*same as above*] ... . Wit: Thomas Hill, Robt Turner, Wm Waller. Proved 1 Jul 1735 & admitted to record. Attest: John Waller clk. (Pg 134)

30 Jun 1735. Deed of Lease. Thomas Sartin of St. George Parish, Spotsylvania Co for 5 shillings leased to Peter Gustavas of same place a 600 a. tr of land being in the parish afsd bounded by James Taylor decd & Thomas Sartin, the same being pt/o a 1,000 a. tr of land granted to the sd Thomas Sartin by patent dated 6 May MDCCXXVII ... during the term of one year paying the rent of one ear of Indian corn if demanded on the feast of St. Michael the Arch Angel ... . Wit: Wm Waller, James Ferry, Thomas Estes. Ackn 1 Jul 1735 & admitted to record. Attest: John Waller clk. (Pg 135)

1 Jul 1735. Deed of Release. Thomas Sartin of St. George Parish, Spotsylvania Co for 300 lbs of tobacco sold & released to Peter Gustavas of same place a 600 a. tr of land ... [*same as above*] ... . Wit: Wm Waller, James Terry, Thomas Estes. Ackn 1 Jul 1735 by Thomas Sartin & Mary the w/o the sd Thomas ackn her right of dower the same is admitted to record. Attest: John Waller clk. (Pg 137)

1 Jul 1735. Deed of Release. Thomas Sartin of St. Georges Parish, Spotsylvania Co for 1600 lbs of tobacco sold to James Terry of same place in his actual possession now being by virtue of a bargain & sail to him made for one year by indentured dated three days before the date hereof [*not recorded before this deed*] a 200 a. tr of land bounded by Thomas Sartin & Peter Gustavase ... . Wit: Wm Waller, Peter Gustavas, Thomas Estes. Ackn 1 Jul 1735 by Thomas Sartin & Mary the w/o the sd Thomas ackn her right of dower & the same is admitted to record. Attest: John Waller clk. (Pg 138)

1 Jul 1735. Deed. The gentlemen trustees for the town of Fredericksburgh for £8:10 sold to Hancock Lee gent of Spotsylvania Co two lotts of land quantity ½ a. each numbered in the platt of the town 35 & 36 being in Charlotte Street ... . Signed Hen Willis, J. Taliaferro, John Waller. Wit: T. Turner, Thos Catlett. Ackn 1 Jul 1735 by Henry Willis & John Waller gent two of the trustees of the town of Fredericksburgh & admitted to record. Attest: John Waller clk. (Pg 140)

30 Jun MDCCXXXV. Deed of Lease. Edward Franklyn of St. Mark Parish, Orange Co, VA leased to George Carter of St. George Parish, Spotsylvania Co a 200 a. tr of land in St. George Parish bounded by Glady Fork Run ... during the term of one year paying the rent of one pepper corn at the feast of St. Michael the Arch Angel if demanded ... . Wit: Wm Waller, David Kinkead, Edmd Pagett, Edwd Herndon Junr. Ackn 1 Jul 1735 by Edward Franklyn & at the motion of William Waller in behalf of the sd Carter is admitted to record. Attest: John Waller clk. (Pg 140)

1 Jul MDCCXXXV. Deed of Release. Edward Franklyn of St. Mark Parish, Orange Co, VA for £20 sold & released to George Carter of St. George Parish, Spotsylvania Co a 200 a. tr of land, which sd tr of land is pt/o a pattent granted to John Chew for 608 a. dated 4 Jun MDCCXXVI & by the sd John Chew sold to the sd Edward Franklyn & conveyed by deeds of lease & released ackn 5 Aug MDCCXXIX ... [same as above] ... . Wit: David Kinkead, Edmd Pagett, Edwd Herndon Junr. Ackn 1 Jul 1735 by Edward Franklyn & at the motion of William Waller in behalf of the sd Carter is admitted to record. Attest: John Waller clk. (Pg 141)

30 Jun MDCCXXXV. Deed of Lease. Thomas Chew heir at law & Larkin Chew adminr of the will annexed of Larkin Chew gent decd of St. George Parish, Spotsylvania Co gent for 5 shillings leased to Abraham Mayfeild of same place a messuage & 200 a. tr of land in the parish afsd adj to the lands (formerly) of Major Benja Robinson, the river Po & Philip Brandegan ... during the term of one year paying the yearly rent of one pepper corn at the feast of St. Michael the Arch Angel if demanded ... . Ackn 1 Jul 1735 & admitted to record. Attest: John Waller clk. (Pg 143)

1 Jul MDCCXXXV. Deed of Release. Thomas Chew heir at law & Larkin Chew adminr of the will annexed of Larkin Chew gent decd of St. George Parish, Spotsylvania Co gent for £12 by one James Stewart paid (for the consideration the sd decd did oblige himself to ackn the land & premises to the sd Stewart or his order (per his bond) & afterwards the sd Stewart did assign over the sd bond unto Anthony Foster who hath sold the same to the sd Abraham Mayfield but more especially for & in consideration & complyance of a decree

in chancery obtained by the sd Anthony Foster 6 Mar 1733/4 in Spotsylvania Co Court agt the sd Thomas Chew & Larkin Chew for the making a conveyance of their right to the sd land) have sold & released to Abraham Mayfield of same place a messuage & 200 a. tr of land ... [*same as above*] .... Wit: Chas Smith. Ackn 1 Jul 1735 & admitted to record. Attest: John Waller clk. (Pg 143)

28 May 1735. Deed of Lease. John Parks of St. George Parish, Spotsylvania Co for 5 shillings leased to John True of Gloucester Co planter & Martin True of St. George Parish, Spotsylvania Co planter a 200 a. tr of land in St. George Parish (that is to say) 150 a. thereof unto the afsd John True & 50 a. the residue of the sd 200 a. of land unto the afsd Martin True bounded by William Holloway, Elias Downs Senr & Elias Downs Junr ... during the term of one year paying the yearly rent of one ear of Indian corn at the feast of St. Michael the Arch Angel if demanded .... Wit: M. Battaley, Henry Martin, Henry Martin. Ackn 2 Sep 1735 & admitted to record. Attest: John Waller clk. (Pg 144)

29 May 1735. Deed of Release. John Parks of St. George Parish, Spotsylvania Co blacksmith for £40 sold & released to John True of Gloucester Co planter & Martin True of St. George Parish, Spotsylvania Co planter a 200 a. tr of land ... [*same as above*] .... Wit: M. Battaley, Henry Martin, Henry Martin. Ackn 2 Sep 1735 by John Parkes & Margaret the w/o the sd John Parkes ackn her right of dower & the same is admitted to record. Attest: John Waller clk. (Pg 145)

2 Sep MDCCXXXV. Deed of Gift. Edward Herndon of Caroline Co for naturall love & affection hath given to Edward Herndon Junr (son of the afsd Edward Herndon) a 400 a. tr of land in St. George Parish bounded by the corner of Mrs. Mary Waller (now Zachary Lewis's), Capt Larkin Chew (now Hawkins's) & the Poyson Fields, which tr of 400 a. of land was granted by patent to the sd Edward Herndon dated XXI Jun MDCCXXVII .... Wit: Wm Waller, Jos Brock. Ackn 2 Sep 1735 & admitted to record. Attest: John Waller clk. (Pg 147)

31 Dec 1734. Deed of Lease. Alexander Spotswood esqr for & in consideration of the rents & covenants hereinafter mentioned doth farm let unto William Pannel planter a 172 a. tr of land (except all mines, minerals & quarries whatsoever) in St. Mark Parish on the s side of the River Rapidanne being pt/o a 40,000 a. tr of land granted by letters patent to the sd Alexander Spotswood & called the Spotsylvania Tract the bounds & limits of which 172 a. of land are described by a plot & survey thereof ... to the sd William Pannel during the natural lives of the sd William & Sarah Pannel his wife & for & during the natural life of the longest liver of them paying yearly of the first four years on 25 Dec one ear of Indian corn & every year after the expiration of the sd four first years 816 lbs weight of good sound merchantable top tobacco clear of ground

leaves & trash according to law together with cask & delivering the same at a convenient landing in the co the first of which tobacco paiments to commence & become due on 25 Dec 1739 .... Wit: John Lightfoot, Elliott Benger, Abraham Chambers. (Pg 148)

Survey: 172 a. of land [above] mentioned surveyed by George Home surveyor of Spotsylvania Co by order of Alexr Spotswood esqr for William Pannel adj Thos Jones & Raccoon Br .... Memorandum that on 14 Jul 1735 full quiet & peaceable possession & seizing of all the lands & messuages [above] mentioned was according to the form & effect of the indenture [above] delivered to the sd William Pannell by John Branham atty of the sd Alexander Spotswood for that purpose constituted. Wit: Bryan Sisson, Ambras Jones. Ackn 2 Sep 1735 & admitted to record. Attest: John Waller clk. (Pg 150)

30 Nov 1734. Deed of Lease. Alexander Spotswood esqr for & in consideration of the rents & covenants hereinafter mentioned doth farm let unto John Ingram planter a 172 a. tr of land (except the mines, minerals & quarries whatsoever) being in St. Mark Parish on the s side of the River Rapidanne being pt/o a 40,000 a. tr of land granted by letters patents to the sd Alexander Spotswood & called the Spotsylvania Tract the bounds & limits of which 172 a. of land are described by a plot & survey thereof ... to the sd John Ingram during the natural lives of Hannah Ingram (his wife) & John Ingram Junr (his son) & during the natural life of the longest liver of them paying the yearly rent of the first four years on 25 Dec one ear of Indian corn & every year after the expiration of the sd four first years 816 lbs weight of good sound merchantable top tobacco clear of ground leaves & trash according to law together with cask & delivering the same at a convenient landing in the co the first of which tobacco paiments to commence & become due on 25 Dec 1736 .... Wit: And Landale, James Gibbs, Luke Thornton. (Pg 150)

Survey: 172 a. of land [above] mentioned surveyed by George Home surveyor of Spotsylvania Co by the order of Alexr Spotswood for John Ingram adj Thomas Patty's Spring Br & Ingram's Spring Br .... Memorandum that on 14 Jul 1735 full quiet & peaceable possession & seizen of all the lands & messuages [above] mentioned was according to the form & effects of the indenture [above] delivered to the sd John Ingram by James Chisum atty of the sd Alexander Spotswood for that purpose constituted. Wit: Charles Spoe, Bryan Sisson. Ackn 2 Sep 1735 & admitted to record. Attest: John Waller clk. (Pg 152)

30 Nov 1734. Deed of Lease. Alexander Spotswood esqr for & in consideration of the rents & covenants hereinafter mentioned doth farm letten unto Luke Thornton planter a 200 a. tr of land (except all mines, minerals & quarries

whatsoever) being in St. Mark Parish on the s side of the River Rapidanne being pt/o a 40,000 a. tr of land granted by letters patent to the sd Alexander Spotswood & called the Spotsylvania Tract the bounds & limits which 200 a. of land are described by a plot & survey thereof ... to the sd Luke Thornton during the natural lives of the sd Luke Thornton & John Randell (his brother in law) for & during the natural life of the longest liver of them paying yearly of the first four years on 25 Dec one ear of Indian corn & every year after the expiration of the sd four first years 900 lbs weight of good sound merchantable top tobacco clear of ground leaves & trash according to law together with cask & delivering the same at a convenient landing in the co the first of which tobacco paiments to commence & become due on 25 Dec 1739 ... . Wit: And Landale, James Gibbs, John Ingram. (Pg 153)

Survey: 200 a. of land [*above*] mentioned surveyed by George Home surveyor of Spotsylvania Co by the order of Alexr Spotswood for Luke Thornton adj Rappidanne River, the Naked Mountain, the Rockey Br & Thomas Pattey Junr ... . Memorandum that on 14 Jul 1735 full quiet & peaceable possession & seizen of all the lands & messuages [*above*] mentioned was according to the form & effects of the indenture [*above*] delivered to the sd Luke Thornton by James Chisum atty of the sd Alexander Spotswood for that purpose constituted. Wit: Bryan Sisson, Charles Spoe. Ackn 2 Sep 1735 & admitted to record. Attest: John Waller clk. (Pg 154)

5 Oct MDCCXXXV. Deed of Lease. William Bradburn of St. George Parish, Spotsylvania Co for 5 shillings leased to James Stevens of St. Stephen Parish, King & Queen Co, VA a 200 a. tr of land in St. George Parish bounded by James Samms ... during the term of one year paying the rent of one pepper corn at the feast of St. Michael the Arch Angel if demanded ... . Wit: John Waller, Edwd Herndon Junr, Wm Waller. Ackn 7 Oct 1735 & admitted to record. Attest: John Waller clk. (Pg 155)

6 Oct MDCCXXXV. Deed of Release. William Bradburn of St. George Parish, Spotsylvania Co for £60 sold & released to James Stevens of St. Stephen Parish, King & Queen Co, VA a 200 a. tr of land, which tr of land is pt/o a pattent granted to Larkin Chew decd dated 4 Jun MDCCXXII & by the sd Larkin Chew sold to the sd William Bradburn by deeds of lease & release ackn 6 Oct MDCCXXIII? ... [*same as above*] ... . Wit: John Waller, Edwd Herndon Junr, Wm Waller. Ackn 7 Oct 1735 by William Bradburn & Sarah the w/o the sd William ackn her right of dower & the same is admitted to record. Attest: John Waller clk. (Pg 156)

6 Oct 1735. Deed of Lease. John Holladay gent of Spotsylvania Co for 5 shillings leased to Thomas Pulliam a 200 a. tr of land being pt/o a larger tr

belonging to the sd Holladay bounded by Holladays Swamp & the sd Holladay's lower line ... during the term of one year paying the rent of one ear of Indian corn on the feast of St. Michael if demanded ... . Wit: Joseph Woollfolk, Wm Waller, John Waller. Ackn 7 Oct 1735 & admitted to record. Attest: John Waller clk. (Pg 157)

7 Oct 1735. Deed of Release. John Holladay gent of Spotsylvania Co for 5 shillings & divers other good considerations hath sold & released to Thomas Pulliam a 200 a. tr of land ... [*same as above*] ... . Wit: Joseph Woollfolk, Wm Waller, John Waller. Ackn 7 Oct 1735 & admitted to record. Attest: John Waller clk. (Pg 158)

21 Jul MDCCXXXV. Deed. Henry Willis & John Waller gent two of the directors & trustees for Fredericksburgh Town, Spotsylvania Co for £5:10 sold to John Tennant of co afsd 1 a. or two lotts of land in Fredericksburgh Town numbered 63 & 64 bounded (as per a plat & survey made by George Home surveyor on 13 Aug MDCCXXVIII) on Princess Ann Street & Amelia Street ... provided that the sd John Tennant shall & will erect built & finish on each of the sd lotts one house of brick, stone or of wood well framed of the dimensions of 20' square & 9' pitch within two years otherwise this deed to be void & the lotts herein mentioned to be revested in the sd trustees to be by them sold & conveyed again by auction ... . Wit: Wm Waller, Jas Taliaferro. Ackn 8 Oct 1735 & admitted to record. Attest: John Waller clk. (Pg 159)

2 Oct 1735. Deed. David Woodrof of St. Margarets Parish, Caroline Co for £50 sold to Joseph Woolfolk of same place a 381 a. tr of land in St. George Parish near East North East Bridge bounded by Dennit Abney Junr, John Chiles, John & James Taylor, Honey Swamp, Edmund Waller & Thomas Hill, which sd tr of land was granted to the sd David Woodrof by patent dated 3 Dec 1733 ... . Wit: Thos Dickenson, William Dickenson, John Dickenson. Ackn 7 Oct 1735 by David Woodroof & Anne the w/o the sd David ackn he right of dower & the same is admitted to record. Attest: John Waller clk. (Pg 159)

2 Oct 1735. Bond. I David Woodrof of St. Margarets Parish, Caroline Co am firmly bound unto Joseph Woolfolk of same place in the sum of £100 ... the condition of this obligation is such that if the afsd David Woodrof shall well & truly observe, fulfill & perform all & every the clauses, covenants & agreements mentioned, comprised & contained in an indenture [*see above*] then this obligation to be void ... . Wit: Thos Dickenson, Willm Dickenson, John Dickenson. Ackn 7 Oct 1735 & admitted to record. Attest: John Waller clk. (Pg 160)

A plan of the lands [*drawing not included here*] belonging to Col Henry Willis & John Royston containing in all 1,858 a. who settled their bounds by agreement of both parties this 3rd day of 8br 1735 adj the Rappahannock River (Col Henry Willis 929 a. & John Royston 929 a.) ... . G. Home surveyor Sp Co. At a court held 7 Oct 1735 on motion of Henry Willis & John Royston gent to have this their plan & division of their land recorded is granted. Attest: John Waller clk. (Pg 161)

3 Nov 1735. Deed of Lease. Anthony Thornton gent of Stafford Co for 5 shillings leased to Sharshall Grasty of King & Queen Co a 270 a. tr of land in St. Georges Parish bounded by the road ... during the term of one year paying the rent of one ear of Indian corn at the feast of St. Michael the Arch Angel if demanded ... . Wit: Wm Waller, G. Home, Antho Strother, Edwd Herndon Junr. Ackn & admitted to record. Attest: John Waller clk. (Pg 161)

4 Nov 1735. Deed of Release. Anthony Thornton gent of Stafford Co for £60 sold & released to Sharshall Grasty of King & Queen Co a 270 a. tr of land, being pt/o a patent granted unto the sd Anthony & Francis Thornton for 2,740 a. dated 19 Apr 1720 ... [*same as above*] ... . Wit: Wm Waller, G. Home, Antho Strother, Edwd Herndon Junr. Ackn 4 Nov 1735 & admitted to record. Attest: John Waller clk. (Pg 162)

3 Nov 1735. Deed of Lease. Mary Abney of St. Pauls Parish, Hanover Co for 5 shillings leased to Edwin Hickman of St. George Parish, Spotsylvania Co a 209 ½ a. tr of land in the parrish afsd being pt/o a larger tr of land granted to Thomas Hill & Dannitt Abney by patent dated 28 Sep 1728 adj Zachry Lewis, Honey (Hunny) Swamp & Joseph Woolfolk's line formerly known by the name of Smith's line & Low Ground Swamp ... during the term of one year paying one ear of Indian corn upon the feast of St. Michael the Arch Angell if demanded ... . Wit: Z. Lewis, Edwd Herndon Junr, Wm Waller, Robt Turner. Proved 2 Dec 1735 & recorded. Attest: John Waller clk. (Pg 164)

4 Nov 1735. Deed of Release. Mary Abney of St. Pauls Parish, Hanover Co for £21 sold & released to Edwin Hickman of St. George Parish, Spotsylvania Co a 209 ½ a. tr of land ... [*same as above*] ... . Wit: Zachary Lewis, Edwd Herndon Junr, Wm Waller, Robt Turner. Proved 2 Dec 1735 & admitted to record. Attest: John Waller clk. (Pg 165)

22 10br 1735. Deed of Lease. George Prockter of Spotsylvania Co for 5 shillings farm lett to John Prockter & Elias Sharp of co afsd a 230 a. parcel of land or woodland ground on the brs of the Hasell Run bounded by Feigans Br, Cock's line, Francis & Antony Thornton ... during the term of one year paying the yearly rent of one ear of Indian corn on the feast of St. Michael if demanded

.... Wit: G. Home, Wm Moore, John Manard. Attest: John Waller clk. (Pg 166)

23 10br 1735. Deed of Release. George Prockter of Spotsylvania Co for £100 sold & released to John Prockter & Elias Sharp of co afsd a 230 a. parcel of land ... [*same as above*] .... Wit: G. Home, Wm Moore, John Manard. Ackn 3 Feb 1735/6 & admitted to record. Attest: John Waller clk. (Pg 167)

30 Oct 1735. Deed of Gift. Joseph Brock of St. Georges Parish, Spotsylvania Co in consideration of Rice Curtis Junr intermarrying with one of the sd Joseph Brock's daus & divers other causes & considerations hath given to the sd Rice Curtis Junr of same place planter a 865 a. parcel of land or woodland ground in St. Georges Parish being pt/o two patents formerly granted to Larkin Chew gent decd dated as followeth, viz, one of them for 9,400 a. dated 4 Jun 1722 the other for 1,600 a. dated 12 Jun 1723, the same being sold by the sd Larkin Chew to the sd Joseph Brock by deeds of lease & release dated 17 Oct 1723, bounded by John Waller, Thos Butler, Branagan's line, Bushes Road, Beverleys Main Road & the Salt Pond .... Wit: Wm Bartlett, Anthony Foster, James Stewart. Ackn 3 Feb 1735/6 & admitted to record. Attest: John Waller clk. (Pg 168)

30 Oct 1735. Bond. I Joseph Brock of Spotsylvania Co am firmly bound unto Rice Curtis Junr of Spotsylvania Co in the sum of £500 ... the condition of this obligation is such that if the afsd Joseph Brock shall well & truly perform & keep all the covenants mentioned in an indenture [*see above*] then this obligation to be void .... Wit: Wm Bartlet, Anthony Foster, James Stewart. Ackn 3 Feb 1735/6 & admitted to record. Attest: John Waller clk. (Pg 170)

15 Feb 1726/7. Bond. I Thos Butler of Stafford Co am firmly bound unto Saml Bartlett of Spotsylvania Co in the sum of £30 ... the condition of this obligation is such that whereas the afsd Saml Bartlett hath this day bought of the afsd Thos Butler (that is to say) a sertaine 150 a. tr of land firmly bought of Larkin Chew ajoyning to the land now in the possession of Richard Walker, now if the afsd Thos Butler doe whenever required ackn the afsd land by good deeds such as the law requires unto the afsd Samll Bartlett then this obligation to be void .... Wit: Wm Bartlet, Larkin Chew Junr. 7 Apr 1729 I do assign the within bond from me Saml Bartlet to William Bartlett. Wit: Abram Mayfield, Anthony Foster. I Wm Bartlet do hereby assine all my right & title of the within bond to Rice Curtis Junr 17 Dec 1735. Thomas Butler's bond for the acknowledgment of land unto Samuell Bartlett was proved & the sd Samuel Bartlett's assignment thereto to William Bartlett was proved & the sd William Bartlett ackn that he had assigned his right in & to the sd bond to Rice Curtis Junr gent at whose motion the same is admitted to record. Attest: John Waller clk. (Pg 170)

27 Feb 1735. Deed. William Richerson of St. George Parish, Spotsylvania Co for 850 lbs of tobacco sold to John Wood of St. George Parish, co afsd a 50 a. tr of land or woodland being pt/o a tr formerly belonging to Larkin Chew gent decd & by him sold to the sd William Richerson by deeds dated 2 Oct 1722, it being bounded by John Taliaferro, the sd William Richerson, land that the sd Wood lives on, Jonathan Clark, Thomas Merry & Peter Mountague ... . Wit: Rice Curtis, Peter Mountague, R. Curtis Junr. Ackn 2 Mar 1735/6 by William Richardson & Sarah the w/o the sd William ackn her right of dower & the same is admitted to record. Attest: John Waller clk. (Pg 171)

27 Feb 1735/6. Bond. I William Richerson of Spotsylvania Co am firmly bound unto John Wood of the sd co in the sum of £30 ... the condition of this obligation is such that if the afsd William Richerson shall well & truly performe & keep all the covenants mentioned in a certain deed [see above] then this obligation to be void ... . Wit: Rice Curtis, Peter Mountague, R. Curtis Junr. Ackn 2 Mar 1735/6 & admitted to record. Attest: John Waller clk. (Pg 173)

1 Mar 1735. Deed of Lease. George Home & Elizabeth his wife of St. George Parish, Spotsylvania Co for 5 shillings leased to John Gordon of same place innkeeper a 200 a. tr of land (being the tr whereon the sd Home now liveth) ... during the term of one year paying the rent of one graine of Indian corn at the feast of St. Michael the Arch Angel if demanded ... . Wit: Joseph Thomas, Richd Tutt, Henry Brock. Ackn 2 Mar 1735/6 by George Home & Elizabeth his wife & admitted to record. Attest: John Waller clk. (Pg 173)

2 Mar 1735. Deed of Release. George Home & Elizabeth his wife of St. George Parish, Spotsylvania Co for £80 sold & released to John Gordon of same place a 200 a. tr of land, it being the same tr of land that was conveyed by a deed of gift from George Procter decd to the sd George Home & Elizabeth his wife 3 Jul 1728 ... [same as above] ... . Wit: Joseph Thomas, Richd Tutt, Henry Brock. Ackn 2 Mar 1735/6 by George Home & Elizabeth his wife & admitted to record. Attest: John Waller clk. (Pg 174)

16 Mar 1735. Deed of Lease. Henry Goodloe of Spotsylvania Co for 5 shillings leased to Augustine Owen of co afsd a 100 a. parcel of land in Saint Georges Parish on the n side of North Fork Br bounded by Henry Goodloe ... during the term of one year paying the rent of one ear of Indian corn on the birthday of our Lord God next ensuing if demanded ... . Wit: Geo Goodloe, Robt Durrett, John Buford. Ackn 6 Apr 1736 by Henry Goodloe gent & at the motion of John Buford in behalf of the sd Owen is admitted to record. Attest: John Waller clk. (Pg 176)

17 Mar 1735. Deed of Release. Henry Goodloe of Spotsylvania Co for £15 sold & released to Augustine Owen of co afsd a 100 a. parcel of land ... [*same as above*] ... . Wit: Geo Goodloe, Robert Durret, John Buford. Ackn 6 Apr 1736 by Henry Goodloe gent & at the motion of John Buford in behalf of the sd Owen is admitted to record. Attest: John Waller clk. (Pg 176)

6 Apr 1736. Deed of Gift. I Henery Martin for the love & affection which I bear my well beloved children William Martin & Benjamin Martin I do give unto them a 300 a. parcel of land on the n side of the River Po adj Capt Henry Beaverley ... . Wit: Samuell Long, Thos Ship. Ackn 6 Apr 1736 & admitted to record. Attest: John Waller clk. (Pg 178)

5 Apr 1736. Deed of Lease. Henry Willis esqr of Spotsylvania Co for 5 shillings leased to Thomas Shipp of Essex Co a 400 a. tr of land being a tr of land formerly granted to William Hansford by patent dated 4 May 1723 & lapsed from the sd Hansford for want of a cultivation & then granted to the sd Henry Willis adj Nassaponock Swamp & Augustine Smith ... during the term of one year paying one pepper corn upon the feast of St. Michael the Arch Angel if demanded ... . Wit: Robt Turner, Henry Goodloe, Wm Waller. Ackn 6 Apr 1736 & admitted to record. Attest: John Waller clk. (Pg 178)

6 Apr 1736. Deed of Release. Henry Willis esqr of Spotsylvania Co for £50 sold & released to Thomas Shipp of Essex Co a 400 a. tr of land ... [*same as above*] ... . Wit: Robt Turner, Henry Goodloe, Wm Waller. Ackn 6 Apr 1736 & admitted to record. Attest: John Waller clk. (Pg 179)

5 Apr MDCCXXXVI. Deed of Lease. Vincent Tapp of St. George Parish, Spotsylvania Co for 5 shillings leased to John Ellson of same place a 175 a. tr of land in St. George Parish bounded by William Tapp, sd Vincent Tapp, Charity Wood & a br of Mattapony ... during the term of one year paying yearly on the feast of St. Michael the Arch Angel the rent of one pepper corn if demanded ... . Wit: Henery Sparkes, Jno Curtis. Ackn 6 Apr 1736 & admitted to record. Attest: John Waller clk. (Pg 181)

6 Apr MDCCXXXVI. Deed of Release. Vincent Tapp of St. George Parish, Spotsylvania Co for £21 sold & released to John Ellson of same place a 175 a. tr of land ... [*same as above*] ... . Wit: Jno Curtis, Henery Sparkes. Ackn 6 Apr 1736 & admitted to record. Attest: John Waller clk. (Pg 182)

31 Oct 1735. Power of Attorney. I Wenifred (Winnifred) Thornton w/o Anthony Thornton gent of Stafford Co do appoint my trusty friend Col John Waller of Spotsylvania Co my atty to ackn & convey my right of dower in & to a 270 a. tr of land unto Sharshall Grasty of King & Queen Co as by the deeds of

lease & release for the sd 200 a. of land from my sd husband Anthony Thornton
sold unto the sd Sharshall Grasty ... . Wit: Wm Thornton Junr, Anthony
Strother. Proved 4 May 1736 & admitted to record. Attest: John Waller clk.
(Pg 183)

1 May 1736. Deed of Gift. Henry Goodloe of Saint George Parish,
Spotsylvania Co gent for naturall love & affection have given unto my well
beloved dau Elizabeth the now w/o Robert Durret (Durrett) of parish afsd a 190
a. tr of land in the parish afsd bounded by the sd Robert Durrett, George
Goodloe & Robert Goodloe ... . Wit: Jno [?], Wm Waller. Ackn 1 Jun 1736 &
admitted to record. Attest: John Waller clk. (Pg 183)

1 Jun 1736. Deed of Gift. I Francis Thornton of St. Maries Parish, Caroline Co,
VA gent for divers good causes & valuable considerations but more especially
for naturall love & affection have given unto my beloved son Frans Thornton
Junr 41 a. of land lying at the falls of Rappa River it being a tr of land I took up
myself the patent dated 25 Feb 1720 & is bounded by the Rappahannock River,
Vicaris Island, the sd Francis & Rowland Thornton & included the sd island ... .
Wit: Thos Meriwether, Nicho Battaile, John Thornton. Ackn 1 Jun 1736 &
admitted to record. Attest: John Waller clk. (Pg 185)

13 Jan 1735. Power of Attorney. I Thomas Giffin of Leaden Hall Street,
London merchant have appointed Francis Thornton the elder of Caroline Co in
Rappahannock River in VA merchant & Francis Thornton the younger of
Spotsilvania Co in Rappahannock River afsd merchant or either of them to be
my atty to aske, demand & receive of & from all & every person whatsoever
whome it shall or may concerne all manner of goods, wares, merchandizes &
effects of any sort or kind whatsoever & also all & every debt & sumes of
money which is or are now due oweing or belonging to me from every or any
person whomsoever ... . Wit: T. Dove, Thos Dove Junr. Proved 1 Jun 1736 &
admitted to record. Attest: John Waller clk. (Pg 185)

7 Jul 1736. Deed of Lease. William Johnston of St. George Parish,
Spotsylvania Co & Ann his wife for 5 shillings leased to John Hoard of Essex
Co a 223 a. tr of land adj Col John Lewis, on the ridge between the River Ny &
the brs of Nassaponix ... during the term of one year paying the yearly rent of
one pepper corn at the feast of St. Michael the Arch Angel if demanded ... .
Wit: Anthony Foster, Fra Smith, Thomas Foster. Ackn 6 Jul 1736 by William
Johnston gent & Ann his wife & admitted to record. Attest: John Waller clk.
(Pg 186)

6 Jul 1736. Deed of Release. William Johnston of St. George Parish,
Spotsylvania Co for £26 sold & released to John Hoard of Essex Co a 223 a. tr

of land ... [*same as above*] ... . Wit: Anthony Foster, Fra Smith, Thomas Foster. Ackn by William Johnston & Ann his wife 6 Jul 1736 & admitted to record. Attest: John Waller clk. (Pg 187)

7 Jul 1736. Deed of Lease. William Johnston & Ann his wife of St. George Parish, Spotsylvania Co for 5 shillings leased to Thomas Red of King & Queen Co a 377 a. tr of land adj Col Lewis, Holloway's line & Elias Downs, lying in the parish afsd on the brs of Nasaponix ... during the term of [?] paying the rent of one peper corn at the feast of St. Michael the Arch Angel if demanded ... . Wit: Anthony Foster, Fra Smith, Thomas Foster. Ackn 6 Jul 1736 by William Johnston gent & Ann his wife & admitted to record. Attest: John Waller clk. (Pg 188)

6 Jul 1736. Deed of Release. William Johnston of St. George Parish, Spotsylvania Co for £50 sold & released to Thomas Red a 377 a. tr of land, which land & premises being pt/o a patent granted to the sd William Johnston dated 28 Sep 1728 ... [*same as above*] ... . Wit: Anthony Foster, Fras Smith, Thomas Foster. Ackn 6 Jul 1736 by William Johnston gent & Ann his wife & admitted to record. Attest: John Waller clk. (Pg 189)

6 Jul MDCCXXXVI. Deed. Joseph Brock of St. George Parish, Spotsylvania Co for £8 sold to John Durrett of same place planter a 64 a. tr of land in the parish afsd bounded by the sd John Durrett & the River Ta ... . Wit: Wm Waller. Ackn 6 Jul 1736 & admitted to record. Attest: John Waller clk. (Pg 190)

3 May 1736. Deed of Lease. Henry Chiles of Spotsylvania Co & John Chiles of King William Co for 5 shillings leased to Humphrey Hill of St. Margaret Parish, King William Co merchant a 400 a. tr of land in St. George Parish adj the sd Chiles, Thomas Graves, land which the sd Humphrey Hill lately purch of Dennet Abney the elder & Dennet Abney the younger & the East North East River, being a parcel of a patent for 2,000 a. granted to Henry Webber 28 Oct 1723 ... during the term of one year paying the rent of one ear of Indian corn only on the last day of the sd term if demanded ... . Wit: John Waller, Wm Waller, Thomas Robinson, Wm Hansford, Chs Barrett. Ackn 6 Jul 1736 by Henry Chiles & John Chiles & at the motion of Benjamin Hubbard in behalf of the sd Hill is admitted to record. Attest: John Waller clk. (Pg 192)

4 May 1736. Deed of Release. Henry Chiles of Spotsylvania Co & Mercy his wife & John Chiles of King William Co for £80 sold & released to Humphrey Hill of St. Margaret Parish, King William Co merchant a 400 a. tr of land ... [*same as above*] ... . Wit: John Waller, Wm Waller, Thomas Robinson, Wm Hansford, Chs Barrett. Ackn 6 Jul 1736 by Henry Chiles & Mercy his wife &

John Chiles & at the motion of Benjamin Hubbard in behalf of the sd Hill is admitted to record. Attest: John Waller clk. (Pg 193)

3 Aug 1736. Deed of Gift. Edward Pigg of Saint George Parish, Spotsylvania Co for naturall love & affection have given to my well beloved dau Ann the now w/o John Clark of Saint Margarets Parish, Caroline Co a 130 a. tr of land in St. George Parish on the n side of the River Tay bounded by the sd river, which sd land is pt/o a larger tr & now in the tenor & occupation of the sd Edward Pigg ... . Wit: Archd Mcpherson, Anthony Foster, John Ward. Ackn 3 Aug 1736 & admitted to record. Attest: John Waller clk. (Pg 195)

5 Jul 1736. Deed of Lease. Philemon Cavenaugh for 5 shillings leased to Henry Willis esqr a 150 a. parcel of land in St. Georges Parish bounded by a br of Hazel Run & Henry Reeves & also 275 a. of land granted to Philemon Cavenaugh by pattent dated [blank] lying on the lower side of Wilderness Run & surrounded by lands of Alexr Spotswood esqr ... during the term of one year paying one pepper corn upon the feast of St. Michael the Arch Angel if demanded ... . Wit: John Taliaferro, Jno Tennent, Zachary Lewis, James Porteus. Proved 3 Aug 1736 & at the motion of the sd Porteus in behalf of the sd Willis is admitted to record. Attest: John Waller clk. (Pg 197)

6 Jul 1736. Deed of Release. Philemon Cavenaugh for £100 sold & released to Henry Willis esqr a 150 a. tr of land & a 275 a. tr of land ... [same as above] ... . Wit: John Taliaferro, Zachary Lewis, Jno Tennent, James Porteus. Proved 3 Aug 1736 & at the motion of the sd Porteus in behalf of the sd Willis is admitted to record. Attest: John Waller clk. (Pg 198)

30 Sep 1736. Deed of Lease. George Woodroof of Saint Georges Parish, Spotsylvania Co planter for 5 shillings leased to William Davenport & Anne his wife of Saint Martin Parish, Hanover Co a 200 a. tr of land being pt/o 380 a. granted to the sd George Woodroof by patent dated 17 Apr 1728 bounded by the Northanna, John Minor & the East North East ... during the term of one year paying the rent of one ear of Indian corn if demanded ... . Wit: John Minor, John Waller Junr, Myles Potter, Wm Waller. Proved 5 Oct 1736 & admitted to record. Attest: John Waller clk. (Pg 200)

1 Oct 1736. Deed of Release. George Woodroof & Jane his wife of Saint George Parish, Spotsylvania Co for natural love & affection & £5 have given to William Davenport & Anne his wife of Saint Martin Parish, Hanover Co a 200 a. tr of land ... [same as above] ... . Wit: John Minor, John Waller Junr, Myles Potter, Wm Waller. Proved 5 Oct 1736 & Jane Woodroff's power of atty to John Waller gent was proved & the sd Waller ackn her right of dower & is admitted to record. Attest: John Waller clk. (Pg 200)

1 Oct MDCCXXXVI. Power of Attorney. I Jane Woodroof the w/o George Woodroof of Spotsylvania Co do appoint Col John Waller to be my atty to appear before the court of Spotsylvania & relinquish my right of dower in & to 200 a. of land this day made over by my sd husband to William Davenport & Anne his wife of Hanover Co ... . Wit: John Waller Junr, John Minor. Proved 5 Oct 1736 & admitted to record. Attest: John Waller clk. (Pg 202)

5 Oct 1736. Deed of Lease. William Davenport & Anne his wife of St. Martin Parish, Hanover Parish in consideration of the rents herein reserved & contained hath lett unto Francis Arnold & Rachel his wife of St. George Parish, Spotsylvania Co a 100 a. tr of land adj John Minor, to include the plantation whereon the sd Francis Arnold & Rachel his wife now lives ... during the naturall lives of the sd Francis Arnold & Rachell his wife paying one ear of Indian corne yearly on the feast of All Saints if demanded ... . Wit: John Minor, Wm Spencer, Wm Wilson Hollmes. Ackn 5 Oct 1736 by William Davenport & Anne his wife & at the motion of John Minor gent in behalf of the sd Arnold is admitted to record. Attest: John Waller clk. (Pg 202)

7 Sep 1736. Deed of Lease. John Jones of Spotsylvania Co for 5 shillings leased to William Hensley of co afsd a 520 a. tr of land in St. George Parish bounded by Robert Baylor, Harry Beverley, Capt John Camm & Saml Smith ... during the term of one year paying one pepper corn upon the feast of St. Michael the Arch Angel if demanded ... . Wit: Adam Gordon, Samll Hensley, Robert King. Ackn 5 Oct 1736 & admitted to record. Attest: John Waller clk. (Pg 203)

7 Sep 1736. Deed of Release. John Jones of Spotsylvania Co for £5 & divers other good consideration sold & released to William Hensley of co afsd a 520 a. tr of land ... [same as above] ... . Wit: Adam Gordon, Sam Hensley, Robert King. Ackn 5 Oct 1736 by John Jones & Agness the w/o the sd John ackn her right of dower & the same is admitted to record. Attest: John Waller clk. (Pg 204)

4 Oct 1736. Deed of Lease. Robert Slaughter of Orange Co gent for 5 shillings leased to George Doggett of Lancaster Co planter a 470 a. tr of land being granted to the afsd Robt Slaughter by patent dated 20 Feb 1719 & granted & conveyed to his son Robert Slaughter party hereof by deed of lease & release, bounded by the river & Hunting Run ... during the term of one year paying the rent of one ear of Indian corn at the feast of St. Michael the Arch Angell if demanded ... . Wit: Thos Slaughter, Frans Thornton Junr, Frans Taliaferro. Ackn 5 Oct 1736 & admitted to record. Attest: John Waller clk. (Pg 206)

5 Oct 1736. Deed of Release. Robert Slaughter of Orange Co gent for £57:15 sold & released to George Doggett planter of Lancaster Co a 470 a. tr of land ...

[*same as above*] ... . Wit: Thos Slaughter, Frans Thornton Junr, Frans Taliaferro. Ackn 5 Oct 1736 by Robert Slaughter gent & Mary the w/o the sd Robert ackn her right of dower & the same is admitted to record. Attest: John Waller clk. (Pg 206)

5 Dec 1736. Deed of Lease. John Foster of Saint Georges Parish, Spotsylvania Co for 5 shillings leased to Cornelius Vaughan & Martin Vaughan infants (the two youngest sons of Cornelius Vaughan late decd) of Drysdale Parish, King & Queen Co a 465 a. tr of land being pt/o a 665 a. tr granted to the sd John Foster by pattent dated 19 Oct 1736 being in St. Georges Parish bounded by Thomas Benson & Capt William Johnston ... during the term of 6 months ... . Wit: Anthony Foster, John Chapman, Ignatious Stureman. Proved 7 Dec 1736 & at the motion of Robert Turner in behalf of the sd Vaughan's is admitted to record. Attest: John Waller clk. (Pg 208)

6 Dec 1736. Deed of Release. John Foster of St. Georges Parish, Spotsylvania Co for £25 paid by Cornelius Vaughan decd in his lifetime the father of Cornelius & Martin Vaughan sold & released to the sd Cornelius Vaughan & Martin Vaughan infants the two youngest sons of Cornelius Vaughan late decd of Drysdale Parish, King & Queen Co a 465 a. tr of land ... [*same as above*] ... . Wit: Anthony Foster, John Chapman, Ignatious Stureman. Proved 7 Dec 1736 & at the motion of Robert Turner in behalf of the sd Vaughan's is admitted to record. Attest: John Waller clk. (Pg 208)

3 Dec MDCCXXVI. Deed of Lease. John Waller of Spotsylvania Co gent for 5 shillings leased to Zachary Lewis of same co gent a 414 a. tr of land on the ridge between the Rivers of Mattapony & Pamunkey bounded by the sd Lewis, sd Waller, Edmond Waller, John Wilkins, John Trusty, William Waller, Cattail Run & Robinsons Run ... ... during the term of one year paying the yearly rent of one pepper corn at the feast of St. Michael the Arch Angel if demanded ... . Wit: Wm Waller, Thomas Robinson, Edmund Waller. Ackn 7 Dec 1736 by John Waller gent & at the motion of William Waller in behalf of the sd Lewis is admitted to record. Attest: John Waller clk. (Pg 210)

4 Dec MDCCXXXVI. Deed of Release. John Waller of Spotsylvania Co for £49:13:7 sold & released to Zachary Lewis of same co gent a 414 a. tr of land, 397 a. part thereof being pt/o a tr of land granted to John Waller Junr by patent dated XXVIII Sep MDCCXXVIII & by him conveyed to the afsd John Waller by deeds of lease & release dated XXIII & XXIV Jun MDCCXXX ackn in Spotsylvania Co Court 7 Jul MDCCXXX, 17 a. the residue thereof is pt/o a tr of 400 a. granted to the sd John Waller by patent dated 21 Feb MDCCXX then in King William Co now Spotsylvania ... [*same as above*] ... . Wit: Wm Waller, Thomas Robinson, Edmund Waller. Ackn 7 Dec 1736 by John Waller gent & at

the motion of William Waller in behalf of the sd Lewis is admitted to record. Attest: John Waller clk. (Pg 211)

4 Apr MDCCXXXVII. Deed of Lease. David Moore & Sarah his wife of Spotsylvania Co for 5 shillings leased to George Carter of same co a 183 a. tr of land in St. George Parish … during the term of one year paying the yearly rent of one pepper corn at the feast of St. Michael the Arch Angel … . Wit: Wm Waller. Ackn 5 Apr 1737 by David Moore & Sarah his wife & at the motion of William Waller in behalf of the sd Carter is admitted to record. Attest: Wm Waller dep clk. (Pg 212)

5 Apr MDCCXXXVII. Deed of Release. David Moore & Sarah his wife of Spotsylvania Co for 2,000 lbs weight of tobacco sold & released to George Carter of same co a 183 a. tr of land, which 183 a. of land is pt/o a greater tr granted by patent to Larkin Chew gent decd & by him sold to Lazarus Tilly & conveyed to the sd Tilley by deeds of lease & release ackn in the co court of Spotsylvania 4 Jul MDCCXXVII & by the sd Tilley sold to the sd David Moore & conveyed by deeds of lease & release ackn in the co court 2 Nov MDCCXXXI … [same as above] … . Wit: Wm Waller. Ackn 5 Apr 1737 by David Moore & Sarah his wife & at the motion of William Waller in behalf of the sd Carter is admitted to record. Attest: Wm Waller dep clk. (Pg 213)

8 Apr MDCCXXXVII. Deed of Lease. William Johnston of Spotsylvania Co gent for 5 shillings leased to John Wiglesworth of same co a 519 a. tr of land in St. George Parish bounded by William Richason & Warner's line … during the term of one year paying the yearly rent of one pepper corn at the feast of St. Michael the Arch Angel if demanded … . Wit: Peter Mountague, Anthony Foster, Edwd Dickinson. Ackn 3 May 1737 & admitted to record. Attest: John Waller clk. (Pg 215)

9 Apr MDCCXXXVII. Deed of Release. William Johnston of Spotsylvania Co gent for £27:10 sold & released to John Wiglesworth of same co a 519 a. tr of land, which tr of land was granted to the sd William Johnston by pattent dated 15 Mar MDCCXXXV … [same as above] … . Wit: Peter Mountague, Anthony Foster, Edwd Dickinson. Ackn 3 May 1737 & admitted to record. Attest: John Waller clk. (Pg 216)

2 May MDCCXXXVII. Deed of Lease. Henry Rice of St. Marks Parish, Orange Co gent for 5 shillings leased to William Bradburn of St. Georges Parish, Spotsylvania Co planter a 200 a. tr of land in St. George Parish bounded by Col John Robinson esqr, Capt Larkin Chew & Col Jno Waller … during the term of 6 months … . Wit: Edwd Franklyn, Themothy Doaelton, John Gordon. Ackn 3 May 1737 & admitted to record. Attest: John Waller clk. (Pg 217)

3 May MDCCXXXVII. Deed of Lease. Henry Rice of St. Marks Parish, Orange Co gent for £20 sold & released to William Bradburn of St. Georges Parish, Spotsylvania Co planter a 200 a. tr of land … [*same as above*] … . Wit: Edwd Franklyn, Themoty Dolton, John Gordon. Ackn 3 May 1737 by Henry Rice & Margeret the w/o the sd Henry's power of atty to John Waller gent was proved by the oaths of Edward Franklyn & Timothy Dalton wits thereto & the same is referred to the next court for the sd Waller to relinquish her right of dower. Attest: John Waller clk. (Pg 218)

At a court held 7 Jun 1737 John Waller gent by virtue of Margaret Rice's power of atty came into court & ackn her right of dower to the [*above*] tr of land sold by her husband Henry Rice to William Bradburn which was ordered to be recorded. Attest: John Waller clk. (Pg 219)

3 May 1737. Power of Attorney. Margaret the w/o Henry Rice hath of her own free will acquitted all her right of dowry of a 200 a. tr of land in St. Georges Parish unto William Bradburn sold by her husband & doth appoint her beloved friend Col John Waller to ackn the same … . Wit: Edwd Franklyn, Thimothy Dolton. Proved 3 May 1737 & admitted to record. Attest: John Waller clk. (Pg 219)

12 Mar 1736. Deed. John Anderson of King William Co for £30 sold to Robert Williamson of Caroline Co a 400 a. tr of land bounded by Col Gawin Corbin, Robinson Run & Taliaferro Crags, granted unto the sd John Anderson by pattent dated 10 Jan 1735 … . Wit: John Haley, Thos Sparks, Thos Holcombs. Ackn 7 Jun 1737 by John Anderson gent & at the motion of Henry Willis gent in behalf of the sd Williamson is admitted to record. Attest: John Waller clk. (Pg 220)

12 Mar 1736. Bond. I John Anderson of St. Margarets Parish, King Wm Co am firmly bound unto Robert Williamson of afsd parish in Caroline Co in the sum of £60 … the condition of this bond is such that if the afsd John Anderson shall well & truly fulfil, performe & observe all the clauses, bonds, covenants & agreements made in an indenture of 400 a. [*see above*] then this obligation to be void … . Wit: Thos Sparks, John Haley, Thomas Holcombs. Ackn 7 Jun 1737 by John Anderson gent & at the motion of Henry Willis gent in behalf of the sd Williamson is admitted to record. Attest: John Waller clk. (Pg 221)

7 Jun 1737. Deed. Robert Goodloe of Saint Georges Parish, Spotsylvania Co for £8 sold to Robert Brown of same place an 89 a. parcel of land in Saint Georges Parish adj to the lands of Thomas Hill, Joseph Carter, Robinsons Swamp & Robinson's line now Bell's or Hill's & is pt/o a greater tr granted to the sd Robert Goodloe by pattent … . Wit: Chr Curtis, Wm Connor. Ackn 7 Jun 1737 & admitted to record. Attest: John Waller clk. (Pg 222)

7 Jun 1737. Deed of Lease. John Miller of Essex Co for 5 shillings leased to William Miller of Spotsylvania Co a 260 a. tr of land or woodland ground on the brs of Nassaponax bounded by a pattent granted to Chisly Corbin Thacker, Symon Miller & John Quarrell ... during the term of one year paying yearly the rent of one ear of Indian corn on the feast of St. Michael if demanded .... Wit: John Parrish, Peter Mountague. Ackn 7 Jun 1737 & admitted to record. Attest: John Waller clk. (Pg 223)

6 Jun 1737. Deed of Release. John Miller of Essex Co for £50 sold & released to William Miller of Spotsylvania Co a 260 a. tr of land ... [*same as above*] .... Wit: John Parrish, Peter Mountague. Ackn 7 Jun 1737 & admitted to record. Attest: John Waller clk. (Pg 224)

7 Jun MDCCXXXVII. Deed. John Tennent of St. George Parish, Spotsylvania Co gent for £5:7:6 sold to Francis Thornton Junr of same place gent two lotts or ½ acres of land in the town of Fredericksburgh marked & distinguished in the plat of the sd town by the numbers 63 & 64 bounded by Princess Ann Street & Amelia Street & by the back lines of the sd town .... Wit: Jno Taliaferro (Taliferro), Anthony Francis Duttond. Ackn 7 Jun 1737 & admitted to record. Attest: John Waller clk. (Pg 225)

23 Mar 1736. Deed of Lease. John Rogers of Drysdale Parish, King & Queen Co for 5 shillings leased to Abraham Rogers of St. Georges Parish, Spotsylvania Co a 228 a. tr of land it being pt/o an 1860 a. tr of land granted to John Madison, John Rogers, Peter Rogers, Henry Pigg, Edward Pigg & John York by patent dated 1 Apr 1717 lying part in Spotsylvania Co & part in Caroline Co & is bounded by the County Line Br of the Middle River of Mattapony & the Mill Run, & also all that tr of land that was given by my brother Peter Rogers decd in his will unto his son John Rogers decd that is not included within the bounds afsd (only reserving & keeping to myself & to my heirs an equal right in the ½ of 6 a. of land adj to the mill for the use & benefit of the mill that is held in copartnership between the sd Abraham Rogers & me the sd John Rogers) ... during the term of 6 months .... Wit: Wm Connor, Wm Smither Junr, Walter Fitzgarrell Junr. Proved 7 Jun 1737 & admitted to record. Attest: John Waller clk. (Pg 226)

24 Mar 1736. Deed of Release. John Rogers of Drysdale Parish, King & Queen Co for £10 sold & released to Abraham Rogers of St. Georges Parish, Spotsylvania Co a 228 a. tr of land ... [*same as above*] .... Wit: Wm Conner, Wm Smither Junr, Walter Fitzgarrell Junr. Proved 7 Jun 1737 & admitted to record. Attest: John Waller clk. (Pg 227)

7 Jun MDCCXXXVII. Deed. The feoffees or trustees for the land appropriated for the building & erecting the town of Fredericksburgh for 55 shillings sold to Joseph Hawkins of Spotsylvania Co gent a ½ a. lot of land in the sd town of Fredericksburgh described in the platt of the sd town by the figure 38 on Princess Ann Street & Charlotta Street ... if the sd Joseph Hawkins shall not within two years next ensuing begin to build & finish upon the sd lot one good dwelling house of such demensions & to be placed in such manner as by one Act of Assembly made 1 Feb MDCCXXXII then it shall be lawfull for the sd feoffees or trustees into the sd granted premises & the same to have again as their former estate as if these presents had never been made .... Wit: None. Ackn 7 Jun 1737 by Henry Willis & John Waller gent two of the feoffees & trustees unto Joseph Hawkins gent at whose motion the same is admitted to record. Attest: John Waller clk. (Pg 228)

7 Jun 1737. Deed of Lease. William Tapp & Christian his wife of St. Marks Parish, Orange Co for 5 shillings leased to William McWilliams of St. George Parish, Spotsylvania Co planter a 716 a. tr of land in St. George Parish being the tr patented by the sd William Tapp 28 Sep 1728 ... during the term of one year paying the rent of one grain of Indian corn at the feast of St. Michael the Arch Angel if demanded .... Wit: Edwd Herndon Junr, Jos Neavill, Joshua Thomas. Ackn 7 Jun 1737 by William Tapp & Christian his wife & admitted to record. (Pg 230)

7 Jun 1737. Deed of Release. William Tapp & Christian his wife of Saint Marks Parish, Orange Co for £60 sold & released to William McWilliams of St. George Parish, Spotsylvania Co a 716 a. tr of land lying on Gravel Run in St. George Parish bounded by Francis & Anthony Thornton's old patent, John Martin, Henry Reins, John Sutten, William Howard & Otterdam Swamp ... [same as above] .... Wit: Edwd Herndon Junr, Jos Neavill, Joshua Thomas. Ackn 7 Jun 1737 by William Tapp & Christian his wife & admitted to record. Attest: John Waller clk. (Pg 230)

28 Feb 1736. Deed of Lease. William Tapp of St. Mark Parish, Orange Co planter for 5 shillings leased to George Nix of St. George Parish, Spotsylvania Co planter a 175 a. tr of land in St. George Parish bounded by the sd William Tapp, Vincent Tapp & a br of Mattapony, the sd parcel of land formerly given to the sd William Tapp by his mother Elizabeth Tapp by deed of gift dated 31 Oct 1724 & was by the sd Elizabeth purch of Francis Thornton & Mary his wife & Anthony Thornton & Winifred his wife by deeds dated 24 & 25 Aug 1722 which sd deeds last mentioned was for a larger tr of land containing 450 a. whereof the sd 175 a. hereby sold is a part ... during the term of one year paying the yearly rent of one ear of Indian corn at the feast of St. Michael the Arch Angel if demanded .... Wit: Elias Sharp, Henery Sparkes, Thomas Elson. Ackn 7 Jun

1737 by William Tapp & Christian Tapp his wife & admitted to record. Attest: John Waller clk. (Pg 232)

1 Mar 1736. Deed of Release. William Tapp of St. Mark Parish, Orange Co planter for £20 sold & released to George Nix of St. George Parish, Spotsylvania Co planter a 175 a. tr of land ... [same as above] ... . Wit to receipt: Henery Sparkes, Elias Sharp, Thomas Elson. Ackn 7 Jun 1737 by William Tapp & Christian his wife & admitted to record. Attest: John Waller clk. (Pg 233)

2 Aug MDCCXXXVII. Deed. The feoffees or trustees for the land appropriated for the building & erecting the town of Fredericksburg for £5:5 sold to John Rucker of Orange Co gent ½ a. or lot of land in the town of Fredericksburgh described in the platt of the sd town by the figure No. 5 on the River Rappahannock (being one of the river side lots) & on Sophia Street, William Street & George Street ... if the sd John Rucker shall not within the space of two years next ensuing begin to build & finish upon the sd lot one good dwelling house that then the sd feoffees or trustees & it shall & may be lawfull to & for them into the sd granted premises to enter & the same to have again as their former estate as if these presents had never been made, in wit whereof Henry Willis & John Waller gent two of the sd trustees have set their hands & seals ... . Wit: Wm Waller. Ackn 2 Aug 1737 & admitted to record. Attest: John Waller clk. (Pg 235)

1 Aug 1737. Deed of Lease. George Prockter now of King George Co planter for 5 shillings farm let unto John Prockter & Elias Sharpe both of Spotsylvania Co planters a 436 a. parcel of land whereon my father George Prockter did dwell at the time of his death on the brs of Hasel Run being the residue & remainder undisposed of by my father & by myself since his death of 1500 a. of land formerly purch by my sd father of William Strother of King George Co the sd 436 a. of land being designed by my father to be given to his son John Prockter one of the parties to these presents & his dau Margaret Prockter w/o Elias Sharp the other party to these presents but by the fault of the writer of his will the words heirs forever was omitted & by that means the reversion descends to me as eldest son & heir at law ... during the term of one year paying the rent of Indian corn on the birthday of our Lord God next coming if demanded ... . Wit: Davis Bronaugh, John Steward, James Strother, Jno Hobby. Proved 2 Aug 1737 & admitted to record. Attest: John Waller clk. (Pg 236)

2 Aug 1737. Deed of Release. George Prockter of King George Co planter for £100 sold & released to John Prockter & Elias Sharpe both of Spotsylvania Co planters a 436 a. tr of land ... [same as above] ... . Wit: David Bronaugh, John Steward, James Strother, Jno Hobby. Proved 2 Aug 1737 & admitted to record. Attest: John Waller clk. (Pg 237)

4 Jul 1737. Deed of Lease. George Poole (Pool) of Spotsylvania Co for 5 shillings leased to James Brown of co afsd a 140 a. parcel of land or woodland ground bounded by a br of Nassaponax ... during the term of one year paying the rent of one ear of Indian corn on the feast of St. Michael if demanded .... Wit: G. Home, William Stevens. Ackn 6 Sep 1737 & admitted to record. Attest: John Waller clk. (Pg 239)

5 Jul 1737. Deed of Release. George Poole of Spotsylvania Co for £15:9 sold & released to James Brown of co afsd a 140 a. tr of land ... [same as above] .... Wit: G. Home, William Stevens. Ackn 6 Sep 1737 by George Poole & Elizabeth the w/o the sd George ackn her right of dower & is admitted to record. Attest: John Waller clk. (Pg 240)

3 Oct 1737. Deed of Lease. Abraham Mayfield of Spotsylvania Co planter for 5 shillings leased to Blomfeild Long of Essex Co black smith a 200 a. parcel of land whereon the sd Mayfeild now liveth bounded by Phillip Brandagon & Major Robinson, which sd tr of land is pt/o a greater tr granted by pattent to Larkin Chew gent decd 4 Jun MDCCXXXII ... during the term of one year paying the rent of one ear of Indian corn at the feast of St. Michael if demanded .... Wit: Wm Bartlet, Jno Parrish, A. Foster. Ackn 4 Oct 1737 & admitted to record. Attest: John Waller clk. (Pg 241)

4 Oct 1737. Deed of Release. Abraham Mayfield of Spotsylvania Co planter for £30 sold & released to Blomfeild Long of Essex Co black smith a 200 a. parcel of land ... [same as above] .... Wit: Wm Bartlet, Jno Parrish, A. Foster. Ackn 4 Oct 1737 by Abraham Mayfield & Elizabeth the w/o the sd Abraham ackn her right of dower & is admitted to record. Attest: John Waller clk. (Pg 242)

4 Oct MDCCXXXVII. Deed. The feoffees or trustees for the land appropriated for the building & erecting the town of Fredericksburgh of the one part & Matthias Gale & William Gale merchants in Whitehaven of the other part, wit that the sd feoffees or trustees for & in consideration of £7:5 which was paid by Henry Willis gent for lot number 2 (as the sd Henry Willis brought by outcry of the sd trustees & now relinquishes unto the sd Matthias Gale & William Gale for a consideration by them paid to the sd Willis) have sold unto the sd Matthias Gale & William Gale ½ a. or lot of land in the sd town of Fredericksburgh described in the plat of the sd town by the figure 2 being on Rappahannock River being one of the water side lots & bounded by Sophia Street & Charlotta Street ... if the sd Matthias Gale & William Gale shall not within the space of two years next ensuing begin to build & finish upon the sd lot one good dwelling house that then the sd feoffees or trustees & it shall & may be lawfull to & for them into the sd granted premises to enter & the same to have again as their

former estate as they might have done if these presents had never been made ... .
Wit: John Chew, Wm Waller, Edmund Waller. Ackn 4 Oct 1737 by Henry
Willis & John Waller gent two of the feoffees or trustees & admitted to record.
Attest: John Waller clk. (Pg 243)

30 Sep 1737. Deed of Lease. John Gordon & Elizabeth his wife of St. George
Parish, Spotsylvania Co for 5 shillings leased to Thomas Hill of same place a
200 a. tr of land in the afsd parish & on the brs of the Deep Run bounded by
William Smith, Thomas Morriss, Piney Br & a pattent granted to Catsby Cock
... during the term of one year paying the rent of one ear of Indian corn on the
feast of St. Michael the Arch Angel if demanded ... . Wit: G. Home, Wm
Cowne, And Rosse. Ackn 4 Oct 1737 by John Gordon & Elizabeth Gordon &
admitted to record. Attest: John Waller clk. (Pg 244)

1 Oct 1737. Deed of Release. John Gordon & Elizabeth his wife of St. George
Parish, Spotsylvania Co for £90 sold & released to Thomas Hill of same place a
200 a. tr of land ... [same as above] ... . Wit: G. Home, Wm Cowne, And
Rosse. Ackn 4 Oct 1737 by John Gordon & Elizabeth his wife & admitted to
record. Attest: John Waller clk. (Pg 245)

1 Nov 1737. Deed. John Snall of St. George Parish, Spotsylvania Co for £100
sold to Anthony Foster of same place a 200 a. parcel of land in the parrish afsd
on the n side the River Po being pt/o 300 a. of land purch by John Snal the elder
decd of Capt Larkin Chew gent decd & bounded by the river bank at the mouth
of Greens Br, Snel's tr of land & Capt John Taliaferro, together with 1 a. of land
on the s side the River Po granted to John Snal decd for the building a water mill
... . Wit: William Johnston, Tho Graves, John Walden. Ackn 1 Nov 1737 &
admitted to record. Attest: John Waller clk. (Pg 246)

10 Oct 1737. Deed. James Tirrey (Terrey) (Terry) of St. Georges Parish,
Spotsylvania Co for £20 sold to John Holliday Senr of same place in his actual
possession now being by virtue of a sail to him made for one year by indenture
dated three days before the date hereof a 200 a. tr of land bounded by a swamp
in Thomas Sertain's line & Peter Gustavas's line ... . Wit: Thos Sertain, Wm
Holliday, Ed Lankford. Proved 6 Dec 1737 & Margaret the w/o the sd Terry
ackn her right of dower which was ordered to be recorded. Attest: John Waller
clk. (Pg 247)

5 Feb 1738. Deed of Lease. John Prockter & Sarah his wife of Spotsylvania Co
for 5 shillings farm let unto Thomas Hill gent of co afsd a 116 a. parcell of land
or woodland ground being pt/o a 1500 a. tr of land ackn by William Strother to
George Prockter in Spotsylvania Court 1 Oct 1735 the sd 116 a. being the sd
John Prockter's pt/o the sd land being left to the sd John Prockter by the will of

George Prockter bounded by Feigons Br, Elias Sharp & Hasell Run ... during the term of one year paying the yearly rent of one ear of Indian corn at the feast of St. Michael if demanded .... Wit: G. Home, William Marshall, James Nelson. Ackn 7 Feb 1737 by John Prockter & Sarah his wife & is admitted to record. Attest: John Waller clk. (Pg 249)

6 Feb 1738. Deed of Release. John Prockter & Sarah his wife of Spotsylvania Co for £50 sold & released to Thomas Hill gent of co afsd a 116 a. tr of land ... [same as above] .... Wit: G. Home, William Marshall, James Nelson. Ackn 7 Feb 1737 by John Prockter & Sarah his wife & is admitted to record. Attest: John Waller clk. (Pg 249)

6 Feb MDCCXXXVII. Deed of Lease. George Carter of St. George Parish, Spotsylvania Co for 5 shillings leased to Isaac (Isac) Darnell of same place a 200 a. tr of land in St. George Parish bounded by Glady Run ... during the term of one year paying the rent of one pepper corn at the feast of St. Michael the Arch Angel if demanded .... Wit: Joseph Adcock, John Stubblefield, Edmund Waller. Ackn 7 Feb 1737 by George Carter & Joseph Adcock & John Stubblefield two of the wits to this deed proved that they saw the sd Elizabeth Carter sign & execute this deed & is admitted to record. Attest: John Waller clk. (Pg 250)

7 Feb MDCCXXXVII. Deed of Release. George Carter of St. George Parish, Spotsylvania Co for £23 sold & released to Isaac (Isac) Darnell of same place a 200 a. tr of land, which sd tr of land is pt/o a patent granted to John Chew for 608 a. dated 4 Jun MDCCXXVI & by the sd John Chew sold unto Edward Franklyn & conveyed by deeds of lease & released ackn in the co court 5 Aug MDCCXXIX & conveyed by deeds of lease & release to the sd George Carter 1 Jul MDCCXXXV ... [same as above] .... Wit: Joseph Adcock, John Stubblefield, Edmund Waller. Ackn 7 Feb 1737 by George Carter & Joseph Adcock & John Stubblefield two of the wits to this deed proved that they saw the sd Elizabeth Carter sign & execute this deed & is admitted to record. Attest: John Waller clk. (Pg 251)

30 Jan 1737. Deed of Lease. John Chew of Spotsylvania Co for 5 shillings leased to Henry Martin Junr & John Colquit Junr of same co planter all that 400 a. parcel of land being pt/o a pattent granted unto the sd John Chew dated 4 Jun 1726 lying in St. George Parish adj the lands of John Bush, Michel Guaney & Glady Fork Run ... during the term of one year paying the yearly rent of one pepper corn at the feast of St. Michall the Arch Angel if demanded .... Wit: Henry Martin, Martin True. Ackn 7 Feb 1737 by John Chew gent & at the motion of Henry Martin Senr in behalf of Henry Martin Junr & John Colquit Junr is admitted to record. Attest: John Waller clk. (Pg 252)

31 Jan 1737. Deed of Release. John Chew of Spotsylvania Co for £20 sold & released to Henry Martin Junr & John Colquit Junr of same co planters a 400 a. tr of land ... [*same as above*] ... . Wit: Henry Martin, Martin True. Ackn 7 Feb 1737 by John Chew gent & at the motion of Henry Martin Senr in behalf of Henry Martin Junr & John Colquit Junr is admitted to record. Attest: John Waller clk. (Pg 253)

14 Dec 1737. Deed of Lease. Henry Willis gent of St. George Parish, Spotsylvania Co for 5 shillings leased to Francis Thornton Junr gent of same place a 150 a. tr of land in St. George Parish it being a certain tr of land called Birams & is bounded by a br of Hazell Run & Henry Rieves ... during the term of one year paying the rent of one ear of Indian corn if demanded ... . Wit: James Belsches, John Gordon, Elisabeth Gordon. Ackn 7 Mar 1737 & admitted to record. Attest: John Waller clk. (Pg 254)

15 Dec 1737. Deed of Release. Henry Willis gent of St. George Parish, Spotsylvania Co for £25 sold & released to Francis Thornton gent of same place a 150 a. tr of land ... [*same as above*] ... . Wit: James Belsches, John Gordon, Elisabeth Gordon. Ackn 7 Mar 1737 & admitted to record. Attest: John Waller clk. (Pg 255)

6 Mar MDCCXXXVII. Deed of Lease. Amey Sutton of Saint George Parish, Spotsylvania Co for 5 shillings leased to John Talbert of same place a 73 a. tr of land in St. George Parish bounded by James Samms, William Bradburn & Cattail Lick Run, being pt/o a patent formerly granted to Larkin Chew gent decd dated 4 Jun MDCCXXII ... during the term of one year paying the rent of one pepper corn at the feast of St. Michael the Arch Angel if demanded ... . Wit: Edmund Waller, Wm Waller. Ackn 7 Mar 1737 & admitted to record. Attest: John Waller clk. (Pg 256)

7 Mar MDCCXXXVII. Deed of Release. Amey Sutton of Saint George Parish, Spotsylvania Co for £12 sold & released to John Talbert of same place a 73 a. tr of land ... [*same as above*] ... . Wit: Edmund Waller, Wm Waller. Ackn 7 Mar 1737 & admitted to record. Attest: John Waller clk. (Pg 257)

5 Dec 1737. Deed of Lease. John Wilkins of Spotsylvania Co for 5 shillings leased to John Wiglesworth of same co a 220 a. tr of land it being the remainder of a patent granted to the sd John Wilkins for 420 a. dated 16 Jun 1727 whereof the afsd John Wiglesworth bought 200 a. by deeds dated 5 Aug 1728 ... during the term of one year ... . Wit: Z. Lewis, Wm Waller. Ackn 2 May 1738 & admitted to record. Attest: John Waller clk. (Pg 259)

6 Dec 1737. Deed of Release. John Wilkins of Spotsylvania Co for £70 sold & released to John Wiglesworth of same co a 220 a. tr of land ... [*same as above*] .... Wit: Z. Lewis, Wm Waller. Ackn 2 May 1738 by John Wilkins & Mary the w/o the sd John Wilkins ackn her right of dower & is admitted to record. Attest: John Waller clk. (Pg 259)

2 May MDCCXXXVIII. Deed. The feoffees or trustees for the land appropriated for the building & erecting the town of Fredericksburgh for 55 shillings paid by John Grame gent sold to Adam Read of the town of Falmouth in King George Co merchant Lot No. 14 (as the sd John Grame bought by out cry of the sd trustees & now relinquishes unto the sd Adam Read for a consideration by him paid to the sd Grame) being ½ a. of land in the sd town of Fredericksburgh described in the plat of the sd town by the figure 14 bounded by Caroline Street & Charlotta Street ... if the sd Adam Read shall not within the space of two years next ensuing begin to build & finish upon the sd lot one good dwelling house then the sd feoffees or trustees & it shall & may be lawfull to & for them into the sd granted premises & every part thereof to enter & the same to have again as their former estate as they might have done if these presents had never been made .... Wit: Joshua Thomas, John Gordon. Ackn 2 May 1738 by John Taliaferro & John Waller gent two of the feoffees or trustees & admitted to record. Attest: John Waller clk. (Pg 261)

5 Apr 1738. Deed of Lease. Thomas Binson (Benson) & Sarah his wife of St. Georges Parish, Spotsylvania Co for 5 shillings leased to Edward Levill (Levell) of Drysdale Parish, King & Queen Co a 200 a. tr of land on the brs of Massaponax bounded by Capt William Johnston ... during the term of 6 months paying the rent of one ear of Indian corn at the feast of St. Michael the Arch Angell if demanded .... Wit: George Nix, Matthew Gayle, Martin Trew. Proved 6 Jun 1738 & admitted to record. (Pg 262)

6 Apr 1738. Deed of Release. Thomas Binson (Benson) & Sarah his wife of St. Georges Parish, Spotsylvania Co for £30 sold & released to Edward Levill (Levell) of Drysdale Parish, King & Queen Co a 200 a. tr of land ... [*same as above*] .... Wit: George Nix, Matthew Gayle, Martin Trew. Proved 6 Jun 1738 & admitted to record. Attest: John Waller clk. (Pg 263)

28 Apr 1738. Deed of Lease. William Fantleroy of Luninsburg Parish, Richmond Co gent for 5 shillings leased to Thomas Edmondson of St. Anne Parish, Essex Co gent two trs of land purch by the sd William Fantleroy from Edward Price & Augustine Smith that purch of Edward Price in St. George Parish containing 200 a. & bounded by a patent granted to John Buckner & John Royston, the other tr of land purch by the sd William Fantleroy from Augustine Smith is bounded by Humphrey Hill, William Thornton & the line of Buckner &

Royston … during the term of one year paying the rent of one peper come at the feast of St. Michael the Arch Angel if demanded … . Wit: Hannah Fantleroy, John Lewis, James Samuell. Ackn 6 Jun 1738 & admitted to record. Attest: John Waller clk. (Pg 264)

29 Apr 1738. Deed of Release. William Fantleroy of Luninsburgh Parish, Richmond Co gent for £170:10:10 sold & released to Thomas Edmondson of St. Anne Parish, Essex Co gent two trs of land … [*same as above*] … . Wit: Hannah Fantleroy, John Lewis, James Samuell. Ackn 6 Jun 1738 & admitted to record. Attest: John Waller clk. (Pg 265)

To Thomas Wright Belfield, William Jordan & William Fantleroy Junr of Richmond Co gent greeting, whereas William Fantleroy gent lately in our co court of Spotsylvania 6 Jun MDCCXXXVIII ackn certain deeds of lease & release dated 28 & 29 Apr 1738 for two trs of land the whole being 746 a. in Saint George Parish to Thomas Edmondson gent … & the sd Thomas Edmondson having insinuated to us that Apphiah the w/o the sd William Fantleroy by reason of the great distance from our sd co court of Spotsylvania & the infirmity of her health was not capable to travel to the sd court to ackn her right in the sd land & prayed that a commission might issue for her privy examination as the Act of Assembly in that cause provided doth direct, now known ye that wee trusting to your fidelity & provident circumspection in the premises we have assigned & impower you the sd Thomas Wright Belfield, William Jordan & William Fantleroy Junr or any two of you to cause the sd Apphiah to come before you to examine privily & apart from her husband touching her consent of conveying her right in the sd land to the sd Edmondson … . Wit Henry Willis esqr judge of our sd court at the sd courthouse 4 Jul MDCCXXXVIII. Richmd: Pursuant to the above commission wee T.W. Belfield & William Fantleroy Junr have caused to come before us the afsd Mrs. Apphiah Fantleroy & hath privily examined her wheather she is willing to relinquish her right of dower to the afsd two trs of land who answered that she was & that she did it of her own free will … . Certified 21 Jul 1738. The within commission being returned last court it is now admitted to record 5 Sep 1738. Attest: John Waller clk. (Pg 268)

24 Apr 1738. Deed of Lease. Anthony Golston for 5 shillings leased to William Crosthwait a 115 a. tr of land in St. George Parish bounded by George Dowdy & Col Corbin … during the term of one year paying one pepper corn upon the feast of St. Michael the Arch Angel if demanded … . Wit: Richard Pickering, James Rallings, Adam Gordon. Ackn 5 Jul 1738 & admitted to record. Attest: John Waller clk. (Pg 269)

25 Apr 1738. Deed of Release. Anthony Golston of Spotsylvania Co for £8 sold & released to William Crosthwait of Orange Co a 115 a. tr of land ... [same as above] .... Wit: Richard Pickering, James Rallings, Adam Gordon. Ackn 5 Jul 1738 & admitted to record. Attest: John Waller clk. (Pg 269)

29 Jul 1738. Deed of Lease. William Coleman of Saint Johns Parish, King William Co for 5 shillings leased to Edward Pigg of Saint Georges Parish, Spotsylvania Co a 100 a. tr of land on the brs of the Middle River of Mattapony bounded by land that Francis Smith bought of Peter Rogers decd (pt/o this sd land being already in the possession of the sd Edward Pigg by right of survivorship) ... during the term of 6 months paying the rent of one ear of Indian corn at the feast of St. Michael the Arch Angell if demanded .... Wit: Wm Johnston, Charles Filks Pigg, Barnett Paine. Ackn 1 Aug 1738 & admitted to record. Attest: John Waller clk. (Pg 271)

30 Jul 1738. Deed of Release. William Coleman of St. Johns Parish, King William Co (son & heir to Darbey Coleman of King & Queen Co decd) for £12:6:10 sold & released to Edward Pigg of St. Georges Parish, Spotsylvania Co a 100 a. tr of land ... [same as above] .... Wit: Wm Johnston, Charles Filkes Pigg, Barnet Paine. Ackn 1 Aug 1738 & admitted to record. Attest: John Waller clk. (Pg 272)

1 Aug MDCCXXXVIII. Deed. The feoffees or trustees for the land appointed for the building & erecting the town of Fredericksburgh for £3:15 sold to Thomas Dowdall of Spotsylvania Co ½ a. or lot of land in the town of Fredericksburgh described in the plat of the sd town by the figure 18 being on Caroline Street & Hanover Street ... if the sd Thomas Dowdall shall not within the space of two years build & finish upon the sd lot one good dwelling house that then the feoffees or trustees & it shall & may be lawfull to & for them into the sd granted premises to enter & the same to have again as their former estate as they might have done if these presents had never been made .... Wit: Edmund Waller. Ackn by Henry Willis & John Waller gent two of the feoffees or trustees & at the motion of Patrick Dowdall in behalf of the sd Thomas is admitted to record. Attest: John Waller clk. (Pg 273)

4 Sep 1738. Deed of Lease. Achilles Bowker of St. Stephens Parish, King & Queen Co for 5 shillings leased to Robt Coleman of St. George Parish, Spotsylvania Co a 400 a. tr of land bounded by the sd Bowker's upper corner of another tr adj to the same on the s side Elstons Run (it being a patent granted to Ralph Bowker for 400 a. dated 20 Feb 1719 & since renewed by Bird Bowker by a patent dated 20 Jul 1736) & the Barren Fields ... during the term of one year paying the rent of one ear of Indian corn only on the last day of the sd term

if demanded ... . Wit: Arth Watts, William Johnston, Larkin Chew. Ackn 5
Sep 1738 & admitted to record. Attest: John Waller clk. (Pg 274)

5 Sep 1738. Deed of Release. Achilles Bowker of St. Stephens Parish, King &
Queen Co for £40 sold & released to Robt Coleman of St. Georges Parish,
Spotsilvania Co a 400 a. tr of land ... [same as above] ... . Wit: Arth Watts,
William Johnston, Larkin Chew. Ackn 5 Sep 1738 & admitted to record.
Attest: John Waller clk. (Pg 275)

4 Sep 1738. Deed of Lease. Joseph Brock gent & Mary his wife of
Spotsylvania Co for 5 shillings leased to Ignatius Turman of same place afsd a
350 a. tr of land in St. George Parish bounded by the sd Brock's patent &
Nathaniel Sanders ... during the term of one year paying the rent of one pepper
corn at the feast of St. Michael the Arch Angel if demanded ... . Wit: Thos
Duerson, William Cowne, R. Curtis Junr. Ackn 5 Sep 1738 by Joseph Brock
gent & Mary his wife & admitted to record. Attest: John Waller clk. (Pg 277)

5 Sep 1738. Deed of Release. Joseph Brock gent & Mary his wife of St. George
Parish, Spotsylvania Co for £35 sold & released to Ignatious (Ignatius) Turman
(Tureman) of same place a 350 a. tr of land, it being pt/o a patent granted to the
sd Joseph Brock dated [blank] 1738 ... [same as above] ... . Wit: Thos
Duerson, William Cowne, R. Curtis Junr. Ackn 5 Sep 1738 by Joseph Brock
gent & Mary his wife & admitted to record. Attest: John Waller clk. (Pg 278)

5 Sep 1738. Bond. I Joseph Brock of Spotsylvania Co am firmly bound unto
Ignatius Turman of same co in the sum of £70 ... the condition of this obligation
is such that if the afsd Joseph Brock shall well & truly perform & keep all the
covenants mentioned & comprised in an indenture of lease & release [see above]
then this obligation to be void ... . Wit: Thos Duerson, William Cowne, R.
Curtis Junr. Ackn 5 Sep 1738 & admitted to record. Attest: John Waller clk.
(Pg 279)

4 Sep 1738. Deed. Anthony Foster of Saint George Parish, Spotsylvania Co for
£50 sold to John Snell of same place a 100 a. tr of land in St. George Parish on
River Po being a parcel of land purch by the sd Anthony Foster of Robert King
bounded by Thomas Salmon, Robt King & John Foster ... . Wit: William
Johnston, Charles Filks Pigg, Isabell Foster. Ackn 5 Sep 1738 & admitted to
record. Attest: John Waller clk. (Pg 280)

26 Jan 1737. Deed of Lease. Thomas Grayson of Deal in Kent eldest son of
John Grayson of Spotsylvania Co lately decd for 5 shillings leased to Thomas
Turner of King George Co, VA gent a 500 a. tr of land lying near the falls of
Rappahannock River adj Francis Taliaferro & Man Page esqr decd ... during the

term of one year paying the rent of one ear of Indian corn on the birthday of our Lord next ensuing if demanded ... . Wit: James Hume, John Graham, John Moncure, Ignats Semmes, Peter Simms, Henry Donaldson, John Bean. Proved 4 Jul 1738 by John Graham & John Moncure two of the wits & ordered that it lye in the clerks office for proof of a third wit. Proved 5 Sep 1738 by Ignatius Semmes one other wit to the sd deed & is admitted to record. Attest: John Waller clk. (Pg 281)

27 Jan 1737. Deed of Release. Thomas Grayson of Deal in Kent eldest son of John Grayson of Spotsylvania Co lately decd for £250 sold & released to Thomas Turner of King George Co, VA gent a 500 a. tr of land, moreover in consideration of the above £250 the sd Thomas Grayson hereby impowers the sd Thomas Turner to demand & receive to his own use all the Negroes & personal estate to the sd Thomas Grayson belonging as eldest son of the decd John Grayson, the late John Grayson's widow's dower only excepted, ... [same as above] ... . Wit: James Hume, John Graham, John Moncure, Ignats Semmes, Peter Simms, Henry Donaldson, John Bean. London 27 Jan 1737/8 recd of Thomas Turner by the hands of William Stevenson merchant in London £250. Tho Grayson. Proved 4 Jul 1738 by the oaths of John Graham & John Moncure two of the wits & ordered that it lye in the clerks office for the proof of a third wit. Proved 5 Sep 1738 by Ignatius Semmes one other wit & is admitted to record. Attest: John Waller clk. (Pg 282)

5 Aug 1738. Deed of Mortgage. I John Wood of St. George Parish, Spotsylvania Co am firmly bound unto Joseph Woolfork of St. Margarets Parish, Caroline Co in the sum of £22:9:2 & 60 lbs of tobacco to be paid unto the sd Joseph Woolfork at or upon 1 Jun next, for the payment whereof I bind myself to the sd Joseph Woolfolk under the penal sum of £44 & 120 lbs of the like merchantable tobacco & for the further securing & more certain payment of the sd several sums know also that I hereby sell & make over unto the sd Joseph Woolfork the following goods & chattels, viz: one Negro woman named Kate & one Negro girle also named Kate with all their future increase, 3 cows, 9 home hoggs, & all my outlying hoggs, 3 feather beds & rugs, sheets & blankets thereto belonging & all other my personal estate (except 3 horses & 1 mare which I determine to sell in order more readily to discharge the afsd debt) ... provided that if the sd John Wood or any person in my behalf pay the afsd several sums at the time afsd then this sale & mortgage to be void & null ... . Wit: John Holladay, Chs Stevens, Joseph Roberts. Ackn 4 Oct 1738 & admitted to record. Attest: John Waller clk. (Pg 284)

4 Oct MDCCXXXVIII. Deed. The feoffees or trustees for the land appropriated for the building & erecting the town of Fredericksburgh for 55 shillings sold to John Waller Junr of Spotsylvania Co gent ½ a. or lot of land in the sd town of

Fredericksburgh described in the plat of the sd town by the figure 56 lying on
Princess Ann Street & Hanover Street ... if the sd John Waller Junr shall not
within the space of two years begin to build & finish upon the sd lot one good
dwelling house that then the sd feoffees or trustees & it shall & may be lawfull
to & for them into the sd granted premises to enter & the same to have again as
their former estate as if these presents had never been made .... Wit: Edmund
Waller. Ackn 4 Oct 1738 by Henry Willis & John Waller gent two of the
feoffees or trustees & admitted to record. Attest: John Waller clk. (Pg 285)

30 Nov MDCCXXXVIII. Deed. John Waller Junr of St. George Parish,
Spotsylvania Co gent for £2:15 sold to Henry Downs of St. Mark Parish, Orange
Co a ½ a. lot of land in the town of Fredericksburgh described in the plan of the
sd town by the figure 56 on Princess Ann Street & Hanover Street (the same
being ackn to the sd John Waller Junr & conveyed by deed of sale from the
feoffees or trustees of the sd town 4 Oct MDCCXXXVIII) .... Wit: John
Waller, Edwd Herndon Junr, Robt Huddleston, Z. Lewis. Ackn 6 Feb 1738 &
ordered to be recorded. Attest: John Waller clk. (Pg 286)

23 Nov 1738. Deed of Lease. Edward Pigg & Abraham Rogers of Spotsylvania
Co planters for 5 shillings leased to William Hawkins of Orange Co planter a
100 a. parcel of land formerly sold to the sd Edward Pigg by William Colman by
deeds of lease & release dated 29 & 30 Jul 1738 & 10 a. pt/o a tr of land
belonging to Abraham Rogers in St. George Parish on the brs of the Middle
River of Mattapony bounded by Edward Ware ... during the term of one year
paying the yearly rent of one pepper corn at the feast of St. Michael the Arch
Angell if demanded .... Wit: John Chew, Charles Filks Pigg, Barnet Paine,
Wm Paine. Ackn 6 Feb 1738 & admitted to record. Attest: John Waller clk.
(Pg 287)

24 Nov 1738. Deed of Release. Edward Pigg & Abraham Rogers of
Spotsylvania Co planters for £20 sold & released to William Hawkins of Orange
Co planter a 100 a. tr of land ... [same as above] .... Wit: John Chew, Charles
Filks Pigg, Barnet Paine, Wm Paine. Ackn 6 Feb 1738 & admitted to record.
Attest: John Waller clk. (Pg 288)

XXIV Nov MDCCXXXVIII. Bond. Wee Edward Pigg & Abraham Rogers of
Spotsylvania Co are firmly bound unto William Hawkins of Orange Co in the
sum of £40 ... the condition of this obligation is such that whereas the afsd
Edwd Pigg & Abraham Rogers hath sold unto the afsd William Hawkins a 100
a. tr of land by deeds of lease & release [see above] now if the afsd Edwd Pigg
& Abraham Rogers do forever defend the sd William Hawkins title to the sd
land agt all persons that may lay any claim whatsoever to the sd land & premises
that then this obligation to be void .... Wit: John Chew, Charles Filks Pigg,

Barnet Paine, Wm Paine. Ackn 6 Feb 1738 & admitted to record. Attest: John Waller clk. (Pg 289)

5 Mar 1738. Deed of Lease. Thomas Chew gent of St. Mark Parish, Orange Co, VA for 5 shillings leased to Nicholas Hawkins of St. George Parish, Spotsylvania Co a 298 a. tr of land in St. George Parish adj the lands of the sd Nicholas Hawkins, Robert Thomas, Francis Smith, William Richerson, Jonathan Clark, John & George Pen & Augustine Smith of Gloster Co, the sd 298 a. of land have been ackn in Spotsylvania Co Court by the sd Thomas Chew to the sd Nicholas Hawkins by deeds of lease & release dated 5 & 6 Apr 1731, the sd Nicholas Hawkins being advised that there was a defect in the sd deeds ackn as afsd being the reason of making these presents to make the sd land more sure unto the sd Nicholas Hawkins ... during the term of one year paying the yearly rent of one pepper corn at the feast of St. Michael the Arch Angel if demanded ... . Wit: John Waller, A. Foster, Edmund Waller. Ackn 6 Mar 1738 & admitted to record. Attest: John Waller clk. (Pg 289)

6 Mar 1738. Deed of Release. Thomas Chew of St. Marks Parish, Orange Co, VA for £5 & 2,750 lbs of tobacco with cask conveniency to him sold & released to Nicholas Hawkins of St. Georges Parish, Spotsylvania Co a 298 a. tr of land adj the sd Nicholas Hawkins, Robert Thomas, Frances Smith, Augustine Smith of Gloster Co, William Richason, Jonathan Clark, John & George Pen, Warner's line & sd Thomas Chew ... [same as above] ... . Wit: John Waller, A. Foster, Edmund Waller. Ackn 6 Mar 1738 & admitted to record. Attest: John Waller clk. (Pg 290)

2 Apr 1739. Deed of Lease. Henry Willis of St. George Parish, Spotsylvania Co for 5 shillings farm letten unto John Allen of same place two lots or ½ acres of ground & houses in the town of Fredericksburgh bounded by Caroline Street & Amelia Street numbered 30 & 32 as appears by a plan returned by George Home surveyor of afsd co XIII Aug MDCCXXXI ... during the term of one year paying the yearly rent of one ear of Indian corn on 10 Oct if demanded ... . Wit: Edmund Waller. Ackn 3 Apr 1739 by Henry Willis gent & at the motion of Zachary Lewis gent in behalf of the sd Allen is admitted to record. Attest: John Waller clk. (Pg 292)

3 Apr 1739. Deed of Release. Henry Willis of St. George Parish, Spotsylvania Co for £105 sold & released to John Allen of same place two lots or ½ acres of ground & houses ... [same as above] ... . Wit: Edmund Waller. Ackn 3 Apr 1739 by Henry Willis gent & at the motion of Zachary Lewis gent in behalf of the sd Allen the same is admitted to record. Attest: John Waller clk. (Pg 292)

18 Mar 1738. Deed of Lease. John Hobson of Charles Co, MD leased to Griffin Fantleroy of St. Stephens Parish, Northumberland Co gent a 400 a. tr of land being on the head of the River Ta in St. Georges Parish bounded by the afsd Fantleroy's line & John Bush's mill path, which sd tr of land was granted by pattent to Daniell Brown of Spotsylvania Co under the hand of William Gooch esqr Lt Governor of the Collony dated 24 Feb 1730 ... during the term of one year paying the rent of one ear of Indian corn at the expiration of the sd term if demanded ... . Wit: Wm Johnston, John Waller, Anthony Foster, Edmund Waller, Benjamin Martin. Proved 3 Apr 1739 & ordered to be recorded. Attest: John Waller clk. (Pg 293)

19 Mar 1738. Deed of Release. John Hobson of Charles Co, MD for £20 sold & released to Griffin Fantleroy of St. Stephens Parish, Northumberland Co, VA gent a 400 a. tr of land ... [*same as above*] ... . Wit: William Johnston, John Waller, Anthony Foster, Edmund Waller, Benjamin Martin. Proved 3 Apr 1739 & admitted to record. Attest: John Waller clk. (Pg 294)

1 May 1739. Deed. Henry Willis & John Waller gent directors & trustees for Fredericksburgh Town in Spotsylvania Co for £8 sold to Harry Turner of King George Co a ½ a. or lot of land in Fredericksburgh Town numbered 4 bounded (as per plot & survey made by George Home surveyor on 13 Aug 1728) on Sophia Street, Hanover Street & George Street ... if the sd Harry Turner shall & will erect, build & finish on the sd lot one house of brick, stone or wood well framed of the demensions of £20' square & 9' pitch within two years otherwise this deed to be void & the lot herein mencond to be revested in the sd trustees to be by them sold again by auction to the highest bidder ... . Wit: Edmund Waller. Ackn 1 May 1739 by Henry Willis & John Waller gent & at the motion of Henry Willis gent in behalf of the sd Turner is admitted to record. Attest: John Waller clk. (Pg 296)

28 Apr 1739. Deed. Joseph Brock of St. Georges Parish, Spotsylvania Co gent & Mary Brock his wife for £36:1:6 sold to Joseph Pen of Drysdale Parish, Caroline Co planter a 350 a. tr of land or woodland ground the same being pt/o a patent granted to Larkin Chew decd for 9,400 a. dated 4 Jun 1722 & by him sold unto the sd Joseph Brock by deeds dated 17 Oct 1723, the sd deeds specifying 7,420 a. as pt/o the afsd patent & hath since been resurveyed by the sd Joseph Brock & a patent obtained in his own name which is dated 12 Sep 1738, bounded by Nathl Sanders & Ignatius Turman ... . Wit: Thos Duerson, Mary Lyne, R. Curtis Junr. Ackn 1 May 1739 by Joseph Brock gent & Mary his wife & at the motion of Thomas Duerson in behalf of the sd Pen is admitted to record. Attest: John Waller clk. (Pg 297)

28 Apr 1739. Bond. I Joseph Brock of St. George Parish, Spotsylvania Co am firmly bound unto Joseph Pen of Drysdale Parish, Caroline Co in the sum of £72 ... the condition of this obligation is such that if the afsd Joseph Brock shall well & truly observe, perform, fulfill, accomplish & keep all the covenants, grants, articles, clauses, conditions & agreements whatsoever mentioned in a deed of feofment [*see above*] then this obligation to be void ... . Wit: Thos Duerson, Mary Lyne, R. Curtis Junr. Ackn 1 May 1739 by Joseph Brock gent & at the motion of Thomas Duerson in behalf of the sd Pen is admitted to record. Attest: John Waller clk. (Pg 299)

1 May 1739. Deed. Joseph Brock of St. Georges Parish, Spotsylvania Co gent & Mary Brock his wife for £21:1:6 sold to James Lee of St. Stevens Parish, King & Queen Co planter a 200 a. parcel of land or woodland ground being pt/o a patent granted to Larkin Chew decd for 9,400 a. dated 4 Jun 1722 & by him sold unto the sd Joseph Brock by deeds of sale dated 17 Oct 1723, the sd deeds being for 7,420 a. pt/o the afsd patent & hath since been resurveyed by the sd Joseph Brock & patented in his own name which sd patent bears dated 12 Sep 1738, bounded by James Stevens, John Talbert & John MyCow ... . Wit: Edmund Waller. Ackn 1 May 1739 by Joseph Brock & Mary his wife & was admitted to record. Attest: John Waller clk. (Pg 299)

1 May 1739. Bond. I Joseph Brock of St. George Parish, Spotsylvania Co am firmly bound unto James Lee of St. Stevens Parish, King & Queen Co in the sum of £42 ... the condition of this obligation is such that if the afsd Joseph Brock shall well & truly observe, perform, fulfill, accomplish & keep all the covenants, grants, articles, clauses, conditions & agreements whatsoever mentioned in one deed of feofment [*see above*] then this obligation to be void ... . Wit: None. Ackn 1 May 1739 & admitted to record. Attest: John Waller clk. (Pg 301)

28 Apr 1739. Deed of Gift. Joseph Brock of St. Georges Parish, Spotsylvania Co gent for & of his own free will & consideration of Thomas Duerson's intermarrying with one of the sd Joseph Brock's daus hath given unto the sd Thomas Duerson of same place a 720 a. parcel of land or woodland ground in St. Georges Parish being pt/o a patent granted to Larkin Chew decd for 1,600 a. dated 12 Jun 1723 & by him sold unto the sd Joseph Brock by deeds dated 17 Oct 1723, bounded by the Mattapony Church, the Main Road that leads from Snall Bridge to Col John Waller's, a patent of Henry Beverley's, sd Chew's patent, Rice Curtis Junr, Snales Road & near Bushes Road ... . Wit: R. Curtis Junr, John Wells, Phillemon Richards. Ackn by Joseph Brock gent & Mary the w/o the sd Joseph ackn her right of dower & is admitted to record. Attest: John Waller clk. (Pg 302)

28 Apr 1739. Bond. I Joseph Brock of St. George Parish, Spotsylvania Co am firmly bound unto Thomas Duerson of same place in the sum of £500 ... the condition of this obligation is such that if the afsd Joseph Brock shall well & truly observe, perform, fulfill, accomplish & keep all the covenants, grants, articles, clauses, conditions & agreements whatsoever mentioned in a deed of feeofment [*see above*] then this obligation to be void ... . Wit: R. Curtis Junr, John Wells, Philo Richards. Ackn 1 May 1739 & admitted to record. Attest: John Waller clk. (Pg 303)

1 May 1739. Deed. John Smith of St. George Parish, Spotsylvania Co planter for 1200 lbs of tobacco convenient in the sd co & three barrels of Indian corn sold to Thomas Dillard of same place planter a 200 a. tr of land in St. George Parish bounded by John Tyre, Ralph Williams, Thomas Hubbard, William Pruet, Thomas Carr gent decd, John Robinson esqr now Humphry Bell's, which sd tr of land is pt/o a greater tr of land granted by pattent to the sd John Smith 28 Sep MDCCXXXVIII for 300 a. (100 a. pt/o the sd pattent being given & ackn by deed of gift by the sd John Smith to his grandson the afsd John Tyre 3 Sep MDCCXXXIII) ... . Wit: Robart Holloway, Mary Asmon. Ackn 1 May 1739 by John Smith & Margaret the w/o the sd John ackn he right of dower & is admitted to record. Attest: John Waller clk. (Pg 304)

1 May 1739. Bond. I John Smith of Spotsylvania Co am firmly bound unto Thomas Dillard of same co in the penal sum of 2,400 lbs of tobacco convenient in the sd co & six barrels of Indian corn ... the condition of this obligation is such that if the afsd John Smith shall well & truly observe, perform, fulfill, accomplish & keep all the covenants, grants, articles, clauses, conditions & agreements whatsoever mentioned in one indenture of feofment [*see above*] then this obligation to be void ... . Wit: Robart Holloway, Mary Asmon. Ackn 1 May 1739 & admitted to record. Attest: John Waller clk. (Pg 306)

3 Jul MDCCXXXVIII. Deed. The feofees or trustees for the land appropriated for the building & erecting the town of Fredericksburgh for £4:10 sold to George Chapman of the sd town sadler ½ a. or lot of land in the sd town of Fredericksburgh described in the plan of the sd town by the figure 49 & is bounded by Caroline Street & Amelia Street ... if the sd George Chapman shall not within the space of two years begin to build & finish upon the sd lot one good dwelling house then the sd feofees or trustees & it shall & may be lawfull to & for them into the sd granted premises to enter & the same to have again as their former estate as if these presents had never been made ... . Wit: Edmund Waller. Wit to receipt: Larkin Chew. Ackn 3 Jul 1739 by John Taliaferro & John Waller gent two of the feofees or trustees & admitted to record. Attest: John Waller clk. (Pg 306)

1 Jun 1739. Bill of Sale. For the valuable consideration of £14 to me James Garton paid by Col Henry Willis I have & do sell to the sd Willis two Negros, viz, Ben a boy & Moll a girl. Wit: John Allan, Alexr Cumings. Proved 3 Jul 1739 & admitted to record. Attest: John Waller clk. (Pg 307)

1 Jun 1739. Deed. Peter Gustavas & Mary his wife of Amelia Co for £25 sold to William Sandidge of Spotsylvania Co a 450 a. tr of land in St. Georges Parish bounded by James Taylor, Joseph Peterson & Thomas Sartin .... Wit: Thomas Cartwright, George Willcox, George Sheppard. Proved 3 Jul 1739 & Mary the w/o the sd Peter ackn her right of dower in the sd land & is admitted to record. Attest: John Waller clk. (Pg 308)

22 Apr 1739. Deed. Peter Gustavas & Mary his wife of Amelia Co for £16 sold to Joseph Peterson of Spotsylvania Co a 150 a. tr of land bounded by Thomas Sartin .... Wit: Thomas Cartwright, George Willcox, George Sheperd. Proved 3 Jul 1739 & Mary the w/o the sd Peter ackn her right of dower in the land & is admitted to record. Attest: John Waller clk. (Pg 309)

7 Aug MDCCXXXIX. Deed. The feoffees or trustees for the land appropriated for the building & erecting the town of Fredericksburgh for £6:15 sold to Lawrence Washington of Prince William Co gent two ½ acres or lots of land in the sd town of Fredericksburgh described in the plan of the sd town by the figures 37 & 39 bounded by Caroline Street, Charlotta Street & Hanover Street as by the plan of the sd town ... if the sd Lawrence Washington shall not within the space of two years begin to build & finish upon each of the sd lots one good dwelling house that then the sd feoffees or trustees & it shall & may be lawfull to & for them into the sd granted premises to enter & the same to have again as their former estate as they might have done if these presents had never been made .... Wit: Elliott Benger, Wm Woodford, Dan Crump, John Pagan. Wit to receipt: Edmund Waller. Ackn 8 Aug 1739 by Henry Willis & John Waller gent two of the feoffees or trustees & at the motion of Edmund Waller in behalf of the sd Washington is admitted to record. Attest: John Waller clk. (Pg 310)

6 Aug 1739. Deed of Lease. Anthony Foster of Spotsylvania Co for 5 shillings leased to John Snale (Snell) of Orange Co planter a 100 a. tr of land (the sd land being pt/o a patent granted to Larkin Chew decd &c & by the sd Chew sold to Robert King by deed &c & by the sd King sold unto the sd Anthony Foster by deed &c) bounded by Thos Solmon, the sd King's line, Johnston's race ground & John Foster ... during the term of one year paying the rent of one ear of Indian corn on the last day of the sd term if demanded .... Wit: R. Curtis Junr, Henery Rogers, Jno Foster. Ackn 7 Aug 1739 & admitted to record. (Pg 311)

7 Aug 1739. Deed of Release. Anthony Foster of Spotsylvania Co & Martha his wife for £50 sold & released to John Snall (Snell) of Orange Co planter a 100 a. tr of land ... [*same as above*] ... . Wit: R. Curtis Junr, Henery Rogers, Jno Foster. Ackn 7 Aug 1739 by Anthony Foster & Martha his wife & admitted to record. Attest: John Waller clk. (Pg 312)

6 Aug 1739. Deed of Lease. John Foster of Orange Co planter for 5 shillings leased to Rice Curtis Senr of Spotsylvania Co an 84 a. tr of land being pt/o a patent granted to Larkin Chew gent since decd dated 26 Apr 1712 (it being also sold by the afsd Chew to Robert King by deeds &c & by the sd King sold to the sd John Foster by deed dated 6 Dec 1721) the sd deed specifying to containe 100 a. with the bounds thereof but it appears by resurvey to containe only 84 a. as afsd, adj the River Po & William Solomon ... during the term of one year paying on the last day of the sd terme the rent of one ear of Indian corn if demanded ... . Wit: Wm Bartlet, Jas Beuford, R. Curtis Junr. Ackn 7 Aug 1739 & admitted to record. Attest: John Waller clk. (Pg 314)

7 Aug 1739. Deed of Release. John Foster of Orange Co planter & Isabella his wife for £25:4 sold & released to Rice Curtis Senr of Spotsylvania Co an 84 a. tr of land ... [*same as above*] ... . Wit: Wm Bartlet, Jas Beuford, R. Curtis Junr. Ackn 7 Aug 1739 by John Foster & Isabella his wife & the sd Isabella ackn her right of dower & is admitted to record. Attest: John Waller clk. (Pg 315)

7 Aug 1739. Bond. I John Foster of Orange Co am firmly bound unto Rice Curtis Senr of Spotsylvania Co in the sum of £100 ... the condition of this obligation is such that if the afsd John Foster shall well & truly perform & keep all the covenants mentioned & comprised in an indenture of release [*see above*] then this obligation to be void ... . Wit: Wm Bartlet, Jas Beuford, R. Curtis Junr. Ackn 7 Aug 1739 & admitted to record. Attest: John Waller clk. (Pg 317)

7 Aug 1739. Deed of Lease. Susanna Livingston of Spotsylvania Co for 5 shillings leased to John Allan merchant of the town of Fredericksburgh a lott or ½ a. of land in the town of Fredericksburgh distinguished in the plot by number 6 commonly known by the name of the Lease Land Wharf ... during the term of one year paying one pepper corn upon the feast of St. Michael the Arch Angel if demanded ... . Wit: Edmund Waller. Ackn 8 Aug 1739 by Susanna Livingston & at the motion of Henry Willis gent is admitted to record. Attest: John Waller clk. (Pg 318)

8 Aug 1739. Deed of Release. Susanna Livingston of Spotsylvania Co for £10 sold & released to John Allan merchant of the town of Fredericksburgh a lott or ½ a. of land ... [*same as above*] ... . Wit: Edmund Waller. Ackn 8 Aug 1739

by Susanna Livingston & at the motion of Henry Willis gent is admitted to record. Attest: John Waller clk. (Pg 319)

7 Aug 1739. Deed. John Snal of Orange Co, VA & Philadelphia his wife & Anthony Foster of Spotsylvania Co & Martha his wife for £100 sold to John Taliaferro of Caroline Co, VA gent a 200 a. tr of land in St. George Parish on the n side the River Po which sd land being pt/o 300 a. of land formerly purch by John Snal the elder father of the afsd John Snal of Larkin Chew gent decd & bounded by Greens Br, Samuel Hensley & the sd John Taliaferro, together with 1 a. of land on the s side the sd River Po granted to the afsd John Snal the father for the building of a water mill .... Wit: R. Curtis Junr, Henry Rogers, Jno Foster. Memorandum that full & peaceable & quiet seisen & possession of the lands & premises within mentioned was given & delivered by the within named Anthony Foster to the sd John Taliaferro. Wit: Wm Bartlet, Thomas Megee. Ackn 7 Aug 1739 by John Snell & Philadelphia his wife & Anthony Foster & Martha his wife the sd Philadelphia & Martha ackn their right of dower in the sd land & admitted to record .... Attest: John Waller clk. (Pg 320)

4 Aug 1739. Deed. John Snall of St. Mark Parish, Orange Co & Philadelphia his wife for £30 sold to Rice Curtis Senr of St. George Parish, Spotsylvania Co a 100 a. tr of land or woodland ground bounded by Abraham Brown, Robert King & John Foster .... Wit: Thos Merry, John Wood, Peter Mountague. Ackn 7 Aug 1739 by John Snell & Philadelphia his wife & Philadelphia ackn her right of dower in the same & admitted to record. Attest: John Waller clk. (Pg 322)

4 Aug 1739. Bond. I John Snall of Orange Co planter am firmly bound unto Rice Curtis Senr of Spotsylvania Co in the sum of £100 ... the condition of this obligation is such that if the afsd John Snall shall well & truly perform & keep all the covenants mentioned & comprised in an indenture of feofment [see above] then this obligation to be void .... Wit: Peter Mountague, Thos Merry, R. Curtis Junr. Ackn 7 Aug 1739 & admitted to record. Attest: John Waller clk. (Pg 323)

28 Aug 1739. Bill of Sale. For the valuable consideration of £7:10 & 202 ½ lbs of neat tobacco to me Francis Arnold paid I do sell unto Humphry Bell of London one mare bay coullar & her colt & six head of cattle & blankets & cotton sheals & one bell mouth spice mortar & one rug, one small table & two iron potts ... Wit: Larkin Chew, John Blake. Proved 4 Sep 1739 & admitted to record. Attest: John Waller clk. (Pg 324)

7 Aug MDCCXXXIX. Deed of Mortgage. I John Hobson bricklayer for £50 sold to Francis Thornton of Spotsylvania Co gent three Negro slaves, to wit, Obay a man, Jonnah a woman & Robin a boy ... provided & upon this condition

that if the sd John Hobson shall well & truly pay to the sd Francis Thornton the sum of £30 at or by 7 Oct MDCCXXXIX that then this sale to be void ... . Wit: Z. Lewis, Anthony Strother, Wm Williams. Proved 4 Sep 1739 & admitted to record. Attest: John Waller clk. (Pg 324)

21 Aug 1739. Bill of Sale. I Nathaniel Holland of Spotsylvania Co carpenter have sold unto Col Henry Willis gent of co afsd three feather beds & all furniture belonging to them with two bedstids & one black walnut table, one chest, one iron pot, one frying pan, three plates, one pewter dish, three rush bottom chairs for the sum of £5 ... . Wit: William Reid, Gabriel Cleaton. Proved 4 Sep 1739 & admitted to record. Attest: John Waller clk. (Pg 325)

7 Aug MDCCXXXVIIII. Deed. The feofees or trustees for the land appropriated for the building & erecting the town of Fredericksburgh for £2:15 sold to John Waller of Spotsylvania Co gent ½ a. or lot of land in the sd town of Fredericksburgh described in the plat of the sd town by the figure 40 bounded by Princess Ann Street & Hanover Street as by the plan of the sd town ... . Wit: Elliott Benger, Andr Craig, John Pagan. Ackn 4 Sep 1739 by Henry Willis & John Taliaferro gent two of the feoffees or trustees & admitted to record. Attest: John Waller clk. (Pg 325)

1 Oct MDCCXXXIX. Deed. John Talbert of St. George Parish, Spotsylvania Co for £14 sold to Thomas Hubbard of same place planter a 100 a. tr of land in St. George Parish bounded by Robert Stubblefield, John Smith & William Pruit, the sd parcel of land is pt/o a greater tr granted by pattent to Henry Haines XXVIII Sep MDCCXXXVIII & by the sd Haines sold to the sd Thomas Hubbard & by the sd Hubard sold 7 May MDCCXXXIV to the sd John Talbert & now for the above consideration conveyed back top the sd Hubbard ... . Wit: Edmund Waller, John Waller. Ackn by John Talbert & Margaret the w/o the sd John's power of atty to John Waller gent being proved the sd Waller by virtue of the sd power ackn he right of dower & is admitted to record. Attest: John Waller clk. (Pg 326)

1 Oct 1739. Power of Attorney. I Margaret Talbert do appoint John Waller gent my trusty friend to ackn all my right & title of dower in & to 100 a. of land sold by my husband to Thomas Hubbard & conveyed by deed of feofment [see above] ... . Wit: Edmund Waller. Proved 2 Oct 1739 & admitted to record. Attest: John Waller clk. (Pg 328)

1 Oct 1739. Deed of Lease. Thomas Smith of Prince William Co for 5 shillings leased to George Reeves of South Farnham Parish, Essex Co a 50 a. tr of land adj the sd George Reeves, land formerly belonging to James Horsenalle but now Capt William Grayson's, Jonathan Gibson, Maine River of Rappahannock &

land formerly patented by John Smith but now belonging to Col Henry Fitzhugh ... during the term of one year paying the yearly rent of one ear of Indian corn on the last day of the sd year if demanded ... . Wit: Jos Reeves, Tho Reeves, Kezia Wise. Ackn 2 Oct 1739 & admitted to record. Attest: John Waller clk. (Pg 328)

2 Oct 1739. Deed of Release. Thomas Smith of Prince William Co for £12 sold & released to George Reeves of South Farnham Parish, Essex Co a 50 a. tr of land ... [same as above] ... . Wit: Jos Reeves, Tho Reeves, Kezia Wise. Ackn 2 Oct 1739 & admitted to record. Attest: John Waller clk. (Pg 329)

6 Nov 1739. Deed. Thomas Sertain (Seartin) (Searton) of St. George Parish, Spotsylvania Co for £25 sold to John Holliday (Holladay) Senr of same place in his actual possession now being by virtue of a bargain & sale to him made for one year by indenture dated three days before the date hereof a 200 a. tr of land with the plantation whereon the sd Seartin now lives it being pt/o 1,000 a. granted to the sd Thomas Searton by pattent dated 6 May 1727 bounded by 2,000 a. of land which the sd Thomas Sertain sold to James Terry which now belongs to the afsd Holliday, James Taylor & Gustavas's line ... . Wit: Joseph Thomas, Daniel Holliday, Elsabeth Holliday. Ackn 6 Nov MDCCXXXIX by Thomas Sertain & Mary the w/o the sd Thomas ackn her right of dower & is admitted to record. Attest: John Waller clk. (Pg 332)

5 Nov 1739. Deed of Lease. Thomas Salmon of St. George Parish, Spotsylvania Co planter for 5 shillings farm letten to William Salmon of same place planter a 100 a. tr of land whereon the sd Thomas Salmon now lives in St. George Parish & on the s side of the River Po adj Robert King, John Snell & John Foster, which 100 a. was formerly in the possession of Robert King & by the sd King sold unto Abraham Brown & by the sd Abraham Brown sold unto the above named Lawrence Franklyn (sic) ... during the term of one year paying the yearly rent of one pepper corn at the feast of St. Michael the Arch Angel if demanded ... . Wit: Edmund Waller, Peter Mountague. Ackn 6 Nov MDCCXXXIX & admitted to record. Attest: John Waller clk. (Pg 333)

6 Nov 1739. Deed of Release. Thomas Salmon of St. Georges Parish, Spotsylvania Co for 500 lbs of good lawfull tobacco in cask sold & released to William Salmon of same place planter a 100 a. tr of land ... [same as above] ... . Wit: Edmund Waller, Peter Mountague. Ackn 6 Nov MDCCXXXIX by Thomas Salmon & Mary the w/o the sd Thomas ackn her right of dower & is admitted to record. Attest: John Waller clk. (Pg 334)

25 Sep 1739. Deed. Rice Curtis of St. George Parish, Spotsylvania Co for 40 shillings sold to William Johnston of same place a 2 a. tr of land in the parish

afsd bounded by the Main Road, land Anthony Foster bought of Robert King & Robert King ... . Wit: Philip Vincent Vass, Jos Stevens, George Moore. Ackn 6 Nov 1739 & admitted to record. Attest: John Waller clk. (Pg 336)

5 Nov 1739. Deed of Lease. Humphry Hill of St. Stephens Parish, King & Queen Co for 5 shillings leased to John Chiles of Hanover Co a 1,000 a. tr of land in St. George Parish adj the n bank of East North East River, in the sd Hill's line of his land bought of Dannit Abney, Henry Chiles, Col Aug Moore, Thos Graves & James Edwards, the sd 1,000 a. being parcel of a pattent for 2,000 a. granted to Henry Webber 28 Oct 1723 ... during the term of one year paying the rent of one ear of Indian corn on the last day of the sd term if demanded ... . Wit: Edwin Hickman, Elizabeth Hill, John Blake. Ackn 6 Nov MDCCXXXIX & admitted to record. Attest: John Waller clk. (Pg 339)

6 Nov 1739. Deed of Release. Humphry Hill of St. Stephens Parish, King & Queen Co for £200 sold & released to John Chiles of Hanover Co a 1,000 a. tr of land ... [same as above] ... . Wit: Edwin Hickman, Elizabeth Hill, John Blake. Ackn 6 Nov MDCCXXXIX & admitted to record. Attest: John Waller clk. (Pg 340)

1 Apr 1740. Deed. Henry Willis esqr & John Waller gent directors & trustees of the town of Fredericksburgh in Spotsylvania Co for £5 sold to William Beverley of Essex Co gent a lot or ½ a. of land in the sd town of Fredericksburg numbered 15 according to the plat thereof made by George Home late surveyor of sd co ... provided that the sd William Beverley do within two years erect, build & finish on the sd lot one house of brick, stone or wood well framed of the demensions of 20' square & 9' pitch at the lease otherwise this grant to be void & the lot granted to be reinvested in the trustees of the sd town & to be liable to the purch of any other person ... . Wit: Jos Brock, Wm Johnston, W. Robinson. Ackn 1 Apr 1740 & admitted to record. Attest: John Waller clk. (Pg 342)

6 Nov 1739. Division of Land. Whereas we Henry Chiles & John Chiles are seized in fee simple as joint tenants in 2,000 a. of land conveyed to us by Henry Webber gent since decd by deed which sd land lies in St. George Parish on both sides of East North East River & we being willing that the sd land should pass as we have & do intent to dispose thereof we have devided the same according to the plan [drawing not included here], that is to say 400 a. up East North East River is the shape of the sd land sold by Henry Chiles to Humphry Hill gent ... the remainder of the sd Henry Chiles share of the sd 2000 a. of land being 600 a. adj Col Moore & Mr. Seaton ... 1,000 a. pt/o the sd 2000 a. being the share of John Chiles is adj Humphry Hill gent formerly Abney's line, Joseph Woolfolk, James Taylor, Henry Chiles, Thomas Graves, James Edwards & the s side of East North East River ... . At a court held 6 Nov 1739 on motion of Henry &

John Chiles the within plan & division of lands between them is admitted to record. Attest: John Waller clk. (Pg 344)

1 Apr 1740. Deed of Gift. I Henry Willis of Spotsylvania Co gent out of good will & natural affection I have to my son Lewis Willis do give unto my sd son two young Negroes or molattoes the one called John the son of Jack Wilshire & Lucy his wife the other called Kate alias True Love the dau of Negro Rose which sd Negroes or mollattoes are to be delivered to him the sd Lewis Willis when he shall attain to the age of 18 .... Wit: None. Ackn 1 Apr 1740 & recorded. Attest: John Waller clk. (Pg 345)

1 Apr 1740. Deed of Gift. I Joseph Brock of Spotsylvania Co for & in consideration of 5 shillings but more especially out of good will & affection towards my two grandsons Giles Curtis & Rice Curtis have given unto the sd Giles Curtis one Negro boy named Corah & unto the sd Rice Curtis one Negro boy named Jamey, provided & it is my intent & meaning that the sd Negroes be & remain in the possession of their father Rice Curtis Junr till my grandsons shall arrive to the age of 21 or day of marriage & the sd Rice Curtis Junr to his own use the produce & crops of corn & tobacco till the time afsd do convert & turn .... Wit: None. Ackn 1 Apr 1740 & recorded. Attest: John Waller clk. (Pg 346)

3 Feb 1739. Deed of Lease. James Garton of Spotsylvania Co for 5 shillings leased to William Bell of sd co a 250 a. tr of land pt/o a 500 a. tr sold formerly sold by Larkin Chew to the sd James Garton & Uriah Garton the sd 250 a. being the sd James Garton's pt/o the sd 500 a. as it was then divided between them by consent bounded by the dividing corner of the sd James Garton & Uriah Garton & Joseph Brocks ... during the term of one year paying the rent of one ear of Indian corn on Lady Day next if demanded .... Wit: Jno Parrish, Nathll Holland, Alexr Cumings. Ackn 1 Apr 1740 & admitted to record. Attest: John Waller clk. (Pg 346)

4 Feb 1739. Deed of Release. James Garton of Spotsylvania Co for £50 sold & released to William Bell of sd co a 250 a. tr of land ... [same as above] .... Wit: Jno Parrish, Nathll Holland, Alexr Cumings. Ackn 1 Apr 1740 & admitted to record. Attest: John Waller clk. (Pg 347)

22 Feb MDCCXXXIX. Deed. Anthony Gholstone of Spotsylvania Co & Jane his wife for £30 sold to Zachary Lewis of same co a messuage & 200 a. tr of land on the s side of Hollidays Swamp being pt/o a patent granted to James Taylor gent decd for 5,000 a. of land dated XXI Jul MDCCXXII & by the sd James Taylors conveyed to the sd Anthony Gholstone by deeds of lease & released dated 5 & 6 Jul MDCCXXV bounded by John Holliday's line, Mr.

Smith, Mr. Thomas & James Taylor ... . Wit: Joseph Thomas, Charles Barrett, John Holliday (Holladay), John Bowles. Ackn 1 Apr 1740 by Anthony Gholstone & Jane his wife & recorded. Attest: John Waller clk. (Pg 349)

18 Dec MDCCXXXIX. Deed. Joseph Thomas of Spotsylvania Co gent & Sarah his wife for £220 sold to Zachary Lewis of same co a 900 a. tr of land on the n side the Northanna in St. George Parish being pt/o a patent granted to Rowland Thomas father of the sd Joseph for 1,000 a. dated 16 Jun MDCCXXVII & by the sd Rowland conveyed to the sd Joseph by deeds of lease & release dated 12 & 13 Jun MDCCXXXV bounded by Woolf Swamp, Robert Turner, Christopher Smith & Hollidays Swamp ... . Wit: Tho Tomkins, Chs Barrett, Henry Lewis. Ackn 1 Apr 1740 & recorded. Attest: John Waller clk. NB that the dedimus for examining Sarah the w/o the sd Joseph Thomas about her dower of the sd land is recorded in folio 398. (Pg 351)

6 May 1740. Deed. Margaret Hamm & Samuel Hamm both of St. George Parish, Spotsylvania Co for £16:10:9 sold to Richard Couzone of same place a messuage & 100 a. tr of land being the same land & plantation which was given to the sd Margaret by her husband Samuel Hamm decd by his will for & during her naturall life & after her death then the land was given to the sd Samuel Hamm his son which land is in the parish afsd on the s side the Middle River of Mattapony, which land is pt/o a greater tr of land granted by patent to John Rogers & several other persons ... . Wit: John Waller, Sharshall Grasty, Wm Waller. Ackn 6 May 1740 by Margaret Hamm & Samuel Hamm & admitted to record. Attest: John Waller clk. (Pg 353)

6 May 1740. Deed. Between Thomas Turner of King George Co of the one part & Benjamin Winslow of Essex Co of the other part, wit that whereas the directors of the town of Fredericksburgh in Spotsylvania Co by their deed did grant, make over & convey unto the sd Thomas Turner one lott or ½ a. of land in the sd town of Fredericksburg numbered 52 according to a plat of the sd town thereof made, now this indenture wit that the sd Thomas Turner for £21:10 sold unto the sd Benjamin Winslow all the estate right, title, interest & demand whatsoever which the sd Thomas Turner now hath, may, might or ought to have of, in or to the sd lot or ½ a. of land numbered 52 in the town of Fredericksburgh ... . Wit: Jos Brock, John Thornton, R. Curtis Junr, M. Battaley, Dav McCulloch. Ackn 6 May 1740 & admitted to record. Attest: John Waller clk. (Pg 354)

29 Jan 1739. Deed. Robert Brown of St. George Parish, Spotsylvania Co for £8 sold to Joseph Carter of same place an 89 a. tr of land in St. George Parish adj to the land of Thomas Hill, the sd Joseph Carter & Robinsons Swamp ... . Wit:

George Goodloe, Isaac Darnell, George Carter. Proved 6 May MDCCXL & admitted to record. Attest: John Waller clk. (Pg 356)

31 Apr 1740. Deed. Joseph Brock of St. Georges Parish, Spotsylvania Co gent & Mary his wife for £41:1:6 sold to Phillip Sanders of St. Drisdale Parish, King & Queen Co planter a 400 a. tr of land or woodland ground in St. Georges Parish being pt/o a patent formerly granted to Larkin Chew gent decd dated 4 Jun 1722 the same being sold & conveyed by the sd Larkin Chew to the sd Joseph Brock by deeds of lease & release dated 17 Oct 1723 & since resurveyed by the sd Joseph Brock & a patent obtained in his own name dated 17 Sep 1738, the 400 a. bounded by John Boswell, the Mine Road, Joseph Pen, Ignatious Turman & the sd Joseph Brocks's patent .... Wit: Wm Bartlet, Thos Merry, Thomas West. Ackn 6 May 1740 by Joseph Brock gent & Mary his wife & admitted to record. Attest: John Waller clk. (Pg 357)

30 Apr 1740. Bond. I Joseph Brock of Spotsylvania Co am firmly bound unto Phillip Sanders of King & Queen Co in the sum of £82:3 ... the condition of this obligation is such that if the afsd Joseph Brock shall well & truly perform & keep all the covenants mentioned & comprised in an indenture of feofment [*see above*] then this obligation to be void .... Wit: Wm Bartlet, Thos Merry, Thomas West. Ackn 6 May 1740 & admitted to record. Attest: John Waller clk. (Pg 359)

5 Mar MDCCXXXIX. Deed. Francis Thornton Junr of St. George Parish, Spotsylvania Co for 500 lbs of lawfull tobacco sold to Larkin Chew of same place gent one lot or ½ a. of land in the town of Fredericksburgh & is one of the outside lots described in the plan of the sd town by the figure 64 bounded by Princess Ann Street & the back lines of the sd town, the sd lot being formerly conveyed by deed 8 Oct MDCCXXXV by the feoffees of the sd town to Dr. John Tennent & by the sd John Tennent sold to the afsd Francis Thornton .... Wit: Wm Johnston, Nathll Chapman, August Washington. Ackn 6 May 1740 & admitted to record. Attest: John Waller clk. (Pg 360)

15 Dec 1739. I Mildred Willis late Mildred Gregory now w/o Henry Willis of Spotsylvania Co gent send greeting, whereas by indenture tripartite dated 5 Jan 1733 made between the sd Henry Willis of the first part, me the sd Mildred of the second part & John Washington of Gloucester Co gent of the third part reciting that a marriage was intended speedily to be solemnized between the sd Henry & me the sd Mildred the sd Henry Willis did covenant & agree to & with the sd John Washington that all the lands, slaves, money, plate, jewels, stocks of cattle & all other goods & chattels whatsoever whereof I the sd Mildred at the time of the sd indenture was in anyway seised, possessed or interested & all profits which should arise therefrom should notwithstanding the sd intended

marriage did take effect be & remain to me the sd Mildred ... & it should & might be lawfull to & for me the sd Mildred to give, devise or dispose of all or any pt/o the lands or chattels therein before mentioned either by my will or by any other writing ... know ye that I the sd Mildred Willis for the advancement of my son Lewis Willis & for the limiting & appointing how the slaves & personal estate of which I am possessed shall go & be disposed of after the death of myself & the sd Henry Willis my husband as also for 5 shillings paid by my sd husband have given to the sd Lewis Willis all & every the slaves, stocks, plate, goods & chattels whatsoever mentioned in the schedule [*see below*] ... from & immediately after the death of the sd Mildred Willis & the sd Henry Willis my husband ... for want of any such limitation direction & appointment that then all & every the sd slaves stocks plate goods & chattels shall at the death of the sd Henry Willis & of me be equally divided between my three daus Frances the w/o Francis Thornton Junr, Mildred & Elizabeth, if I the sd Mildred for the undutifulness of my sd son Lewis Willis or any other cause shall think fit to do .... Wit: August Washington, John Taliaferro. Proved 6 May 1740 & admitted to record. Attest: John Waller clk. (Pg 361)

A list of the slaves &c belonging to Mildred Willis to be annext to her [*above*] deed of gift: Potomack Tom, Venus, Patt, Christian, Venus, Molly, Harry, Charles, Betty, Jenny, Nanny, Judy, Peter, Sambo, Tom, Jo, Mingo, Will, Joan, Mingo, Roger, Robin, Rachel, Toby, Nell, Lucy, Toby, Harry, Nell, Jack, Jack, Grace, Phil, Sarah, Ned, Sarah, Amos, Pender, Dick, Alice, Major, Hannah, Betty, Dick, Billy, Jenny, Judy, Nanny, Sam, Humphry & Kate. 100 head of cattle, 50 sheep & all the plate, household goods &c belonging to the sd Mildred at the time of her marriage. (Pg 363)

6 May 1740. Indenture. I John Becket (Beckett) do ackn myself a servant to Col Henry Willis for 13 months & 20 days & do oblidge myself to serve the sd time whenever he please to demand it either by month or months, week or weeks, day or days untill the sd time of service shall be fully completed, I Henry Willis do give the afsd Jno Becket full liberty to follow his own trade or calling for his own benefit under the above restrictions .... Ackn 6 May 1740 by John Beckett & Henry Willis gent & admitted to record. Attest: John Waller clk. (Pg 364)

7 May 1740. Deed. The feoffees or trustees for the land appropriated for the building & erecting the town of Fredericksburgh for £4:5 sold to Nathll Chapman of Stafford Co gent ½ a. or lot of land in the sd town of Fredricksburgh described in the plan of the sd town by the figure 20 bounded by Caroline Street & George Street ... if the sd Chapman shall not within the space of two years begin to build & finish upon the sd lot one good dwelling house then the sd feoffees or trustees & it shall & may be lawfull to & for them into the

sd granted premises & every part thereof to enter & the same to have again as their former estate as if these presents had never been made .... Wit: Edmund Waller. Recd of Nathll Chapman £4:5 it being the consideration for the lot of land & premises within mentioned sold by us to James Belchaise who afterwards sold the lot to Samll Wharton & by Wm Wharton executor to the sd Saml assigned to Henry Willis & by him to the sd Chapman 7 May 1740. Henry Willis. Wit: Geo Chapman. This deed ackn 6 May 1740 by Henry Willis & John Waller gent two of the feoffees or trustees & the receipt for the consideration money to Nathaniell Chapman gent & at the motion of George Chapman is admitted to record. Attest: John Waller clk. (Pg 384)

4 Feb MDCCXXXIX. Deed of Lease. John Dobbs of St. George Parish, Spotsylvania Co for 5 shillings leased to John Smith of same place a 100 a. tr of land pt/o a 400. tr granted to the sd John Smith by patent dated 13 Jun MDCCXXVI ... during the term of one year paying the rent of one ear of corn if demanded on the feast of St. John the Baptise .... Wit: Robt Huddleston, John Bowles, Isaac Darnell, Ralph Willis, Samuel Matthews. Proved 6 May 1740 & admitted to record. Attest: John Waller clk. (Pg 365)

11 Feb MDCCXXXIX. Deed of Release. John Dobbs of St. George Parish, Spotsylvania Co for £20 sold & released to John Smith of same place a 100 a. tr of land ... [same as above] .... Wit: John Bowles, Isaac Darnell, Ralph Williams, Samuel Matthews, Robt Huddleston. Proved 6 May 1740 & admitted to record. Attest: John Waller clk. (Pg 367)

1 Oct 1739. Deed of Lease. Joseph Brock of Spotsylvania Co gent for 5 shillings leased to William Bartlet of same co planter a 336 a. tr of land (the same being pt/o a pattent granted to Larkin Chew decd dated 4 Jun 1722 & by the sd Larkin Chew sold & conveyed unto the sd Joseph Brock by deeds dated 7 Oct 1723 & hath since been resurveyed by the sd Joseph Brock & regranted to him by patent dated 12 Sep 1738) bounded by Bushes Road, the Iron Mine Road & the land of John Walker ... during the term of one year paying the rent of one ear of Indian corn if demanded .... Wit: R. Curtis Junr, Ann Curtis, John Mountague. Ackn 6 May 1740 & admitted to record. Attest: John Waller clk. (Pg 368)

2 Oct 1739. Deed of Release. Joseph Brock of Spotsylvania Co gent & Mary his wife for £34:13:6 sold & released to William Bartlet of same co planter a 336 a. tr of land ... [same as above] .... Wit: R. Curtis Junr, Ann Curtis, John Mountague. Ackn by Joseph Brock gent & Mary his wife & admitted to record. Attest: John Waller clk. (Pg 369)

2 Oct 1739. Bond. I Joseph Brock of Spotsylvania Co am firmly bound unto William Bartlet of afsd co in the sum of £69:7 ... the condition of this obligation is such that if the afsd Joseph Brock shall well & truly perform & keep all the covenants mencond & comprised in an indenture of release [*see above*] then this obligation to be void ... . Wit: R. Curtis Junr, Ann Curtis, John Mountague. Ackn 6 May 1740 & admitted to record. Attest: John Waller clk. (Pg 372)

29 Apr 1740. Deed of Lease. Joseph Brock of Spotsylvania Co gent for 5 shillings leased to John Boswell of same co planter a 980 a. tr of land, being pt/o a patent granted to Larkin Chew decd dated 4 Jun 1722 & by the sd Larkin Chew sold & conveyed unto the sd Joseph Brock by deeds dated 7 Oct 1723 & hath since been resurveyed by the sd Joseph Brock & regranted to him by patent dated 12 Sep 1738, bounded by the Middle River, Sander's line, Joseph Pen & the mine ... during the term of one year paying on the last day of the sd term the rent of one ear of Indian corn if demanded ... . Wit: R. Curtis Junr, Ann Curtis, Mary Lynes. Ackn 6 May 1740 & admitted to record. Attest: John Waller clk. (Pg 373)

30 Apr 1740. Deed of Release. Joseph Brock of Spotsylvania Co gent & Mary his wife for £100 sold & released to John Boswell of sd co a 980 a. tr of land ... [*same as above*] ... . Wit: R. Curtis Junr, Ann Curtis, Mary Lynes. Ackn by Joseph Brock gent & Mary his wife 6 May 1740 & admitted to record. (Pg 374)

30 Apr 1740. Bond. I Joseph Brock of Spotsylvania Co am firmly bound unto John Boswell of same co in the sum of £200 ... the condition of this obligation is such that if the sd Joseph Brock shall well & truly perform & keep all the covenants mencond & comprised in an indenture of released [*see above*] then this obligation to be void ... . Wit: R. Curtis Junr, Ann Curtis, Mary Lynes. Ackn 6 May 1740 & admitted to record. Attest: John Waller clk. (Pg 376)

3 Jun MDCCXXXX. Deed. The feoffees or trustees for the land appropriated for the building & erecting the town of Fredericksburgh for £9:5 sold to Benjamin Winslow of Essex Co gent ½ a. or lot of land in the sd town of Fredericksburgh described in the plan of the sd town by the figure 55 bounded by Princess Ann Street & Charlotta Street ... if the sd Benjamin Winslow shall not within the space of two years build & finish upon the sd lot one good dwelling house that then the sd feofees or trustees & it shall & may be lawfull to & for them into the sd granted premises to enter & the same to have again as their former estate as they might have done if these presents had never been made ... . Wit: Jno Edwards, Edmund Waller. Ackn 3 Jun 1740 by John Taliaferro & John Waller gent two of the feoffees or trustees & admitted to record. Attest: John Waller clk. (Pg 377)

3 Jun 1740. Deed of Lease. Bartholomew & Charity Wood for 5 shillings farm let unto Richard Chiles a 100 a. parcel of land or woodland ground bounded by Vincent Tapp & the uttermost extent of the bounds of the land as Elizabeth Tapp bought of Francis & Anthony Thornton & ackn by deed of lease & release 4 Sep 1722 ... during the term of one year paying the yearly rent of one ear of Indian corn on the feast of St. Michael if demanded ... . Wit: John Gordon, Wm Spencer, Joshua Thomas. Ackn 3 Jun 1740 by Bartholomew Wood & Charity his wife & admitted to record. Attest: John Waller clk. (Pg 378)

3 Jun 1740. Deed of Release. Bartholomew Wood of Prince William Co for £11 sold & released to Richard Chiles of Spotsylvania Co a 100 a. tr of land ... [*same as above*] ... . Wit: John Gordon, Wm Spencer, Joshua Thomas. Ackn 3 Jun 1740 by Bartholomew Wood & Charity his wife & admitted to record. Attest: John Waller clk. (Pg 380)

3 Jun 1740. Deed. Anthony Foster of St. George Parish, Spotsylvania Co for £200 sold to Hugh Sanders of same place a messuage & 1,657 a. parcel of land being the same land & plantation that was formerly sold by the sd Hugh Sanders to the sd Anthony Foster, except 103 a. of land & plantation whereon the sd Foster lives which is hereby intended to be reserved to the sd Foster & his heirs he having bought the same of the sd Sanders bounded by a patent granted to Joseph Brock gent, Nathaniel Sanders, Humphry Bates, the sd Hugh Sanders, a patent granted to John Chew gent, John Bush, Thomas Chew, Boar Run or Glady Fork Run, Corbin's line, sd Anthony Foster & Glady Run ... . Wit: A. Bowker, Parmenas Bowker. Ackn 3 Jun MDCCXXXX & admitted to record. Attest: John Waller clk. (Pg 381)

1 Jul 1740. Deed. John Chew gent & Margaret his wife of St. George Parish, Spotsylvania Co for £40 sold to Anthony Goldstone planter of same place a 400 a. parcel of land whereof the sd Anthony Goldstone is now in possession bounded by Joseph Hawkins & the Main Br of Terrys Run ... . Wit: John Waller, Wm Waller, M. Battaley. Ackn 1 Jul 1740 & admitted to record. Attest: John Waller clk. (Pg 383)

30 Jun MDCCXL. Deed. Robert Turner of Spotsylvania Co & Catharine his wife for £14:3:6 sold to Zachary Lewis of same co a 58 a. tr of land on the n side the Northanna in St. George Parish being pt/o a patent granted to Rowland Thomas for 1,000 a. dated 16 Jun MDCCXXVII & by the sd Rowland conveyed to the sd Robert by deeds of lease & release dated 5 & 6 Oct MDCCXXX bounded by Wolf Swamp a br of Pamunky River ... . Wit: Thomas Durham, Thomas Gibson, Edmund Waller, John Bowles. At a court held 1 Jul 1740 Robert Turner & Catherine his wife's deed of feoffment for land the sd Robert's

part being proved & the sd Catherine ackn her part in court & is admitted to record. Attest: John Waller clk. (Pg 385)

5 Aug 1740. Deed. Between John Rogers of Drisdale Parish, King & Queen Co of the first part, Edward Pigg of St. George Parish, Spotsylvania Co of the second part, Thomas Gresham of St. Martins Parish, Hanover Co of the third part & Robert Johnston & Elizabeth his wife & Frances Rogers of St. Margrits Parish, Caroline Co & Thomas Warren, John Winill Sanders, John Warren, William Warren, Samuell Warren & Richard Cuzens of St. George Parish, Spotsylvania Co of the fourth part, whereas John Rogers, Peter Rogers, Edward Pigg, John York & Thomas Gresham the 16th day of Jun in 1714 obtained a patent for 1,525 a. of land pt/o it in Caroline Co & part in Spotsylvania Co since which the sd Peter Rogers & John York departed this life & no legal division of the land mentioned in the sd pattent being made & by several conveyances & the will of Peter Rogers & John York the sd Robert Johnston & Elizabeth his wife, Frances Rogers, Thomas Warren, John Winill Sanders, John Warren, William Warren, Samuel Warren & Richard Cuzens are possessed of several parts of the sd tr of land, now this indenture wit that the sd John Roberts, Edward Pigg & Thomas Gresham for 10 shillings by the sd Robert Johnston & Elizabeth his wife, Frances Rogers, Thomas Warren, John Winnell Sanders, John Warren, William Warren, Samuel Warren & Richard Cuzens to them in hand paid for preventing any of the afsd land so conveyed & bequeathed from descending to them or their heirs by survivourship have released & confirm unto the sd Robert Johnston & Eliza his wife, Frances Rogers, Thomas Warren, John Winnell Sanders, John Warren, William Warren, Samuel Warren & Richard Cuzens all their right, title & claim of each of them in & to the sd land so conveyed & bequeathed ... . Wit: John Ashen, Matthew Brooks, John Paine. At a court held 5 Aug 1740 John Rogers, Edward Pigg & Thomas Gresham's deed, the sd Rogers & Gresham ackn their part in court & the sd Pigg's part was proved & is admitted to record. Attest: John Waller clk. (Pg 387)

5 Aug MDCCXL. Deed. The feofees or trustees for the land appropriated for the building & erecting the town of Fredericksburgh for £5:10 sold to Henry Willis gent two lotts or ½ acres of land in the sd town of Fredericksburgh described in the plan of the sd town by the figures 41 & 43 purch by the Rev. Mr. Staige & by him assignd, bounded by Hanover, Caroline & George Streets adj to the lotts No. 42 & 44 ... if the sd Henry Willis shall not within the space of two years begin to build & finish upon each of the sd lotts one good dwelling house that then the sd feofees or trustees shall have full power & it shall & be lawfull to & for them into the sd granted premises to enter & the same to have again as their former estate as they might have done if these presents had never been made ... . Wit: None. Ackn 5 Aug 1740 by John Waller, Francis Thornton Junr & John Allan gent three of the feofees or trustees & at the motion

of Thomas Wood in behalf of the sd Willis is admitted to record. Attest: John Waller clk. (Pg 389)

5 Aug MDCCXL. Deed. The feofees or trustees for the land appropriated for the building & erecting the town of Fredericksburgh for £2:15 sold to Henry Willis gent one lott or ½ a. of land in the sd town of Fredericksburgh described in the plan of the sd town by the figure 8 bounded by Sophia Street, the woods & the river adj to the lott of John Allan merchant described by the figure 7, purch by James Porteus & by him assigned ... if the sd Henry Willis shall not within the space of two years begin to build & finish upon the sd lott one good dwelling house that then the sd feofees or trustees shall have full power & it shall & be lawfull to & for them into the sd granted premises to enter & the same to have again as their former estate as they might have done if these presents had never been made .... Wit: None. Ackn 5 Aug 1740 by John Waller, Francis Thornton Junr & John Allan gent three of the feofees or trustees & at the motion of Thomas Wood in behalf of the s Willis is admitted to record. Attest: John Waller clk. (Pg 390)

5 Aug MDCCL. Deed. The feoffees or trustees for the land appropriated for the building & erecting the town of Fredericksburgh for £5:10 sold to Mildred Willis for seven years, to Henry Willis for his lifetime & then to John Willis the son of Henry & Mildred Willis forever two lotts or ½ acres of land in the town of Fredericksburgh described in the plan of the sd town by the figures 47 & 48 which lott 48 was bought by Capt Giles Cook & by him assignd, bounded by Princess Anne, Amelia & Caroline Streets & adj to the lotts No. 45 & 46 ... if the sd Mildred Willis, Henry Willis & John Willis shall not within the space of two years begin to build & finish upon each of the sd lotts one good dwelling house that then the sd feofees or trustees shall have full power & it shall & be lawfull to & for them into the sd granted premises to enter & the same to have again as their former estate as they might have done if these presents had never been made .... Wit: None. Ackn 5 Aug 1740 by John Waller, Francis Thornton Junr & John Allan gent three of the feofees or trustees & at the motion of Thomas Wood in the behalf of Mildred Willis, Henry Willis & John Willis is admitted to record. Attest: John Waller clk. (Pg 391)

5 Aug MDCCXL. Deed. The feofees or trustees for the land appropriated for the building & erecting the town of Fredericksburgh for £6:15 sold to Henry Willis & Mildred his wife for their life & then to Lewis Willis forever two lotts or ½ acres of land in the town of Fredericksburgh described in the plan of the sd town by the figures 45 & 46 bounded by Caroline, William & Princess Ann Streets & the lotts No. 47 & 48 being the lotts purch by Giles Cook & Stonehouse & by them assigned ... if the sd Henry Willis, Mildred his wife & Lewis Willis shall not within the space of two years begin to build & finish upon

each of the sd lotts one good dwelling house that then the sd feofees or trustees shall have full power & it shall & be lawfull to & for them into the sd granted premises to enter & the same to have again as their former estate as they might have done if these presents had never been made ... . Wit: None. Ackn 5 Aug 1740 by John Waller, Francis Thornton Junr & John Allan gent three of the feofees or trustees & at the motion of Thomas Wood in the behalf of Henry Willis & Mildred his wife & Lewis Willis is admitted to record. Attest: John Waller clk. (Pg 391)

5 Aug MDCCXL. Deed. The feofees or trustees for the land appropriated for the building & erecting the town of Fredericksburgh for £10:15 sold to Henry Willis gent two lotts or ½ acres of land in the town of Fredericksburgh described in the plan of the sd town by the figures 33 & 34 being the two lotts in the same square with Mr. Lee's, bought by Doctor Ballandine & by him assignd, bounded by Caroline, Charlotta & Princess Ann Streets adj to the lotts No. 35 & 36 ... if the sd Henry Willis shall not within the space of two years begin to build & finish upon each of the sd lotts one good dwelling house that then the sd feofees or trustees shall have full power & it shall & be lawfull to & for them into the sd granted premises to enter & the same to have again as their former estate as they might have done if these presents had never been made ... . Wit: None. Ackn 5 Aug 1740 by John Waller, Francis Thornton Junr & John Allan gent three of the feofees or trustees & at the motion of Thomas Wood in the behalf of Henry Willis is admitted to record. Attest: John Waller clk. (Pg 392)

5 Aug MDCCXL. Deed. The feofees or trustees for the land appropriated for the building & erecting the town of Fredericksburgh for £5 sold to Henry Willis gent one lot or ½ a. of land in the sd town of Fredericksburgh described in the plan of the sd town by the figure 59 purch by Nathaniel Chapman & by him assigned, bounded by George & Princess Ann Streets & adj to the lott No. 60 ... if the sd Henry Willis shall not within the space of two years begin to build & finish upon the sd lott one good dwelling house that then the sd feofees or trustees shall have full power & it shall & be lawfull to & for them into the sd granted premises to enter & the same to have again as their former estate as they might have done if these presents had never been made ... . Wit: None. Ackn 5 Aug 1740 by John Waller, Francis Thornton Junr & John Allan gent three of the feofees or trustees & at the motion of Thomas Wood in the behalf of Henry Willis is admitted to record. Attest: John Waller clk. (Pg 393)

5 Aug MDCCXL. Deed. The feofees or trustees for the land appropriated for the building & erecting the town of Fredericksburgh for £5:5 sold to Gowin Corbin esqr one lott or ½ a. of land in the sd town of Fredericksburgh described in the plan of the sd town by the figure 17 bounded by Hanover & Sophia Streets & adj to the lotts 18, 19 & 20 ... if the sd Gowin Corbin shall not within the

space of two years begin to build & finish upon the sd lott one good dwelling house that then the sd feofees or trustees shall have full power & it shall & may be lawfull to & for them into the sd granted premises to enter & the same to have again as their former estate as if these presents had never been made .... Wit: None. Ackn 5 Aug 1740 by John Waller, Francis Thornton Junr & John Allan gent three of the feofees or trustees & at the motion of Thomas Wood in behalf of the sd Corbin is admitted to record. Attest: John Waller clk. (Pg 393)

26 Jul 1740. Deed. Rice Curtis of St. George Parish, Spotsylvania Co for £60 sold to Peter Mountague of same place (son of Thomas Mountague) a 182 a. tr of land being the land that the sd Curtis bought of John Foster & John Sneles bounded by the River Po, William Sollemon, Capt William Johnston & a corner formerly marked between John Foster & Anthony Foster .... Wit: William Johnston, Thos Merry, Ann Johnston. Ackn 5 Aug 1740 & admitted to record. Attest: John Waller clk. (Pg 394)

6 Jul 1740. Bond. I Rice Curtis of Spotsylvania Co am firmly bound unto Peter Mountague of same co in the sum of £120 ... the condition of this obligation is such that if the afsd Rice Curtis shall well & truly perform & keep all the covenants mentioned & comprised in an indenture [see above] then this obligation to be void .... Wit: William Johnston, Thos Merry, Ann Johnston. Ackn 5 Aug 1740 & admitted to record. Attest: John Waller clk. (Pg 395)

30 Jun 1740. Deed of Lease. Henry Goodloe & Elizabeth his wife & Robert Goodloe of St. George Parish, Spotsylvania Co for 5 shillings leased to John Scandland Crane of St. Stephens Parish, King & Queen Co a 554 a. tr of land in St. Georges Parish bounded by Robert Durratt & Joseph Carter ... during the term of one year paying the rent of one pepper corn upon the feast of St. Michael the Arch Angel if demanded .... Wit: Edwd Herndon Junr, Wm Miller, Tho Estes. Wit to Elizabeth Goodloe: Daniel Ramsey, Elizabeth Durratt, Aniclina Seales. Ackn 5 Aug 1740 by Henry Goodloe & Robert Goodloe & Elizabeth the w/o the sd Henry ackn her right of dower & at the motion of Thomas Estes in behalfe of the sd John Scandland Crane is admitted to record. Attest: John Waller clk. (Pg 395)

1 Jul 1740. Deed of Release. Henry Goodloe & Elizabeth his wife & Robert Goodloe of St. Georges Parish, Spotsylvania Co for £72 sold & released to John Scandland Crane of St. Stephens Parish, King & Queen Co a 554 a. tr of land ... [same as above] .... Wit: Edward Herndon Junr, Wm Miller, Tho Estes. Wit to Elizabeth Goodloe: David Ramsey, Elizabeth Durrat, Aniclina Seales. Ackn 5 Aug 1740 by Henry Goodloe & Robert Goodloe & Elizabeth the w/o the sd Henry ackn her right of dower & at the motion of Thomas Estes in behalfe of the

sd John Scandland Crane is admitted to record. Attest: John Waller clk. (Pg 396)

Commission. To William Johnston, John Chew, William Robinson & Henry Goodloe gent greeting, whereas Joseph Thomas & Sarah his wife by their indenture of feofment dated 18 Dec 1739 have convey'd unto Zachary Lewis the fee simple estate of 900 a. of land in Spotsylvania Co & whereas the sd Sarah cannot conveniently travel to our co court to make acknowledgment of the sd conveyance, therefore wee do give unto you or any two or more of you power to receive the sd acknowledgment which the sd Sarah shall be willing to make before you of the conveyance afsd, we do therefore command you that you do personally go to the sd Sarah & receive her acknowledgment of the same & examine her privily & apart from the sd Joseph Thomas her husband wither she doeth the same freely & voluntary & wither she be willing that the same should be recorded in our co court .... Wit: John Waller clerk of court 12 Aug 1740. XVI Aug 1740 wee William Johnston & Henry Goodloe do hereby certifie that pursuant to the within commission wee personally went to Sarah the w/o Joseph Thomas & examiner her privily & apart from the sd Joseph Thomas who ackn before us that she freely & voluntary did make & execute the indenture of feofment & that she was willing & freely consent that the same should be recorded .... (Pg 398)

21 Aug 1740. Receipt. I Henry Willis hereby ackn that I have recd of James Garton the full balance of all accts, bills, bond, mortgages, but more especially give this my receipt in barr of a mortgage of two Negroes, viz, the one named Ben & the other Moll which sd mortgage bears date in 1739 for which I ackn to recd full satisfaction. Attest: Jas Marye. Proved 2 Sep 1740 by the oath of the Rev. James Marye & is admitted to record. Attest: John Waller clk. (Pg 398)

2 Sep MDCCCL. Deed. The feoffees or trustees for the land appropriated for the building & erecting the town of Fredericksburgh for £5 sold to John Edwards of Spotsylvania Co gent one lot or ½ a. of land in the sd town of Fredericksburgh described in the plan of the sd town by the figure 54 purch by Henry Willis gent & by him assigned, bounded by Princess Ann Street & by the back line of the sd town adj to lot numbered 53 ... if the sd John Edwards shall not within the space of two years build & finish upon the sd lot one good dwelling house then the sd feoffees or trustees shall have full power & it shall & may be lawfull to & for them into the sd granted premises & the same to have again as their former estate as if these presents had never been made .... Wit: Edmund Waller. Ackn 2 Sep 1740 by John Taliaferro, John Waller & Francis Thornton gent three of the feoffees or trustees & admitted to record. Attest: John Waller clk. (Pg 399)

21 Aug 1740. Deed. George Dowdy of St. George Parish, Spotsylvania Co planter for £45 sold to William Marsh of same place a 600 a. tr of land in St. George Parish being all the remaining pt/o a tr of 1,000 a. which was granted to the sd George Dowdy by pattent except 200 a. which the sd George Dowdy sold to William Stephens & 200 a. to Alexander Hill & the sd 600 a. are bounded by William Stephens, Anthony Golson, Alexander Hill, sd Dowdy & Col Corbin ... . Wit: James Jones, John Howaton, Jos Collins. 4 Feb 1735 full & peaceable possession & seisin of the land within granted was delivered by the sd George Dowdy to the sd William Marsh ... Wit: William Garris. Proved 7 Oct 1740 & admitted to record. Attest: John Waller clk. (Pg 400)

6 Oct 1740. Deed of Lease. William Dyer of St. Georges Parish, Spotsylvania Co for 5 shillings leased to Robert Spilsbe Coleman of Essex Co a 100 a. tr of land in St. Georges Parish on the brs of Pamunkey River & is pt/o a greater patent granted to Roger Tandy 30 Oct 1727 for 520 a. & by the sd Tandy ackn unto the sd Dyer 6 Nov 1733 ... during the term of one year paying the yearly rent of one barley corn at the feast of St. Michael the Arch Angell if demanded .... Wit: Wm Waller, Edmund Waller. Ackn 7 Oct MDCCXL & admitted to record. Attest: John Waller clk. (Pg 401)

7 Oct 1740. Deed of Release. William Dyer of St. George Parish, Spotsylvania Co for £10 sold & released to Robert Spilsbe Coleman of Essex Co a 100 a. tr of land ... [same as above] .... Wit: Wm Waller, Edmund Waller. Ackn 7 Oct MDCCXL by William Dyer & Mary the w/o the sd William ackn her right of dower & is admitted to record. Attest: John Waller clk. (Pg 402)

Commission. To Thomas West, Francis West & Richard Gregory of King William Co gent greeting, whereas Roger Tandy lately in our co court of Spotsylvania ackn a deed of sale for a 100 a. tr of land in St. George Parish in the brs of Pidgeon River to William Dyer of the afsd co [see above] & the sd William Dyer having insinuated to us that Sarah Tandy the w/o the sd Roger Tandy by reason of the distance from our sd co court is uncapable of traveling there to ackn her right of dower in the sd land ... now know ye that we have assigned & impowered you to cause the sd Sarah Tandy the w/o Roger Tandy to come before you & then & there the sd Sarah to examine privily touching her consent of conveying her right in the sd land to the sd William Dyer ... wit John Waller clerk of court this 5th day of Jul MDCCXL. King Wm Co, 29 Aug 1740 pursuant to the within order we Thos West & Fra West have privately exam'd the sd Sarah Tandy concerning acknowledgment of her right of dower to which she freely & willingly doth consent. At the request of William Dyer the above commission is recorded. (Pg 404)

4 Aug 1740. Deed of Lease. James Roy of St. George Parish, Spotsylvania Co planter for 5 shillings leased to Thomas Edmondson of St. Anne Parish, Essex Co gent a 107 a. tr of land purch by the sd James Roy from George Procter in St. George Parish bounded by Haslee Run & Edward Price ...during the term of one year paying the rent of one pepper corn at the feast of St. Michael the Arch Angel if demanded .... Wit: John Waller, John Gordon, John Wiglesworth, Will Reid, Andr Craig. Ackn 7 Oct 1740 & admitted to record. Attest: John Waller clk. (Pg 405)

5 Aug 1740. Deed of Release. James Roy of St. George Parish, Spotsylvania Co planter for £24 sold to Thomas Edmondson of St. Anne Parish, Essex Co gent a 107 a. tr of land ... [same as above] .... Wit: John Waller, John Gordon, John Wiglesworth, Will Reid, Andr Craig. Wit to receipt: Jas Marye, William Hunter, Dav McCullough. Ackn 7 Oct 1740 by James Roy & Elizabeth the w/o the sd James ackn her right of dower & admitted to record. Attest: John Waller clk. (Pg 406)

6 Oct 1740. Deed. Joseph Brock of St. George Parish, Spotsylvania Co gent & Mary his wife for £21:1:6 sold to Thomas West of same place a 250 a. tr of land (it being pt/o a pattent granted to Larkin Chew decd & by the sd Larkin sold & convey'd unto the sd Joseph Brock by deeds of lease & release & since surveyed by the sd Joseph & a pattent obtained in his own name which bears date 12 Sep 1738) bounded by William Bartlett, Ironmines Road, Bushes Road, Phillip Sanders & Achilles Br .... Wit: John Durret, William Long, George Trible. Ackn 7 Oct 1740 & admitted to record. At a court held 7 Dec 1742 Mary Brock the w/o Joseph Brock gent ackn this her deed for land to Thomas West & is admitted to record. Wit: Edmund Waller. Attest: John Waller clk. (Pg 409)

6 Oct 1740. Bond. I Joseph Brock of Spotsylvania Co am firmly bound unto Thomas West of same co in the sum of £42:3 ... the condition of this obligation is such that if the afsd Joseph Brock shall well & truly perform & keep all the covenants mentioned & comprised in an indenture [see above] then this obligation to be void .... Wit: John Durret, William Long, George Trible. Ackn 7 Oct 1740 & admitted to record. Attest: John Waller clk. (Pg 410)

6 Aug 1740. Deed. Robert King of St. George Parish, Spotsylvania Co planter & Mary his wife for £57:15 sold to Edward Cason of St. Marys Parish, Caroline Co a 231 a. tr of land or woodland ground bounded by the river bank, William Sallomon, Rice Curtis & the sd King's back line .... Wit: Rice Curtis, Thos Merry, Thomas West. Ackn 7 Oct 1740 by Robert King & Mary his wife ackn her right of dower & is admitted to record. Attest: John Waller clk. (Pg 410)

6 Aug 1740. Bond. I Robert King of Spotsylvania Co planter am firmly bound unto Edward Cason of Caroline Co in the sum of £200 ... the condition of this obligation is such that if the afsd Robert King shall well & truly perform & keep all the covenants mentioned & comprised in an indenture [*see above*] then this obligation to be void ... . Wit: Rice Curtis, Thos Merry, Thomas West. Ackn 7 Oct 1740 & admitted to record. Attest: John Waller clk. (Pg 411)

1 May MDCCXXXX. Deed of Lease. Ralph Williams of St. George Parish, Spotsylvania Co for 5 shillings leased to William Williams of same place a messuage & 100 a. tr of land where the sd Ralph Williams now lives bounded by Pappau Run, Benjamin Mathews, the sd Ralph Williams, William Williams, John Williams, John Smith now Tyre's corner ... during the term of one year paying the yearly rent of one peper corn at the feast of St. Michal the Arch Angel ... . Wit: Robert Huddleston, Thomas Dillard. Ackn 7 Oct 1740 & admitted to record. Attest: John Waller clk. (Pg 412)

2 May MDCCXXXX. Deed of Release. Ralph Williams of St. George Parish, Spotsylvania Co for £30 sold & released to William Williams of same place a 100 a. tr of land, being first taken up & surveyed for Nicholas Lankford & by him sold to John Collier Junr of King & Queen Co & by the sd Collier sold to Robert Stubblefield & from the sd Stubblefield (sold) to the sd Ralph Williams by deeds ackn in Spotsylvania Co Court 5 Jul 1734 ... [*same as above*] ... . Wit: Robt Huddleston, Thomas Dillard. Ackn 7 Oct 1740 & admitted to record. Attest: John Waller clk. (Pg 412)

1 May MDCCXXXX. Deed of Lease. Ralph Williams of St. George Parish, Spotsylvania Co for 5 shillings leased to John Williams of same place a messuage & 100 a. tr of land bounded by a corner of Mathews & Stubblefield's, William Williams & John Williams ... during the term of one year paying the yearly rent of one pepper corn at the feast of St. Michael the Arch Angel if demanded ... . Wit: Robert Huddleston, Thos Dillard. Ackn 7 Oct 1740 & admitted to record. Attest: John Waller clk. (Pg 414)

2 May MDCCXXXX. Deed of Release. Ralph Williams of St. George Parish, Spotsylvania Co for £10 sold to John Williams of same place a 100 a. tr of land, the sd land was first taken up & surveyed for Nicholas Lankford & by him sold to John Collier Junr of King & Queen Co & by the sd Collier conveyed to the sd Robert Stubblefield by deeds ackn in Spotsylvania Co Court 6 Oct 1730 ... [*same as above*] ... . Wit: Robert Huddleston, Thomas Dillard. Ackn 7 Oct 1740 & admitted to record. Attest: John Waller clk. (Pg 414)

Commission. To Henry Goodloe, William Johnston & William Robinson gent greeting, whereas John Chew gent & Margaret his wife of Spotsylvania Co by their indenture of sale dated 1 Jul MDCCXL have conveyed unto Anthony Golston of same co planter the fee simple estate of 400 a. of land & whereas the sd Margaret cannot conveniently travel to our co court to make acknowledgement of the sd conveyance, we do give unto you power to receive the acknowledgment which the sd Margaret shall be willing to make before you, we therefore command that you personally go to the sd Margaret & receive her acknowledgment & examine her privily & apart from the sd John Chew her husband whither she doth the same freely & voluntarily & whither she be willing that the same should be recorded ... wit John Waller clerk of court 5 Jul 1740. 30 Aug 1740 Margaret Chew after being privily examined did sign, seal & ackn the indenture unto Anthony Golston & desires the same may be recorded. Signed Henry Goodloe, W. Robinson. At the request of Anthony Golston this commission & return is recorded. Attest: John Waller clk. (Pg 416)

2 Oct 1740. List of slaves upon the Mine Tract & by Butler Spotswood, Elliott Benger & Robt Ross annex'd to it pursuant to the will of the late Honorable Alexander Spotswood esqr. Tamerlane, Paris, Sarah, Bristoll, Daphne, Blunt, Juno, Pedro, Oliver, Hector, Dick, Daniell, Shirbridge, Sharper, Noah, Piero, Tom, Ben, Billy, Toney, Peter, London, Paulo, Frank (young), Prince, Stran, Frank (old), Hester, Ampthill, Dido, Kate Lawrel, Sue, Judie (old), Judie (young), Bess, Polly, Joe, Castor, Sambo, Isaac, Flora, Pallas, Bob, Sorrell, Cesar, Yarrico, Lawrence, Hazard, Adain, Marcus, Sevellah, Leo, Pompey, Sarah, Polly, Little Moll, Beauty, Sarah, Hannah, Lady, Jenny, Charles, Bembo, Prince, Dover, Mowyarrow, Bridge, Mingo, Damon, Conrie, Calais, Simon, Dick, Cary, Manzor, Will, Jolly, Betty, Ness, Humphry. Charles, Rose, Amy, Doll (Juno's children), George, Parish, Patty (Sarah's children), Simon, Juno, Boson (Kate's children), Dinah, Edie, Scipio (Sue's children), Sue (Judy's child), Beck (Polly's child), Frank, Ned, Billy (Jenny's children), Sam (Pallas's child), Duke (Dido's child). The within list of Negroes belonging to the estate of the Honble Alexander Spotswood esqr decd at the motion of his executors is admitted to record 7 Oct 1740. Attest: John Waller clk. (Pg 417)

12 Sep 1740. Deed. Edward Pigg of St. George Parish, Spotsylvania Co for £5 sold to Charles Filks Pigg of same place a 150 a. tr of land in the parrish afsd bounded by Capt Johnston's mill damm, Mill Path, old Mr. Pigg's back line & Stony Run ... . Wit: Wm Johnston, Robt Johnston, James Atkins, Wm Power. Proved 7 Oct 1740 & admitted to record. Attest: John Waller clk. (Pg 418)

4 Oct 1740. Deed. Hugh Sanders of St. George Parish, Spotsylvania Co planter & Catey Sanders his wife for £24:10 sold to Dudley Gatewood of same place a 235 a. tr of land (it being pt/o a patent granted to Nathaniell Sanders decd & by the sd Nathll give to the sd Hugh Sanders by his will) being on Glady Fork bounded by Ignatius Turman, Joseph Pen, Stony Run, Thos Sanders & Joseph

Brock .... Wit: Robt King Junr, William Long, William Walding. Ackn 7 Oct 1740 by Hugh Sanders & Catey his wife & admitted to record. Attest: John Waller clk. (Pg 420)

6 Oct MDCCXL. Deed of Lease. Mary Hawkins widow of John Hawkins late decd & Joseph Hawkins, George Smith & Elizabeth his wife & Phebe Hawkins for 5 shillings leased to Phillemon Hawkins a 132 a. tr of land (& all the personal estate of the sd John Hawkins which the sd Philemon Hawkins hath now in his possession) together with the land & premises which being pt/o what the sd John Hawkins decd left by his will to his wife & children being in St. Georges Parish on the n side the North Fork of Northanna & on the n side of Terrys Run bounded by the land of Harry Beverley decd ... paying the yearly rent of one pepper corn at the feast of St. Michael the Arch Angell if demanded .... Wit: Thos Chew, Jos Morton, Charles Smith. Ackn 7 Oct 1740 by Mary Hawkins, George Smith & Elizabeth his wife & Phebe Hawkins & admitted to record. Attest: John Waller clk. (Pg 422)

7 Oct MDCCXL. Deed of Release. Mary Hawkins widow of John Hawkins late decd & Joseph Hawkins, George Smith & Elizabeth his wife & Phebe Hawkins for £50 sold & released to Philemon Hawkins a 132 a. tr of land ... [same as above] .... Wit: Thos Chew, Jos Morton, Charles Smith. Ackn 7 Oct 1740 by Mary Hawkins, George Smith & Elizabeth his wife & Phebe Hawkins & admitted to record. Attest: John Waller clk. (Pg 423)

7 Oct 1740. Deed of Lease. Robert Biscoe of Lancaster Co for 5 shillings leased to James Brown of Spotsylvania Co a 97 a. tr of land granted by pattent to Joseph Delanie dated 28 Sep 1728 & by the sd Delanie convey'd unto the afsd Robert Biscoe by deeds dated 28 & 29 Jun 1734 the sd land bounded by a br of Nassaponack Swamp, Stephen Sharp, Lawrence Smith & Francis Thornton ... during the term of one year paying the rent of one ear of Indian corn at the feast of St. Michael the Arch Angel if demanded .... Wit: Matthew Gayle, Francis Turnley. Ackn 7 Oct 1740 & admitted to record. Attest: John Waller clk. (Pg 425)

7 Oct 1740. Deed of Release. Robert Biscoe of Lancaster Co for £6 sold & released to James Brown of Spotsylvania Co a 97 a. tr of land ... [same as above] .... Wit: Matthew Gayle, Francis Turnley. Ackn 7 Oct 1740 & admitted to record. Attest: John Waller clk. (Pg 426)

31 Oct 1740. Deed of Lease. Griffin Fantleroy of Northumberland Co gent for 5 shillings farm let unto Peter How & Richard Kelsick of Whitehaven merchants one lot in the town of Fredericksburgh described in the plat of the sd town by the figure 16 lying on Caroline Street & Hanover Street ... during the term of one

year paying the yearly rent of one grain of Indian corn on 10 Oct if demanded ...
. Wit: John Taliaferro, Richard Griffith, Jno Hobby. Proved 2 Dec 1740 &
admitted to record. Attest: John Waller clk. (Pg 428)

1 Nov 1740. Deed of Release. Griffin Fantleroy of Northumberland Co gent for
£20 sold & released to Peter How & Richard Kelsick of Whitehaven merchants
one lot in the town of Fredericksburgh No. 16 ... [same as above] .... Wit:
John Taliaferro, Richard Griffith, Jno Hobby. Proved 2 Dec 1740 & admitted to
record. Attest: John Waller clk. (Pg 429)

1 Dec 1740. Deed. Robert Turner & Katherine his wife of St. George Parish,
Spotsylvania Co for £20 sold to James Rawlins of same place a 40 a. parcel of
land whereon he now lives pt/o 100 a. ackn unto the sd Turner by Rowland
Thomas which sd 100 a. was pt/o 1,000 a. granted to the afsd Rowland Thomas
by pattent dated 16 Jun 1727, bounded by James Rawlins, the Northanna River
& Wolf Swamp .... Wit: Edmund Waller, Z. Lewis, George Woodroof.
Robert Turner's part proved 2 Dec 1740 & Catherine ackn her part & is ordered
to be recorded. Attest: John Waller clk. (Pg 430)

5 Aug MDCCXL. Deed. The feoffees or trustees for the land appropriated for
the building & erecting the town of Fredericksburgh for £8 sold to Henry Willis
gent two lots or ½ acres of land in the sd town of Fredericksburgh described in
the plan of the sd town by the figures 9 & 10 purch by Francis Willis gent & by
him assign'd, bounded by Sophia, Charlotta & Caroline Streets & adj to lots No.
11 & 12 ... if the sd Henry Willis shall not within the space of two years begin
to build & finish upon each of the sd lots one good dwelling house then the sd
feoffees or trustees shall have full power & it shall & may be lawfull to & for
them into the sd granted premises to enter & the same to have again as their
former estate as if these presents had never been made .... Wit: Edmund
Waller. Ackn 3 Dec 1740 by John Waller, Francis Thornton Junr & John Allan
gent three of the feoffees or trustees & at the motion of Thomas Wood is
admitted to record. Attest: John Waller clk. (Pg 432)

5 Aug MDCCXL. Deed. The feoffees or trustees for the land appropriated for
the building & erecting the town of Fredericksburgh for £8 sold to Henry Willis
& John the son of Henry & Mildred Willis two lots or ½ acres of land in the
town of Fredericksburgh described in the plan of the sd town by the figures 11 &
12 purch by William Gooch esqr & by him assigned, bounded by Sophia,
Charlotta & Caroline Streets & adj lots No. 9 & 10 ... if the sd Henry Willis
shall not within the space of two years begin to build & finish upon each of the
sd lots one good dwelling house then the sd feoffees or trustees shall have full
power & it shall & may be lawfull to & for them into the sd granted premises to
enter & the same to have again as their former estate as if these presents had

never been made ... . Wit: Edmund Waller. Ackn 3 Dec 1740 by John Waller, Francis Thornton Junr & John Allan gent three of the feoffees or trustees & at the motion of Thomas Wood is admitted to record. Attest: John Waller clk. (Pg 433)

5 Aug MDCCXL. Deed. The feofees or trustees for the land appropriated for the building & erecting the town of Fredericksburgh for £4:10 sold to Henry Willis gent one lot or ½ a. of land in the town of Fredericksburgh described in the plan of the sd town by the figure 53 purch by Francis Willis & by him assigned, being the corner back lott bounded by Princess Ann Street adj to Lot 54 ... if the sd Henry Willis shall not within the space of two years begin to build & finish upon the sd lot one good dwelling house then the sd feoffees or trustees shall have full power & it shall & may be lawfull to & for them into the sd granted premises to enter & the same to have again as their former estate as if these presents had never been made ... . Wit: Edmund Waller. Ackn 3 Dec 1740 by John Waller, Francis Thornton Junr & John Allan gent three of the feoffees or trustees & at the motion of Thomas Wood is admitted to record. Attest: John Waller clk. (Pg 434)

5 Aug MDCCXXXX. Deed. The feoffees or trustees for the land appropriated for the building & erecting the town of Fredericksburgh for £5:10 sold to Henry Willis gent two lots or ½ acres of land in the town of Fredericksburgh described in the plan of the sd town by the figures 57 & 58 purch by Col John Taliaferro & by him assigned, bounded by Hanover, Princess Ann & George Streets ... if the sd Henry Willis shall not within the space of two years begin to build & finish upon each of the sd lots one good dwelling house then the sd feoffees or trustees shall have full power & it shall & may be lawfull to & for them into the sd granted premises to enter & the same to have again as their former estate as if these presents had never been made ... . Wit: Edmund Waller. Ackn 3 Dec 1740 by John Waller, Francis Thornton Junr & John Allan gent three of the feoffees or trustees & at the motion of Thomas Wood is admitted to record. Attest: John Waller clk. (Pg 435)

1 Dec 1740. Deed of Lease. Thomas Shipp (Ship) of Spotsylvania Co for 5 shillings leased to Richard Shipp (Ship) of Caroline Co a 194 a. tr of land being pt/o a tr of land purch by the sd Thomas Shipp of Henry Willis gent by deeds dated 6 Apr 1736 adj Chiswells Mine Road & Smith's line ... during the term of one year paying the rent of one ear of Indian corn at the feast of St. Michael if demanded ... . Wit: Jno Parrish, Thomas West, Patrick Dowdall. Ackn 2 Dec 1740 & admitted to record. Attest: John Waller clk. (Pg 436)

2 Dec 1740. Deed of Release. Thomas Ship of Spotsylvania Co for £24:5 sold to Richard Ship of Caroline Co a 194 a. tr of land ... [same as above] ... . Wit:

Jno Parrish, Thomas West, Patrick Dowdall. Ackn 2 Dec 1740 & admitted to record. Attest: John Waller clk. (Pg 437)

1 Dec 1740. Deed of Lease. Parmenas Bowker of St. George Parish, Spotsylvania Co for 5 shillings leased to James Gardner of St. Stephens Parish, King & Queen Co a 500 a. tr of land bounded by Larkin Chew ... during the term of one year paying the rent of one ear of Indian corn on the last day of the sd term if demanded ... . Wit: Wm Allcock, A. Foster, Saml Hensley. Ackn 2 Dec 1740 & admitted to record. Attest: John Waller clk. (Pg 438)

2 Dec 1740. Deed of Release. Parmenas Bowker of St. George Parish, Spotsylvania Co for £65 sold & released to James Gardner of St. Stephens Parish, King & Queen Co a 500 a. tr of land ... [*same as above*] ... . Wit: Wm Allcock, A. Foster, Saml Hensley. Ackn 2 Dec 1740 & admitted to record. Attest: John Waller clk. (Pg 440)

6 Feb MDCCXL. Deed. Edmund Waller of Spotsylvania Co & Mary his wife for £7:6:4 sold to Zachary Lewis of same co a 61 a. tr of land granted to the sd Edmund Waller for 1,000 a. dated 28 Sep MDCCXXVIII, the sd 61 a. is bounded by the sd Lewis, John Waller gent, Mr. Holliday, the Mill Road & John Wiglesworth ... . Wit: Thos Cowper, Anne Lewis, John Lewis. Ackn 3 Mar 1740 by Edmund Waller & admitted to record. Look to page 551 in this book & there is the acknowledgment of the feme covert recorded. Attest: John Waller clk. (Pg 442)

23 Jan MDCCXL. Deed. Edmund Waller of St. George Parish, Spotsylvania Co & Mary his wife for £12:10 sold to John Wiglesworth of same place a 110 a. tr of land in St. George Parish & is pt/o a 1,000 a. tr of land granted by pattent to the sd Edmund Waller XXVKKK Sep MDCCXXVIII bounded by Zachary Lewis, the sd Wiglesworth, Honey Swamp ... . Wit: John Waller, John Cockburn, George Atkinson. Ackn 7 Apr 1741 by Edmund Waller & admitted to record. Look to page 551 in this book & there is the acknowledgment of the feme covert recorded. Attest: John Waller clk. (Pg 444)

6 Apr 1741. Deed of Lease. Henry Ealley (Elley) of Spotsylvania Co founder for 5 shillings leased to Robert Spilsbe Coleman of Essex Co a 200 a. tr of land in St. George Parish lying on both sides of Plentifull Run & is pt/o a greater pattern granted to Thomas Allen & George Musick 28 Sep 1728 for 1,000 a. & by the sd Allen ackn to William Taylor by Thomas Allen & George Musick of St. Georges Parish, & the sd Taylor ackn to Henry Elley 3 Feb 1732 & is bounded by Mr. Jarman's line & Thomas Allen ... during the term of one year paying the yearly rent of one barly corn at the feast of St. Michael the Arch

Angel if demanded ... . Wit: Edwd Herndon, Thos Stubblefield. Ackn 7 Apr 1741 & admitted to record. Attest: John Waller clk. (Pg 445)

7 Apr 1741. Deed of Release. Henry Ealley (Elley) of Spotsylvania Co founder for 5 shillings sold & released to Robert Spilsbe Coleman a 200 a. tr of land ... [*same as above*] ... . Wit: Edwd Herndon, Thos Stubblefield. Ackn by Henry Ealley & Mary the w/o the sd Henry ackn her right of dower & is admitted to record. Attest: John Waller clk. (Pg 446)

6 Apr 1741. Deed of Lease. Henry Elley (Elly) of Spotsylvania Co founder for 5 shillings leased to Robert Spilsbe Coleman of Essex Co an 87 a. tr of land in St. George Parish on both sides of Plentifull (Run) it being a pattern granted to Thomas Jarman 20 Jun 1733 & by the sd Jarman ackn to Henry Elly 31 Aug 1733 & is bounded by Thomas Allen, Capt John Camm & Henry Beverley ... during the term of one year paying the yearly rent of one barley corn at the feast of St. Michael the Arch Angell if demanded ... . Wit: Edwd Herndon, Thos Stubblefield. Ackn 7 Apr 1741 & admitted to record. Attest: John Waller clk. (Pg 447)

7 Apr 1741. Deed of Release. Henry Elley of Spotsylvania Co founder for £5 sold & released to Robert Spilsbe Coleman of Essex Co an 87 a. tr of land ... [*same as above*] ... . Wit: Edwd Herndon, Thos Stubblefield. Ackn 7 Apr 1741 by Henry Elley & Mary the w/o the sd Henry ackn her right of dower & is admitted to record. Attest: John Waller clk. (Pg 448)

6 Feb 1740. Deed of Mortgage. I Thomas Hill of St. George Parish, Spotsylvania Co merchant send greeting, whereas the sd Thomas Hill by obligation under his hand & seal dated with these presents became bound unto Humphry Bell of London merchant in the penalty sum of £382:16:2 conditioned for the payment of £191:8: 1 penny within the space of 10 years, now these presents wit that the sd Thomas Hill in consideration of the sd sum of £191:8 1 penny paid & lent to him by the sd Humphry Bell & for which the recited bond is given, the sd Thomas Hill doth hereby ackn & as further security unto the sd Humphry Bell for the more sure payment of the sd sum of £191:8 1 penny the sd Thomas Hill hath sold unto the sd Humphry Bell all the Negroes, cattle, stock & household stuff mentioned in the schedule hereunto annexed ... provided that if the sd Thomas Hill shall truly pay unto the sd Humphry Bell the sum of £191:8 1 penny according to the condition of the sd recited obligation then these presents & everything herein contained shall cease & be void ... . Wit: Wm Cowne, John Blake, Benja Hubbard. Proved 7 Apr 1741 & admitted to record. Attest: John Waller clk. (Pg 449)

A schedule referr'd to by the [*above*] instrument of writing. Negroes: Cupid, Maria, Venus, London, Truelove, Lancaster, Pompy, Maria, 1 molatto girl named Betty. 3 mares, 3 colts, 33 head of cattle, 55 head of hoggs, 2 horses, 17 sheep, 2 looking glasses, 3 feather beds, bolsters & 4 pillows, 2 pair of curtains, 4 quilts, 2 counter paines, 2 large seal skin trunks, 3 midling leather ditto, 1 desk, 1 tea table, 1 chest of drawers. Thos Hill. (Pg 450)

6 Feb 1740. Deed of Mortgage. Thomas Hill of St. George Parish, Spotsylvania Co merchant for £50 sold to Humphry Bell merchant of London a tr of land in Spotsylvania Co & also all those plantations & trs of land in Orange Co ... for the term of 500 years paying yearly during the sd term the yearly rent of one pepper corn if demanded provided & upon condition that if the sd Thomas Hill shall well & truly pay unto the sd Humphry Bell the full sum of £250 within the space of 10 years that then this indenture shall cease & be void .... Wit: Wm Cowne, John Blake, Benja Hubbard. Memo: The lands in the within indenture mentioned & designed are 3,033 a. in Orange Co & 315 a. in Spotsylvania Co on the brs of Deep Run. Proved 7 Apr 1741 & admitted to record. Attest: John Waller clk. (Pg 451)

6 Feb 1740. Bond. I Thomas Hill of Spotsylvania Co am firmly bound unto Humphry Bell of London merchant in the penal sum of £382:16:2 ... the condition of this obligation is such that if the afsd Thos Hill do pay unto the sd Humphry Bell the full & just sum of £192:8 1 penny within the space of 10 years then this obligation to be void .... Wit: Wm Cowne, John Blake, Benja Hubbard. Proved 7 Apr 1741 & admitted to record. Attest: John Waller clk. (Pg 452)

13 Apr 1741. Deed of Lease. Thomas Hill of Spotsylvania Co gent for 5 shillings leased to Humphry Hill of King & Queen Co, VA gent two lotts or ½ acres of land in the town of Fredericksburgh marked & distinguished in the town plat by the numbers 21 & 22 being bounded, that is to say, the lot number 21 bounded by Sophia Street, George Street, lot number 22 & a lot of Humphry Hill marked number 23 & the sd lot number 22 being bounded by lot number 21, George Street, Caroline Street & a lot of Humphry Hill number 24 ... during the term of one year paying the yearly rent of one pepper corn at the feast of St. Michael the Arch Angel if demanded .... Wit: Wm Williams, Robt Jackson, John Blake. Proved 5 May 1741 & admitted to record. Attest: John Waller clk. (Pg 452)

14 Apr 1741. Deed of Release. Thomas Hill gent & Elizabeth his wife of Spotsylvania Co for £50 sold & released to Humphry Hill of King & Queen Co, VA gent two lots in the town of Fredericksburgh numbers 21 & 22 ... [*same as*

above] ... . Wit: Wm Williams. Rob Jackson, John Blake. Proved 5 May 1741 for Thomas Hill gent & admitted to record. Attest: John Waller clk. (Pg 453)

24 Nov 1740. Deed of Lease. Hugh Sanders of Spotsylvania Co planter for 5 shillings leased to Joseph Pen of Caroline Co planter a 105 a. tr of land pt/o a patent granted to Nathll Sanders decd by the will of Nathll Sanders given unto the afsd Hugh Sanders & by the sd Hugh Sanders sold & conveyed unto Antho Foster by deed & by the sd Antho Foster conveyed unto the sd Hugh Sanders by deed dated 3 Jun 1740, bounded by Ignatious Turman & the patent granted to Nathll Sanders afsd ... during the term of one year paying on the last day of the sd term the rent of one ear of Indian corn if demanded ... . Wit: Thos Merry, Dudley Gatewood, John Hoskins. Ackn 5 May 1741 by Hugh Sanders & at the motion of Robert Coleman in behalf of the sd Pen is admitted to record. Attest: John Waller clk. (Pg 455)

25 Nov 1740. Deed of Release. Hugh Sanders of Spotsylvania Co planter & Katey his wife for £15:15 sold & released to Joseph Pen of Caroline Co planter a 105 a. tr of land ... [*same as above*] ... . Wit: Thos Merry, Dudley Gatewood, John Hoskins. Ackn 5 May 1741 by Hugh Sanders & at the motion of Robert Coleman in behalf of the sd Pen is admitted to record. Carr'd to 476 per feme covert acknowledgment. Attest: John Waller clk. (Pg 456)

4 May 1741. Deed of Lease. Larkin Chew of St. George Parish, Spotsylvania Co gent for 5 shillings leased to John Allan of same place gent one lot or ½ a. of land in the town of Fredericksburgh & is one of the outside lots described in the plan of the sd town by the figure 64 bounded by Princess Ann Street & the back line of the sd town ... during the term of one year paying the yearly rent of one ear of Indian corn on Lady day next if demanded ... . Wit: Edmund Waller. Ackn 5 May 1741 & admitted to record. Attest: John Waller clk. (Pg 458)

5 May 1741. Deed of Release. Larkin Chew of St. George Parish, Spotsylvania Co gent for £25:10 sold & released to John Allan of same place gent one lot of land in the town of Fredericksburgh number 64 ... [*same as above*] ... . Wit: Edmund Waller. Ackn 5 May 1741 & admitted to record. Attest: John Waller clk. (Pg 459)

14 Apr MDCCXXXXI. Deed. John Robinson of Strutton Major Parish, King & Queen Co esqr for £20 sold to Joseph Collins of Spotsylvania Co planter a 400 a. tr of land which is now in the possession & occupation of the sd Joseph Collins it being pt/o a tr of 5,059 a. of land belonging to the sd John Robinson lying in the fork & on the n side the River Po which sd 400 a. was laid off by James Cox surveyor of the sd co ... . Wit: Humphry Hill, Benja Hubbard, Thos

Collins. Proved 2 Jun 1741 & admitted to record. Attest: John Waller clk. (Pg 460)

1 Jun 1741. Deed of Lease. Peter Mountague of St. George Parish, Spotsylvania Co planter for 5 shillings leased to John Blake of the town of Fredericksburgh merchant a 242 a. tr of land in the parish afsd bounded by Greens Br, Thomas Merry, Wm Richerson, John Wood & Warner's line ... during the term of one year .... Wit: Edmund Waller, Willm Barber. Ackn 2 Jun 1741 & admitted to record. Attest: John Waller clk. (Pg 462)

2 Jun 1741. Deed of Release. Peter Mountague of St. George Parish, Spotsylvania Co planter & Elizabeth his wife for £40 sold & released to John Blake of the town of Fredericksburgh merchant a 242 a. tr of land ... [same as above] .... Wit: Edmund Waller, Willm Barber. Ackn 2 Jun 1741 by Peter Mountague & Elizabeth his wife & admitted to record. Attest: John Waller clk. (Pg 462)

4 May 1741. Deed. Rice Curtis of St. George Parish, Spotsylvania Co for £50 sold to John Parrish of same place a 200 a. tr of land or woodland ground bounded by Greens Br, Lawrence Battaile & Peter Mountague .... Wit: Philip Vincent Vass, Thos Merry, R. Curtis Junr. Ackn 2 Jun 1741 & admitted to record. Attest: John Waller clk. (Pg 464)

1 Jun 1741. Deed of Mortgage. For the valuable consideration of £25 to me Francis Arnold in hand paid I do by this instrument of writing sell unto Thomas Graves, Richard Phillips & John Minor my lease & all the title I have to 100 a. of land whereon I now live & one bay mare, one bay horse, three cows & calves, 10 head of hoggs, three beds, two rugs, blankets, sheets, one bell mettle spice mortar & pestle, one small table, one chest, two iron pots, one box iron & heaters, three pewter basons & two dishes, 6 pewter plates & four head of sheep & one saddle & bridle & one set of wedges .... Wit: Thomas Graves Junr, John Graves. Proved 7 Jul 1741 & admitted to record. Attest: John Waller clk. (Pg 466)

4 Oct 1741. Bond. I Hugh Sanders of Spotsylvania Co am firmly bound unto Anthony Foster of Spotsylvania Co in the sum of £100 ... the condition of this obligation is such that if the afsd Hugh Sanders shall well & truly perform & keep all the covenants mentioned & comprised in an indenture [see above] then this obligation to be void .... Wit: Owen Thomas, Benjamin Martin, Wm Lindsay. Ackn 7 Jul 1741 & admitted to record. Attest: John Waller clk. (Pg 467)

12 Jun 1741. Deed of Gift. Robert Coleman of Drysdale Parish, King & Queen Co for natural love & paternal affection have given to my well beloved & dutiful son Robert Coleman the younger of St. George Parish, Spotsylvania Co a 444 ½ a. tr of land being pt/o a pattent granted to me the sd Robert Coleman the elder dated 7 Sep 1723 the sd land lying on the s side of Robinsons Run adj the land sold by me to George Carter … . Wit: Z. Lewis, Wm Waller, E. Pendleton. Proved 7 Jul 1741 & admitted to record. Attest: John Waller clk. (Pg 467)

6 Jul 1741. Deed of Lease. John Robinson esqr of Essex Co, VA for 5 shillings leased to William Robinson gent of Spotsylvania Co a 500 a. tr of land being pt/o a pattent granted unto the sd John Robinson esqr dated 23 Apr 1718 called Clesby Tract in St. George Parish in the fork of the River Ta adj the Beaver Dam & Pike Run … during the term of one year paying the yearly rent of one pepper corn at the feast of St. Michael the Arch Angel if demanded … . Wit: Edmund Waller. Ackn 7 Jul 1741 & admitted to record. Attest: John Waller clk. (Pg 468)

7 Jul 1741. Deed of Release. John Robinson esqr of Essex Co, VA for £150 sold & released to William Robinson gent of Spotsylvania Co a 500 a. tr of land … [same as above] … . Wit: Edmund Waller. Ackn 7 Jul 1741 & admitted to record. Attest: John Waller clk. (Pg 469)

2 Jun 1741. Deed. John Smith of St. George Parish, Spotsylvania Co for £60 sold to John Farish of St. Stephens Parish, King & Queen Co a 400 a. patten of land dated 30 June 1726 lying upon the head brs of South River adj the lands of Robert Baylor & William Prewit … . Wit: Robert Farish, Jas Martin, Samuell Poe. Ackn 7 Jul 1741 by John Smith & Margaret his wife & admitted to record. Attest: John Waller clk. (Pg 471)

7 Jul MDCCXLI. Deed of Gift. George Carter of Spotsylvania Co for naturall love & affection hath given to my son Henry Carter of same co a 183 a. tr of land being the same tr of land that the sd George Carter purch of David Moore & Sarah his wife & by them conveyed to the sd George Carter by deeds of lease & release ackn in the co court 5 Apr MDCCXXXVII since which purch the sd land hath been resurveyed by the sd George Carter & lies in St. George Parish on the s side the Middle River or River Ta a br of Mattapony River & now bounded by James or Uriah Garton & a pattent granted to John Robinson esqr … . Wit: Wm Waller, Jos Adcock, Edwd Ware. Ackn 7 Jul 1741 & admitted to record. Attest: John Waller clk. (Pg 473)

5 Jul ----. Deed. The feoffees or trustees for the land appropriated for the building & erecting the town of Fredericksburgh for £5:15 sold to Augustine Moore of King William Co & John Baylor of Caroline Co, VA gent ½ a. or lot

of land in the sd town of Fredericksburgh described in the plan of the sd town by the figure 19 bounded by Sophia Street, George Street & lots number 17 & 20 ... if the sd Augustine Moore & John Baylor shall not within the space of two years build & finish upon the sd lot one good dwelling house that then the sd feoffees or trustees & it shall & may be lawfull to & for them into the sd granted premises & the same to have again as their former estate as if these presents had never been made ... . Wit: Edmund Waller, Henry Pendleton. Ackn 7 Jul 1741 by John Waller & Francis Thornton Junr gent two of the feoffees or trustees & at the motion of Edmund Waller in behalf of the sd Moore & Baylor is admitted to record. Attest: John Waller clk. (Pg 474)

4 Aug 1741. Deed. William Marsh (Mash) of St. Georges Parish, Spotsylvania Co for £18 sold to Erasmus Weathers (Wethers) Allen of St. Anns Parish, Essex Co a 304 a. tr of land bounded by Col Corban (Corbin) & Anthony Street's line ... . Wit: Larkin Chew, Tho Reeves. Ackn 4 Aug 1741 by William Marsh & Elizabeth the w/o the sd William ackn her right of dower & is admitted to record. Attest: John Waller clk. (Pg 476)

3 Aug MDCCXLI. Deed of Gift. James Edwards Senr of St. John Parish, King William Co for natural love & affection hath given to his son James Edwards now of the same place a 200 a. tr of land being pt/o a 400 a. tr of land which the sd James Edwards Senr purch of Richard Phillips by deeds ackn 4 Jun 1734 the land being on the n side of the Northanna in St. George Parish adj to the lands of Thomas Graves, John Graves & Humphry Hill ... . Wit: John Waller, Edmund Waller, Zachary Lewis, Henry Pendleton. Proved 4 Aug 1741 & admitted to record. Attest: John Waller clk. (Pg 477)

4 Jun 1741. Deed. Between the Honble John Grymes of Middlesex Co esqr & Francis Willis of Glocester Co esqr executors of the will of Henry Willis late of Spotsylvania Co esqr decd of the one part & John Allan of Spotsylvania Co merchant & Nathaniel Chapman of Stafford Co gent of the other part, whereas the sd Henry Willis by his will dated 27 Jul 1740 did give full power to his executors to make an absolute right in fee to such persons as they shall think proper to all or any pt/o his estate that his debts might be paid & if any estate remained that they would dispose of it to his children ... now this indenture wit that the sd John Grymes & Francis Willis for £141 sold to the sd John Allan & Nathaniel Chapman (who were the highest bidders for the same at a public sale) a parcel of land in the town of Fredericksburgh bounded by the Public Warehouses, a parcel of ground sold by the sd John Grymes & Francis Willis to William Hunter, Caroline Street, lot number 10, lot number 12, lot number 9, Sophia Street, lot number 11 & the town land ... . Wit: Benja Hubbard, William Hunter, Thos Wood, John Thornton. Proved 4 Aug 1741 by the oaths

of William Hunter & John Thornton two of the wits & admitted to record.
Further proved look to page 515 in this book. Attest: John Waller clk. (Pg 479)

4 Jun 1741. Deed. Between the Honble John Grymes of Middlesex Co esqr &
Francis Willis of Glocester Co esqr executors of the will of Henry Willis late of
Spotsylvania Co esqr decd of the one part & William Hunter of Spotsylvania Co
merchant of the other part, whereas the sd Henry Willis by his will dated 27 Jul
1740 did give full power to his executors to make an absolute right in fee to such
persons as they shall think proper to all or any pt/o his estate that his debts might
be paid & if any estate remained that they would dispose of it to his children ...
now this indenture wit that the sd John Grymes & Francis Willis for £250:10
sold to the sd William Hunter (who was the highest bidder for the same at a
public sale) a parcel of land adj to the town of Fredericksburgh bounded by the
river according to a late survey made by William Waller gent by the mutual
agreement & consent of the feoffees of the sd town & the sd Henry Willis, the
Public Warehouses sold by the sd John Grymes & Francis Willis to John Allan
& Nathaniel Chapman & one of the houses now in the possession of Thomas
Thornton, land of Richard Tutt gent & an acre of land purch by the sd Henry
Willis of James Williams decd .... Wit: John Allan, Nathll Chapman, John
Thornton, Thos Wood. Proved 4 Aug 1741 & admitted to record. Attest: John
Waller clk. (Pg 481)

4 Jun 1741. Deed. Between the Honble John Grymes of Middlesex Co esqr &
Francis Willis of Glocester Co esqr executors of the will of Henry Willis late of
Spotsylvania Co esqr decd of the one part & John Thornton of Spotsylvania Co
gent of the other part, whereas the sd Henry Willis by his will dated 27 Jul 1740
did give full power to his executors to make an absolute right in fee to such
persons as they shall think proper to all or any pt/o his estate that his debts might
be paid & if any estate remained that they would dispose of it to his children ...
now this indenture wit that the sd John Grymes & Francis Willis for £268 sold to
the sd John Thornton (who was the highest bidder for the same at a public sale)
two lots or ½ acres of land in the town of Fredericksburgh described in the plan
of the sd town by the numbers 41 & 43 purch by the Rev Mr. Staige & by him
assigned to the sd Henry Willis to whom the same were conveyed by John
Waller, Fras Thornton & John Allan gent feoffees or trustees of the sd town by
deed dated 5 Aug 1740 which sd lots are now in the possession of Joseph
Calvert & are bounded by Hanover, Caroline & George Streets & the lots No. 42
& 44 .... Wit: Nathll Chapman, Benja Hubbard, William Hunter, Thos Wood,
John Allan. Proved 4 Aug 1741 & admitted to record. Attest: John Waller clk.
(Pg 483)

5 Jun 1741. Deed. Between the Honble John Grymes of Middlesex Co esqr &
Francis Willis of Glocester Co esqr executors of the will of Henry Willis late of

Spotsylvania Co esqr decd of the one part & Philip Rootes of King & Queen Co gent of the other part, whereas the sd Henry Willis by his will dated 27 Jul 1740 did give full power to his executors to make an absolute right in fee to such persons as they shall think proper to all or any pt/o his estate that his debts might be paid & if any estate remained that they would dispose of it to his children ... now this indenture wit that the sd John Grymes & Francis Willis for £12 sold to the sd Philip Rootes (who was the highest bidder for the same at public sale) one lot or ½ a. of land in the town of Fredericksburgh described in the plan of the sd town by the number 8 purch by the sd Henry Willis of John Waller, Francis Thornton & John Allan gent feoffees & trustees for the sd town by deed dated 5 Aug 1740 bounded by Sophia Street, the woods, the river & adj to the lot of John Allan merchant described by the figure 7 ... . Wit: August Washington, John Thornton, Henry Willis. Proved 5 Aug 1741 & admitted to record. Attest: John Waller clk. (Pg 485)

5 Jun 1741. Deed. Between the Honble John Grymes of Middlesex Co esqr & Francis Willis of Glocester Co esqr executors of the will of Henry Willis late of Spotsylvania Co esqr decd of the one part & Andrew Craig of Spotsylvania Co chirgeon of the other part, whereas the sd Henry Willis by his will dated 27 Jul 1740 did give full power to his executors to make an absolute right in fee to such persons as they shall think proper to all or any pt/o his estate that his debts might be paid & if any estate remained that they would dispose of it to his children ... now this indenture wit that the sd John Grymes & Francis Willis for £31:10 sold to the sd Andrew Craig (who was the highest bidder for the same at a publick sale) a lot or ½ a. of land in the town of Fredericksburgh described in the plan of the sd town by the number 62 ... . Wit: John Taliaferro, John Thornton, Henry Willis, Thos Wood, August Washington. Proved 1 Sep 1741 & admitted to record. Attest: John Waller clk. (Pg 487)

4 Jun 1741. Deed. Between the Honble John Grymes of Middlesex Co esqr & Francis Willis of Glocester Co esqr executors of the will of Henry Willis late of Spotsylvania Co esqr decd of the one part & Benjamin Hubbard of King William Co merchant of the other part, whereas the sd Henry Willis by his will dated 27 Jul 1740 did give full power to his executors to make an absolute right in fee to such persons as they shall think proper to all or any pt/o his estate that his debts might be paid & if any estate remained that they would dispose of it to his children ... now this indenture wit that the sd John Grymes & Francis Willis for £11:10 sold to the sd Benjamin Hubbard (who was the highest bidder for the same at a publick sale) a lot or ½ a. of land in the town of Fredericksburgh described in the plat of the sd town by the number 53 ... . Wit: John Allan, Nathll Chapman, Thos Wood, John Thornton. Proved 1 Sep 1741 by the oaths of John Allan & John Thornton two of the wits & is admitted to record. Further proved look to page 515. Attest: John Waller clk. (Pg 489)

5 Jun 1741. Deed. Between the Honble John Grymes of Middlesex Co esqr & Francis Willis of Glocester Co esqr executors of the will of Henry Willis late of Spotsylvania Co esqr decd of the one part & Augustine Washington of King George Co gent of the other part, whereas the sd Henry Willis by his will dated 27 Jul 1740 did give full power to his executors to make an absolute right in fee to such persons as they shall think proper to all or any pt/o his estate that his debts might be paid & if any estate remained that they would dispose of it to his children ... now this indenture wit that the sd John Grymes & Francis Willis for £44 sold to the sd Augustine Washington (who was the highest bidder for the same at a public sale) two lotts or acre in the town of Fredericksburgh described in the plan of the sd town by the numbers 33 & 34 being the two lots in the sd square with Mr. Lee's bought by Doctor Ballendine & by him assigned, bounded by Caroline, Charlotta & Princess Ann Streets & adj to lots No. 35 & 36 which were purch by the sd Henry Willis of John Waller, Frans Thornton & John Allan gent feoffees & trustees of & for the sd town by deed dated 5 Aug 1740 ... . Wit: John Taliaferro, John Thornton, Henry Willis, Thos Wood, Andr Craig. Proved 1 Sep 1741 & admitted to record. Attest: John Waller clk. (Pg 490)

6 Oct 1741. Deed. James Jones planter & Mary his wife of St. George Parish, Spotsylvania Co for £10 sold to Joseph Hawkins planter of same place a 200 a. parcel of land whereof the sd Joseph Hawkins is now in possession ... . Wit: Larkin Chew, Isaac Darnell. Ackn 6 Oct 1741 & admitted to record. Attest: John Waller clk. (Pg 492)

7 Jul MDDCCXLI. Deed. The feofees or trustees for the land appropriated for the building & erecting the town of Fredericksburgh for £5 sold to John Allan merchant one lot or ½ a. of land in the sd town of Fredericksburgh described in the plan of the sd town by the figure 7 bounded by Sophia Street & Lots No. 6 & 8 ... if the sd John Allan shall not within the space of two years begin to build & finish upon the sd lot one good dwelling house that then the sd feofees or trustees shall have full power & it shall be lawfull to & for them to enter the same to have again as their former estate ... . Wit: Edmund Waller. Ackn 6 Oct 1741 by John Taliaferro, John Waller & Francis Thornton Junr gent three of the feoffees or trustees & admitted to record. Attest: John Waller clk. (Pg 494)

6 Oct 1741. Deed. Joseph Hawkins now of Hanover Co, VA gent for £25 sold to Robert Jackson of Fredericksburgh Town gent one lot or ½ a. of land in the town of Fredericksburgh & is one of the sd town lots described in the plan of the sd town by the figure 38 bounded by Princess Ann Street & Charlotta Street, the same being ackn to the sd Joseph Hawkins & conveyed by deed from the trustees of the sd town 7 Jun MDCCXXXVII ... . Wit: John Thornton, Wm Bartlett, John Word, William Pollard. Ackn 6 Oct 1741 by Joseph Hawkins & Jane his wife & admitted to record. Attest: John Waller clk. (Pg 495)

29 Sep 1741. Deed. John Wiglesworth of Spotsylvania Co carpenter & Mary his wife for £8:12 sold to Benjamin Waller of the City of Williamsburgh gent a 50 a. parcel of land in St. George Parish bounded by the Main Run of Raccoon Swamp, the land of the sd Wiglesworth, Capt Humphry Hill (formerly Chiles's), sd Waller's line & land of John Trustee, the sd parcel of land being pt/o a larger tr of land granted by patent unto John Wilkins 16 Jun MDCXXVII & is all the land which he held on the w side of the swamp afsd & by him sold & conveyed unto the sd John Wiglesworth ... . Wit: John Waller, Edmund Waller, Thos Cowper, Henry Pendleton, Beery Lewis. Ackn 7 Oct 1741 by John Wiglesworth & ordered to be recorded. Attest: John Waller clk. (Pg 497)

4 Jun 1741. Deed. Between the Honble John Grymes of Middlesex Co esqr & Francis Willis of Glocester Co esqr executors of the will of Henry Willis late of Spotsylvania Co esqr decd of the one part & Humphry Hill of King & Queen Co gent of the other part, whereas the sd Henry Willis by his will dated 27 Jul 1740 did give full power to his executors to make an absolute right in fee to such persons as they shall think proper to all or any pt/o his estate that his debts might be paid & if any estate remained that they would dispose of it to his children ... now this indenture wit that the sd John Grymes & Francis Willis for £15:10 sold to the sd Humphry Hill (who was the highest bidder for the same at a public sale) a lott or ½ a. of land in the town of Fredericksburgh known & described in the plat of the sd town by the number 59 ... . Wit: John Allan, Nathl Chapman, John Thornton, Thos Wood. Proved 6 Oct 1741 by the oaths of John Allan & John Thornton two of the wits & admitted to record. Further prov'd look to page 515 in this book. Attest: John Waller clk. (Pg 498)

3 Nov 1741. Deed of Lease. John Hord Junr of Hamilton Parish, Prince William Co, VA for 5 shillings leased to Joseph Redd of Drisdale Parish, King & Queen Co, VA a 223 a. tr of land bounded by Col John Lewis, in St. Georges Parish on the ridge between the River Ny & the brs of Nassaponax ... during the term of one year paying the yearly rent of one pepper corn at the feast of St. Michael the Arch Angel if demanded ... . Wit: Thomas Dickenson, John Carter. Ackn 3 Nov 1741 & admitted to record. Attest: John Waller clk. (Pg 500)

3 Nov 1741. Deed of Release. John Hord Junr of St. Hambleton Parish, Prince William Co, VA for £30 sold & released to Joseph Redd of Drysdale Parish, King & Queen Co a 223 a. tr of land ... [same as above] ... . Wit: John Dickenson, John Carter. Ackn 3 Nov 1741 & John Hord Junr & Sarah the w/o the sd John ackn her right of dower & is admitted to record. Attest: John Waller clk. (Pg 501)

3 Nov MDCCXLI. Deed. Anthony Thornton of Stafford Co, VA gent for £5 sold to Richard Childs of Spotsylvania Co a 50 a. tr of land in St. George Parish adj the land of the sd Richard Childs & William McWilliams & is pt/o a greater tr of land belonging to the sd Anthony Thornton which sd 50 a. is bounded by the sd Childs, John Elson, sd Thornton, sd Thornton's line now Childs's line & Gravelly Run ... . Wit: Edmd Pendleton. Ackn 3 Nov 1741 & admitted to record. Attest: John Waller clk. (Pg 503)

10 Oct 1741. Deed. Thomas Dillard of St. George Parish, Spotsylvania Co & Elizabeth his wife for £9:10 sold to Robert Huddleston of same place a 113 a. parcel of land in St. George Parish pt/o a 300 a. tr of land granted by patent to John Smith XXVIII Sep MDCCXXVIII & is bounded by Wm Pruit, Zachary Lewis, Thos Carr gent decd, George Carter & John Tyre ... . Wit: Thos Hubbard, Catherine Hubbard, Janet Hubbard. Ackn 3 Nov 1741 by Thomas Dillard & Elizabeth his wife & ordered to be recorded. Attest: John Waller clk. (Pg 504)

2 Nov 1741. Deed of Lease. Joseph Brock of Spotsylvania Co gent for 5 shillings leased to George Stubblefield of co afsd gent a 538 a. tr of land being pt/o a pattent granted to the sd Joseph Brock for 7467 a. & dated 12 Sep 1738 bounded by James Lea, James Stevens, Rice Curtis Junr & a Poison Field ... during the term of one year paying on the last day of the sd term the rent of one ear of Indian corn if demanded ... . Wit: None. Ackn 3 Nov 1741 & admitted to record. Attest: John Waller clk. (Pg 507)

3 Nov 1741. Deed of Release. Joseph Brock of Spotsylvania Co gent & Mary his wife for £54:6 sold & released to George Stubblefield of co afsd gent a 538 a. tr of land ... [*same as above*] ... . Wit: None. Ackn 3 Nov 1741 by Joseph Brock gent & Mary his wife & admitted to record. Attest: John Waller clk. (Pg 508)

28 Nov 1741. Deed. James Stevens of St. Georges Parish, Spotsylvania Co & Mary his wife for £15 sold to Jeremiah Stevens of same place planter a 71 a. tr of land in St. Georges Parish the same being pt/o a pattent granted unto the sd James Stevens dated 13 Dec 1738 bounded by the sd James Stevens's Mill Pond ... . Wit: Thos Duerson, John Talbert, Samuell Brown. Ackn 1 Dec 1741 & admitted to record. Look to page 552 per the feme coverts acknowledgment. Attest: John Waller clk. (Pg 510)

19 Nov MDCCXLI. Deed. Phebee Hobson of St. Mark Parish, Orange Co, VA widow for £20 sold to Robert Coleman the younger of St. George Parish, Spotsylvania Co a 50 a. tr of land or woodland ground in St. George Parish & is pt/o a greater tr of land granted by pattent 2 Dec 1723 to Robert Coleman Senr

father to the afsd Robert Coleman & by him sold to George Carter & by the sd
Carter sold to the sd Phebee Hobson, the 50 a. is bounded by Col John
Robinson, Humphry Bell, George Carter & Col John Robinson's now Bell's line
.... Wit: Joseph Adcock, George Carter, David Roy. Proved 1 Dec 1741 by
the oaths of Joseph Adcock & David Roy two of the wits & is admitted to
record. NB look to page 530 in this book where the deed was further proved.
Attest: John Waller clk. (Pg 511)

1 Feb MDCCXLI. Deed of Lease. Benjamin Winslow of Essex Co gent for 5
shillings leased to John Allan of Spotsylvania Co merchant a lot or ½ a. of
ground in the town of Fredericksburgh described by the plan of the sd town by
the figure 52 bounded by Princess Anne Street & lots numbered 50, 49 & 51 ...
during the term of one year paying the yearly rent of one ear of Indian corn on
Lady day next if demanded .... Wit: Rob Jackson, William Hunter, John
Thornton, Andr Craig. Proved 3 Feb 1741 & admitted to record. Attest: John
Waller clk. (Pg 513)

2 Feb MDCCXLI. Deed of Release. John Allan of Spotsylvania Co merchant
for £22:10 sold & released to John Allan of same co merchant a lot or ½ a. of
ground in the town of Fredericksburgh number 52 ... [same as above] .... Wit:
Rob Jackson, William Hunter, John Thornton, Andr Craig. Proved 3 Feb 1741
& admitted to record. Attest: John Waller clk. (Pg 514)

At a court held 2 Feb 1741 John Grymes & Francis Willis esqr executors &c of
Henry Willis gent decd deed &c for land to John Allan & Nathaniel Chapman
gent was further proved by the oath of Thomas Wood one of the wits thereto &
is admitted to record. Attest: John Waller clk. (Pg 515)

At a court held 2 Feb 1741 John Grymes & Francis Willis esqr exrs &c of Henry
Willis gent decd deed &c for land to Benjamin Hubbard gent was further proved
by the oath of Thomas Wood one of the wits thereto & is admitted to record.
Attest: John Waller clk. (Pg 515)

9 Dec 1741. Deed. Bernat (Barnet) (Bernerd) (Bernard) Paine of Drysdale
Parish, King & Queen Co for £103 sold to John Farish of St. Stephens Parish in
King & Queen Co a 350 a. tr of land lying on the n side Middle River & adj to
the lands of Wm Johnston & Charles Pigg .... Wit: Robert Farish, James
Martin, John Warren. Ackn 2 Feb 1741 & ordered to be recorded. Attest: John
Waller clk. (Pg 515)

28 Feb 1741. Deed. Charles Filks Pigg of St. George Parish, Spotsylvania Co
for £32:15 sold to William Johnston of same place a 131 a. tr of land in St.
George Parish bounded by the sd Johnston, the sd Pigg, the Glebe land & John

Clark .... Wit: John Chew, Larkin Chew, A. Foster. Ackn 2 Mar 1741 by Charles Filks Pigg & Sarah the w/o the sd Charles ackn her right of dower & is admitted to record. Attest: John Waller clk. (Pg 517)

1 Mar MDCCXLI. Deed. John Waller Junr of Spotsylvania Co gent & Agnes his wife for £45 sold to James Shackleford of same co a 400 a. tr of land bounded by a Poyson Field & Col John Waller, the sd land being granted to Thomas Carr Junr of King William Co by patent dated 16 Jun MDCCXXVII & by him conveyed to the sd John & Agnes by deed of gift dated 26 Nov MDCCXXXI .... Wit: Z. Lewis, Anne Lewis, Mary Lewis. Ackn 6 Apr 1742 by John Waller Junr gent & at the motion of Zachary Lewis gent is admitted to record. Attest: John Waller clk. (Pg 519)

Commission. To Joseph Brock, William Robinson & Larkin Chew gent greeting, whereas John Waller Junr gent & Agnes his wife by their indenture of feofment [see above] have conveyed unto James Shackleford the fee simple estate of 400 a. of land & whereas the sd Agnes cannot conveniently travel to our co court to make acknowledgment of the sd conveyance, therefore we do give unto you or any two or more of you power to receive the acknowledgment which the sd Agnes shall be willing to make before you & we do command that you do personally go to the sd Agnes & receive her acknowledgment & examine her privily & apart from the sd John Waller her husband whether she doth the same freely & voluntarily & whether she be willing that the same should be recorded .... Wit John Waller clerk of court 26 Mar MDCCXLII. XXXI Mar 1742 we Jos Brock & Larkin Chew hereby certify that pursuant to the within commission we personally went to Agnes the w/o John Waller Junr & examiner her privily & apart from her sd husband who ackn before us that she freely & voluntarily did make & execute the indenture of feofment within mentioned & that she was willing that the same should be recorded .... At the request of Zachary Lewis gent in behalf of James Shackleford the within commission is admitted to record. Attest: John Waller clk. (Pg 520-521)

XXV Feb 1741. Deed of Lease. Jonathan Gibson of Orange Co for 5 shillings leased to John Allan merchant of Spotsylvania Co a 400 a. tr of land bounded by the Rappahannock River, which sd land was granted to the sd Jonathan Gibson by deeds of lease & release from Augustine Smith dated XXVIII & XXIX Oct MDCCXXVI ... during the term of one year paying one pepper corn upon the feast of St. Michael the Arch Angel if demanded .... Wit: Geo Chapman, John Blake, Jno Edwards, Henry Willis. Proved 6 Apr 1742 & admitted to record. Attest: John Waller clk. (Pg 521)

XXVI Feb 1741. Deed of Release. Jonathan Gibson of Orange Co for £218 sold to John Allan merchant of Spotsylvania Co a 400 a. tr of land ... [same as *above*] ... . Wit: Geo Chapman, Henry Willis. Proved 6 Apr 1742 & admitted to record. Attest: John Waller clk. (Pg 522)

5 Apr 1742. Deed of Lease. Nicholas Copeland (Copland) of Orange Co for 5 shillings leased to Benjamin Martin of Spotsylvania Co a 100 a. tr of land in St. George Parish bounded by William Lindsey, John Chew & Col Spotswood ... during the term of one year paying the yearly rent of one pepper corn at the feast of St. Michael the Arch Angell if demanded ... . Wit: John Chew, Archd McPherson, John Allan. Ackn 6 Apr 1742 & admitted to record. Attest: John Waller clk. (Pg 524)

6 Apr 1742. Deed of Release. Nicholas Copeland (Copland) of Orange Co for £20 sold to Benjamin Martin of Spotsylvania Co a 100 a. tr of land ... [*same as above*] ... . Wit: John Chew, Archd McPherson, John Allan. Ackn 6 Apr 1742 & admitted to record. Attest: John Waller clk. (Pg 525)

6 Apr 1742. Bond. I Nicholas Copland (Copeland) of Orange Co am firmly bound unto Benjamin Martin of Spotsylvania Co in the sum of £40 ... the condition of this obligation is such that if the afsd Nicholas Copeland shall well & truly perform & keep all the covenants mentioned & comprised in an indenture of release [*see above*] then this obligation to be void ... . Wit: John Chew, Archd McPherson, John Allan. Ackn 6 Apr 1742 & admitted to record. Attest: John Waller clk. (Pg 526)

5 Apr 1742. Deed of Lease. Nicholas Copeland (Copland) of Orange Co for 5 shillings leased to John Sutton of Spotsylvania Co a 100 a. tr of land in St. George Parish bounded by Wm Lindsey, Benjamin Martin & Col Spotswood ... during the term of one year paying the yearly rent of one peper corn at the feast of St. Michael the Arch Angel if demanded ... . Wit: John Chew, Wm Lindsey, Benjamin Martin. Ackn 6 Apr 1742 & admitted to record. Attest: John Waller clk. (Pg 527)

6 Apr 1742. Deed of Release. Nicholas Copland (Copeland) of Orange Co for £20 sold & released to John Sutton of Spotsylvania Co a 100 a. tr of land ... [*same as above*] ... . Wit: John Chew, Wm Lindsey, Benjamin Martin. Ackn 6 Apr 1742 & admitted to record. Attest: John Waller clk. (Pg 528)

6 Apr 1742. Bond. I Nicholas Copeland of Orange Co am firmly bound unto John Sutton of Spotsylvania Co in the sum of £40 ... the condition of this obligation is such that if the afsd Nicholas Copeland shall well & truly perform & keep all the covenants mentioned & comprised in an indenture of release [*see above*] then this obligation to be void ... . Wit: John Chew, Wm Lindsey,

Benjamin Martin. Ackn 6 Apr 1742 & admitted to record. Attest: John Waller clk. (Pg 529)

At a court held 4 May 1742 Phebe Hobson's deed &c for land to Robert Coleman the younger was further proved by the oath of George Carter one of the wits thereto & is admitted to record. Attest: Edmund Waller clk. (Pg 530)

4 May 1742. Deed. Between Robert Coleman Junr of St. George Parish, Spotsylvania Co of the one part & George Carter of same place of the other part, wit that whereas Robert Coleman Senr the father of the sd Robert party to these presents in the year MDCCXXV for £25 had agreed to sell & convey to the sd George Carter in fee simple a 200 a. tr of land & pursuant to the sd agreement the sd Robert Coleman Senr by deeds of lease & release dated 5 & 6 Apr MDCCXXV & ackn in the court of Spotsylvania Co 6 Apr MDCCXXV did convey in fee simple to the sd George Carter 200 a. of land bounded as in the sd deeds are mentioned, & whereas on a resurvey of the sd land it is found to contain but 165 a. & the sd Robert Coleman Senr being willing that the residue of the sd land sold being 35 a. be conveyed to the sd George Carter to compleat the agreement afsd but he the sd Robert having given & conveyed the land adj to the sd Carter's to his son the sd Robert party to these presents by his deed of gift dated XII Jun MDCCXLI & proved 7 Jul next following cannot convey the same to the sd Carter, therefore the sd Robert Coleman Junr for & in consideration of the money afsd on the agreement afsd being paid to his father as afsd hath sold unto the sd George Carter all that messuage & 35 a. tr of land in St. George Parish adj to the land of the sd George Carter .... Wit: Thos Duerson, Edmund Waller, John Carter. Ackn 4 May 1742 & admitted to record. Attest: Edmund Waller clerk. (Pg 530)

4 May 1742. Deed of Lease. George Stubblefeild of St. Georges Parish, Spotsylvania Co & Catherine his wife for 5 shillings leased to George Cook of same place a 200 a. tr of land being pt/o a patent granted to Harry Beverley decd & by the will of the sd Beverley bequeathed that his sd dau Catherine have a certain part or dividend of the sd patent bounded by the sd George Stubblefeild, John Chew, Parmunkey River & the mouth of Plentifull ... during the term of one year paying on the last day of the sd term the rent of one ear of Indian corn if demanded .... Wit: None. Ackn 4 May 1742 by George Stubblefeild & Catherine his wife & admitted to record. Attest: Edmund Waller clk. (Pg 531)

4 May ----. Deed of Release. George Stubblefeild of St. Georges Parish, Spotsylvania Co & Catherine his wife for £21:10 sold & released to George Cook of same place a 200 a. tr of land ... [same as above] .... Wit: None. Ackn 4 May 1742 & admitted to record. Attest: Edmund Waller clk. (Pg 533)

6 Apr 1742. Deed. Francis Thornton of King George Co gent & Elizabeth his wife for £500 sold to John Lewis of Glocester Co gent all that lower ½ pt/o a tr of land containing 812 ¼ a. in St. George Parish bounded by land lately sold by Thomas Hawkins & Ann his wife to Francis Thornton of Spotsylvania Co gent & Rappahannock River, which sd tr of land was sold by the sd Thomas Hawkins & Ann his wife to the sd Francis Thornton party to these presents by indenture dated 26 Apr 1738 ... . Wit: None. Ackn 6 Apr 1742 & admitted to record. Attest: Edmund Waller clk. (Pg 535)

Commission. To Joseph Strother, John Champe & Samuel Skinker of King George Co gent greeting, whereas Francis Thornton of King George Co gent & Elizabeth his wife have by their indenture of feofment [see above] conveyed unto John Lewis of Gloucester Co gent the fee simple estate of ½ pt/o 812 ¼ a. of land, & whereas the sd Elizabeth cannot conveniently travel to our co court to make acknowledgment of the sd conveyance & also to sign the sd deed, therefore we do give unto you or any two or more of you power to receive the acknowledgement which she shall be willing to make before you & we do command that you do personally go to the sd Elizabeth & receive her acknowledgment of the same & examine her privily & apart from the sd Francis Thornton her husband whether she doth the same freely & voluntarily & whether she be willing the same should be recorded ... . Wit John Waller clerk of court 6 Apr 1742. 1 May 1742 We Jos Strother & John Champe doe hereby certifie that this day we went to the house of Francis Thornton & pursuant to the above writ to us directed have examined the afsd Elizabeth Thornton who freely ackn her consent. At a court held 1 Jun 1742 the within commission being returned it is admitted to record. Attest: Edmund Waller clk. (Pg 537)

4 May 1742. Deed of Lease. John Sertain of St. George Parish, Spotsylvania Co & Anna his wife for 5 shillings leased to George Cook of same place a 200 a. parcel of land being pt/o a pattent granted to the sd John Sertain dated 28 Sep 1728 bounded by James Taylor decd & Thomas Sartin ... during the term of one year paying on the last day of the sd term the rent of one ear of Indian corn if demanded ... . Wit: None. Ackn 4 May 1742 by John Sartin & Anna his wife & admitted to record. Attest: Edmund Waller clk. (Pg 538)

4 May ----. Deed of Release. John Sertain of St. George Parish, Spotsylvania Co & Anna his wife for £12 sold & released to George Cook of same place a 200 a. tr of land ... [same as above] ... . Wit: None. Ackn 4 May 1742 by John Sartin & Anna his wife & admitted to record. Attest: Edmund Waller clk. (Pg 539)

31 May 1742. Deed of Lease. Philip Sanders of Drisdale Parish, King & Queen Co for 5 shillings leased to Mary Curtis of St. George Parish, Spotsylvania Co a

200 a. tr of land being pt/o a pattent granted to Larkin Chew decd dated 4 Jun 1722 & by the sd Chew sold to Joseph Brock gent by deeds dated 17 Oct 1723 & the same granted to the sd Joseph Brock by pattent dated 17 Sep 1738 the same being pt/o a sale made by the sd Joseph Brock to the sd Philip Sanders 30 Apr 1740, bounded by John Boswell, the Mine Road, Joseph Pen & Ignatious Tureman ... during the term of one year paying on the last day of the sd term the rent of one ear of Indian corn if demanded ... . Wit: R. Curtis Junr, Philip Vincent Vass, John Graves. Ackn 1 Jun 1742 & admitted to record. Attest: Edmund Waller clk. (Pg 541)

1 Jun 1742. Deed of Release. Philip Sanders of Drisdale Parish, King & Queen Co & Mary his wife for £20:10 sold & released to Mary Curtis of St. George Parish, Spotsylvania Co a 200 a. tr of land ... [same as above] ... . Wit: R. Curtis Junr, Philip Vincent Vass, John Graves. Ackn 1 Jun 1742 by Philip Sanders & Mary his wife & admitted to record. Attest: Edmund Waller clk. (Pg 542)

31 May 1742. Deed of Lease. Philip Sanders of Drysdale Parish, King & Queen Co for 5 shillings leased to Richard Coleman of Caroline Co a 200 a. tr of land pt/o a pattent granted to Larkin Chew decd dated 4 Jun 1722 & by the sd Chew sold to Joseph Brock gent by deeds dated 17 Oct 1723 & the same granted to the sd Joseph Brock by pattent dated 17 Sep 1738 the same being pt/o a sale made by the sd Joseph Brock to the sd Philip Sanders by deed dated 30 Apr 1740 bounded by the Mine Road, Thomas West, Mary Curtis & John Boswell ... during the term of one year paying on the last day of the sd term the rent of one ear of Indian corn if demanded ... . Wit: Rice Curtis, R. Curtis Junr, Philip Vincent Vass. Ackn 1 Jun 1742 & admitted to record. Attest: Edmund Waller clk. (Pg 545)

1 Jun 1742. Deed of Release. Philip Sanders of Drysdale Parish, King & Queen Co & Mary his wife for £20:10 sold & released to Richard Coleman of Caroline Co a 200 a. tr of land ... [same as above] ... . Wit: Rice Curtis, R. Curtis Junr, Philip Vincent Vass. Ackn 1 Jun 1742 by Philip Sanders & Mary his wife & admitted to record. Attest: Edmund Waller clk. (Pg 546)

1 May MDCCXLII. Deed. Edmund Waller & Mary his wife of St. George Parish, Spotsylvania Co for £20:10 sold to Samuel Brown of same place a 170 a. tr of land in St. George Parish pt/o a greater tr of land containing 1,000 a. granted by patent to the sd Edmund Waller 28 Sep 1728 bounded by the Mill Road, Zach Lewis, Col John Waller, John Wiglesworth, Honey Swamp & Edmund Waller ... . Wit: Henry Pendleton, Michael Lawless. Ackn 1 Jun 1742 by Edmund Waller & Mary his wife & admitted to record. Look to page

552 per the feme cover to acknowledgment. Attest: Edmund Waller clk. (Pg 549)

Commission. To William Robinson, John Minor & John Waller Junr gent greeting, whereas Edmund Waller of Spotsylvania Co & Mary his wife by their deed dated 23 Jan 1740 have conveyed unto John Wiglesworth of the sd co the fee simple estate of 110 a. of land, & whereas the sd Mary cannot conveniently travel to our co court to make acknowledgment of the sd conveyance, therefore we do give unto you or any two or more of you power to receive the acknowledgment which the sd Mary shall be willing to make before you, & we do command that you do personally go to the sd Mary & receive her acknowledgment of the same & examine her privily & apart from her husband whether she doth the same freely & voluntarily & whether she be willing that the same should be recorded .... Wit Edmund Waller clerk of court 28 Jun 1742. 28 Jul 1742 we John Minor & Jno Waller Junr do hereby certifie that pursuant to the within commission we personally went to Mary the w/o the sd Edmund Waller & examined her privily & apart from her husband who ackn before us that she freely & voluntarily did make & execute the indenture of feofment & that she was willing that the same should be recorded. The within commission being returned is admitted to record. Attest: Edmund Waller clk. (Pg 551)

Commission. To William Robinson, John Minor & John Waller Junr gent greeting, whereas Edmund Waller of Spotsylvania Co & Mary his wife by their deed dated 6 Feb 1740 have conveyed unto Zachary Lewis of the sd co the fee simple estate of 61 a. of land, & whereas the sd Mary cannot conveniently travel to our co court to make acknowledgment of the sd conveyance, therefore we do give unto you or any two or more of you power to receive the acknowledgment which the sd Mary shall be willing to make before you, & we do command that you do personally go to the sd Mary & receive her acknowledgment of the same & examine her privily & apart from her husband whether she doth the same freely & voluntarily & whether she be willing that the same should be recorded .... Wit Edmund Waller clerk of court 28 Jun 1742. 28 Jul 1742 we John Minor & Jno Waller Junr do hereby certifie that pursuant to the within commission we personally went to Mary the w/o the sd Edmund Waller & examined her privily & apart from her husband who ackn before us that she freely & voluntarily did make & execute the indenture of feofment & that she was willing that the same should be recorded. The within commission being returned is admitted to record. Attest: Edmund Waller clk. (Pg 551)

Commission. To William Robinson, John Minor & John Waller Junr gent greeting, whereas Edmund Waller of Spotsylvania Co & Mary his wife by their deed dated 31 May 1742 have conveyed unto Samuel Brown of the sd co the fee simple estate of 170 a. of land, & whereas the sd Mary cannot conveniently travel to our co court to make acknowledgment of the sd conveyance, therefore we do give unto you or any two or more of you power to receive the acknowledgment which the sd Mary shall be willing to make before you, & we do command that you do personally go to the sd Mary & receive her acknowledgment of the same & examine her privily & apart from her husband whether she doth the same freely & voluntarily & whether she be willing that the same should be recorded ... . Wit Edmund Waller clerk of court 28 Jun 1742. 28 Jul 1742 we John Minor & Jno Waller Junr do hereby certifie that pursuant to the within commission we personally went to Mary the w/o the sd Edmund Waller & examined her privily & apart from her husband who ackn before us that she freely & voluntarily did make & execute the indenture of feofment & that she was willing that the same should be recorded. The within commission being returned is admitted to record. Attest: Edmund Waller clk. (Pg 552)

Commission. To William Robinson, John Minor & John Waller Junr gent greeting, whereas James Stevens of St. George Parish, Spotsylvania Co & Mary his wife by their deed dated 28 Nov 1741 have conveyed unto Jeremiah Stevens of same place the fee simple estate of 71 a. of land, & whereas the sd Mary cannot conveniently travel to our co court to make acknowledgment of the sd conveyance, therefore we do give unto you or any two or more of you power to receive the acknowledgment which the sd Mary shall be willing to make before you, & we do command that you do personally go to the sd Mary & receive her acknowledgment of the same & examine her privily & apart from her husband whether she doth the same freely & voluntarily & whether she be willing that the same should be recorded ... . Wit Edmund Waller clerk of court 28 Jun 1742. 28 Jul 1742 we John Minor & Jno Waller Junr do hereby certifie that pursuant to the within commission we personally went to Mary the w/o the sd Edmund Waller & examined her privily & apart from her husband who ackn before us that she freely & voluntarily did make & execute the indenture of feofment & that she was willing that the same should be recorded. The within commission being returned is admitted to record. Attest: Edmund Waller clk. (Pg 552)

3 Jul 1742. Deed. Hugh Sanders of Spotsylvania Co for £11 sold to Henry Gatewood of King & Queen Co a 207 a. tr of land in St. George Parish on the brs of Mattapony River bounded by Robert Coleman, William Johnston, Anthony Foster, land Ignatious Stureman bought of Joseph Brock & the sd Joseph Brock ... . Wit: Robert Coleman, Henry Gatewood, Sarah Coleman. Ackn 6 Jul 1742 by Hugh Sanders & Catey his wife & admitted to record. Attest: Edmund Waller clk. (Pg 553)

6 Jul MDCCXLII. Deed of Gift. Thomas Allen of St. George Parish, Spotsylvania Co for natural love & affection hath given unto his son Thomas Allen Junr a 100 a. tr of land being pt/o a patent granted to the sd Thomas Allen

& George Musick for 1,000 a. dated 28 Sep MDCCXXVIII in St. George Parish bounded by Robert Spilsbe Coleman, Edward Ware & Edward Coleman .... Wit: Edmund Waller, Henry Pendleton. Ackn 6 Jul 1742 & admitted to record. Attest: Edmund Waller clk. (Pg 554)

27 Feb 1741. Deed. John Wells of St. George Parish, Spotsylvania Co planter & Frances his wife for £21 sold to Bloomfield Long Senr of same place a tr of land being pt/o a pattent granted to Larkin Chew gent decd of same place dated 4 Jun 1722 & made over to Phillip Brandegon from the sd Larkin Chew by indenture of release dated 5 Mar 1722 & by the sd Phillip Brandegon sold to the afsd John Wells 6 Oct 1730 in St. George Parish adj John Walker & Bloomfeild Long .... Wit: Larkin Chew, A. Foster, John Durret, Igs Turman. Proved 6 Jul 1742 & admitted to record. Attest: Edmund Waller clk. (Pg 555)

4 Jul 1742. Deed of Lease. Daniel Brown of St. Marks Parish, Orange Co, VA for 5 shillings leased to Thomas Brown of same place a tr of land whereon the sd Daniel Brown formerly lived in St. Georges Parish on the s side of Pike Run being pt/o 800 a. of land which the sd Daniel Brown purch of Larkin Chew, the sd land being pt/o a greater tr granted to Larkin Chew by pattent dated 4 Jun 1722 ... during the term of one year .... Wit: Jas Pendleton, Philip Clayton, John Nalle, John Parks. Proved 6 Jul 1742 & admitted to record. Attest: Edmund Waller clk. (Pg 557)

5 Jul 1742. Deed of Release. Daniel Brown of St. Marks Parish, Orange Co, VA for £40 sold & released to Thomas Brown of same place a tr of land ... [same as above] .... Wit: Jas Pendleton, Philip Clayton, John Nalle, John Parks. Proved 6 Jul 1742 & admitted to record. Attest: Edmund Waller clk. (Pg 558)

SPOTSYLVANIA COUNTY, VIRGINIA
DEED BOOK D
1742-1751

6 Jul 1742. Deed of Gift. Mary Gresham for love, good will & affection haven given to my children Mary Johns, William Gresham & Rachel Gresham to be equally divided between them two cows after my death & calves, one heifer, one stear, two new feather beds with bolsters, one new flock bed & fether bolster, two iron pots, one iron skillet, four large & one small pewter dishes, ½ dozen supe plates, eight shallow plates, one large pewter tankard, one large pewter two handled mugg, one large cupboard, one frying pan, one box iron & heaters, one pair of fire tongs, two chests, one box, three new stone pans, one sow bigg with pigg, five barrows, six chairs, three bed steds, & all other things to me belonging both moveable & immoveable both real & personal .... Wit: John Waller, John Gordon, James Allan. Ackn 7 Jul 1742 & admitted to record. Attest: Edmund Waller clk. (Pg 1)

5 Jun 1742. Deed. Andrew Craig of Spotsylvania Co chirgeon for £32 sold to John Allan of co afsd merchant a lot or ½ a. of land in the town of Fredericksburgh described in the plan of the sd town by the number 62 which lot formerly did belong to Henry Willis decd & by his executors sold to the sd Andrew Craig .... Wit: John Thornton, Henry Willis, Wm Barber, Thos Wood, Roger Malory (Mallory). Proved 7 Jul 1742 & admitted to record. Attest: Edmund Waller clk. (Pg 1)

3 Mar MDCCXLI. Deed. John Waller of Spotsylvania Co gent for £26:17:6 sold to Augustine Washington of King George Co gent a lot or ½ a. of land & house in the town of Fredericksburgh bounded by Princess Ann Street & Hanover Street described in the plan of the sd town by the figure 40 the same being ackn in Spotsylvania Co Court 4 Sep 1739 by the trustees of the sd town by deed of sale to the sd John Waller .... Wit: John Allan, Geo Chapman, Henry Willis, Roger Malory, James Allan. Ackn 7 Jul 1742 & admitted to record. Attest: Edmund Waller clk. (Pg 3)

3 Jul 1742. Deed. George Musick of Spotsylvania Co & Ann his wife for £10 sold to Nicholas Randall (Randolph) of same co planter a 170 a. tr of land in St. George Parish bounded by the Mine Road, John Sartin & a line that old Musick made, being pt/o a larger tr of land granted by patent unto the sd Musick & by him sold & conveyed unto the sd Nicholas Randolph .... Wit: Francis Gouldman, W. Russell, John Wetherall. Ackn 3 Aug 1742 by George Musick & Ann his wife & admitted to record. Attest: Edmund Waller clk. (Pg 5)

3 Aug 1742. Deed. Francis Thornton of St. George Parish, Spotsylvania Co gent for £27 sold to David Alexander of Petsworth Parish, Gloucester Co gent a lot or ½ a. of land in the town of Fredericksburgh & is one of the outside lotts described in the plan of the sd town by the figure 63 bounded by Princess Ann Street & the back lines of the sd town being formerly conveyed by deed 8 Oct MDCCXXXV by the feoffees of the sd town to Doctor John Tennent & by the sd Tennent sold to the afsd Francis Thornton ... . Wit: John Waller, Philip Rootes, Jno Sutton. Ackn 3 Aug 1742 & admitted to record. Attest: Edmund Waller clk. (Pg 7)

9 Aug 1742. Deed of Lease. Robert Williams of St. Thomas Parish, Orange Co for 5 shillings leased to Thomas Hayden (Haydon) of Brunswick Parish, King George Co a 100 a. parcel of land in St. Georges Parish bounded by the mouth of the South Br of Massaponnax Swamp, Mott's patent, patent granted to James Canney, James Atkins & the Massaponnax Main Run ... during the term of one year paying one ear of Indian corn upon the fest of St. Michael the Arch Angel if demanded ... . Wit: Linefield Sharpe, William Burbadge, Thomas Morris. Ackn 7 Sep 1742 & admitted to record. Attest: Edmund Waller clk. (Pg 8)

10 Aug 1742. Deed of Release. Robert Williams of St. Thomas Parish, Orange Co for £40 sold & released to Thomas Hayden (Haydon) of Brunswick Parish, King George Co a 100 a. parcel of land ... [same as above] ... . Wit: Lincefeild Sharpe, Wm Burbadge, Thomas Morris. Ackn 7 Sep 1742 by Robert Williams & Mary the w/o the sd Robert ackn her right of dower & is admitted to record. Attest: Edmund Waller clk. (Pg 9)

6 Sep 1742. Deed of Lease. Thomas Ship & Elizabeth his wife of Orange Co for 5 shillings leased to William Carr of Caroline Co gent a 357 a. tr of land in St. George Parish being a tr of land formerly granted to Henry Willis decd bounded by a br of Massaponax Swamp, Augustine Smith & Chiswell's Mine Road ... during the term of one year paying one pepper corn upon the feast of St. Michael the Arch Angel if demanded ... . Wit: Thos Roy, Geo Taylor, Wm Burnett. Ackn 7 Sep 1742 by Thomas Ship & Elizabeth his wife & admitted to record. Attest: Edmund Waller clk. (Pg 11)

7 Sep 1742. Deed of Release. Thomas Ship & Elizabeth his wife of Orange Co for £70 sold & released to William Carr of Caroline Co gent a 357 a. tr of land ... [same as above] ... . Wit: Thos Roy, Geo Taylor, Wm Burnett. Ackn 7 Sep 1742 by Thomas Ship & Elizabeth his wife & admitted to record ... . Attest: Edmund Waller clk. (Pg 12)

7 Sep 1742. Deed. Abraham Rogers & Barbary (Barbra) his wife of St. George Parish, Spotsylvania Co for 2,228 lbs of tobacco sold to Abraham Eastes (Estes)

Junr of St. Stephen Parish, King & Queen Co an 83 a. tr of land or woodland ground bounded by the land of the sd Rogers ... . Wit: Abraham Estes Senr, Matthew Brooke, Robert Johnston. Ackn 7 Sep 1742 by Abraham Rogers & Barbary his wife & admitted to record. Attest: Edmund Waller clk. (Pg 14)

15 Jul MDCCXLII. Deed of Gift. Robert King of St. George Parish, Spotsylvania Co for natural love & affection hath given unto his son Robert King Junr of same place a 150 a. tr of land whereon the sd Robert lately dwelt & where the sd Robert King Junr doth now dwell in St. George Parish bounded by the River Po which divides this land from Edward Cason's & Dalton's land ... . Wit: William Johnston, James Taylor, Thos Minor, Wm Login. Proved 7 Sep 1742 & at a court held 2 Nov 1742 was further proved & admitted to record. Attest: Edmund Waller clk. (Pg 16)

2 Nov MDCCXLII. Deed . Between Joseph Hawkins (son & heir of John Hawkins late decd) of Spotsylvania Co of the one part & Philemon Hawkins of same co of the other part, wit that the sd John Hawkins father of the sd Joseph & Philemon Hawkins by his will duly proved & recorded in King William Co Court by which sd will certain lands are given to the sd Philemon Hawkins & others the children of the sd John Hawkins decd & the sd lands was intended by the sd John Hawkins to be devised in fee simple to his sd children but by the wording of the sd will occasioned by the ignorance of the writer thereof the sd land is not devised in fee simple & it is doubted what estate the sd Philemon Hawkins & others the children of the sd John Hawkins decd (except the sd Joseph) have in the sd lands & the sd Philemon Hawkins having lately bought several pts/o the sd land of others, his mother & sisters, to whom the same was devised, so that the sd Philemon Hawkins is now possessed of the several pts/o Mary Hawkins (his mother), George Smith & Elizabeth his wife & Phebe Hawkins amounting to 200 a. & upwards which the sd land lieth in St. George Parish bounded by Harry Beverley gent decd, Terrys Run & the North Fork of the Northanna ... now this indenture wit that the sd Joseph Hawkins knowing the intent of his father the sd John Hawkins, therefore for the quiet & peaceable possession of the sd Philemon Hawkins & his heirs forever in the sd land & more especially in consideration of that the sd Philemon Hawkins hath agreed to convey all his right & title in certain lands in Caroline Co which the sd Joseph Hawkins hath sold to Augustine Moore gent & also the sd Philemon Hawkins paying & allowing to Mary Hawkins (the mother of the sd Joseph & Philemon) yearly & every year during her natural life the sum of 500 lbs of lawfull tobacco & five barrels of Indian corn hath sold & released unto the sd Philemon Hawkins a tr of land bounded as above mentioned containing 200 a. ... . Wit: Edwd Herndon, W. Miller, Thos Pritchett. Ackn 2 Nov 1742 & admitted to record. Attest: Edmund Waller clk. (Pg 17)

2 Nov 1742. Deed. William Johnston of St. Georges Parish, Spotsylvania Co gent & Anne his wife for £44 sold to Thomas Minor of same place planter a 220 a. tr of land or woodland ground in St. Georges Parish the same being pt/o a patent formerly granted to William Johnston dated 28 Sep 1728 bounded by Col John Lewis, John Hoard & John Martin ... . Wit: None. Ackn 2 Nov 1742 by William Johnston gent & admitted to record. Attest: Edmund Waller clk. (Pg 19)

Commission. To Henry Goodloe, John Chew & Larkin Chew gent greeting, whereas William Johnston of Spotsylvania Co gent by his indenture [*see above*] hath conveyed unto Thomas Minor of sd co the fee simple estate of 220 a. of land, & whereas Ann Johnston the w/o the sd William Johnston by means of her indisposition cannot conveniently travel to our co court to make acknowledgment of her thirds in the sd land, therefore we do give unto you or any two of you power to receive the acknowledgment which the sd Ann shall be willing to make before you, we do therefore command you that you do personally go to the sd Ann & receive her acknowledgment & examine her privily & apart from the sd William Johnston her husband whether she doth the same freely & voluntarily & whether she be willing that the sd deed should be recorded ... . Wit Edmund Waller clerk of court 25 Nov 1742. 6 Dec 1742 by vertue of the within commission we John Chew & Lark Chew did personally go to the within named Ann & did privily examine her apart from her sd husband & she doth freely & voluntarily ackn her thirds in the sd 220 a. of land & desires the same may be recorded ... . The within commission being returned is admitted to record. Attest: Edmund Waller clk. (Pg 21)

2 Nov 1742. Bond. I William Johnston of Spotsylvania Co am firmly bound unto Thomas Minor of co afsd in the sum of £88 ... the condition of this obligation is such that if the afsd William Johnston shall well & truly perform & keep all the covenants mentioned & comprised in an indenture of feofment [*see above*] then this obligation to be void ... . Wit: None. Ackn 2 Nov 1742 & admitted to record. Attest: Edmund Waller clk. (Pg 22)

2 Nov MDCCXLII. Deed. Henry Elley of Hambleton Parish, Prince William Co, VA for £21 sold to Edward Ware of St. George Parish, Spotsylvania Co a 300 a. tr of land in St. George Parish on both sides of Assforemast Run a br of Pamunkey River & is pt/o a greater tr of land containing 1,000 a. granted by pattent to Thomas Allen & George Musick 28 Sep MDCCXXVIII which tr of land is adj John London ... . Wit: Edwd Herndon, Robt Huddleston, Edmund Foster. Ackn 2 Nov 1742 & admitted to record. Attest: Edmund Waller clk. (Pg 23)

2 Nov MDCCXLII. Deed. Henry Elley of Hambleton Parish, Prince William Co for £14 sold to Edward Coleman of St. George Parish, Spotsylvania Co a 200 a. tr of land or woodland ground pt/o a greater tr of land containing 1,000 a. granted by pattent to Thomas Allen & George Musick 28 Sep MDCCXXVIII ... . Wit: Edwd Herndon, Robt Huddleston, Edmund Foster. Ackn 2 Nov 1742 & admitted to record. Attest: Edmund Waller clk. (Pg 25)

1 Nov 1742. Deed. William Hawkins of St. Thomas Parish, Orange Co planter & Mary his wife for £24 sold to Abraham Estes Junr of St. Stephens Parish, King & Queen Co a 110 a. tr of land or woodland ground being pt/o a tr of land sold by Edward Pigg decd & Abraham Rogers both of Spotsylvania Co to the sd William Hawkins by deeds of lease adj John Clark ... . Wit: Lark Chew, George Smith, Richd Bradley. Ackn 2 Nov 1742 by William Hawkins & admitted to record. (Pg 27)

7 Dec 1742. Deed of Lease. Joseph Brock gent of St. George Parish, Spotsylvania Co for 5 shillings leased to Henry Lines of Drisdale Parish, King & Queen Co a 1,075 a. tr of land it being pt/o a patent granted unto the sd Joseph Brock dated 12 Sep 1738 & is bounded by Garton's & Micou's line, James Lee, George Stubblefeild & the Black Rock Swamp ... during the term of one year paying on the last day of the sd term the rent of one ear of Indian corn if demanded ... . Wit: None. Ackn 7 Dec 1742 by Joseph Brock gent & admitted to record. Attest: Edmund Waller clk. (Pg 28)

7 Dec 1742. Deed of Release. Joseph Brock gent of St. George Parish, Spotsylvania Co & Mary his wife for £107:10 sold & released to Henry Lines of Drisdale Parish, King & Queen Co a 1,075 a. tr of land ... [same as above] ... . Wit: None. Ackn 7 Dec 1742 by Joseph Brock gent & Mary his wife & admitted to record. Attest: Edmund Waller clk. (Pg 30)

1 Feb MDCCXLII. Deed of Gift. Thomas Allen of St. George Parish, Spotsylvania Co for natural love & effection hath given to his son John Allen of same place a 1/3 pt/o all the profits which accrues by the sd Thomas Allen's water grist mill, together with 100 a. of land whereon the sd Thomas Allen now lives & whereon the sd mill now stands, after the reservations & exceptions herein mentioned, that is to say, the sd John Allen shall have & enjoy the 1/3 pt/o the sd grist mill from this day forever hereafter & shall enjoy the sd land, plantation & premises belonging to the sd 100 a. after the death of the sd Thomas Allen & Elizabeth his present wife but not to enjoy or claim the sd land during their natural lives, this 100 a. is pt/o a pattent granted to the sd Thomas Allen 28 Sep 1728 & is bounded by the lines of the land now belonging to the Honble Wm Gooch esqr, James Jones & Thomas Allen Junr ... . Wit: Edmund

Waller, Henry Pendleton. Ackn 1 Feb 1742 & admitted to record. Attest: Edmund Waller clk. (Pg 32)

31 Jan 1742. Deed of Lease. Richard Ship of Spotsylvania Co for 5 shillings leased to William Carr of Caroline Co gent a 194 a. tr of land being a tr of land purch of Thomas Ship adj Chiswells Mine Road & Smith's line ... during the term of one year paying the yearly rent of one grain of Indian corn at the feast of St. Michal the Arch Angel if demanded ... . Wit: Lark Chew, Robt Seayres, Patrick Dowdall. Ackn 1 Feb 1742 & admitted to record. Attest: Edmund Waller clk. (Pg 34)

1 Feb 1742. Deed of Release. Richard Ship of Spotsylvania Co for £30 sold & released to William Carr of Caroline Co gent a 194 a. tr of land ... [same as above] ... . Wit: Lark Chew, Robt Seayres, Patrick Dowdall. Ackn 1 Feb 1742 by Richard Ship & Elizabeth the w/o the sd Richard ackn her right of dower & is admitted to record. Attest: Edmund Waller clk. (Pg 35)

30 Dec 1742. Deed of Mortgage. Between Wm Read of the town of Fredericksburgh, Spotsylvania Co of the one part & Jno Gordon of same place in trust for John Thornton, John Allan, John Parrish, William Picket, John Edwards, Rd Tutt & Joseph Calvert, the afsd Reid's securities in a bond payable for £80 to John Grame of Williamsburgh which sd bond hath been due from 17 Apr 1741 with interest on the same, also in trust for the sd Jno Grame for £5:3:7 ½ penny due with interest from the above time, now whereas the afsd William Read holds now in his possession one Negro man named Casar Strange & all the tools & other things bought of the afsd John Grame amounting to £85:3:7 ½ penny & also sundry household goods, viz, one feather bed & furniture, one flock bed with ditto, one black walnut table, four chairs, one iron pott, one frying pan, three pewter dishes, five pewter plates, one sorrel horse with saddle & bridle, four chests & one square table, this indenture wit that the sd William Reid for the above considerations hath sold & made over to Jno Gordon in trust afsd all the above sd Negro man, tools &c & household goods afsd, now lastly it is agreed by the sd parties that if the sd Reid shall indemnifie the afsd John Thornton, John Allan, John Parrish, William Picket, John Edwards &c from any suit to be brought agt them or their being his securities as afsd or shall discharge the sd bond or give such securities as the above persons shall think sufficient to indemnifie them & discharge the afsd sd sum of £5:3:7 ½ penny due to the afsd Grame on or before 25 Dec next then this deed of sale to be void ... . Wit: Dorothy Tennant, James Allanach, Alexander Lamb. Ackn 2 Feb 1742 & admitted to record. Attest: Edmund Waller clk. (Pg 38)

23 Feb 1742. Deed. Charles Filks Pigg of St. George Parish, Spotsylvania Co planter & Sarah Pigg his wife for £30 sold to Bloomfeild Long of same place a

118 ½ a. parcel of land formerly belonging to Edward Pigg decd in St. George Parish adj the land of John Clerk, Stony Run & River Ta .... Wit: Wm Johnston, A. Foster, Jos Stevens, Larkin Johnston. Proved 1 Mar 1742 & Sarah the w/o the sd Charles ackn her right of dower & is admitted to record. Attest: Edmund Waller clk. (Pg 39)

1 Mar 1742. Deed of Lease. Francis Thornton gent of Spotsylvania Co for & in consideration of the covenants & agreements together with the yearly rents hereafter mentioned have farm lett unto Abraham Darnell of co afsd a 180 a. tr of land adj Hasell Run, John Prockter, sd Thornton & Henry Martain ... during the natural lives of the sd Abraham Darnell, Elizabeth Darnell his wife & David Darnell his son & for & during the natural life & lives of the longest liver of them ... if any of the afsd Abraham Darnell, Eliza Darnell & David Darnell should depart this life that then it shall & may be lawfull for the sd Abraham Darnell to put in a new life into the lease paying the sd Francis Thornton a double rent for that year, & that the sd Abraham Darnell shall hold the above premises during the above term paying yearly 530 lbs of neet tobacco or the value thereof in cash during the term .... Wit: G. Home, Jno Parrish. Ackn 1 Mar 1742 & admitted to record. Attest: Edmund Waller clk. (Pg 41)

1 Mar 1742. Deed of Lease. Francis Thornton gent of Spotsylvania Co for & in consideration of the covenants & agreements together with the yearly rents hereafter mentioned have farm lett unto John Prockter of afsd co planter a 169 a. tr of land being on the n side of the Tub Lick Br, adj William Prockter, Hasell Run, Henry Martain & the Publick Br ... during the naturall lives of the sd John Prockter, Sarah Proctor his wife & John Proctor Junr & for & during the naturall life & lives of the longest liver of them ... if any of the above named lives, viz, John Prockter, Sarah Prockter & John Prockter Junr should depart this life that then it shall & may be lawfull for the sd John Proctor to put in a new life into this lease paying the sd Francis Thornton double rent for that year ... paying the yearly rent of 530 lbs of neet tobo or the value thereof in cash during the sd term .... Wit: G. Home, Abraham Darnell. Ackn 1 Mar 1742 & admitted to record. Attest: Edmund Waller clk. (Pg 43)

3 May 1743. Deed. Robert King & Mary his wife of St. Peter Parish, Orange Co for £35 sold to John Carter of St. George Parish, Spotsylvania Co planter a 140 a. tr of land in St. George Parish bounded by the lands of Edward Cason, Capt Thruston & Robert King Junr .... Wit: Jno Parrish, Robt King Junr, George Moore. Memorandum: Full & peaceable sisin in the tr of land was given & delivered by turf & twig by the sd Robert King unto the sd John Carter 2 May 1743. Wit: George Moore, Robt King Junr, John Brammar. Ackn 3 May 1743 by Robert King & admitted to record. Look to page 89 in this book per the feme coverts acknowledgment. Attest: Edmund Waller clk. (Pg 45)

25 Apr 1743. Deed of Lease. William Lindsey of St. George Parish, Spotsylvania Co for 5 shillings leased to Nicholas Hawkins of same place a 200 a. tr of land bounded by a br of River Po & a small island (being pt/o a grant to Larkin Chew for 3800 a. & since sold by the sd Chew to the sd Lindsey by deed dated 5 Nov 1722) ... during the term of one year paying the rent of one ear of Indian corn on the last day of the sd term if demanded ... . Wit: William Martin, Parmenas Bowker, John Hutcherson, John Sutton, James Hawkins, Nathan Hawkins, Alexander Hawkins. Proved 7 Jun 1743 & admitted to record. Attest: Edmund Waller clk. (Pg 46)

26 Apr 1743. Deed of Release. William Lindsey of St. George Parish, Spotsylvania Co for £45 sold & released to Nicholas Hawkins of same place a 200 a. tr of land ... [*same as above*] ... . Wit: Parmenas Bowker, John Hutcheson, William Martin, John Sutton, James Hawkins, Nathan Hawkins, Alexander Hawkins. Proved 7 Jun 1743 & admitted to record. Attest: Edmund Waller clk. (Pg 47)

3 Jun 1743. Deed of Lease. Diana Goodloe executrix of the will of George Goodloe late of St. Margarets Parish, Caroline Co gent decd for 5 shillings leased to Robert Goodloe of St. Georges Parish, Spotsylvania Co a 160 a. tr of land in St. Georges Parish bounded by William Smethers, Nathll Sanders, Henry Goodloe & Col Robinson ... during the term of one year paying the yearly rent of one grain of Indian corn at the feast of St. Michael the Arch Angel if demanded ... . Wit: John Durrett, Wm Long, Jno Crane. Ackn 7 Jun 1743 & admitted to record. Attest: Edmund Waller clk. (Pg 50)

4 Jun 1743. Deed of Release. Diana Goodloe executrix of the will of George Goodloe late of St. Margrets Parish, Caroline Co gent decd for £16 sold & released to Robert Goodloe of St. George Parish, Spotsylvania Co a 160 a. tr of land ... [*same as above*] ... . Wit: John Durrett, Wm Long, Jno Crane. Ackn 7 Jun 1743 & admitted to record. Attest: Edmund Waller clk. (Pg 51)

26 Jan 1742. Bond. I Nathanal (Nathanel) Sanders of North Hampton Co, NC am firmly bound unto Robert Coleman of Spotsylvania Co, VA in the sum of £500 ... the condition of this obligation is such that whereas the afsd Nathanal Sanders had left by his decd father Nathanal Sanders 400 a. of land in Spotsylvania Co & for non payment of the quitrents due to his Majesty the afsd Robert Coleman petitioned & has a grant for the same (now know yee) that if the sd Nath Sanders supposing the sd grant granted to the sd Robt Coleman should not be good in the law then the sd Nath Sanders or his heirs to make good & lawfull deeds to the sd Robert Coleman for the better securing the sd 500 a. of land then this obligation to be void ... . Wit: John Wynill Sanders, George

Chapman. Proved 7 Jun 1743 & admitted to record. Attest: Edmund Waller clk. (Pg 53)

22 Feb MDCCXLII. Deed of Gift. Charles Filks (Filkes) Pigg of St. George Parish, Spotsylvania Co for love & natural affection hath given to my beloved wife Sarah Pigg & to my dau Jane Pigg in the following manner, to my sd wife during her natural life the use of one Negro woman named Dinah & also a feather bed & furniture for the support & maintainance of my sd wife, to descend & go as the law doth direct to my heirs & not to be the property of the sd Sarah's heir or future husband, & also I give unto my dau Jane one Negro boy named Jack to her & her heirs forever ... . Wit: Wm Waller, J. Brock Junr. Proved 7 Jun 1743 & admitted to record. Attest: Edmund Waller clk. (Pg 54)

7 Jun 1743. Deed. Daniel Holladay & Angess his wife of St. George Parish, Spotsylvania Co for £59:3:6 sold to Thomas Pulliam of same place a plantation & 197 ¼ a. tr of land devised to the sd Daniel Holladay by his father John Holladay gent by his will dated 4 Nov MDCCXLII which tr of land is in parish afsd on the w side of the East North East River bounded by Chapple Bridge, George Seaton, sd Thomas Pulliam, Holladays Swamp & Joseph Holladay ... . Wit: Josias Baker, Patterson Pulliam, Anthony Gholston. Ackn 7 Jun 1743 by Daniel Holladay & Angess his wife & admitted to record. Attest: Edmund Waller clk. (Pg 55)

6 Jun MDCCXLIII. Deed of Lease. Anthony Golston (Gholston) Junr of Spotsylvania Co planter for 5 shillings leased to William Lea of King & Queen Co a 500 a. tr of land in St. George Parish bounded by the land of Musick & Allen & Capt Clowder ... during the term of one year paying the rent of one ear of Indian corn at the feast of St. Michael the Arch Angell if demanded ... . Wit: Saml Coleman, Anthony Strother, Robert Goodloe. Ackn 7 Jun 1743 & admitted to record. Attest: Edmund Waller clk. (Pg 57)

7 Jun MDCCXLIII. Deed of Release. Anthony Gholson (Gholston) Junr of Spotsylvania Co planter for £50 sold & released to William Lea of King & Queen Co a 500 a. tr of land ... [same as above] ... . Wit: Saml Coleman, Antho Strother, Robert Goodloe. Ackn 7 Jun 1743 by Anthony Gholson Junr & Mary the w/o the sd Anthony ackn her right of dower & is admitted to record. Attest: Edmund Waller clk. (Pg 58)

6 Jun 1743. Deed of Lease. Thomas Todd of St. Stephens Parish, King & Queen Co gent for 5 shillings farm let to Richard Todd of same co all his pt/o a lot of ground in the town of Fredericksburgh described in the plat of the sd town by the figure 60 which was devised to him by the will of his father Col Wm Todd decd being on Princess Ann Street & William Street ... during the term of

one year paying the yearly rent of one grain of Indian corn on 10 Oct if demanded ... . Wit: John Latane, Patrick Dowdall, Joshua Thomas. Ackn 7 Jun 1743 & admitted to record. Attest: Edmund Waller clk. (Pg 60)

7 Jun 1743. Deed of Release. Thomas Todd of St. Stephens Parish, King & Queen Co gent for £15 sold & released to Richard Todd of same co a lot in the town of Fredericksburgh numbered 60 ... [same as above] ... . Wit: John Latane, Patrick Dowdall, Joshua Thomas. Ackn 7 Jun 1743 & admitted to record. Attest: Edmund Waller clk. (Pg 60)

5 Jul 1743. Deed. John Sartin & Anna his wife of Spotsylvania Co for £70 sold to the Rev. James Marye clerk of same co a plantation & 800 a. tr of land whereon the sd John Sartin now lives & is pt/o a patent granted to the sd John Sartin dated XXVIII Sep MDCCXXVIII for 1,000 a. in St. George Parish bounded by George Cook (a sale out of this patent), Edward Herndon, Col John Waller & Thos Sartin ... . Wit: John Waller, Richd Tutt, Wm Hughes. Ackn 5 Jul 1743 by John Sartin & Anna his wife & admitted to record. Attest: Edmund Waller clk. (Pg 62)

5 Jul 1743. Deed. Lawrence Washington now of Fairfax Co, VA gent for £42:10 sold to Robert Jackson of the town of Fredericksburgh gent one lot or ½ a. of land in the town of Fredericksburgh & is one of the sd town lots described in the plan of the sd town by the figure 37 & is bounded by Caroline Street, Charlotta Street, Lot No. 38 & Lot No. 39, the same ackn to the sd Lawrance Washington & conveyed by deed from the trustees of the sd town 7 Aug 1739 ... . Wit: Hancock Lee, Archd Mcpherson, Thos Slaughter. Ackn 5 Jul 1743 & admitted to record. Attest: Edmund Waller clk. (Pg 64)

21 Apr 1743. Deed. John Wiglesworth of St. George Parish, Spotsylvania Co for £103 sold to William Johnston of same place a 519 a. tr of land in St. George Parish bounded by William Richerson & Warner's line, the sd 519 a. of land out of which the sd John Wiglesworth doth reserve to himself 140 a. of land at the lower end as it was laid off for Benjamin Martin ... . Wit: Jas Taylor, Stephen Johnston, John Mountague. Proved 5 Jul 1743 & admitted to record. Attest: Edmund Waller clk. (Pg 65)

20 Jun 1743. Deed. Charles Filks Pigg of St. George Parish, Spotsylvania Co for £35 sold to William Johnston of same place a 94 a. tr of land in the parish afsd bounded by Pains Swamp or Stony Run, sd Johnston & an old mill dam ... . Wit: Robert King Junr, Thos Estes Junr, Larkin Johnston, Robert Farish, Samuel Warren. Ackn 5 Jul 1743 & admitted to record. Attest: Edmund Waller clk. (Pg 67)

9 Jun 1743. Deed. Humphrey Hill of King & Queen Co gent & Frances his wife for £310 sold to William Lynn of Fredericksburgh, Spotsylvania Co doctor of physic a lott or ½ a. of land in the sd town of Fredericksburgh known & described in the plan of the sd town by the number 22 bounded by a lot belonging to the sd Humphery Hill number 21 & now in the tenure of William Reid, George Street, Caroline Street & lot belonging to the sd Humphry Hill number 24 ... . Wit: John Champe, George Morton, Wm Hughes, John Taliaferro Junr. Ackn 5 Jul 1743 by Humphrey Hill gent & admitted to record. Attest: Edmund Waller clk. (Pg 69)

Commission. To John Camm, George Braxton Junr & Maurice Smith gent of King & Queen Co greeting, whereas Humphry Hill of King & Queen Co gent & Frances his wife by their deed of feofment [*see above*] have conveyed unto Doctor William Lynn of Spotsylvania Co the fee simple estate of one lot or parcel of land in Fredericksburgh town described by the figure 22, & whereas the sd Frances cannot conveniently travel to our co court to make acknowledgment of the sd conveyance, therefore we do give unto you or any two or more of you power to receive the acknowledgment which the sd Frances shall be willing to make before you & we do command that you do personally go to the sd Frances & receive her acknowledgment & examine her privily & apart from the sd Humphry Hill her husband whether she doth the same freely & voluntarily & whether she be willing that he same should be recorded ... . Wit Edmund Waller clerk of court 11 Jun MDCCXLIII. 1 Jul 1743 pursuant to the within commission wee John Camm & Maurice Smith went to the sd Frances Hill who ackn the indenture in our presence & declared she did the same freely & voluntarily ... . The within commission being duly returned in court 5 Jul 1743 is admitted to record. Attest: Edmund Waller clk. (Pg 72)

8 Jun 1743. Quit Claim. Elizabeth Hill of Fredericksburgh, Spotsylvania Co widow & relict of Thomas Hill late of Fredericksburg afsd gent decd for 5 shillings quit claim unto Humphrey Hill of King & Queen Co gent all manner of dower & right & title of dower whatsoever which the sd Elizabeth Hill now hath or may have in, to or out of all those two lotts or ½ acres of land in the sd town of Fredericksburg known in the plan of the sd town by the numbers 21 & 22 which the sd Humphrey Hill purch of the sd Thomas Hill decd in his lifetime ... . Wit: None. Ackn 5 Jul 1743 & admitted to record. Attest: Edmund Waller clk. (Pg 72)

1 Aug 1743. Deed. Robert Hutcherson of St. Mark Parish, Orange Co & Ann his wife sold to Peter Mountague of St. George Parish, Spotsylvania Co a 121 a. tr of land or woodland ground in St. Georges Parish the same being pt/o a pattent granted to Larkin Chew gent decd of St. George Parish, Spotsylvania Co dated 4 Jun 1722 & sold by the sd Larkin Chew to John Roye & bounded by Lewis's

line & Robert Beverlie .... Wit: John Wood, William Richerson, Thos Merry. Ackn 2 Aug 1743 by Robert Hutcherson & Ann his wife & admitted to record. Attest: Edmund Waller clk. (Pg 73)

2 Aug MDCCXLIII. Deed. William Holladay of St. George Parish, Spotsylvania Co & Judey his wife for £30 sold to John Holladay of same place a 200 a. tr of land in the parish afsd bounded by 200 a. of land which Thomas Sertain sold to James Terry which now belongs to the afsd John Holladay, James Taylor & Gustavas's line, the sd 200 a. of land is pt/o a patent granted to Thomas Sertain for 1,000 a. dated 6 May MDCCXXVII & by the sd Sertain sold to John Holladay gent decd father of the sd William Holladay ackn in co court 6 Nov MDCCXXXIX & the sd John Holladay gent decd in his will devised to the sd William Holladay .... Wit: Edmund Waller, Henry Pendleton, Reuben Daniel. Ackn 2 Aug 1743 by William Holladay & Judah his wife & admitted to record. Attest: Edmund Waller clk. (Pg 75)

1 Aug 1743. Deed of Lease. George Doggett of Orange Co for 5 shillings leased to William Ellis of Gloucester Co & Robert Ellis of Spotsylvania Co a 470 a. tr of land granted to Robert Slaughter of Essex Co by patent dated 20 Feb 1719 & conveyed to his son Robert Slaughter gent of Orange Co & by him conveyed to the afsd George Doggett by deeds of lease & released, bounded by the riverside & the Hunting Run ... during the term of one year paying the rent of one ear of Indian corn at the feast of St. Michal the Arch Angel if demanded .... Wit: H. Pendleton, Joel Parrish, John Gordon. Ackn 2 Aug 1743 & admitted to record. Attest: Edmund Waller clk. (Pg 78)

2 Aug 1743. Deed of Release. George Doggett of Orange Co for £100 sold & released to William Ellis of Gloucester Co & Robert Ellis of Spotsylvania Co a 470 a. tr of land ... [same as above] .... Wit: H. Pendleton, Joel Parrish, Jno Gordon. Ackn 2 Aug 1743 by George Doggett & Ann the w/o the sd George ackn her right of dower & is admitted to record. Attest: Edmund Waller clk. (Pg 79)

1 Jul 1743. Deed. John Williams of St. George Parish, Spotsylvania Co & Jannet (Jennet) his wife for £10 sold to Thomas Dillard of same place a 100 a. tr of land in St. George Parish & is pt/o a greater tr of Ralph Williams' that he had of Robert Stubblefeild & is bounded by the land of Matthews, Williams & Stubblefeild & the dividing line between the sd Mr. Williams & the afsd Dillard .... Wit: Robert Huddleston, Thomas Shurley. Ackn 2 Aug 1743 by John Williams & Jannet his wife & admitted to record. Attest: Edmund Waller clk. (Pg 81)

2 Aug 1743. Deed. Between John Allan of the town of Fredericksburgh in Spotsylvania Co of the one part & George Chapman of the same place of the other part, wit that whereas the directors of the town of Fredericksburgh by their deed did grant & convey unto the sd John Allan one lott or ½ a. of land in the sd town numbered 7 according to the plan of the sd town, now this indenture wit that the sd John Allan for £2:10 paid by the sd George Chapman hath sold & set over unto the sd George Chapman 20' square on the lower corner of the sd lott No. 7 next to the river bank adj Amelia Street ... . Wit: None. Ackn 3 Aug 1743 & admitted to record. Attest: Edmund Waller clk. (Pg 83)

6 Sep 1743. Deed. George Cook & Sarah his wife of St. George Parish, Spotsylvania Co for £13 sold to the Rev. James Marye clerk of same place a 200 a. tr of land in the parish afsd pt/o a patent granted to John Sertain dated XXVIII Sep MDCCXXVIII for 1,000 a. & is bounded by the land of James Taylor decd & Thomas Sertain ... . Wit: Cuthbert Sandys, C. Boreman. Ackn 6 Sep 1743 by George Cook & Sarah his wife & admitted to record. Attest: Edmund Waller clk. (Pg 84)

6 Sep 1743. Deed. Robert King Junr & Mary his wife of Spotsylvania Co for £80 sold to John Carter of co afsd a 150 a. tr of land bounded by a br of the River Po, Edward Carson, sd King's & Dalton's land ... . Wit: Robt Dudley, George Moore, Thomas Watts. Ackn 6 Sep 1743 by Robert King Junr & admitted to record. Attest: Edmund Waller clk. (Pg 85)

6 Sep MDCCXLIII. Deed. George Cook of St. George Parish, Spotsylvania Co & Sarah his wife for £12 sold to Henry Lewis of same place a 400 a. tr of land or woodland ground in St. George Parish bounded by the New Mine Bank Road, Griffin Fantleroy, Thomas Shelton, Joseph Roberts, Devils Ditch Swamp, George Musick & Nicholas Randall, which land was granted by patent 12 Feb MDCCXLII to the sd George Cook ... . Wit: None. Ackn 6 Sep 1743 by George Cook & Sarah his wife & admitted to record. Attest: Edmund Waller clk. (Pg 87)

At a court held 6 Sep 1743 Mary King the w/o Robert King ackn her deed [see above] to John Carter which is admitted to record. Attest: Edmund Waller clk. (Pg 89)

4 Oct 1743. Deed. John Clark & Ann his wife of St. Margarets Parish, Caroline Co for £32 sold to Abraham Estis Junr of St. Stephens Parish, King & Queen Co a 130 a. tr of land in St. George Parish on the n side the River Tay ... . Wit: Henry Brock, Wm Bartlet, A. Foster. Recorded further on by mistake. Attest: Edmund Waller clk. (Pg 90)

1 Oct 1743. Deed of Lease. Thomas Edmundson gent & Dorothy his wife of Essex Co for 5 shillings leased to James Garnett gent an 853 a. tr of land in St. George Parish & bounded as followeth that is to say 546 a. part thereof purch by William Fantleroy of Augt Smith adj Humphrey Hill, Major Wm Thornton, Buckner & Royston's line, & also 200 a. part thereof purch of Ed Price by the sd Wm Fantleroy adj a patent granted to John Buckner & John Royston, & also 107 a. the residue of sd 853 a. adj Hasel Run & Ed Price, the two parts mentioned was purch by the sd Thomas Edmundson of Wm Fantleroy & the last 107 a. purch by the sd Thomas Edmundson of James Roy ... during the term of one year paying the rent of one peper corn at the feast of St. Michael the Arch Angel if demanded ... . Wit: John Seyres, Jas Davis, John Levingston. Ackn 4 Oct 1743 by Thomas Edmondson gent & admitted to record. Attest: Edmund Waller clk. (Pg 91)

2 Oct 1743. Deed of Release. Thomas Edmondson & Dorothy his wife of Essex Co gent for £213 sold & released to James Garnett of co afsd gent an 853 a. tr of land ... [same as above] ... . Wit: John Seayres, Jas Davis, Jno Levingston. Ackn 4 Oct 1743 by Thomas Edmondson gent & admitted to record. Attest: Edmund Waller clk. (Pg 93)

4 Oct 1743. Deed. William Hansford & Sarah his wife of St. Georges Parish, Spotsylvania Co for £200 sold to the Rev. James Marye clerk of same place two trs of land, the one in parish afsd & whereon the sd William Hansford now lives containing 400 a. as appears by a patent granted unto James Canne for the same dated 15 Jul 1717 the sd 400 a. bounded by Francis Thornton, a br of Massaponax Swamp & a br of Hasle Run, the second tr of land in the parish afsd adj pt/o the 400 a. above mentioned contains 100 a. as appears by a deed of John Blackle to James Atkins dated 4 Apr MDCCXXIV & by another deed of James Atkins to William Hansford dated XI Aug MDCCXXVII the sd 100 a. bounded by Massapponax Run, Francis Thornton & Canne's line, it being pt/o a larger tr of land containing 180 a. by a deed dated 9 Feb MDCCXXIII ... . Wit: Jos Morton, George Morton, Jno Edwards. Ackn 4 Oct 1743 by William Hansford gent & Sarah his wife & admitted to record. Attest: Edmund Waller clk. (Pg 97)

4 Oct 1743. Deed. John Clark (Clerke) & Ann his wife of St. Margrets Parish, Caroline Co for £32 sold to Abraham Estis Junr of St. Stephens Parish, King & Queen Co a 130 a. tr of land in St. George Parish on the n side the River Tay ... . Wit: Henry Brock, Wm Bartlet, A. Foster. Ackn 4 Oct 1743 by John Clark & Ann his wife & admitted to record. Attest: Edmund Waller clk. (Pg 99)

3 Oct 1743. Deed of Lease. Edward Herndon Junr of St. George Parish, Spotsylvania Co for 5 shillings leased to George Stubblefeild of same place a

400 a. tr of land being a patent granted to Edward Herndon of King & Queen Co dated 16 Jun 1727 & bounded by Mrs. Mary Waller, Capt Larkin Chew & a Poyson Field ... during the term of one year paying on the last day of the sd term the rent of one ear of Indian corn if demanded .... Wit: None. Ackn 4 Oct 1743 by Edward Herndon & Elizabeth his wife & admitted to record. Attest: Edmund Waller clk. (Pg 101)

4 Oct 1743. Deed of Release. Edward Herndon Junr of St. George Parish, Spotsylvania Co & Elizabeth his wife for £41:1:6 sold to George Stubblefeild of same place a 400 a. tr of land ... [*same as above*] .... Wit: None. Ackn 4 Oct 1743 by Edward Herndon & Eliza his wife & admitted to record. Attest: Edmund Waller clk. (Pg 102)

5 Dec 1743. Deed. Joseph Red (Redd) of King & Queen Co, VA for £35 sold to James Red of the sd co a 223 a. tr of land bounded by Col John Lewis on the ridge between the River Ny & the brs of Nasaponix .... Wit: Samuel Hipkins, Margaret Hipkins, Suca Jones. Ackn 6 Dec 1743 & admitted to record. Attest: Edmund Waller clk. (Pg 105)

22 Aug MDCCXLIII. Deed. William Smither of Essex Co, VA planter for £9:16:9 sold to William Waller of Spotsylvania Co gent a 61 ½ a. tr of land bounded by the sd Waller, Robert Goodloe, Lawrence Anderson, Lick Swamp & Thomas Warren .... Wit: Wm Smither Junr, Robt Smither, Joseph Foster, John Wynill Sanders, John Warren. Proved 6 Dec 1743 & admitted to record. Attest: Edmund Waller clk. (Pg 107)

5 Dec 1743. Deed. Thomas Red of King & Queen Co, VA for £125 sold to Joseph Red of sd co a 377 a. tr of land upon the brs of Nassaponnax adj Col Lewis, Holloway's line & Elias Downes .... Wit: Saml Hipkins, James Redd, Suca Jones. Ackn 6 Dec 1743 & admitted to record. Attest: Edmund Waller clk. (Pg 109)

27 Jan 1743. Deed. Nicholas Randolph of Spotsylvania Co & Margarett his wife for £25 sold to John Graves of co afsd a plantation & 170 a. tr of land in St. George Parish bounded by the Mine Road, Wyatt's line, John Sartin & a road old Musick made, being pt/o a larger tr of land granted by pattent unto the sd Musick & by him sold unto the sd Nicholas Randolph .... Wit: Henry Chiles, Ambrose Musick, John Davis. Ackn 7 Feb 1743 by Nicholas Randall & Margaret his wife & admitted to record. Attest: Edmund Waller clk. (Pg 111)

7 Feb 1744. Deed. Henry Martin Junr of St. Margarets Parish, Caroline Co planter & Susanna his wife for £12:7:9 sold to Alexander Spencehead of St. George Parish, Spotsylvania Co planter a 166 a. tr of land or woodland ground

in St. Georges Parish the same being pt/o a patent formerly granted unto John Chew gent dated 4 Jun 1726 & sold unto Henry Junr & John Colquit Junr by a lease & release dated 31 Jan 1737 bounded by the Glady Run .... Wit: Joseph Hawkins, Isaac Darnell, Martin True. (Pg 112)

7 Feb 1743/4. Bond. I Henry Martin Junr of Caroline Co planter am firmly bound unto Alexander Spencehead planter of Spotsylvania Co in the sum of £24:15:6 ... the condition of this obligation is such that if the afsd Henry Martin Junr shall well & truly keep all the covenants mentioned & comprised in an indenture of feofment [see above] then this obligation to be void .... Wit: Joseph Hawkins, Martin True, Isaac Darnell. The deed ackn 7 Feb 1743 by Henry Martin Junr & Susanna his wife & the sd Martin ackn his bond & admitted to record. Attest: Edmund Waller clk. (Pg 113)

5 Mar 1743/4. Commission. Elliott Benger esqr sole deputy post master general of all his Majesty's Dominions in America have deputed & appointed the Honourable George Grame of the Island of Barbadoes esqr to be my lawfull & sufficient deputy to execute the office of postmaster of the Island of Barbadoes .... At a court held 6 Mar MDCCXLIII Elliott Benger esqr came into court & ackn this his commission to the Honble George Grame esqr of Barbadoes which is admitted to record. Attest: Edmund Waller clk. (Pg 114)

5 Mar 1743/4. Power of Attorney. I Elliott Benger of Newpost, VA sole deputy postmaster general of all his Majestys Dominions in North America & the West Indies have appointed the Honorable George Grame of the Island of Barbadoes esqr my true & lawfull atty to receive all such sums of money, debts, duties & demands whatsoever now due or hereafter to become due or payable unto me by Messrs William Cook & William Dunken or any other person who have had the direction or management of the post office in sd island since 24 Jun 1740 .... At a court held 6 Mar 1743 Elliott Benger esqr came into court & ackn this his power of atty to the Honble George Grame esqr of Barbadoes which is admitted to record. Attest: Edmund Waller clk. (Pg 115)

1 Mar 1743. Deed. Lawrance Washington now of Fairfax Co, VA gent for £42:10 sold to Francis Thornton of Spotsylvania Co gent a lot or ½ a. of land in the town of Fredericksburgh & is one of the sd town lots described in the plan of the sd town by the figure 39 bounded by Caroline Street & Hanover Street, the same being ackn to the sd Lawrance Washington & conveyed by deed from the trustees of the sd town 7 Aug MDCCXXXIX .... Wit: Mildred Willis, John Thornton, Henry Willis. Ackn 6 Mar 1743 by Lawrance Washington gent & Ann his wife & admitted to record. Attest: Edmund Waller clk. (Pg 116)

6 Mar 1743. Deed. James White & Sarah his wife of Hanover Co, VA for £29 sold to Thomas White of Spotsylvania Co a 300 a. tr of land devised to the sd James White by his father John White decd by the will of the sd John White duly proved & recorded in King William Co Court which sd land adj the land of the sd Thomas White, William Lea, Chilion White & Mr. Baylor ... . Wit: John Graves, William Lea. Ackn 6 Mar 1743 by James White & Sarah his wife & admitted to record. Attest: Edmund Waller clk. (Pg 117)

10 Feb 1743/4. Deed of Mortgage. Thomas Sanders of St. George Parish, Spotsylvania Co mason for £53:3 sold to Charles Coulston (Colson) of same place (as security for the above sum for me advanced) all manner of my personall estate which consists of one servant man named John Welch, two feather beds & furniture, five pewter basons, three pewter dishes, five pewter plates, two iron pots, one small iron kettle, four chairs, one square table with a frame drawer in it, one square cross legged table, four milch cows, five yearlings, two horses, one mare, five head of hoggs, 15 piggs, 1 frying pan, two pair of pot hooks, one hilling hoe, two wedges, three narrow axes, a bedtick & rug ... . Wit: Joseph Steward, Joshua Thomas. Ackn 6 Mar 1743 & admitted to record. Attest: Edmund Waller clk. (Pg 118)

2 Apr MDCCXLIV. Deed. Edmund Waller & Mary his wife of St. George Parish, Spotsylvania Co for £6 sold to John Sartin of same place a 200 a. tr of land pt/o a 552 a. tr of land granted by pattent to the sd Edmund Waller XXV Nov MDCCXLIII being in Devils Ditch in the parish afsd bounded by Griffin Fantleroy & George Cook ... . Wit: Thos Duerson, H. Pendleton. Ackn 3 Apr 1744 by Edmund Waller gent & admitted to record. Attest: Edmund Waller clk. (Pg 119)

1 May 1744. Deed. Thomas Foster of St. Marks Parish, Orange Co for 3,500 lbs of tobacco of VA sold to Thomas Salman (Solman) of St. George Parish, Spotsylvania Co a 400 a. tr of land which is now in the possession & occupation of the sd Thomas Salmon lying amongst the brs of Mattapony River bounded by Taliaferro Crag & Col Robinson ... . Wit: Ignatious Turman, Edmund Foster. Ackn 1 May 1744 & admitted to record. Attest: Edmund Waller clk. (Pg 121)

1 May 1744. Deed. Thomas West & Catherine his wife of Over Wharton Parish, Stafford Co, VA for £30 sold to William Long of St. George Parish, Spotsylvania Co a 250 a. tr of land or woodland ground in St. George Parish & is pt/o a patent granted to Joseph Brock gent decd & by him sold to the sd Thos West bounded by William Bartlet, Iron Mine Road, Bushes Road, Philip Sanders & Ackillis Br ... . Wit: Edmund Waller. Ackn 1 May 1744 by Thomas West & Catherine his wife & admitted to record. Attest: Edmund Waller clk. (Pg 122)

5 Jun 1744. Deed. Edward Ware of St. George Parish, Spotsylvania Co & Lucy his wife for £55 sold to Erasmus Wethers Allen of St. Anns Parish, Essex Co a plantation & 300 a. tr of land in St. George Parish which lyeth on both sides the Assforemost Run a br of Pamunkey River which being pt/o a 1,000 a. tr of land granted by pattent to Thomas Allen & George Musick 28 Sep 1728 which sd land adj John London ... . Wit: Benja Winslow, Hugh Sanders, Richd Phillips. Ackn 5 Jun 1744 by Edward Ware & admitted to record. Attest: Edmund Waller clk. (Pg 124)

27 Jul 1744. Deed of Lease. Cornelius Sale of Essex Co, VA for 5 shillings leased to Francis Thornton of Spotsylvania Co a 200 a. parcel of land being a tr of land purch by the sd Cornelius Sale of Augustine Smith 8 Apr 1731 & bounded by land sold by Augustine Smith to Peter Byrom, Fall Br, Henry Reaves, Henry Byrom (Byrum) & a br of Hazel Run ... during the term of one year paying the rent of one ear of Indian corn if demanded ... . Wit: Richard Childs, James Sale, Anthony Sale. Proved 7 Aug 1744 & admitted to record. Attest: Edmund Waller clk. (Pg 125)

28 Jul 1744. Deed of Release. Cornelius Sale of Essex Co, VA for £50 sold to Francis Thornton of Spotsylvania Co a 200 a. tr of land ... [same as above] ... . Wit: Richard Childs, James Sale, Anthony Sale. Proved 7 Aug 1744 & admitted to record. Attest: Edmund Waller clk. (Pg 126)

6 Aug 1744. Deed. Peter Mountague Junr of St. George Parish, Spotsylvania Co & his wife Anthorit for £40 sold to Roger Cason (Cayson) of Caroline Co an 84 a. tr of land or woodland ground being the same land as was John Foster's bounded by the River Po & Wm Solmon ... . Wit: William Johnston, Robert King Junr. Ackn 7 Aug 1744 by Peter Mountague Junr & admitted to record. At a court held 1 Oct 1745 Anthorit the w/o Peter Mountague Junr ackn this deed to Roger Cason. Attest: Edmund Waller clk. (Pg 128)

6 Aug 1744. Deed. Peter Mountague Junr of St. George Parish, Spotsylvania Co & Anthorit his wife for £40 sold to William Johnston of same place a 98 a. tr of land or woodland ground bounded by land of Abraham Brown now William Solmon's, land that was John Foster's now the sd Mountague's, Johnstons Ordinary & the plantation where John Snall lived ... . Wit: Robert King Junr, Roger Cason. Ackn 7 Aug 1744 by Peter Mountague Junr & admitted to record. At a court held 5 Aug 1746 Anthorit Mountague late the w/o Peter Mountague decd came into court & ackn this deed to Wm Johnston gent & the same is recorded. Attest: Edmund Waller clk. (Pg 130)

3 Sep 1744. Deed of Lease. Henry Chiles of St. George Parish, Spotsylvania Co planter for 5 shillings leased to George Seaton of St. John Parish, King

William Co gent a messuage & 600 a. tr of land in St. George Parish bounded by East North East River & land of Col Moore ... during the term of one year paying the rent of one ear of Indian corn upon the last day of the sd term if demanded .... Wit: George Morton, William Sandige, John Graves. Ackn 4 Sep 1744 & admitted to record. Attest: Edmund Waller clk. (Pg 133)

4 Sep 1744. Deed of Release. Henry Chiles of St. George Parish, Spotsylvania Co planter & Marcy his wife for £180 sold to George Seaton of St. John Parish, King William Co gent a 600 a. tr of land, pt/o a tr of land that was granted to the sd Henry Chiles & John Chiles as joint tenants whereof they made partition ... [same as above] .... Wit: George Morton, William Sandige, John Graves. Ackn 4 Sep 1744 by Henry Chiles & Mercy his wife & admitted to record. Attest: Edmund Waller clk. (Pg 134)

4 Sep 1744. Deed. Patterson Pulliam of Spotsylvania Co planter & Elizabeth his wife for £90 sold to Henry Chiles of same co planter a 250 a. tr of land lying on the n side of Pamunkey River in St. George Parish adj the land of Col Moore .... Wit: George Seaton, George Morton, John Graves. Ackn 4 Sep 1744 by Patterson Pulliam & Elizabeth his wife & admitted to record. Attest: Edmund Waller clk. (Pg 136)

24 Aug 1744. Deed of Lease. James Taylor of St. Stephens Parish, King & Queen Co for 5 shillings leased to Joseph Temple of St. Margarets Parish, King William Co an 800 a. tr of land in St. Georges Parish on both sides of Arnolds Run below the East North East on the n side the North Anna bounded by Arnold's line & Capt Christr Smith, the same being granted to John Taylor & James Taylor by pattent dated XXX Jun MDCCXXVI ... during the term of one year paying the rent of one pepper corn upon the feast of St. Michael the Archangel now next coming if demanded .... Wit: Michael Wharton, William Temple, Hannah Temple. Ackn 4 Sep 1744 & admitted to record. Attest: Edmund Waller clk. (Pg 138)

25 Aug 1744. Deed of Release. James Taylor of St. Stephens Parish, King & Queen Co & Martisha his wife for £40 & a 593 a. tr of land on the brs of Bever Dam Swamp in Hanover Co, being the same granted to the sd Joseph Temple by pattent dated 12 Mar MDCCXXXIX & ackn in Hanover Co Court by the sd Joseph Temple, the sd James Taylor hath sold & released unto the sd Joseph Temple of St. Margarets Parish, King William Co an 800 a. tr of land ... [same as above] .... Wit: Michael Wharton, William Temple, Hannah Temple. Ackn 4 Sep 1744 by James Taylor & admitted to record. N.B. look to page 168 for the feme coverts acknowledgment. Attest: Edmund Waller clk. (Pg 139)

3 Sep 1744. Deed of Lease. Edward Herndon Junr of St. George Parish, Spotsylvania Co for 5 shillings leased to Thomas Forster surgeon of same place a 337 a. tr of land bounded by Joseph Brock, Mr. Bowker, Achilles Br, Robert Coleman, Hugh Sanders & Ignatius Turman ... during the term of one year paying the rent of one ear of Indian corn the last day of the sd term if demanded .... Wit: William Lynn, Wm Smith, Charles Boreman. Ackn 4 Sep 1744 by Edward Herndon & Elizabeth his wife & admitted to record. Attest: Edmund Waller clk. (Pg 142)

4 Sep 1744. Deed of Release. Edward Herndon Junr of St. George Parish, Spotsylvania Co for £26:6 sold & released to Thomas Forster surgeon of same place a 337 a. tr of land ... [same as above] .... Wit: William Lynn, Wm Smith, Charles Boreman. Ackn 4 Sep 1744 by Edward Herndon & Eliza his wife & admitted to record. Attest: Edmund Waller clk. (Pg 143)

2 Oct 1744. Deed of Lease. William Lea (Lee) of King & Queen Co planter for 5 shillings leased to Anthony Garnett of Spotsylvania Co a 500 a. tr of land in St. George Parish bounded by the land of Musick & Allen & Capt Clowder ... during the term of one year paying the rent of an ear of Indian corn at the feast of St. Michaell the Arch Angel if demanded .... Wit: Jos Brock, John Coffey, Thos Foster. Ackn 2 Oct 1744 by William Lea & admitted to record. Attest: Edmund Waller clk. (Pg 146)

2 Oct 1744. Deed of Release. William Lee of King & Queen Co planter for £55:10 sold & released to Anthony Garnett of Spotsylvania Co a 500 a. tr of land ... [same as above] .... Wit: Jos Brock, Thos Foster, John Coffey. Ackn 2 Oct 1744 by William Lee & Rachel his wife & admitted to record. Attest: Edmund Waller clk. (Pg 147)

2 Oct 1744. Deed. Robert Williamson of Caroline Co & Elizabeth his wife for £50 sold to John Haley of Hanover Co a 400 a. tr of land bounded by Col Goin Corbin, Robinson Run & Taliaferro Cragg (Crag), by patern dated 10 Jan 1735 .... Wit: Wm Barber, William Rolfe, Jos Collins. Ackn 2 Oct 1744 by Robert Williamson & Elizabeth the w/o the sd Robert ackn her right of dower & admitted to record. Attest: Edmund Waller clk. (Pg 150)

2 Oct 1744. Bond. I Robert Williamson of St. Margarets Parish, Caroline Co am firmly bound unto John Haley in Hanover Co in the sum of £90 ... the condition of this obligation is such that if the afsd Robert Williamson shall well & truly fulfill, perform & observe all the clauses, bonds, covenants & agreements made & comprised in an indenture [see above] then this obligation to be void .... Wit: Wm Barber, Jos Collins, William Rolfe. Ackn 2 Oct 1744 & admitted to record. Attest: Edmund Waller clk. (Pg 151)

1 Oct 1744. Deed of Lease. John Thornton of the town of Fredericksburg in Spotsylvania Co gent for 5 shillings leased to David Bell of Henrico Co merchant a lot & ½ of a lot of land in the town of Fredericksburg whereon the Long Ordinary now stands & is the lot described in the plan of the sd town by the number 41 & ½ of the lot described by the number 43 & were purch by the sd John Thornton of the executors of Henry Willis esqr late decd by deed dated 4 Jun 1741 ... during the term of one year paying one pepper corn upon the feast of St. Michael the Arch Angel if demanded ... . Wit: William Hunter, Tho Prestwood Junr, Tully Choice. Ackn 2 Oct 1744 & admitted to record. Attest: Edmund Waller clk. (Pg 152)

2 Oct 1744. Deed of Release. John Thornton of the town of Fredericksburg in Spotsylvania Co gent for £290 sold & released to David Bell of Henrico Co merchant lot No. 41 & ½ of lot No. 43 in the town of Fredericksburg ... [same as above] ... . Wit: William Hunter, Thos Prestwood Junr, Tully Choice. Ackn 2 Oct 1744 & admitted to record. Attest: Edmund Waller clk. (Pg 153)

2 Oct 1744. Deed. Griffin Fantleroy Junr of Northumberland Co gent for £40 sold to Henry Lewis of Spotsylvania Co planter a 400 a. tr of land on the head of the River Ta in St. Georges Parish the sd tr of land being granted to Daniel Brown by pattent dated 24 Feb 1730 & bounded by Griffin Fantleroy Senr, John Bushes Mill Path & the Main Road ... . Wit: Wm Hughes, John Holladay. Ackn 2 Oct 1744 & admitted to record. Attest: Edmund Waller clk. (Pg 155)

2 Oct 1744. Deed. Henry Lewis of Spotsylvania Co & Martha his wife for £55 sold to Patterson Pulliam of sd co planter a 400 a. tr of land on the head of the River Ta in St. Georges Parish the sd tr of land being granted to Daniel Brown by pattent dated 24 Feb 1730 bounded by Griffin Fantleroy, John Bushes Mill Path & the Main Road ... . Wit: John Holladay, Wm Hughes. Ackn 2 Oct 1744 by Henry Lewis & Martha his wife & admitted to record. Attest: Edmund Waller clk. (Pg 157)

2 Oct 1744. Deed. Anthony Goldstone (Gholdston) & Jane his wife of St. Georges Parish, Spotsylvania Co for £50 sold to William Pollard of St. Thomas Parish, Orange Co a 120 a. parcel of land adj Terrys Run, it being pt/o a tr of land where the sd Anthony now lives which he formerly bought of John Chew ... . Wit: Edwd Herndon, A. Foster, Edmd Foster. Ackn 2 Oct 1744 & admitted to record. Attest: Edmund Waller clk. (Pg 159)

6 Nov 1744. Deed. William Gains of St. Thomas Parish, Orange Co, VA & Isabell his wife for £7 & 2,600 lbs of tobacco sold to Joseph Hawkins of St. George Parish, Spotsylvania Co a 442 ½ a. tr of land in St. George Parish being pt/o a tr containing 1,000 a. granted by pattent to Anthony Gholston dated 28

Sep 1728 ... . Wit: James Mills, James Jones, Jos Collins, William Collins.
Ackn 6 Nov 1744 by William Gains & Isabella his wife & admitted to record.
Attest: Edmund Waller clk. (Pg 160)

3 Dec 1744. Deed of Lease. John Mennefee & Mary his wife, James Stevens &
Alice his wife & James Kennerley & Elizabeth his wife planters for 5 shillings
leased to James Ball of White Chappell Parish, Lancaster Co gent an 850 a. tr of
land in St. George Parish adj a pattent formerly granted to Robert Taliaferro &
Lawrance Smith called Nassaponax Pattent, Stephen Sharp, a br of Nassaponex
& Francis & Anthony Thornton ... during the term of one year paying the rent of
one ear of Indian corn upon the last day of the sd term if demanded ... . Wit:
None. Ackn by the parties 4 Dec 1744 & admitted to record. Attest: Edmund
Waller clk. (Pg 162)

4 Dec 1744. Deed of Release. John Mennefee & Mary his wife, James Stevens
& Alice his wife & James Kennerley & Elizabeth his wife planters for £70 sold
& released to James Ball of White Chappell Parish, Lancaster Co gent an 850 a.
tr of land, granted to John James by pattent from the Secretarys office dated 30
Jun 1726 ... [same as above] ... . Wit: None. Ackn by the parties 4 Dec 1744
& admitted to record. Attest: Edmund Waller clk. (Pg 163)

4 Dec 1744. Bond. We John Mennefee, James Stevens & James Kennerley are
joyntly & severally bound unto James Ball of Lancaster Co in the sum of £200
... the condition of this obligation is such that if the afsd John Menefee, James
Stevens & James Kennerley & Mary, Alice & Elizabeth their wives do well &
truly observe, perform, fullfill & keep all the covenants, articles, conditions &
agreements mentioned in an indenture of release [see above] then this obligation
to be void ... . Wit: None. Ackn by the parties 4 Dec 1744 & admitted to
record. Attest: Edmund Waller clk. (Pg 165)

4 Dec 1744. Deed of Lease. John Menefee & Mary his wife, James Stevens &
Alice his wife & James Kennerley & Elizabeth his wife planters for £10 sold to
James Ball of White Chappell Parish, Lancaster Co gent a 249 a. tr of land in St.
George Parish adj a pattent formerly granted to Robert Taliaferro & Lawrence
Smith called Nassaponnax Pattent & Stephen Sharp ... during the respective
natural lives of the afsd Mary Menefee, Alice Stevens & Elizabeth Kennerley ...
. Wit: None. Ackn 4 Dec 1744 by the parties & admitted to record. Attest:
Edmund Waller clk. (Pg 165)

6 Nov 1744. Deed. Joseph Roberts of Spotsylvania Co & Susanna his wife for
£140 sold to William Sandage of sd co a 512 a. tr of land in St. Georges Parish
bounded by Roberts's patent line bought of Col James Taylor, Wyat's line
formerly Col Taylor's, Mr. Baylor's line & Gregory's line, 300 a. were purch of

Col James Taylor & from him conveyed to the sd Joseph Roberts, the other 212 a. were pt/o 1,000 a. granted by pattent unto the sd Joseph Roberts dated 28 Sep 1728 .... Wit: Thos Cowper, John Holladay, Isaac Bradburn. Ackn 6 Nov 1744 by Joseph Roberts & Susannah his wife & admitted to record. Attest: Edmund Waller clk. (Pg 167)

Commission. To John Camm, Humphry Hill, Maurice Smith & William Bird Richards gent greeting, whereas James Taylor of King & Queen Co & Martisha his wife by their deeds of lease & release dated 24 & 25 Aug have conveyed to Joseph Temple of King William Co the fee simple estate of 800 a. of land, & whereas the sd Martisha cannot conveniently travel to our co court to make acknowledgment of the sd conveyance, therefore we do give unto you or any two or more of you power to receive the acknowledgment & examine her privily & apart from the sd James Taylor her husband whether she doth the same freely & voluntarily & whether she be willing that the same should be recorded .... Wit Edmund Waller clerk of court 4 Sep 1744. 27 Nov 1744 pursuant to the commission wee John Camm & Humphry Hill went to the within named Martisha Taylor who ackn the indenture & declared she did the same freely & voluntarily & that she was willing the same should be recorded. The within commission being duly returned to the office is admitted to record. Attest: Edmund Waller clk. (Pg 168)

4 Dec 1744. Deed of Lease. Francis Thornton gent of Spotsylvania Co for & in consideration of the covenants & agreements together with the yearly rent hereafter mentioned have farm lett to George Head of same co planter & Elizabeth his wife a 200 a. tr of land adj John Procter, Abraham Darnell, the division line of the sd Francis & Anthony Thornton & the line of Humphry Bell of London ... during the natural life & lives of George Head & Elizabeth his wife & for & during the natural life of the longest liver of them paying yearly 530 lbs of neat tobacco during the sd term & is to pay the quitrents ... to the performance of the above agreements both parties hereby doth bind themselves to each other in the penal sum of 5,000 lbs of good tobacco .... Wit: John Waller, Richd Tutt, Wm Waller. Ackn 4 Dec 1744 & admitted to record. Attest: Edmund Waller clk. (Pg 169)

4 Dec 1744. Deed. William Samms & Mary his wife of St. George Parish, Spotsylvania Co for £25 sold to John Pain of same place a 100 a. tr of land pt/o a parcel of land devised the sd William by his father in the afsd parish adj Cattail Lick Br & Robinson's line .... Wit: Thos Duerson, Felix Gilbirt, Isaac Davis. Ackn 4 Dec 1744 & admitted to record. Attest: Edmund Waller clk. (Pg 170)

16 Nov 1744. Deed of Lease. William Prewett of Caroline Co planter for 5 shillings leased to John Shurley of same co planter a 200 a. tr of land pt/o a

pattent granted to the sd William Prewit for 400 a. adj John Smith ... during the term of one year paying on the last day of the sd term the rent of one ear of Indian corn if demanded ... . Wit: Wm Emerson, George Stubblefeild, Henry Williamson. Proved 4 Dec 1744 & admitted to record. Attest: Edmund Waller clk. (Pg 172)

17 Nov 1744. Deed of Release. William Prewett of Caroline Co planter for £25 sold to John Shurley of same co planter a 200 a. tr of land ... [same as above] ... . Wit: William Emerson, George Stubblefeild, Henry Williamson. Proved 4 Dec 1744 & admitted to record. Attest: Edmund Waller clk. (Pg 173)

12 Jan MDCCXXXXIV. Deed. George Woodroofe (Woodroof) of St. George Parish, Spotsylvania Co & Jane his wife for £33 sold to Henry Pendleton of same place a 300 a. tr of land or woodland ground granted by patent XXVIII Sep MDCCXXXVIII to William Smith gent decd being in St. George Parish bounded by the Main Road, William Prewit, John Smith & Robert Baylor, which sd land was sold by deeds of lease & release ackn in Spotsylvania Co court 5 Nov MDCCXXXIV by Richard Phillips adminr & Thomas Ballard Smith the heir at law of the sd Wm Smith decd to the sd George Woodroofe ... . Wit: Edwd Jones, Wm Searcy, Wm Woodroofe. Proved 5 Feb 1744 & admitted to record. At a court held 2 Jun 1747 Jane Woodroof the w/o George Woodroof ackn this deed for land to Henry Pendleton & admitted to record. Attest: Edmund Waller clk. (Pg 176)

17 Nov 1744. Deed of Gift. George Woodroof of St. Georges Parish, Spotsylvania Co planter & Jane his wife for naturall love & affection & 5 shillings hath given to George Woodroof Junr planter a 100 a. tr of land bounded by the Haw Br, Spring Br & Benjamin Woodroof, being pt/o a tr granted to the sd George Woodroof for 640 a. by patent dated 24 Jun 1726 ... . Wit: Benjamin Woodroof, William Woodroof, George Wilson. Proved 5 Feb 1744 & 2 Sep 1746 & admitted to record. Attest: Edmund Waller clk. (Pg 177)

20 Dec MDCCXLIV. Deed. John Farish of Spotsylvania Co for 5 shillings sold to William Waller of same co a 1 ½ a. tr of land on the n side the River Ta bounded by the place called Clayhole & the Mill Race ... agt the claim of all persons whatsoever & more especially agt the claim & right of dower of Sarah the now w/o the sd John Farish ... . Wit: Lark Chew, William Johnston, John Mitchell, William Login, Jos Brock. Proved 5 Feb 1744 & admitted to record. Attest: Edmund Waller clk. (Pg 179)

15 Nov 1744. Deed. Edward Coleman & Lucretia his wife of St. George Parish, Spotsylvania Co for £12 sold to Samuel Waggoner of Southfarnham Parish, Essex Co all the right, title, interest & estate whatsoever which is or shall

hereafter become due to them to a 100 a. parcel of land in St. George Parish with plantation bounded by Allen's line & John London .... Wit: James Waggoner, Jos Reynolds, Kerenhappuck Reeves. Ackn 5 Feb 1744 by Edward Coleman & Lucretia his wife & admitted to record. Attest: Edmund Waller clk. (Pg 181)

6 Feb 1744. Deed of Mortgage. John Elson of St. George Parish, Spotsylvania Co am firmly bound unto Anthony Strother of same place gent in the sum of £100 for the payment well & truly to be made by me on or before 10 May next insuing under the penal sum of £200 & for the further securing & confirming unto the sd Anthony Strother the payment of the sd £100 I do hereby sell & assign & make over unto the sd Anthony Strother 175 a. of land in St. George Parish & the following goods & chattels, viz, five cows, four heifers & two calves, one bay horse, one bay mare, 15 head of hoggs, 3 feather beds & furniture ... provided that if the sd John Elson shall well & truly pay the afsd sum of £100 on 10 May then this bond & mortgage to be void .... Wit: Z. Lewis, Wm Waller. Ackn 6 Feb 1744 & admitted to record. Attest: Edmund Waller clk. (Pg 182)

28 Jan 1744. Deed of Mortgage. William Potter of the town of Fredericksburgh barber hath sold unto Anthony Strother of the sd town merchant the following goods, viz, one feather bed,1 pr sheets, one pr blankits, three tables, four chairs, two stools, four chests, one trunk, one spinning wheel, four pails, two bedsteads, two looking glasses, four pewter dishes, 15 pewter plates, one iron pott & one kettle, being now at the time of this sale the property & in the possession of the sd Potter ... if the afsd William Potter shall pay unto the sd Anthony Strother by 10 Feb next ensuing the sum of £10:7:11 then the above goods to revert to the sd Potter as tho the above sale had not been made & the same is to be void .... Wit: Frans Tyler, John Prince. Proved 5 Mar 1744 & admitted to record. Attest: Edmund Waller clk. (Pg 183)

4 Mar 1744. Deed. George Cook & Sarah his wife of St. Georges Parish, Spotsylvania Co for £47 sold to Joseph Allen of Southfarnham Parish, Essex Co a 200 a. tr of land in St. George Parish being pt/o a patent granted to Harry Beverly decd & by his will pt/o the sd patent was bequeathed unto his dau Catharine which being now w/o George Stubblefeild & the afsd 200 a. of land was transferred & sold by the sd George Stubblefeild & Catharine his wife to the afsd George Cook in 1742 & is bounded by the sd George Stubblefeild, John Chew, Pamunkey River & the mouth of Plentifull .... Wit: James Waggoner, John Evans, Leonard Young. Ackn 5 Mar 1744 by George Cook & Sarah his wife & admitted to record. Attest: Edmund Waller clk. (Pg 184)

4 Mar MDCCXLIV. Deed. Between Robert King Junr & Mary his wife of Spotsylvania Co of the one part & Edward Cason of the same co of the other

part, wit that whereas the sd Edward Cason by his deed of gift dated 10 Jul MDCCXXIX ackn in Caroline Co Court did give & convey unto his dau Mary Cason one Negro man named Barbar, one Negro woman named Jenny & one Negro girl named Judey with their increase after the death of the sd Edward & in case the sd Mary (his dau) should die without heirs that then the sd negroes & their increase to return to the sd Edward & his heirs, since which making the deed afsd the sd Negroes are increase four so that their number is now seven & whereas the sd Mary on XXVIII Feb MDCCXXI intermarried with the sd Robert & the sd Robert & Mary having accepted pt/o the sd Negroes which were to them delivered (to wit Jenny a woman, Docter, Billy & Dick boys) XIII Mar year last mentioned instead of the whole number at the death of the sd Edward Cason, now this indenture wit that the sd Robert King Junr & Mary his wife in consideration of the four Negroes Jenny, Docter, Billy & Dick afsd to them delivered have sold unto the sd Edward Cason three Negro slaves named Barber a man, Judey a young woman & Travan a boy together with the increase of the sd Judey ... . Wit: Wm Waller, William Johnston, Edmund Foster, John Mitchell. Ackn 5 Mar 1744 by Robert King Junr & William Waller, William Johnston & John Mitchell gent three of the wits to the sd deed proved that they saw the sd Mary King execute the same & is admitted to record. Attest: Edmund Waller clk. (Pg 186)

21 Feb 1744. Deed of Gift. George Woodroofe of Spotsylvania Co planter & Jane his wife for & in consideration of natural love & affection & 5 shillings have given unto George Woodroofe Junr of co afsd planter a 100 a. tr of land bounded by Spring Br, Benjamin Woodroofe & the sd George Woodroofe Junr ... . Wit: John Minor, George Willson, Thos Graves. Proved 5 Mar 1744 & 2 Apr 1745 & admitted to record. Attest: Edmund Waller clk. (Pg 187)

28 Mar 1745. Deed of Gift. George Woodroofe of St. Georges Parish, Spotsylvania Co planter & Jane his wife for natural love & effection & 5 shillings have given to Benjamin Woodroof planter a 200 a. tr of land lying on both sides of Arnolds Run adj Capt Temple & Thos Hill, being pt/o a tr of 640 a. granted to the sd George Woodroof by patent dated 24 Jun 1726 ... . Wit: John Parrish, W. Miller, John Carter. Ackn 2 Apr 1745 by George Woodroofe & Jane his wife & admitted to record. Attest: Edmund Waller clk. (Pg 189)

8 Sep 1744. Deed. John Allan of Spotsylvania Co merchant for £25 sold to Charles Dick of same co merchant a lot or ½ a. of land in the town of Fredericksburgh & is one of the outside lots described in the plan of the sd town by the figure 51 & is bounded by Caroline Street & Lots No. 49 & 52 ... . Wit: John Thornton, Geo Chapman, Alexr Wright. Ackn 3 Apr 1745 & admitted to record. Attest: Edmund Waller clk. (Pg 190)

1 Apr 1745. Deed of Lease. Edmund Waller of St. George Parish, Spotsylvania Co for the consideration hereafter mentioned farm let unto Alexander Hume of same place during the natural life of the sd Alexander Hume & Mary his wife & for & during the natural life of the longest liver of them 90 a. of land being pt/o the sd tr of land whereon the sd Edmund Waller now lives & was granted by patent to the sd Edmund Waller 28 Sep 1728 & is bounded by the sd Waller, John Wiglesworth, the run side of Honey Swamp & Capt Humphry Hill ... for the first two years shall pay the quitrents of the sd land & plant on the sd premises 100 apple trees & 50 peach trees within the space of three years ... any more than one person they shall for every such person above the number of one pay yearly the rent of 20 shillings ... . Wit: Josias Baker, Edmund Foster. Ackn 3 Apr 1745 by Edmund Waller & Alexander Hume & admitted to record. Attest: Edmund Waller clk. (Pg 192)

6 May MDCCXLV. Deed of Lease. Augustine Owen of Middlesex Co planter for 5 shillings farm let to William Baskett of Caroline Co planter a 100 a. tr of land in St. George Parish bounded by Henry Goodloe & the n side of the North Fork ... during the term of one year paying the yearly rent of one grain of Indian corn on the feast of St. John the Baptist if demanded ... . Wit: John Hughes, Wm Martin. Ackn 7 May 1745 & admitted to record. Attest: Edmund Waller clk. (Pg 193)

7 May MDCCXLV. Deed of Release. Augustine Owen of Middlesex Co planter for £50 sold & released to William Baskett of Caroline Co planter a 100 a. tr of land ... [same as above] ... . Wit: John Hughes, Wm Martin. Ackn 7 May 1745 & admitted to record. Attest: Edmund Waller clk. (Pg 194)

7 May 1744. Deed. William Sandidge & Ann (Anne) his wife of Spotsylvania Co for £35 sold to Anthony Golston (Golson) Junr of same co a 200 a. tr of land in St. George Parish bounded by Sartin's patent line ... . Wit: None. Ackn 7 May 1745 by William Sandige & Ann his wife & admitted to record. Attest: Edmund Waller clk. (Pg 195)

7 May 1745. Deed of Lease. Nicholas Hawkins of St. George Parish, Spotsylvania Co for 5 shillings leased to Nathan Hawkins of same place a 200 a. tr of land bounded by River Po & a small island in the river (it being pt/o a grant to Larkin Chew for 3800 a. & since sold by the sd Chew to William Lindsey by deed dated 5 Nov 1722 & since sold by the sd Lindsey to the sd Hawkins by lease & release dated 25 & 26 Apr 1743) ... . Wit: Parmenas Bowker, Alexander Hawkins, Thomas Cartwright. Ackn 7 May 1745 & admitted to record. Attest: Edmund Waller clk. (Pg 196)

7 May 1745. Deed of Release. Nicholas Hawkins of St. George Parish, Spotsylvania Co for £60 sold to Nathan Hawkins of same place a 200 a. tr of land ... [*same as above*] .... Wit: Parmanas Bowker, Alexander Hawkins, Thomas Cartwright. Ackn 7 May 1745 & admitted to record. Attest: Edmund Waller clk. (Pg 198)

19 Apr 1745. Deed of Lease. Anthony Thornton & Winifred his wife of Stafford Co gent for 5 shillings leased to Sharshall Grasty of Spotsylvania Co a 222 a. tr of land in St. Georges Parish bounded by the sd Grasty, Wm McWilliams, George Nix, John James's patent & sd Thornton's patent ... during the term of one year paying the rent of one ear of Indian corn at the feast of St. Michael the Arch Angel if demanded .... Wit: Wm Waller, John Farish, Wm McWilliams. Ackn 7 May 1745 by Anthony Thornton gent & admitted to record. Attest: Edmund Waller clk. (Pg 200)

20 Apr 1745. Deed of Release. Anthony Thornton & Winifred his wife of Stafford Co gent for £27:15 sold & released to Sharshall Grasty of Spotsylvania Co a 222 a. tr of land, being pt/o a patent granted unto the sd Anthony Thornton & Francis Thornton for 2,740 a. of land dated 19 Apr 1720 ... [*same as above*] .... Wit: Wm Waller, John Farish, Wm McWilliams. Ackn 7 May 1745 by Anthony Thornton gent & admitted to record. Attest: Edmund Waller clk. (Pg 201)

19 Apr 1745. Deed of Lease. Anthony Thornton & his wife Winifred of Stafford Co gent for 5 shillings leased to William McWilliams of Spotsylvania Co a 434 a. tr of land in St. George Parish bounded by the sd McWilliams, Mr. Rains, Mr. Grasty, sd Thornton, George Nix, John Elson & Richard Childs ... during the term of one year paying the rent of one ear of Indian corn at the feast of St. Michael the Arch Angel if demanded .... Wit: Wm Waller, John Farish, Sharshall Grasty. Ackn 7 May 1745 by Anthony Thornton gent & admitted to record. Attest: Edmund Waller clk. (Pg 202)

20 Apr 1745. Deed of Release. Anthony Thornton & Winifred his wife of Stafford Co gent for £43:8 sold & released to William McWilliams of Spotsylvania Co a 434 a. tr of land, being pt/o a patent granted unto the sd Anthony Thornton & Francis Thornton for 2,740 a. of land dated 19 Apr 1720 ... [*same as above*] .... Wit: Wm Waller, John Farish, Sharshall Grasty. Ackn 7 May 1745 by Anthony Thornton gent & admitted to record. Attest: Edmund Waller clk. (Pg 203)

3 Jun 1745. Deed. Dudley Gatewood of St. George Parish, Spotsylvania Co planter & Sarah his wife for £8:10 sold to Henry Gatewood Senr of same place an 83 a. tr of land or woodland ground (it being pt/o a tr the sd Dudley

Gatewood bought of Hugh Saunders) on the Glady Fork bounded by Glady Run, sd Henry Gatewood's Spring Br & Ignatious Tureman ... . Wit: Robert Coleman, Henry Gatewood Junr, Wm Gatewood. Ackn 4 Jun 1745 by Dudley Gatewood & Sarah his wife & admitted to record. Attest: Edmund Waller clk. (Pg 206)

3 Jun 1745. Deed. Robert Coleman of St. George Parish, Spotsylvania Co planter & Sarah his wife for £31:6:6 sold to Henry Gatewood Senr of same place a 174 a. tr of land or woodland ground on the Glady Fork bounded by the Glady Run ... . Wit: Henry Gatewood Junr, Wm Gatewood, Dudley Gatewood. Ackn 4 Jun 1745 by Robert Coleman & Sarah his wife & admitted to record. Attest: Edmund Waller clk. (Pg 207)

4 Jun 1745. Deed of Gift. Nicholas Hawkins of St. George Parish, Spotsylvania Co planter for fatherly love & affection have given to my son James Hawkins one Negro man named Boson & 100 a. of land the same in the parish afsd bounded by Owen Thomas, Francis Smith, William Richerson, William Johnston, Jarmanah Road, Chiswells Mine Road & Oen Thomas ... . Wit: John Parrish, Jacob Fox. Ackn 4 Jun 1745 by Nicholas Hawkins Senr & admitted to record. Attest: Edmund Waller clk. (Pg 208)

4 Jun 1744. Deed. William Samms & Mary his wife of St. George Parish, Spotsylvania Co for £10 sold to James Samms of same place an 18 a. tr of land pt/o a parcel of land devised the sd William by his father in St. George Parish adj Stevens's corner ... . Wit: Wm Carr, John Bigger, John Carr Junr. Ackn 4 Jun 1745 by William Samms & admitted to record. Attest: Edmund Waller clk. (Pg 209)

4 Jun 1745. Deed. James Sams (Samms) & Anne his wife of St. George Parish, Spotsylvania Co for £10 sold to William Sams (Samms) of same place a 34 a. tr of land pt/o a parcel of land devised the sd James by his father in St. George Parish adj the sd Sams, Abel Stears, Cattail Lick Br & Tolbert's line ... . Wit: Wm Carr, John Bigger, John Carr Junr. Ackn 4 Jun 1745 by James Samms & admitted to record. Attest: Edmund Waller clk. (Pg 211)

3 Jun 1745. Deed of Lease. Robert Coleman & Sarah his wife of St. George Parish, Spotsylvania Co for 5 shillings leased to Thomas Forster surgeon of same place a 400 a. tr of land bounded by Achilles Bowker & Elstons Run, it being a patent granted to Ralph Bowker for 400 a. dated 20 Feb 1719 & since renewed by Bird Bowker by a patent dated 20 Jul 1736 & since sold by Achilles Bowker to the sd Robert Coleman ... during the term of one year paying the rent of one ear of Indian corn on the last day of the sd term if demanded ... . Wit:

A. Foster, John Gordon, Jno Parrish. Ackn 4 Jun 1745 by Robert Coleman & Sarah his wife & admitted to record. Attest: Edmund Waller clk. (Pg 212)

4 Jun 1745. Deed of Release. Robert Coleman & Sarah his wife of St. George Parish, Spotsylvania Co for £150 sold & released to Thomas Forster surgeon of same place a 400 a. tr of land ... [*same as above*] ... . Wit: A. Foster, John Gordon, Jno Parrish. Ackn 4 Jun 1745 by Robert Coleman & Sarah his wife & admitted to record. Attest: Edmund Waller clk. (Pg 214)

13 May 1745. Deed of Lease. John Robinson esqr of Strutton Major Parish, King & Queen Co for £36 leased to Thomas Collins planter of St. George Parish, Spotsylvania Co a 300 a. tr of land in St. Georges Parish it being pt/o a grant formerly granted unto the sd John Robinson adj Lewis Conner & the s side of the South Po ... during the term of one year paying the rent of one ear of Indian corn at the feast of St. Michael the Arch Angell if demanded ... . Wit: Humphrey Hill, Jos Collins, Wm Collins, G. Braxton Junr. Proved 4 Jun 1745 & admitted to record. Attest: Edmund Waller clk. (Pg 216)

14 May 1745. Deed of Release. John Robinson esqr of King & Queen Co for £36 sold & released to Thomas Collins of Spotsylvania Co a 300 a. tr of land ... [*same as above*] ... . Wit: Humphrey Hill, Jos Collins, Wm Collins, G. Braxton Junr. Proved 4 Jun 1745 & admitted to record. Attest: Edmund Waller clk. (Pg 217)

14 May 1745. Deed. John Robinson of Strutton Major Parish, King & Queen Co esqr for £15 sold to Joseph Collins of Spotsylvania Co planter a 254 a. tr of land which is now in the possession & occupation of the sd Joseph Collins it being pt/o a tr of 4,059 a. of land belonging to the sd John Robinson in the fork & on the n side of the River Po which sd 254 a. of land was layed off by Owen Thomas & is adj Joseph Collins ... . Wit: Humphrey Hill, Thos Collins, Wm Collins, G. Braxton Junr. Proved 4 Jun 1745 & admitted to record. Attest: Edmund Waller clk. (Pg 218)

13 May 1745. Deed of Lease. John Robinson esqr of Strutton Major Parish, King & Queen Co for £24 leased to William Collins of same place a 200 a. tr of land in St. Georges Parish it being pt/o a grant formerly granted unto the sd John Robinson adj the lands of Corbin, Spotswood & the sd Robinson & Lewis Conner ... during the term of one year paying the rent of one ear of Indian corn at the feast of St. Michell the Arch Angell if demanded ... . Wit: Humphrey Hill, G. Braxton Junr, Jos Collins, Thos Collins. Proved 4 Jun 1745 & admitted to record. Attest: Edmund Waller clk. (Pg 219)

14 May 1745. Deed of Release. John Robinson esqr of King & Queen Co for £24 sold & released to William Collins of same co a 200 a. tr of land ... [*same as above*] ... . Wit: Humphrey Hill, G. Braxton Junr, Jos Collins, Thos Collins. Proved 4 Jun 1745 & admitted to record. Attest: Edmund Waller clk. (Pg 220)

2 Jul MDCCXLV. Deed. William Hunter of Spotsylvania Co gent & Martha his wife for £16:13:4 sold to John Allan of co afsd gent a 10 a. 20 perches tr of land near to the town of Fredericksburgh adj Humphry Hill, Henry Willis decd, John Royston, several lots or ½ acres of land adj to the town of Fredericksburgh formerly laid off & sold by the exrs of Henry Willis gent decd at publick auction & the sd John Allen ... . Wit: Edmund Waller. Ackn 2 Jul 1745 by William Hunter gent & Martha his wife & admitted to record. Attest: Edmund Waller clk. (Pg 222)

2 Jul MDCCXLV. Deed. William Hunter of Spotsylvania Co gent & Martha his wife for £16:13:4 sold to Humphrey Hill of King & Queen Co gent a 10 a. 20 perches tr of land near to the town of Fredericksburgh adj to lands of John Allan, several lots or ½ acres of land that adj to the town of Fredericksburgh formerly laid off & sold at publick auction by the exrs of Henry Willis gent decd, the land of the sd William Hunter & the sd Henry Willis decd ... . Wit: Edmund Waller. Ackn 2 Jul 1745 by William Hunter gent & Martha his wife & admitted to record. Attest: Edmund Waller clk. (Pg 223)

2 Jul 1745. Deed. William Long & Ann his wife of St. George Parish, Spotsylvania Co for £37 sold to Thos Duerson of same place a 250 a. tr of land or woodland ground in St. George Parish pt/o a pattent granted to Joseph Brock gent decd & by him sold & conveyed to Thomas West & by the sd Thomas West sold to the afsd William Long & is bounded by William Bartlett, Iron Mine Road, Bushes Road, Philip Sanders & the Achilles Br ... . Wit: Edmund Waller, Henry Brock, Barbrey Brock. Ackn 2 Jul 1745 & admitted to record. Attest: Edmund Waller clk. (Pg 224)

29 Jun 1744. Deed. Bloomfeild Long of St. George Parish, Spotsylvania Co & Mary his wife for £60 sold to Anthony Foster of same place a 331 a. tr of land in the parish afsd bounded by Joseph Brock, John Walker & William Branagen, the sd land is pt/o a pattent for a larger quantity of land granted to Larkin Chew 4 Jun 1722 & by divers mesne conveyances is become vested in the sd Bloomfeild Long ... . Wit: Henry Brock, Thos Duerson, Hannah Duerson, W. Miller, Peter Mountague Junr. Wit to Livery & Seizen: Henry Brock, William Brock, Wm Long. Ackn 2 Jul 1745 by Bloomfeild Long & Mary his wife & admitted to record. Attest: Edmund Waller clk. (Pg 226)

5 Aug 1744. Deed of Lease. William Marshall of Caroline Co planter for 5 shillings leased to Richard Durrett of Orange Co planter a 400 a. tr of land which sd tr of land was granted by patent to Thomas Allen & by the sd Allen sold & conveyed to the sd William Marshall & is bounded by the sd Marshall, Henry Goodloe, West Side Br, Robert Baylor & the County Line ... during the term of one year paying the rent of one ear of Indian corn on Lady day next if demanded .... Wit: Han Lee, John Willis, Jno Madison. Ackn & admitted to record. Attest: Edmund Waller clk. (Pg 228)

6 Aug 1744. Deed of Release. William Marshall of Caroline Co planter for £5 sold & released to Richard Durrett of Orange Co planter a 400 a. tr of land ... [same as above] .... Wit: Han Lee, John Willis, Jno Madison. Ackn 6 Aug 1745 & admitted to record. Attest: Edmund Waller clk. (Pg 229)

16 Jul MDCCXLV. Deed. Richard Couzens of Spotsylvania Co planter & Elizabeth his wife for £20 sold to William Waller of sd co gent a 100 a. tr of land in St. George Parish on the s side the Middle River of Mattapony, which sd land is pt/o a greater tr of land granted by patent to John Rogers & several other persons .... Wit: Jos Brock, Nicholas Horn, Margret Ship. Ackn 6 Aug 1745 by Richard Couzens & Elizabeth his wife & admitted to record. Attest: Edmund Waller clk. (Pg 230)

6 Aug 1745. Deed. John Pain & Frances his wife of St. George Parish, Spotsylvania Co for £26:5 sold to John Talburt (Talbert) of same place a 100 a. tr of land pt/o a parcel of land devised to the sd Wm Sams (sic) by his father in the sd parish adj the Cattail Lick Br & Robinson's line .... Wit: Jos Brock, James Lea, John Graves. Ackn 6 Aug 1745 & admitted to record. Attest: Edmund Waller clk. (Pg 231)

25 Jun1 1745. Deed. John Talburt (Talbert) of St. George Parish, Spotsylvania Co & Margret his wife for £12 sold to Jeremiah Stevans of same place a 36 a. tr of land in St. George Parish on the Cattail Swamp Br of Mattapony River bounded by Joseph Brock, the orphans of James Samms, Talbert's line, James Stevans, Cattail Run & Cattail Fork Swamp, the same being pt/o a larger tr of land formerly granted unto Larkin Chew by Letters Pattent dated 4 Jun 1722 & by him sold to Amey Sutton & by the sd Sutton sold unto the sd John Talburt ... . Wit: Robt Huddleston, Mathew Hubbard. Ackn 6 Aug 1745 by John Talbert & Margaret his wife & admitted to record. Attest: Edmund Waller clk. (Pg 233)

A 2,946 a. tr of land in Spotsylvania Co devised by Francis Wiatt late of Gloucester Co decd to his children named William, Edward, Thomas & Ann (the sd Ann is since married to John Thurston) which sd tr is divided among the sd Wm, Edwd, Thomas & Ann in the following manner, 667 a. of land now laid off for William Wiat, 667 a. of land now laid off for Edward Wiatt, 667 a. of land now laid off for Thomas Wiatt, 945 a. of land now laid off for John Thurston & Ann his wife. [*Drawing not included here.*]

29 Aug 1745. The plan & division are collected from the works of William Daniel Junr who lately divided the 2,946 a. of land among William Wiat, Edward Wiat, Thomas Wiat & John Thurston & Ann his wife according to the plan. Certified per Wm Waller surveyor. (Pg 235)

Names mentioned in the drawing: Zachary Lewis on the n side Holladays Run. Corner to Joseph Peterson now Wm Sandige's land. Corner to the sd Roberts now Sandige. Mr. Trusty's fence. The s side of East North East now Holladays & formerly Allen's corner. Holladay's line. William Wiatt's line. George Musick's line.
(Pg 236)

XXIX Aug MDCCXLV. Whereas the above mentioned land was devised to us by the will of Francis Wiatt decd & we having in pursuance of the sd devise, lately divided the same among us in the following manner, viz, William Wiat, Edward Wiat & Thomas Wiat each 667 a., John Thurston (in right of Ann his wife) the remainder of the land being 945 a. We do agree that the same is the true division & bounds between us & so shall forever remain & continued between us, our heirs & assigns ... & desire the same may be recorded .... Wit: Wm Waller, Jos Brock, Nicholas Horn. Proved 3 Sep 1745 & admitted to record. Attest: Edmund Waller clk. (Pg 236)

1 Oct 1745. Deed. Edwin Hickman of Albe[?] Co for £22 sold to Giles Tompkins of Spotsylvania Co a 209 ½ a. tr of land on Low Ground Swamp bounded by Zachary Lewis, Hunney Swamp & Woolfolk's line formerly known by the name of Smith's line .... Wit: Chrisr Tompkins, Henry Chiles. Ackn 1 Oct 1745 & admitted to record. Attest: Edmund Waller clk. (Pg 237)

9 Aug 1745. Deed of Gift. Robert Coleman of Drysdale Parish, Caroline Co for natural love & paternal affection have given unto my well beloved & dutiful son Thomas Coleman of same place a 346 a. tr of land being pt/o two patents granted to the sd Robert Coleman dated 2 Dec 1723 & 16 Jun 1727 the sd land lying on the n side of the Robinson Run adj the land of Col John Waller, William Bradburn & Spilsbey Coleman .... Wit: Thos James, Richard Coleman, Joseph Ray. Proved 1 Oct 1745 & admitted to record. Attest: Edmund Waller clk. (Pg 238)

21 Sep 1745. Deed. George Woodroofe Junr of St. Margerits Parish, Caroline Co, VA planter & Ann his wife for 5 shillings sold to Thomas Graves of St. Georges Parish, Spotsylvania Co planter a 200 a. tr of land it being a parcel of land made over to the sd George Woodroofe Junr by his father George

Woodroofe by two deeds the first hundred bounded by the Haw Br, Spring Br & Benjamin Woodroofe, the second hundred is bounded by a fork of the Spring Br, Benja Woodroofe & the sd George Woodroofe Junr ... . Wit: Jno Parrish, Wm Williams, A. Foster. Ackn 1 Oct 1745 & admitted to record. Attest: Edmund Waller clk. (Pg 239)

30 Sep 1745. Deed of Lease. Richard Todd of King & Queen Co gent for 5 shillings leased to William Lynn of the town of Fredericksburgh doctor of physick a lot of ground in the town of Fredericksburgh described in the platt of the town by the figure 60 which sd lot was devised by the will of Col William Todd formerly of King & Queen Co decd unto his son Thomas Todd of the sd co gent who by his deeds of lease & release dated 6 & 7 Jun 1743 did sell & release the sd lott unto the afsd Richard Todd lying on Princess Anne Street & William Street ... during the term of one year paying the rent of one pepper corn on Lady day next if demanded ... . Wit: W. Kelly, Edwd Herndon, Wm Hughes. Ackn 1 Oct 1745 & admitted to record. Attest: Edmund Waller clk. (Pg 241)

1 Oct 1745. Deed of Release. Richard Todd of King & Queen Co gent for £40 sold & released to William Lynn of the town of Fredericksburgh doctor of physic a lot of ground in the town of Fredericksburgh No. 60 ... [*same as above*] ... . Wit: W. Kelly, Edwd Herndon, Wm Hughes. Ackn 1 Oct 1745 & admitted to record. Attest: Edmund Waller clk. (Pg 242)

30 Sep 1745. Deed of Lease. Adam Read (Reid) of Urbanna, Middlesex Co merchant for 5 shillings leased to John Tayloe Junr of Richmond Co ½ a. or lot of land in the town of Fredericksburg described in the plat of the sd town by the figure 14 bounded by Caroline Street & Charlotta Street ... during the term of one year paying the rent of one pepper corn on Lady day next if demanded ... . Wit: Robert Burwell, John Champe, James Hunter, William Black. Ackn 1 Oct 1745 & admitted to record. Attest: Edmund Waller clk. (Pg 244)

1 Oct 1745. Deed of Release. Adam Read (Reid) of the town of Urbanna, Middlesex Co merchant for £141 sold & released to John Tayloe Junr of Richmond Co esqr a lot in the town of Fredericksburg No. 14 ... [*same as above*] ... . Wit: Robert Burwell, John Champe, James Hunter, William Black. Ackn 1 Oct 1745 & admitted to record. Attest: Edmund Waller clk. (Pg 245)

3 Jun 1745. Deed. John Martin of King & Queen Co for 5 shillings sold to Robert Farrish of St. George Parish, Spotsylvania Co a 400 a. tr of land or woodland ground bounded by Prosser's line, Henry Rains & Company, a Poyson Field & Warner's line ... . Wit: William Johnston, John Coleman, Henry May, Richd Coleman. Proved 1 Oct 1745 & admitted to record. Attest: Edmund Waller clk. (Pg 247)

2 Jul MDCCXLV. Deed. Robert Spilsbe Coleman of Essex Co, VA & Sarah his wife for £25 sold to Richard Couzens of Spotsylvania Co a 100 a. tr of land whereon William Dyer formerly dwelt in St. George Parish & on the brs of Pamunkey River .... Wit: John Edmondson, Richd Coleman, John Willson, Richard Shipp. Ackn 2 Jul 1745 by Robert Spilsbee Coleman & admitted to record. Attest: Edmund Waller clk. (Pg 248)

Commission. To Alexander Parker, William Dangerfeild & Benjamin Winslow of Essex Co gent greeting, whereas Robert Spilsbee Coleman of Essex Co & Sarah his wife by their deed [see above] have conveyed unto Richard Couzins of Spotsylvania Co the fee simple estate of 100 a. of land, & whereas the sd Sarah cannot conveniently travel to our co court to make acknowledgment of the sd conveyance, therefore we do give to you or any two or more of you power to receive the acknowledgment which the sd Sarah shall be willing to make before you & we do therefore command that you do personally go to the sd Sarah & receive her acknowledgment & examine her privily & apart from her husband whether she doth the same freely & voluntarily & whether she be willing that the same should be recorded .... Wit Edmund Waller clerk of court VIII Jul 1745. 19 Sep 1745 at Essex in obedience to the within commission to us directed we Alexander Parker & Wm Dangerfield this day repaired to the sd Sarah Coleman & did examine her privily & apart from her husband & she did freely & voluntarily ackn that she was willing the indenture should be recorded. The within commission being returned it is admitted to record. Attest: Edmund Waller clk. (Pg 250)

31 Oct 1745. Deed. Thomas Cartwright of St. George Parish, Spotsylvania Co & Rachel his wife for £25 sold to George Sheppard of same place a 60 a. tr of land whereon the sd George Sheppard now lives it being pt/o a 140 a. tr of land whereon the sd Cartwright now dwells & which the sd Thomas Cartwright bought of Col James Taylor bounded by the e side of the East North East Run ... . Wit: Edmund Waller, Mary Waller, Ephraim Musick. Ackn 5 Nov 1745 by Thomas Cartwright & Rachel his wife & admitted to record. Attest: Edmund Waller clk. (Pg 251)

4 Nov 1745. Deed. Peter Mountague of St. George Parish, Spotsylvania Co & Elizabeth his wife for £70 sold to John Long of Essex Co a 100 a. tr of land or woodland ground bounded by Warner's line & Robert Beverley .... Wit: Owen Thomas, Nicholas Hawkins Junr, Nicholas Hawkins Senr. Ackn 5 Nov 1745 by Peter Mountague & Elizabeth his wife & admitted to record. Attest: Edmund Waller clk. (Pg 252)

5 Nov MDCCXLV. Deed. William Baskett of Spotsylvania Co & Elizabeth his wife for £23 sold to Jeremiah White of same co a 100 a. tr of land in St. George

Parish bounded by Henry Goodloe & the n side of the Northfolk .... Wit:
Edmund Waller. Ackn 5 Nov 1745 by William Baskett & admitted to record.
At a court held 2 Sep 1746 Elizabeth Baskett ackn this deed which is admitted to
record. Attest: Edmund Waller clk. (Pg 254)

4 Feb 1745. Deed of Gift. George Carter of St. George Parish, Spotsylvania Co
& Eliza his wife in consideration of natural love & affection have given to their
son in law John Lea of same place & Ann his wife their dau a 185 a. tr of land in
St. George Parish bounded by John Robinson esqr, Robt Coleman, Paupen
Swamp & Col John Waller ... during the joint & separate lives of the sd John &
Ann & after their decease to the issue of the sd John & Ann if any there be at the
death of the longest liver of them, if the sd Jno Lea & Ann his wife shall depart
this life without leaving any issue behind them then these presents shall cease &
be utterly void .... Wit: None. Ackn 4 Feb 1745 by George Cater & admitted
to record. Attest: Edmund Waller clk. (Pg 255)

--- 1745. Deed of Gift. Robert Coleman of Drysdale Parish, Caroline Co for
natural love & paternal affection have given to my well beloved & dutifull son
John Coleman of Spotsylvania Co a 316 a. tr of land it being pt/o a patent
granted to the sd Robert Coleman dated 2 Dec 1723 lying on the s side the
Robinson Run adj the land of Robert & Richard Coleman .... Wit: Ed Wiat,
Samuel Hawes, Thomas Coleman, Wiat Coleman. Proved 4 Feb 1745 &
ordered to be certifyed. Further proved 3 Jun 1746 & admitted to record. Attest:
Edmund Waller clk. (Pg 256)

5 Nov MDCCXLV. Deed. Benjamin Woodroofe of St. George Parish,
Spotsylvania Co & Mary his wife for £40 sold to William Davenport of St.
Martins Parish, Louisa Co a 200 a. tr of land or woodland ground in St. George
Parish on both sides of Arnolds Run adj to the lands of Capt Joseph Temple &
Thos Hill & is pt/o a greater tr of land granted by patent to George Woodroofe
24 Jun 1726 for 640 a., which was given by George Woodroofe father of the sd
Benjamin to the sd Benjamin Woodroofe by deed 28 Mar 1745 & ackn in
Spotsylvania Co Court 2 Apr 1745 .... Wit: John Minor, Benja Arnold,
Ambrose Arnold, John Davenport. Proved 4 Feb 1745 & recorded. Attest:
Edmund Waller clk. (Pg 258)

4 Dec 1745. Deed of Mortgage. William Searcy of Spotsylvania Co innkeeper
sold to Edmond Waller of sd co gent the following goods & chattels, viz, one
iron coloured grey horse, one other light bay coloured horse, one cow with her
cow calf, one feather bed, bolster, pillow & furniture belonging together with all
& singular my farther estate, in consideration of this my bargain & sale & of my
farther estate hereby also sold I do ackn to have received from the sd Edmond
Waller the sum of £22 ... for performance whereof & making over to the sole

use of the sd Edmund Waller the estate afsd I hereby bind me in the just & full sum of £40 ... . Wit: Edmund Foster, Thos Foster, Wm Hughes. Proved 1 Apr 1746 & admitted to record. Attest: Edmund Waller clk. (Pg 259)

5 Nov 1745. Deed of Gift. Nicholas Hawkins of St. George Parish, Spotsylvania Co planter for the fatherly love & affection which I bear unto my dau Ann Pritchett w/o James Pritchett have given unto my son in law James Pritchett one Negro man named Price & 115 a. of land on the head of Francis Smith's Br in the afsd parish bounded by Owen Thomas, Jarmanna Road & Waggon Road, it being pt/o a patent formerly granted unto Larkin Chew decd as the same was to me sold by the afsd Larkin Chew decd & Thomas Chew his son ... . Wit: James Hawkins, Nicholas Hawkins, Alexander Hawkins, John Hawkins. Ackn 1 Apr 1746 & admitted to record. Attest: Edmund Waller clk. (Pg 260)

5 Nov 1745. Deed of Gift. Nicholas Hawkins of St. George Parish, Spotsylvania Co planter for fatherly love & effection have given unto my son Nicholas Hawkins Junr one Negro named Ned & 100 a. of land being on the ne side of Jarmanna Road bounded by Johnston's line formerly Clark's line, Warner's line & Pen's line, the same as was sold unto me by Thomas Chew by deeds of sale it being pt/o a pattent formerly granted unto Larkin Chew decd ... . Wit: James Hawkins, James Pritchett, Alexander Hawkins, John Hawkins. Ackn 1 Apr 1746 & admitted to record. Attest: Edmund Waller clk. (Pg 262)

6 May 1746. Deed. Joseph Holladay of Spotsylvania Co for £5 sold to Thomas Pulliam of same co a 22 a. tr of land in St. George Parish bounded by Susannah Holladay, East North East River, sd Thomas Pulliam, Daniel Holladay & Holladays Swamp ... . Wit: John Holladay, James Edwards. Ackn 6 May 1746 & admitted to record. Attest: Edmund Waller clk. (Pg 263)

27 Feb MDCCXLV. Deed. James Shackelford & Elizabeth his wife of St. George Parish, Spotsylvania Co for £10:7 sold to Edward Jones of same place a 69 a. tr of land in St. George Parish bounded by Edmund Waller, the Main Road, Pamunkey Road & the sd Shackelford's line ... . Wit: John Wiglesworth, Edmund Waller, Isaac Bradburn. Ackn 6 May 1746 by James Shackelford & admitted to record. Attest: Edmund Waller clk. (Pg 264)

Commission. To John Waller, John Minor & John Waller Junr gent greeting, whereas James Shackelford of Spotsylvania Co & Elizabeth his wife by their deed [see above] have conveyed unto Edward Jones of Spotsylvania Co the fee simple estate of 69 a. of land, & whereas the sd Elizabeth cannot conveniently travel to our co court to make acknowledgment of the sd conveyance, therefore we do give to you or any two or more of you power to receive the acknowledgment which the sd Elizabeth shall be willing to make before you & we do therefore command that you do personally go to the sd Elizabeth & receive her acknowledgment & examine her privily & apart from her husband whether she doth the same freely & voluntarily & whether she be willing that the same should be recorded .... Wit Edmund Waller clerk of court 1 May 1746. 3 May 1746 we do certify that pursuant to the within commission we John Minor & Jno Waller Junr personally went to Elizabeth & did examine her privily & apart from her husband & she did freely & voluntarily ackn that she was willing the indenture should be recorded. The within commission being returned & is admitted to record 6 May 1746. Attest: Edmund Waller clk. (Pg 266)

5 May 1746. Deed of Lease. William Woodford of Caroline Co gent for 5 shillings leased to John Champe of King George Co gent a 1600 a. tr of land purch by the sd William Woodford from Richard Taliaferro & Charles Taliaferro to whom the same was conveyed by their brother Francis Taliaferro by deed dated 28 Sep 1682 granted to their father Robert Taliaferro & Lawrence Smith by patent dated 26 Mar 1666 the sd 1600 a. being bounded by the land of Col John Taliaferro lately decd ... during the term of one year .... Wit: T. Turner, Peter Daniel. Ackn 6 May 1746 & admitted to record. Attest: Edmund Waller clk. (Pg 267)

6 May 1746. Deed of Release. William Woodford of Caroline Co gent & Anne his wife for £640 sold & released to John Champe of King George Co gent a 1600 a. tr of land ... [same as above] ... & also the Negro & Mulatto slaves Cesar, Mulatto Jemmy, Maria, Sarah & her child now about 2 years old, young Maria & her child now about 12 months old, Cato, Juba, Prince, Toby, Matt, Daphne, Daniel a boy about 15 years old, Harry a boy about 8 years old, Mulatto Will, Moll, Judy & Peter with all their future offspring & increase .... Wit: T. Turner, Peter Daniell. Ackn 6 May 1746 by William Woodford gent & admitted to record. Attest: Edmund Waller clk. (Pg 269)

6 May MDCCXLVI. Deed. Henry Downs of St. Thomas Parish, Orange Co, VA gent for £43 sold to Francis Thornton of St. George Parish, Spotsylvania Co gent a lot of land containing ½ a. in the town of Fredericksburgh & is described in the plan of the sd town by the figure 56 on Princess Ann Street & Hanover Street the same being ackn to John Waller Junr gent of Spotsylvania Co & conveyed by deed from the trustees or feoffees of the sd town 4 Oct MDCCXXXVIII & from the sd John Waller Junr the sd lot of land was conveyed to Henry Downs afsd 30 Nov MDCCXXXVIII .... Wit: John Chew, Richd Tutt, Thos Slaughter. Ackn 6 May 1746 & admitted to record. Attest: Edmund Waller clk. (Pg 273)

3 Jun 1746. Deed. Thomas Brown of Orange Co for £58 sold to Richard Stears a 230 a. tr of land or woodland ground bounded by Pike Run ... . Wit: Jno Parrish, Wm Long, Richd Phillips. Ackn 3 Jun 1746 & admitted to record. Attest: Edmund Waller clk. (Pg 275)

30 Jun 1746. Deed of Lease. Thomas Salmon of Orange Co for £50 leased to Thomas Cook of Spotsylvania Co a 300 a. tr of land in St. Georges Parish on the brs of Po River adj Col Robinson & Taliaferro Cragg ... during the term of one year paying the rent of one ear of Indian corn at the feast of St. Michael the Arch Angell if demanded ... . Wit: William Collins, Thomas Collins, Jos Collins. Ackn 1 Jul 1746 & admitted to record. Attest: Edmund Waller clk. (Pg 276)

30 Jun 1746. Deed of Release. Thomas Salmon of St. Thomas Parish, Orange Co for £50 sold & released to Thomas Cook of Spotsylvania Co a 300 a. tr of land, it being pt/o a patent lately granted unto Thomas Foster dated 1 Jun 1741 ... [same as above] ... . Wit: William Collins, Thomas Collins, Jos Collins. Ackn 1 Jul 1746 & admitted to record. Attest: Edmund Waller clk. (Pg 277)

27 Jan MDCCXLV. Deed. William Samms & Mary his wife of St. George Parish, Spotsylvania Co for £8 sold to James Stevens of same place a 34 a. tr of land or woodland ground being pt/o a greater tr of land devised to James Samms by his father James Samms decd & by the sd James Samms conveyed to the sd William Samms 4 Jun 1745 & bounded by the sd William Samms, James Samms, Abel Stears, Cattaile Lick Br & Talbert's line ... . Wit: Jeremiah Stevens, John Talbert, James Samms. Proved 1 Jul 1746 & admitted to record. Attest: Edmund Waller clk. (Pg 279)

1 Jul 1746. Deed. Luke Hambleton of Fredericksvil Parish, Louisa Co & Susanna his wife for £60 sold to Anthony Foster of St. George Parish, Spotsylvania Co a 135 a. tr of land in St. George Parish bounded by Bushes Road, Mr. Brock, Walker's line & the sd Antho Foster, which sd land is pt/o a pattent for a larger quantity of land granted to Larkin Chew 4 Jun 1722 & divers many conveyances is become vested in the sd Luke Hambleton & Susanna his wife ... . Wit: Lark Chew, W. Robinson, Edmund Foster. Ackn 1 Jul 1746 by Luke Hambleton & Susanna his wife & admitted to record. Attest: Edmund Waller clk. (Pg 281)

6 Jun 1746. Deed of Lease. David Bell of Henerico Co for 5 shillings leased to Charles Colson of the town of Fredericksburgh innkeeper a lott or ½ a. of land in the town of Fredericksburgh distinguish'd in the plan of the sd town by the number 41 & likewise ½ of the lot known by the number 43 adj the lot number 41 bounded by Caroline Street & Hanover Street ... during the term of one year paying the rent of one ear of Indian corn on Lady day next if demanded ... .

Wit: John Allan, Alexr Scott, Peter Lucas, Patrick Connelly, William Thomson. Proved 1 Jul 1746 & admitted to record. Attest: Edmund Waller clk. (Pg 283)

7 Jun 1746. Deed of Release. David Bell of Henerico Co for £370 sold to Charles Colson of the town of Fredericksburgh innkeeper a lott of land in the town of Fredericksburgh No. 41 & ½ of lot No. 43 ... [same as above] .... Wit: John Allan, Alexr Scott, Peter Lucas, Patrick Connelly, William Thomson. Proved 1 Jul 1746 & admitted to record. Attest: Edmund Waller clk. (Pg 284)

1 Jul 1746. Deed. Joseph Holladay of Spotsylvania Co for £110 sold to Zachary Lewis of same co a 120 a. tr of land pt/o the lands devised to the sd Joseph Holladay by the will of his father John Holladay decd which sd 120 a. is bounded by the East North East Run, Stoney Br, George Seaton, Mill Pond & the Mill Run, also ½ pt/o that water mill called Holladays Mill adj to the sd land & ½ pt/o the mill house, mill damm, mill stones & other impliments & utensils to the sd mill belonging which was also devised to the sd Joseph Holladay by the sd will of his father .... Wit: M. Battaley, Jos Brock, Jno Holladay. Ackn 1 Jul 1746 & admitted to record. Attest: Edmund Waller clk. (Pg 286)

5 Aug 1746. Deed of Gift. William Bell of Spotsylvania Co planter out of love & affection & in consideration of her duty & obedience to me have given to my dau Lydia Arnold & the heirs of her body the plantation whereon her husband William Arnold & she now live together with 70 a. of land adj & bounded by a water course called Black Rock, Henry Lines, Micow's & Bell's land, Garton's line, Bells Spring & Black Rock Swamp ... together with the priviledge of getting board timber of 100 a. of land I have in like manner bequeathed to her sister Bathsheba Bell .... Wit: Jno Parrish, Philip Vincent Vass. Ackn 4 Sep 1746 & admitted to record. Attest: Edmund Waller clk. (Pg 287)

5 Aug 1746. Deed of Gift. William Bell Spotsylvania Co planter out of love & affection & in consideration of her duty & obedience to me have given to my dau Bathsheba Bell & the heirs of her body the plantation whereon I now live with the land thereto adj & belonging containing 100 a. bounded by the River Ta, Henry Lines, Black Rock, Black Rock Swamp, Lydia Arnold & Garton's line ... I have reserved to Lydia Arnold of getting what board timber she has occasion of for her plantation use ... I do hereby give & bequeath after the decease of me & my wife Catherine to my dau Bathseba Bell .... Wit: Jno Parrish, Philip Vincent Vass. Ackn 2 Sep 1746 & admitted to record. Attest: Edmund Waller clk. (Pg 288)

XVI Sep MDCCXLVI. Deed. Benjamin Winslow gent & Susannah his wife of Essex Co, VA for £28 sold to the Rev. James Marye minister of St. George Parish, Spotsylvania Co ½ a. or lot of land in the town of Fredericksburg described in the plan of the sd town by the figure 55 bounded by Princess Ann Street & Charlotta Street ... . Wit: John Nicholas, Thos Walker, Rob Jackson, Geo Taylor, Hen Downs, Taverner Beale, John Willis, Jas Barbour, Thos Scott. Proved 7 Oct 1746 & admitted to record. Attest: Edmund Waller clk. (Pg 289)

6 Oct 1746. Deed of Lease. Henry Lewis of Spotsylvania Co for 5 shillings leased to John Parrish of same co a 400 a. tr of land bounded by the New Mine Bank Road, Griffin Fantleroy, Thomas Shelton, Joseph Roberts, Devils Ditch Swamp, George Musick & Nicholas Randall ... during the term of one year paying the rent of one pepper corn on Lady day next if demanded ... . Wit: Edmund Waller. Ackn 7 Oct 1746 & admitted to record. Attest: Edmund Waller clk. (Pg 290)

7 Oct 1746. Deed of Release. Henry Lewis of Spotsylvania Co for £30 sold & released to John Parrish of same co a 400 a. tr of land, being first granted by patent dated 12 Feb 1742 to George Cook who conveyed the same to the sd Henry Lewis ... [same as above] ... . Wit: Edmund Waller. Ackn 7 Oct 1746 by Henry Lewis & Martha the w/o the sd Henry relinquished her right of dower & recorded. Attest: Edmund Waller clk. (Pg 291)

17 Sep 1746. Deed. Mary Belfeild widow & John Belfeild & William Jordan gent all of Richmond Co, VA executors of the will of Thomas Wright Belfeild gent decd of the one part & Charles Dick of the town of Fredericksburgh, Spotsylvania Co merchant of the other part, whereas Henry Willis & John Waller gent two of the feoffees & trustees for the town of Fredericksburg by deed dated 2 Aug MDCCXXXVII did convey to John Rucker of Orange Co gent in fee simple ½ a. or lott of land in the sd town described in the platt of the town by the figure 5 being on the River Rappahannock & on Sophia Street, William Street & George Street, by virtue whereof the sd John Rucker entered into the sd lott of land & being thereof seized made his will & devised the sd lott of land to the sd Thos Wright Belfeild & his heirs forever & soon after died seised of the sd lott after whose death the sd Thomas Wright Belfeild in his lifetime entered into the sd lott & being thereof seised made his will dated 6 Dec MDCCXLIII by which he declared his will to be that his executors dispose of any pt/o his lands wherever situated as they should think fitt for the discharging his debts & appointed the afsd Mary Belfeild, John Belfeild & William Jordan executors as by the sd will proved in Richmond Co & soon after making the sd will the sd Thomas Wright Belfeild died seised of the sd lott of land ... now this indenture wit that the sd Mary Belfeild, John Belfeild & William Jordan for £40 have sold unto the sd Charles Dick the afsd ½ a. or lott of land No. 5 in the town of Fredericksburgh ... . Wit: T. Turner, Thos Turner Junr, James Dun, Archd Gordon. Proved 7 Oct 1746 & admitted to record. Attest: Edmund Waller clk. (Pg 293)

7 Oct 1746. Deed. Edward Wyat of Glocester Co for £10 sold to Joseph
Peterson of Spotsylvania Co a tr of land in St. George Parish bounded by the sd
Wyat's line ... . Wit: Thos White, John Graves, Thomas Fagg. Ackn 7 Oct
1746 & admitted to record. Attest: Edmund Waller clk. (Pg 295)

6 Sep 1746. Deed. William Williams of St. George Parish, Spotsylvania Co &
Elizabeth his wife for £35 sold to John Williams of same place a 100 a. tr of land
in St. George Parish pt/o a greater tr first taken up by Nicholas Lankford & by
him sold to John Coller Junr of King & Queen Co & by the sd Coller to Robert
Stubblefield & to Ralph Williams & after ackn William Williams & sold to John
Williams of the sd co bounded by Pappan Run, Benjamin Matthews, the sd
William Williams, land that was John Williams & now is Dillard's, Smith's line
& line of John Smith now Tyre ... . Wit: Robt Huddleston, Danl Pruit, John
Huddleston. Ackn 4 Nov 1746 by William Williams & Elizabeth his wife &
admitted to record. Attest: Edmund Waller clk. (Pg 297)

4 Nov 1746. Deed of Gift. Bloomfeild (Bloumfeild) Long of St. George Parish,
Spotsylvania Co for love & affection have given to my son Rubin Long of same
place a 118 ½ a. tr of land whereon I now live only reserving mine & my wifes
life in the sd land being in the parish afsd bounded by Stony Run, Abraham Estis
& the River Ta ... the sd granted land & premises unto the sd Rubin Long agt
the sd Bloomfeild Long & his heirs by a former wife & every person whatsoever
shall & will warrant & former by these presents defend ... . Wit: Thomas
Graves, Robt Moor, William Johnston. Proved 4 Nov 1746 & admitted to
record. Attest: Edmund Waller clk. (Pg 299)

3 Mar MDCCXLVI. Deed. Benjamin Matthews & Ann his wife of
Spotsylvania Co for £8 sold to Joseph Carter of same co a 100 a. tr of land in St.
George Parish adj the lands of Humphry Bell merchant, Robert Goodloe,
Thomas Dillard (formerly Ralph Williams) & Robert Stubblefeild ... . Wit:
Abraham Estes, Tho Megee, Edmund Foster. Ackn 3 Mar 1746 by Benjamin
Matthews & Ann his wife & admitted to record. Attest: Edmund Waller clk.
(Pg 300)

3 Mar MDCCXLVI. Deed. Richard Phillips of Louisa Co gent & Katherine his
wife for £200 sold to Oswald Smith of Orange Co a 380 a. tr of land with one
water grist mill thereon bounded by the Northanna & the East North East River,
which tr of land was granted to William Smith gent by patent dated 31 Oct 1726
... . Wit: John Waller, John Minor, Edmund Waller. Ackn 7 Apr 1747 by
Richard Phillips & recorded. Attest: Edmund Waller clk. (Pg 302)

Commission. To John Waller, William Robinson & John Minor of Spotsylvania
Co gent greeting, whereas Richard Phillips of Louisa Co gent & Katherine his

wife by their indenture [*see above*] have conveyed unto Oswald Smith late of Orange Co the fee simple estate of 380 a. of land, & whereas the sd Katherine cannot conveniently travel to our co court to make acknowledgment of the sd conveyance, therefore we do give unto you or any two of you power to receive the acknowledgment which the sd Katherine shall be willing to make before you, & we do command that you do personally go to the sd Katherine & receive her acknowledgment & examine her privily & apart from her husband whether she doth the same freely & voluntarily & whether she be willing to the recording the same ... . Wit Edmund Waller clerk of court 6 Apr 1747. 6 Apr 1747 we John Waller & John Minor do hereby certifie that pursuant to the within commission we personally went to the sd Katherine w/o Richard Phillips & examined her privily & apart from her husband who ackn before us that she freely & voluntarily did make & execute the indenture & that she was willing that the same should be recorded. The within commission being duly returned into court is admitted to record. Attest: Edmund Waller clk. (Pg 305)

7 Apr 1747. Deed. Toliver Cragg & Mary his wife of St. George Parish, Spotsylvania Co for £5 sold to Joseph Hawkins of same place all their right & title of a 200 a. tr of land being on both sides of Terys Run in parish afsd the same being left by the will of John Hawkins decd to be equally divided between Mary his wife & four of his children (viz) Elizabeth Smith, Philemon Hawkins, Phebe Smith & the sd Mary Cragg ... . Wit: A. Foster, Edmund Foster, Larkin Johnston. Ackn 7 Apr 1747 by Taliaferro Cragg & Mary his wife & admitted to record. Attest: Edmund Waller clk. (Pg 305)

12 Feb 1746. Deed of Lease. Margret Morriss (Morris) of Spotsylvania Co widdow for & in consideration of the yearly rent & covenants hereinafter mentioned have farm letten unto Mosley Battaley of same co gent a plantation & 200 a. tr of land whereon the sd Margret Morriss now lives ... during the natural life of the sd Margret Morriss paying yearly the rent of 40 shillings upon 12 Feb ... the sd Mosley Battaley to allow her the liberty of as much ground as she & her son Thomas Morriss can tend & the use of the houses which are now upon the sd plantation during the sd term ... . Wit: John Wheeler, J. Battaley, Joseph Brookes. Proved 5 May 1747 & admitted to record. Attest: Edmund Waller clk. (Pg 307)

4 May 1747. Deed of Gift. Henry Goodloe of St. George Parish, Spotsylvania Co gent for natural love & affection hath given unto his son Robert Goodloe of same place planter a 150 a. tr of land or woodland ground the same being in St. George Parish pt/o a patent granted to the sd Henry Goodloe for 400 a. dated 21 May 1726, bounded by Larence Anderson, Augustine Owen, sd Robert Goodloe, Mark Wheeler & the North Fork Swamp ... . Wit: Geo Eastham, John

Spallding. Ackn 5 May 1747 & admitted to record. Attest: Edmund Waller clk. (Pg 308)

30 Apr 1747. Deed. Henry Goodloe of St. George Parish, Spotsylvania Co for £37 sold to Thomas Coats of St. Margarets Parish, Caroline Co a 303 a. tr of land amongst the brs of the North Fork of the South Fork of the South River bounded by Baylor's line, sd Goodloe, Col Robinson & Lankford's line … . Wit: Robt Stubblefield, John Crane, Richard Stubblefield. Ackn 5 May 1747 & admitted to record. Attest: Edmund Waller clk. (Pg 310)

18 Dec 1746. Deed of Lease. Thomas Chew of St. Thomas's Parish, Orange Co gent & Martha his wife for 5 shillings leased to John Penn of Drysdale Parish, Caroline Co a 307 a. tr of land on some of the s brs of the North Fork of Mattapony River called Lewis River bounded by the Poison Field, Augustine Smith, Col Spotswood, Nicholas Hawkins, Garmanna Road, George Penn & Loyds Br … during the term of 6 months paying the rent of one ear of Indian corn at the fest of St. Michael the Arch Angel if demanded … . Wit: John Ray, Joseph Hoomes, Eusebins Stone, Augustin Muse, Moses Penn. Proved 2 Jun 1747 & admitted to record. Attest: Edmund Waller clk. (Pg 312)

19 Dec 1746. Deed of Release. Thomas Chew of St. Thomas's Parish, Orange Co gent & Martha his wife for £20 sold & released to John Penn of Drysdale Parish, Caroline Co a 307 a. tr of land … [same as above] … . Wit: John Ray, Joseph Hoomes, Eusebins Stone, Augustin Muse, Moses Penn. Proved 2 Jun 1747 & admitted to record. Attest: Edmund Waller clk. (Pg 313)

18 Dec 1746. Deed of Lease. Thomas Chew of St. Thomas's Parish, Orange Co gent & Martha his wife for 5 shillings leased to George Penn of Drysdale Parish, Caroline Co a 307 a. tr of land on some of the s brs of the North Fork of Mattapony River called Lewis River bounded by land that Nicholas Hawkins bought of Robt Hutcheson, Augustine Smith, Loyds Br & John Penn … during the term of 6 months paying the rent of one ear of Indian corn at the feast of St. Michael the Arch Angel if demanded … . Wit: John Ray, Joseph Hoomes, Eusebins Stone, Augustine Muse, Moses Penn. Proved 2 Jun 1747 & admitted to record. Attest: Edmund Waller clk. (Pg 316)

19 Dec 1746. Deed of Release. Thomas Chew of St. Thomas's Parish, Orange Co gent for £20 sold & released to George Penn of Drysdale Parish, Caroline Co a 307 a. tr of land … [same as above] … . Wit: John Ray, Joseph Hoomes, Eusebins Stone, Augustine Muse, Moses Penn. Proved 2 Jun 1747 & admitted to record. Attest: Edmund Waller clk. (Pg 317)

2 Jun 1747. Deed of Mortgage. Joseph Venable (Vennable) for 15:15:8 sell
unto John Minor of Spotsylvania Co 2 beds & furniture, 3 iron pots & frying
pan, 1 pot rack, 2 piggins, 1 spinning wheel, 2 chests, 1 small looking glass, 2
cows & calves & 4 yearlings, 3 sows, 13 piggs, 6 barrows, 1 black mare & 1
gray horse. Wit: Peter Daniel, James Sparks. Ackn 2 Jun 1747 & admitted to
record. Attest: Edmund Waller clk. (Pg 319)

2 Jun 1747. Deed. Beverley Randolph of Kingston Parish, Gloucester Co, VA
gent for £45:5 sold to James Garnett of St. Anne Parish, Essex Co, VA gent a
parcel of land or woodland ground containing one lott in the town of
Fredericksburg number 3 being all the lands within the bounds of the sd
Beverley Randolph's lot according to the sd town plat surveyed by George
Home .... Wit: John Livingston Junr, Cha Dick, Alexr Wright. Ackn 2 Jun
1747 by Charles Carter esqr atty for Beverley Randolph esqr & is admitted to
record. Attest: Edmund Waller clk. (Pg 320)

1 Jun 1747. Deed of Lease. William Wyatt mariner for £5 shillings leased to
Joseph Herndon of Caroline Co a 667 a. tr of land which was given & devised to
the sd William Wyatt by the will of his late father Francis Wyatt decd bounded
by a corner formerly of Rowland Thomas, Allen's corner & Holliday's line ...
during the term of on year paying the rent of a pepper corn on the feast of the
Annunciation of the Blessed Virgin Mary if demanded .... Wit: James Taylor,
Joseph Russel, Richard Todd. Ackn 2 Jun 1747 & admitted to record. Attest:
Edmund Waller clk. (Pg 322)

2 Jun 1747. Deed of Release. William Wyatt mariner for £133:8 paid to Samuel
Coleman legal atty of the sd William Wyatt for the use of the sd William Wyatt
hath sold to Joseph Herndon of Caroline Co a 667 a. tr of land ... [same as
above] .... Wit: James Taylor, Joseph Russel, Richard Todd. Ackn 2 Jun 1747
& admitted to record. Attest: Edmund Waller clk. (Pg 323)

4 Aug 1747. Deed. William Hensley & Jane his wife of St. George Parish,
Spotsylvania Co for £35 sold to Robert Spilsby Coleman of Southfarnham
Parish, Essex Co a 420 a. tr of land in St. George Parish being pt/o a tr granted
to Roger Tandy by patent dated 13 Oct 1727 for 520 a. the sd Tandy has since
sold to William Dyer of Spotsylvania Co 100 a. pt/o the sd tr & the remainder to
John Jones founder who has since conveyed it to William Hensley, bounded by
Robert Baylor, Harry Beverley, Capt John Camm & Samuel Smith .... Wit: A.
Bowker, Thomas Coleman, Hugh Sanders. Ackn 4 Aug 1747 by William
Hensley & Jane his wife & recorded. Attest: Edmund Waller clk. (Pg 326)

4 Aug 1747. Deed. John Allan of the town of Fredericksburgh, Spotsylvania Co
merchant for £20 sold to Charles Dick of the same town merchant two lotts or ½

acres of land numbered 5 & 6 in a plan of land laid off into lotts by the sd John Allan & is pt/o a tr of land purch of the executors of Henry Willis gent decd by William Hunter gent & by the sd Hunter conveyed to the sd John Allan the sd two lotts are bounded by pt/o Allans Street, Hanover Street, a lott laid off by the exrs of the sd Willis No. 3 which joins to the town of Fredericksburgh, land of Humphrey Hill gent & Lot No. 7 now belonging to the sd John Allan .... Wit: None. Ackn 4 Aug 1747 & recorded. Attest: Edmund Waller clk. (Pg 327)

4 Aug 1747. Deed. John Allan of Spotsylvania Co gent for £20 sold to the Rev. Robert Rose of Essex Co, VA clerk two lotts or ½ acres of land near the town of Fredericksburgh the sd lotts are numbered 3 & 4 bounded by lott No. 2 purch by John Mitchel, John Royston's line, the remaining pt/o the sd John Allan's tr of land & Allans Street, which sd lotts are pt/o 10 a. 20 perches of land conveyed to the sd John Allan by William Hunter & Martha his wife by deed dated 2 Jul MDCCXLV .... Wit: None. Ackn 4 Aug 1747 & recorded. Attest: Edmund Waller clk. (Pg 328)

1 Sep 1747. Deed of Gift. William Bartlet of St. George Parish, Spotsylvania Co planter for fatherly love & affection which I beare unto my son in law Clement Mountague & Ann his wife have given to my sd son in law & my dau Ann during their natural lives, & after their decease to return unto my granddau Susanna Mountague & if in case she dies without heir then to go to the next surviving child they have then living, I the sd William Bartlet do give unto my sd granddau after the decease of my son in law & dau a 56 a. tr of land in the afsd parish bounded by Chissells Wagon Road & Achillis Bowker, the same was to me granted by patent dated 12 Mar 1739 under the hand of Sir William Gooch knt then governor of VA .... Wit: Francis Miller, Edmund Foster. Ackn 1 Sep 1747 & recorded. Attest: Edmund Waller clk. (Pg 330)

3 Jun MDCCXLVI. Deed of Gift. George Musick Senr & Ann his wife of St. George Parish, Spotsylvania Co & William Sandige & Ann his wife of same place for the natural love the sd George Musick & Ann his wife bear to William Trustee of same place their son in law & Elizabeth his wife their dau have given to the sd William & Elizabeth Trustee a 50 a. parcel of land bounded by Wyat's line, sd Musick's old patent & sd Sandige's line, & the sd William Sandige & Anne his wife for £4 sold to the sd William Trustee 15 a. of land adj the 50 a. which sd 15 a. is bounded by Wyat's line & sd Sandige's line .... Wit: Thos White, William Lea, Phillip Ballard. George Musick's deed was proved 3 Jun 1746 by Thomas White & Phillip Ballard & ordered to be certifyed & Ann Musick w/o the sd George came into court & ackn her right of dower to the sd land & is recorded. William Sandige came into court 3 Jun 1746 & ackn his pt/o the within deed & recorded. The within deed was further proved 6 Oct

1747 by William Lea & is admitted to record. Attest: Edmund Waller clk. (Pg 331)

4 May MDCCXLVI. Deed. George Musick Senr & Ann his wife of Spotsylvania Co for £7 sold to Robert Beadles now of same co a 50 a. tr of land in St. George Parish bounded by the Mine Road, Wyat's line, sd George Musick & John Graves, the same being pt/o a greater tr of land whereon the sd George Musick now liveth & was given by him to his son George Musick Junr but never ackn to him & by the sd George Musick Junr sold to the sd Robert Beadles ... . Wit: Thos White, William Lea, Phillip Ballard. Proved 3 Jun 1746 by Thomas White & Philip Ballard & certified & Ann Musick the w/o the sd George came into court & ackn her right of dower & is recorded. Deed further proved 6 Oct 1747 by William Lea & recorded. Attest: Edmund Waller clk. (Pg 333)

17 Apr 1747 in Tappahanock Town, Essex Co. Power of Attorney. I Alexander Scott late of the town of Fredericksburg, Spotsylvania Co have appointed my trusty & well beloved friend Charles Colston of the town of Fredericksburg my atty to ask, demand, sue for & receive all manner of debt, sums of money, rents, gifts, legacies & bequests whatsoever now to me due or that shall hereafter become due to me from any person whatsoever ... . Wit: Samuel Ritchie, Saml Martin, W. Woodward. Ackn 6 Oct 1747 & recorded. Attest: Edmund Waller clk. (Pg 335)

6 Oct 1747. Deed. John Allan of Spotsylvania Co gent for £10 sold to the Rev. John Thompson of Orange Co, VA clerk a lott or ½ a. of land in the town of Fredericksburg bounded by Lot No. 6 belonging to Charles Dick, Allan Street, Lott No. 8 not yet sold, Humphry Hill & the sd John Allan which sd lott is pt/o 10 a. 20 perches of land conveyed to the sd John Allan by William Hunter & Martha his wife by deed dated 2 Jul MDCCXLV ... . Wit: Z. Lewis, Charles Colson, Tho Houison. Ackn 6 Oct 1747 & recorded. Attest: Edmund Waller clk. (Pg 336)

6 Oct 1747. Deed. George Woodroof of Spotsylvania Co & Jane his wife for £33:15 sold to Zachary Lewis of same co a 135 a. tr of land on both sides of Arnolds Run bounded by Haw Br, land that George Woodroof Junr sold to Thos Graves, sd George Woodroof, sd Zachary Lewis & Thomas Hill, which sd land is pt/o a patent dated 24 Jun MDCCXXVI granted to the sd George Woodroof for 640 a. ... . Wit: William Talliaferro, Harbin Moor, Anne Sandige. Ackn 6 Oct 1747 by George Woodroof & Jane his wife & recorded. Attest: Edmund Waller clk. (Pg 337)

30 Oct MDCCXLVII. Deed. Edmund Waller of St. George Parish, Spotsylvania Co & Mary his wife for £13 sold to Phillip Ballard now of the

same place a 352 a. tr of land pt/o a 552 a. tr of land granted by patent to the sd Edmund Waller 25 Nov 1743 lying on the Devils Ditch in the parish afsd bounded by John Sartin, William Sandige decd formerly Roberts's, George Cook's now Parrish's & John Chew's line .... Wit: J. Pendleton, Richd Phillips Junr. Ackn 3 Nov 1747 & admitted to record. Attest: Edmund Waller clk. (Pg 339)

4 Oct 1747. Deed. Benjamin Holladay of Spotsylvania Co & Susanna his wife for £180 sold to Zachary Lewis of same co a 295 ½ a. tr of land being the land devised to the sd Benjamin Holladay by the will of his father John Holladay decd & is bounded by Wyat's line, Susannah Holladay & the East North East River, also ½ pt/o that water grist mill called Holladays Mill adj to the sd land & ½ pt/o the mill house, mill dam, mill stones & other impliments & utensils to the sd mill belonging .... Wit: George Wythe, A. Bowker, Edmund Waller. Ackn 3 Nov 1747 by Benjamin Holladay & admitted to record. Wit to Susanna 1 Oct 1751: Edmd Waller, Edwd Herndon Junr, Jno Battaley. See page 559 for the womans ackmt. Attest: Edmund Waller clk. (Pg 341)

17 Nov 1747. Deed. Jeremiah White of Spotsylvania Co & Mary his wife for £23 sold to William Waller of same co gent a 100 a. tr of land bounded by Henry Goodloe & the North Fork .... Wit: Edmund Waller, George Wythe, Benja Davis. Proved 2 Feb 1747 & admitted to record. Attest: Edmund Waller clk. (Pg 343)

3 Feb 1747. Deed. John Allan of the town of Fredericksburgh, Spotsylvania Co merchant for £20 sold to John Mitchell of same town merchant an acre or two lots of land No. 1 & 2 in a plan of several lots of land lately laid out by the sd John Allan which sd lots are pt/o a tr of land purch by the sd John Allan, Humphrey Hill & William Hunter gent of the executors of Henry Willis gent decd & by the exrs conveyed to the sd Hunter & by him conveyed to the sd John Allan adj John Royston & several lots laid out by the sd Willis's executors (which join to the town of Fredericksburgh) & now belong to William Waller & Zachary Lewis, Allans Street & Lot No. 3 .... Wit: Archd Gordon, Patrick Mitchell, James Miller. Ackn 3 Feb 1747 & admitted to record. Attest: Edmund Waller clk. (Pg 345)

1 Feb 1747. Deed of Lease. William Marshall of St. Margarets Parish, Caroline Co planter for 5 shillings leased to Charles Dick of the town of Fredericksburg, Spotsylvania Co merchant a 150 a. tr of land in St. George Parish (being pt/o a tr of land formerly belonging to Charles Taliaferro called Motts Run Tract & transferred by the sd Taliaferro to the sd Marshall) bounded by John Bowsee's patent (now the land of John Allan) & Phillip Roots (Rootts) ... during the term of one year paying the rent of one Indian ear of corn at the feast of St. Michael

the Archangel if demanded ... . Wit: Anthony Strother, Alexr Wright, John Jones. Ackn 2 Feb 1747 & admitted to record. Attest: Edmund Waller clk. (Pg 347)

2 Feb 1747. Deed of Release. William Marshall of St. Margarets Parish, Caroline Co planter for £66 sold & released to Charles Dick of the town of Fredericksburg, Spotsylvania Co merchant a 150 a. tr of land ... [same as above] ... . Wit: Anthony Strother, Alexr Wright, John Jones. Ackn 2 Feb 1747 & admitted to record. Attest: Edmund Waller clk. (Pg 348)

1 Feb 1747. Deed of Lease. Edward Wiat of Gloucester Co, VA for 5 shillings leased to Benjamin Holladay of Spotsylvania Co a 597 a. tr of land bounded by Joseph Peterson, the East North East Run, Zachary Lewis formerly Allan's & Holladay's & William Wiat ... during the term of one year paying the yearly rent of one pepper corn at the feast of St. Michael the Arch Angel if demanded ... . Wit: None. Ackn 2 Feb 1747 & admitted to record. Attest: Edmund Waller clk. (Pg 350)

2 Feb 1747. Deed of Release. Edward Wiat of Gloucester Co, VA for £110 sold to Benjamin Holladay of Spotsylvania Co a 597 a. tr of land, which tr of land is pt/o a greater tr of land conveyed by James Taylor gent to Francis Wiat father of the sd Edward & by the sd Francis Wiat's will devised to the sd Edward his son ... [same as above] ... . Wit: None. Ackn 2 Feb 1747 & admitted to record. Attest: Edmund Waller clk. (Pg 351)

520 a. of land in St. George Parish, Spotsylvania Co granted to George Musick & John Graves by pattent dated 10 Jul 1745 & at the request of the sd George Musick & the sd John Graves Jos Brock divides this land into equal parts ... [drawing not included here] ... surveyed 19 Feb 1747 by Jos Brock. 260 a. for John Graves & 260 a. for George Musick. Names mentioned: The fork of the devils Ditch a corner of Joseph Robert's land, Wyatt's line, Musick's old land, Sartin's line being Wm Harris's corner, Fieldour's line. This plan & division of land between George Musick & John Graves being proved in court 2 Feb 1747 is recorded. Attest: Edmund Waller clk. (Pg 353)

3 May 1748. Deed. John Holladay of St. George Parish, Spotsylvania Co & Elizabeth his wife for £45 sold to John Wiglesworth of same place a 200 a. tr of land or woodland ground & plantation in parish afsd bounded by 200 a. which Thomas Sertain sold to James Tery which now belongs to the afsd John Holladay, James Taylor & Gustavus's line, which 200 a. of land is pt/o a patent granted to Thomas Sertain for 1,000 a. dated 6 May MDCCXXVII & by the sd Sertain sold to Thom Holladay gent decd father of the sd John Holladay & from the sd Holladay to John Wiglesworth ... . Wit: Joel Parrish, Benja Martin,

Thomas Stubblefield. Ackn 3 May 1748 by John Holladay & Elizabeth his wife & admitted to record. Attest: Edmund Waller clk. (Pg 354)

3 May 1748. Deed. Robert Coleman of St. George Parish, Spotsylvania Co & Elizabeth his wife for £45 sold to John Pain of same place a 140 a. tr of land or woodland ground & plantation whereon the sd Robert Coleman now liveth, pt/o the same the sd Robert Coleman bought of Phebe Hobson the other remaining part was given to him by his father Robert Coleman decd, bounded by George Carter & Humphry Bell of London .... Wit: Edmund Waller, Richd Phillips Junr. Ackn 3 May 1748 by Robert Coleman & Elizabeth his wife & admitted to record. Attest: Edmund Waller clk. (Pg 356)

5 Feb 1748. Deed. Abraham Rogers & Barbary his wife of St. George Parish, Spotsylvania Co planter for £30 sold to Henry Bartlett of same place a 100 a. parcel of land or woodland ground in St. George Parish being pt/o a patent formerly granted unto Peter Rogers, adj William Rogers & Abraham Estis .... Wit: Owen Thomas, William Rogers, John Griffen Junr. Ackn 3 May 1748 by Abraham Rogers & Barbary his wife & admitted to record. Attest: Edmund Waller clk. (Pg 358)

8 Oct 1747. Deed of Lease. William Hawkins of St. Ann Parish, Essex Co gent for 5 shillings leased to Rice Curtis Junr of St. Margret Parish, Caroline Co a 501 a. tr of land it being pt/o a patent granted to Larkin Chew 4 Jun 1722 & sold by the sd Larkin Chew (since decd) to John Hawkins of Essex Co gent decd by indenture dated 3 Nov 1724 & by a devise in the sd John Hawkins' will it is devised to the afsd William Hawkins as will more fully appear by the sd will on the records of Essex Co Court, bounded by sd Larkin Chew, Major Willm Todd, Mrs. Mary Waller, James Samm & Wm Bradburn ... during the term of one year paying on the last day of the sd term the rent of one ear of Indian corn if demanded .... Wit: Wm Connor, Thos Scott, Jas Dismukes, John Garrett, John Hudgens, John Boutwell. Proved 3 Nov 1747 & admitted to record. Attest: Edmund Waller clk. (Pg 360)

9 Oct 1747. Deed of Release. William Hawkins of St. Ann Parish, Essex Co gent & Margret his wife for £50 sold & released to Rice Curtis Junr of St. Margret Parish, Caroline Co a 501 a. tr of land ... [same as above] .... Wit: Wm Connor, Thos Scott, Jas Dismukes, John Garrett, John Hudgens, John Boutwell. Proved 3 Nov 1747 & admitted to record. Attest: Edmund Waller clk. (Pg 361)

Commission. To Mungo Roy, Simon Miller & Samuell Hipkins of Essex Co gent greeting, whereas Williams Hawkins of Essex Co & Margaret his wife by their deeds [see above] have conveyed unto Rice Curtis Junr of Caroline Co the fee simple estate of 501 a. of land, & whereas the sd Margaret cannot conveniently travel to our co court to make acknowledgment of the sd conveyance, therefore we do give to you or any two or more of you power to receive the acknowledgment which the sd Margaret shall be willing to make before you & we do therefore command that you do personally go to the sd Margaret & receive her acknowledgment & examine her privily & apart from her husband whether she doth the same freely & voluntarily & whether she be willing that the same should be recorded ... . Wit Edmund Waller clerk of court 7 Nov 1747. 11 Mar 1747/8 persuant to the within commission we Simon Miller & Saml Hipkins have examined Margaret Hawkins & doe hereby certifie that she doth freely & voluntarily assent to the sd deeds within mentioned & is willing the same shall be admitted to record. The within commission being duly returned is admitted to record. Attest: Edmund Waller clk. (Pg 364)

5 Jul 1748. Deed. Robert Coleman of Orange Co & Sarah his wife for £31 sold to William Hucheson of St. George Parish, Spotsylvania Co a 226 a. tr of land on the s side of Glady Run bounded by Doctor Forster & Mr. Brock, it being pt/o a patent granted to the sd Robert Coleman dated 30 Aug 1744 ... . Wit: John Chew, Samll Major, A. Foster. Ackn 5 Jul 1748 by Robert Coleman & Sarah his wife & admitted to record. Attest: Edmund Waller clk. (Pg 365)

2 Aug 1748. Deed. Whereas Henry Goodloe of Spotsylvania Co did by his deed dated 30 May 1736 convey or intended to convey unto George Goodloe of Caroline Co gent now decd the fee simple estate of 800 a. of land in the sd deed mentioned lying in Caroline Co & Spotsylvania Co which sd 800 a. of land is devised by the will of the sd George Goodloe decd dated 4 Oct MDCCXLI unto his three sons Henry, George & Robert, & on a survey lately made of the sd land it appears there is several mistakes in describing the bounds in the sd deed which may hereafter occasion disputes which the sd Henry Goodloe being willing to prevent & also desirous that the sd land should be conveyed according to the afsd deed & will. Now this indenture wit that the sd Henry Goodloe for 5 shillings do hereby exonerate & discharge & sell to the sd Henry, George & Robert Goodloe the 800 a. tr of land bounded by the sd Henry Goodloe, Paul Pigg, Stoney Lick Run & Mark Wheeler ... . Wit: Edmund Waller, John Fox, Nich Hawkins, Rob Jackson, Thos Turner Junr, Benjamin Woodward. Ackn 2 Aug 1748 & admitted to record. Attest: Edmund Waller clk. (Pg 367)

3 Sep 1748. Deed. Between Mary Brock widow & executrix of Joseph Brock late of Spotsylvania Co gent decd of the one part & Henry Brock of sd co planter of the other part, wit that whereas the sd Joseph Brock by his will dated 3 Mar 1742 did devise to his son the sd Henry Brock for & during the term of his natural life 650 a. of land including the plantation & improvements thereunto belonging that he now lives on, bounded by the run of Middle River, John

Boswell, Mine Road, Bushes Road, his son Joseph's dividend of land &
Garton's line, the sd land he did give to his son Henry as afsd except a small
piece thereof which he had sold to Henry Lyne & also did devise unto his sd son
Henry five Negro slaves named Mingo, Nan, Pat, Will & Juno for & during the
term of his natural life only & after if he should depart this life (it is his will) that
his wife have full power to dispose of the sd 650 a. of land & slaves & their
future increase either to the futer children of the sd Henry to be born among his
four children William, Joseph, Mary & Susannah ... whereas after the death of
the sd Joseph Brock the testator the sd Henry Brock brought his suit in chancery
in the General Court of VA agt the sd Mary Brock & the sd Joseph's children
William Brock, Joseph Brock & Susanna Brock & thereupon at a General Court
held at the courthouse in Williamsburgh XI Apr MDCCXLVII the following
decree was made in the sd suit by the mutual consent of the partys & on their
motion it is decreed & ordered that the def Mary do make & execute a deed of
confirmation & release to the plaintiff & his heirs of the 650 a. of land & four
slaves named Mingo, Little Nan, Patt & Will, in the bill mentioned given to the
sd plt by his father Joseph Brock gent decd ... . Now this indenture wit that the
sd Mary Brock in pursuance of the sd decree & the trust reposed in her by the sd
will & for 5 shillings hath given & released unto the sd Henry Brock the 650 a.
of land & the several Negro slaves ... . Wit: Elizabeth Blake, W. Robinson,
Zachary Boughan, Jos Brock. Proved 6 Sep 1748 & admitted to record. Attest:
Edmund Waller clk. (Pg 369)

6 Sep MDCCXLVIII. Deed. John Allen of Spotsylvania Co gent for £10 sold to
Elliott Benger of same co esqr a lott or ½ a. of land No. 8 near to the town of
Fredericksburg (being pt/o a tr of land containing 10 a. 20 perches granted to the
sd Allen by William Hunter gent by deed dated 2 Jul 1745) which lott is
bounded by the Rev. John Thomson, Allens Street, pt/o the remaining tr of 10 a.
20 perches & Humphrey Hill gent ... . Wit: Ambrose Ballard, W. Russell.
Ackn 6 Sep 1748 & admitted to record. Attest: Edmund Waller clk. (Pg 371)

6 Dec 1748. Deed of Gift. Pattison Pulliam of Spotsylvania Co for natural love
& affection & 5 shillings hath given unto his son Joseph Pulliam a 130 a. tr of
land bounded by the Mine Road & sd Pattison Pulliam ... . Wit: Edmund
Waller, Jno Holladay, Benjamin Pulliam. Ackn 6 Dec 1748 & admitted to
record. Attest: Edmund Waller clk. (Pg 373)

6 Dec 1748. Deed. Pattison Pulliam of Spotsylvania Co & Elizabeth his wife
for £22:10 sold to John Holladay of same co a 150 a. tr of land bounded by the
Mine Road ... . Wit: Edmund Waller, Benjamin Woodward. Ackn 6 Dec 1748
by Patterson Pulliam & Elizabeth his wife & admitted to record. Attest:
Edmund Waller clk. (Pg 374)

6 Dec 1748. Deed. Pattison Pulliam of Spotsylvania Co & Elizabeth his wife
for £25 sold to George Wilcocks (Willcocks) of same co a 114 a. tr of land
bounded by the sd Pattison Pulliam .... Wit: Edmund Waller, Jno Holladay.
Ackn 6 Dec 1748 by Patterson Pulliam & Elizabeth his wife & admitted to
record. Attest: Edmund Waller clk. (Pg 376)

20 May 1748. Deed. Thomas Chew of Orange Co gent for £10:15 sold to
William Waller of Spotsylvania Co gent a 171 a. tr of land bounded by John
Thruston gent formerly Dolton's, Robert Moor formerly Samuel Moor now in
possession of Robert Moor, William Johnston gent & Edward Cason .... Wit:
Stephen Chenault, Edmund Waller, Jos Redd, Ambrose Foster. Proved 6 Sep
1748 & ordered to be certifyed. This deed was further proved 6 Dec 1748 &
admitted to record. Attest: Edmund Waller clk. (Pg 378)

8 Feb 1748. Deed. Between Thomas Chew of Orange Co gent son & heir of
Larkin Chew late of Spotsylvania Co gent decd & Larkin Chew of Spotsylvania
Co gent son & devisee of the sd Larkin Chew decd of the one part & John
Thruston of Gloucester Co gent of the other part, wit that whereas the sd Larkin
Chew decd in his life time, to wit, 1 & 2 Apr 1721 for £100 by his deeds of lease
& released ackn 29 Apr the year last mentioned did convey unto William Dolton
of Gloucester Co the fee simple estate of a 996 a. tr of land bounded as in the sd
deeds are mentioned & described, that some time afterwards the sd Wm Dalton
died intestate & the sd tr of land descended to Wm Dolton his son & heir who
was thereof seized & possessed & being so seized made his will dated 8 Dec
1733 which is contained this clause, Item by my will afsd do make over all my
estate both real & personal the legacys hereafter mentioned only excepted to
Sarah Dalton my beloved spouse the heirs made of her body & in case of no
issue & after the death of my afsd spouse I give the same to my brother Michael
Dalton & the heirs of his body & in case of such failure to my sister Margrett
Dalton, that soon after making the sd will the sd William Dalton died seized of
the lands & premises after whose death the sd will was duly proved in
Gloucester Co Court, that some time after the sd John Thruston intermarried
with the sd Sarah Dalton widow & relict of the sd testator & the sd John
Thruston in right of the sd Sarah is now possessed of the sd land & premises &
having lately caused the same to be surveyed it is found that the land intended to
be conveyed as afsd from the sd Larkin Chew to the first named Wm Dalton is
not included in the bounds mentioned in the sd deeds, & the sd Thos Chew,
Larkin Chew & John Thruston being willing & desirous that the sd land intended
to be conveyed as afsd should descend to the will of the sd Wm Dalton. Now
this indenture wit that the sd Thomas Chew & Larkin Chew as well for & in
consideration of the afsd £100 to the sd Larkin Chew decd & also 5 shillings to
them in hand paid by the sd John Thruston have sold the 103 a. tr of land
bounded by John Carter formerly Robert King, the River Po, Edward Casone,

Robert Moore, Stony Run, Capt Thos Duerson, Capt Rice Curtis, the Main
Road, the Salt Pond & Walker's formerly Major Benja Robinson's line ... .
Wit: Thos Chew, Wm Carr, Roger Dixon, A. Foster, Edmund Waller. Ackn 7
Mar 1748 & recorded. Attest: Edmund Waller clk. (Pg 379)

20 Sep 1748. Patent. Sir William Gooch Barronet Lt. Governor & Commander
in Chief of VA at Williamsburg have given unto John Chew & Francis
Taliaferro church wardens of St. George Parish, Spotsylvania Co for a Glebe a
577 a. tr of land on the s side of the River Po bounded by Roger Casone,
William Johnston gent, land formerly Edward Pigg's, Harry Beverley & the
New Land Tract, 512 a. being pt/o a patent granted to Larkin Chew gent 26 Apr
1712 & 32 a. the residue being pt/o a patent granted unto Harry Beverley gent 23
Mar 1715 & by divers mesne conveyances become vested in the afsd church
wardens in right of the sd parish ... paying unto us, our heirs & successors for
every 50 a. of land the rent of 1 shillings yearly to be paid upon the feast of St.
Michael the Arch Angel ... . At a court held 8 Mar 1748 at the motion of
Zachary Lewis gent one of the churchwardens of St. George Parish it is ordered
that the within patent for the Glebe Land of this parish be recorded. Attest:
Edmund Waller clk. (Pg 382)

14 Jan 1748. Agreement. Then appeared before William Waller, Nicholas
Seward & his servant woman Margaret Hart & the sd Margaret confessing that
she was infected with a disease called the Pox which she caught before the sd
Seward bought her & the sd Margaret being desirous to be cured, therefore in
consideration that the sd Seward imploys Doctor Wm Lynn & he makes a cure
of her she the sd Margaret doth promise & oblige herself to serve the sd Seward
one whole year after her time of servitude is expired. At a court held 7 Mar
1748 Nicholas Seward & his servant woman Margaret Hart agreement being
approved of by the court it is recorded. Attest: Edmund Waller clk. (Pg 383)

6 Nov MDCCXLVIII. Deed of Gift. Henry Chew late of Calvert Co, MD gent
for natural love & affection which I have & do bear unto my dau Jane Chew &
also in consideration of her going with me to NC have given unto my sd dau
three Negroes named Abigal, Grace & Fender & their future increase provided
that I the sd Henry Chew shall have the use of the sd Negroes during the term of
my natural life & also the sum of £200 I give to my sd dau which sd sum of
£200 is to be paid out of my estate after my decease ... . Wit: Larkin Chew,
Joseph Brock, Jno Spooner, Patrik Carey. Proved 6 Dec 1748 & 7 Mar 1748 &
admitted to record. Attest: Edmund Waller clk. (Pg 384)

13 Feb 1748. Deed. Henry Brock & Barbara his wife of St. George Parish,
Spotsylvania Co for £25 sold to Thos Brock of same place a 150 a. tr of land or
woodland ground pt/o a tr of land whereon the sd Henry Brock now lives

bounded by Bushes Road, Joseph Brock, Garton's land & Mr. Lynes's land … .
Wit: George Trible, Wm Waller, Nicho Horn, Martin True. Ackn 4 Apr 1749 &
admitted to record. Attest: Edmund Waller clk. (Pg 385)

4 Apr 1749. Deed. Thomas Wyatt (Wiat) of Essex Co & Sukey his wife for
£153 sold to Henry Chiles of Spotsylvania Co a 667 a. tr of land bounded by
George Musick & William Wyatt … . Wit: Jos Brock, Thos Estes, Nicho Horn.
Ackn 4 Apr 1749 by Thomas Wiat & admitted to record. Attest: Edmund
Waller clk. At a court held 7 May 1754 Sukey the w/o Thomas Wiatt ackn this
deed which is recorded. Attest: Wm Waller clk. (Pg 387)

22 Jul 1748. Deed. John Corbin of Essex Co, VA gent & Lettice his wife for
£30 sold to Anthony Foster of Spotsylvania Co a 223 a. tr of land or woodland
ground in St. George Parish adj the land of the sd Foster, Glady Run,
Gatewood's land, the sd Corbin & Hugh Sanders, which sd 223 a. is pt/o a
greater tr belonging to the sd John Corbin … . Wit: Samll Major, John Carter,
James Zachry. Proved 6 Sep 1748 & certifyed. The deed was further proved 2
May 1749 & admitted to record. Attest: Edmund Waller clk. (Pg 388)

2 May 1749. Deed. John Haley of Spotsylvania Co & Mary his wife for £50
sold to John Faulconer of Orange Co a 200 a. tr of land bounded by Robinson
Run & Tallever Cragg, being pt/o a pattent dated 10 Sep 1735 … . Wit: Henry
Rains Junr, Thomas Massey, James Debrise. Ackn 2 May 1749 by John Haley
& Mary his wife & admitted to record. Attest: Edmund Waller clk. (Pg 390)

30 Nov 1748. Deed. Between William Davenport of Louisa Co & Ann his wife
of the one part & George Woodroof of Spotsylvania Co of the other part,
William Davenport & Ann his wife for & in consideration that the sd George
Woodroof & Jane his wife shall & will jointly with the sd William Davenport &
Ann his wife make over, ackn & convey unto Joel Parrish 200 a. of land part
whereof was formerly sold by Benjamin Woodroofe to the sd William
Davenport have sold unto the sd George Woodroof a 94 a. tr of land … . Wit:
Ambrose Arnold, Benja Woodroof, Jane Woodroof Junr, Rachel Arnold. Ackn
6 Jun 1749 by William Davenport & Ann his wife & admitted to record. Attest:
Edmund Waller clk. (Pg 391)

30 Nov 1748. Deed. William Davenport of Louisa Co & Ann his wife of the
first part, George Woodroof of Spotsylvania Co & Jane his wife of the second
part & Joel Parrish of Spotsylvania Co of the third part, wit that the sd William
Davenport & Ann his wife & the sd George Woodroof & Jane his wife for £58
to the sd William Davenport in hand paid have sold unto the sd Joel Parrish a
200 a. tr of land … . Wit: Ambrose Arnold, Benjamin Woodroofe, Jane
Woodroof Junr, Rachel Arnold. Ackn 6 Jun 1749 by William Davenport & Ann

his wife & George Woodroof & Jane his wife & admitted to record. Attest: Edmund Waller clk. (Pg 393)

6 Jun 1749. Deed. John Healey (Haley) of St. George Parish, Spotsylvania Co for £30 sold to Ambrose Healey (Haley) of St. Thomas Parish, Orange Co in his actual possession now being containing one pt/o a 200 a. tr of land in St. Georges Parish which is pt/o a tr of land granted by patent to him bounded by Col Gawin Corbin, Robinson Run, John Faulkner, Thomas Wisdom & Robert Gaines ... . Wit: Wm Barber, Geo Wells, James Stevens. Ackn 6 Jun 1749 by John Haley & Mary his wife & admitted to record. Attest: Edmund Waller clk. (Pg 395)

6 Jun 1749. Deed. Thomas Cartwright of Spotsylvania Co & Rachel his wife for £43 sold to Joseph Holladay of sd co an 80 a. tr of land whereon the sd Thos Cartwright now dwelleth in St. George Parish bounded by the East North East Run, sd Holladay's line, Joseph Peterson, sd Thos Cartwright & George Sheppard ... . Wit: John Crittendon Webb, Wm Gholeston, Henry Sparks. Ackn 6 Jun 1749 by Thomas Cartwright & Rachel his wife & admitted to record. Attest: Edmund Waller clk. (Pg 397)

31 Oct 1748. Deed of Lease. Robert Stubblefield of St. George Parish, Spotsylvania Co for 5 shillings leased to Richard Baylor of King & Queen Co merchant a 400 a. tr of land in St. George Parish which was granted by patent dated 30 Jun 1726 unto John Collier Junr & by him sold to the sd Robert Stubblefield 5 Oct 1730 bounded by the North Fork of the South Fork of the South River, James Taylor, Punch Br & Nicholas Langford ... during the term of one year paying the rent of one peper corn upon the last day of the sd term if demanded ... . Wit: Joseph Hawkins, Richard Woolfolk, Richard Dobson, Humphrey Wallis (Willis), Wm Barber. Proved 6 Jun 1749 & admitted to record. Release recorded in page 407 & commission by a mistake. Attest: Edmund Waller clk. (Pg 398)

4 Jul 1749. Deed. Henry Chiles of Spotsylvania Co planter & Marcy his wife for £90 sold to James Rawllings Senr of sd co planter a 250 a. tr of land on the n side of Permunkey River in St. George Parish bounded by Col Moor ... . Wit: Ben Johnson, John C. Webb, Jos Brock. Ackn 4 Jul 1749 by Henry Chiles & Marcy his wife & admitted to record. Attest: Edmund Waller clk. (Pg 400)

4 Jul 1749. Deed. Henry Chiles of Spotsylvania Co & Marcy his wife for £23 sold to William Webb of same co a tr of land bounded by the Lick Br, Joseph Herndon formerly Capt William Wyatt's line & the East North East Run ... . Wit: Ben Johnson, James Rallings, Jos Brock. Ackn 4 Jul 1749 by Henry Chiles & Mary his wife & recorded. Attest: Edmund Waller clk. (Pg 401)

4 Jul 1749. Deed. Henry Chiles of Spotsylvania Co & Marcy his wife for £23 sold to John Crittenden Webb of same co a 100 a. tr of land bounded by Lick Br & Joseph Herndon formerly Capt William Wyatt's line ... . Wit: Ben Johnson, James Rawllings, Jos Brock. Ackn 4 Jul 1749 by Henry Chiles & Marcy his wife & recorded. Attest: Edmund Waller clk. (Pg 403)

2 Jul 1749. Deed. John Farish of Spotsylvania Co & Sarah his wife for £120 sold to Nicholas Horn of same co a 400 a. tr of land on both sides of the South Fork of the South River bounded by Robert Baylor & William Prewett ... . Wit: Jeremiah White Junr, James Younger, John Farish Junr. Ackn 4 Jul 1749 by John Farish & Sarah his wife & admitted to record. Attest: Edmund Waller clk. (Pg 405)

1 Nov 1748. Deed of Release. Robert Stubblefield & Ann his wife of St. George Parish, Spotsylvania Co for £100 sold & released to Richard Baylor of King & Queen Co merchant in his actual possession now being by virtue of one indenture to him made for one year by the sd Robert a 400 a. tr of land in St. George Parish which was granted by patent dated 30 Jun 1726 unto John Collier Junr & by him sold to the sd Robert Stubblefield 5 Oct 1730 bounded by North Fork of the South Fork of the South River, James Taylor, Punch Br & Nicholas Langford ... . Wit: Joseph Hawkins, Richd Woolfolk, Richd Dobson, Humphry Wallis, Wm Barbar. Proved 6 Jun 1749 & admitted to record. N.B. The lease recorded in page 399 by mistake. Attest: Edmund Waller clk. (Pg 407)

Commission. To John Waller, Larkin Chew & William Waller Junr gent of Spotsylvania Co greeting, whereas Robert Stubblefield & Ann his wife by their deed [see above] have conveyed unto Richard Baylor of King & Queen Co the fee simple estate of 400 a. of land, & whereas the sd Ann cannot conveniently travel to our co court to make acknowledgment of the sd conveyance, therefore we do give to you or any two or more of you power to receive the acknowledgment which the sd Ann shall be willing to make before you & we do therefore command that you do personally go to the sd Ann & receive her acknowledgment & examine her privily & apart from her husband whether she doth the same freely & voluntarily & whether she be willing that the same should be recorded ... . Wit Edmund Waller clerk of court 28 Jun 1749. 28 Jun 1749 in compliance of the within dedimus we John Waller & Lark Chew went to the house of the sd Robert Stubblefield & privately examined the sd Ann w/o the sd Robt whether she willingly made & signed the conveyance of the deed of released, answered that she freely & willingly signed the sd release & desired that her right of dower & conveyance might be ackn in court ... . The within commission being duly returned to the clerks office it is admitted to record. Attest: Edmund Waller clk. (Pg 409)

16 Nov MDCCXLXVIII. Deed of Lease. John Robinson Junr of King & Queen Co, VA esqr for 5 shillings leased to John Allan of Spotsylvania Co gent a messuage & 1,000 a. tr of land on the head brs of Mattapony River bounded by the Main Run of the River Po, Alexander Spotswood esqr, Corbin's land & John Allan ... during the term of one year paying the yearly rent of one peper corn at the feast of St. Michaell the Arch Angel if demanded .... Wit: Nathl Harrison, Wm Waller, Henry Willis, Chas Dick. Proved 7 1748 & 1 Aug 1749 & admitted to record. Attest: Edmund Waller clk. (Pg 410)

17 Nov MDCCXLXVIII. Deed of Release. John Robinson Junr of King & Queen Co, VA esqr for £65 sold & released to John Allan of Spotsylvania Co gent a 1,000 a. tr of land ... [same as above] .... Wit: Nathl Harrison, Wm Waller, Henry Willis, Chas Dick. Proved 7 Feb 1748 & 1 Aug 1749 & admitted to record. Attest: Edmund Waller clk. (Pg 412)

20 Jul 1749. Deed. John Willis of Culpepper Co, VA son of Henry & Mildred Willis decd & Nanny his wife for £50 sold to Henry Willis of Spotsylvania Co gent two lotts or ½ acres of land in the town of Fredericksburg described in the plan of the sd town by the figures 11 & 12 which sd lotts by the feoffees of the sd town by deed dated 5 Aug MDCCXL were conveyed to the sd Henry Willis decd for term of his life & then to the sd John Willis & are bounded by Sophia, Charlotta & Caroline Streets & the lots numbered 9 & 10 .... Wit: Will Lynn, John Willis, Geo Livingston, Humphry Wallis. Ackn 1 Aug 1749 by John Willis Junr & admitted to record. (Pg 414)

20 Jul 1749. Deed. John Willis of Culpepper Co, VA son of Henry & Mildred Willis decd & Nanny his wife for £50 sold to Henry Willis of Spotsylvania Co gent two lotts or ½ acres of land in the town of Fredericksburg described in the plan of the sd town by the figures 47 & 48 which sd lotts by the feoffees of the sd town by deed dated 5 Aug MDCCXL were conveyed to the sd Mildred Willis decd for term of 7 years & to the sd Henry Willis decd for term of his life & then to the sd John Willis & are bounded by Princess Ann, Amelia & Caroline Streets adj to the lotts numbered 45 & 46 .... Wit: Will Lynn, John Willis, George Livingston, Humphry Wallis. Ackn 1 Aug 1749 & admitted to record. (Pg 415)

16 Jun 1749. Deed of Sale. Thomas Howell (Howel) of the town of Fredericksburgh, Spotsylvania Co blacksmith do hereby sell unto John Fox of the sd town one feather bed, boulster & rug, one anvil, one pair of Smiths bellows, one Smiths vice, two sledge hammers, one hand hammer, bick iron & four pair of Smiths tongs for & in consideration of £9 .... Wit: David Mitchell, John Innis, John Simpson, Wm Hughes. Proved 1 Aug 1749 & admitted to record. Attest: Edmund Waller clk. (Pg 417)

25 Apr 1748. Deed of Lease. James Shakelford of St. George Parish, Spotsylvania Co for natural love & affection hath farm lett unto Richard Shakelford & Mary his wife of same place during their natural lives a tr of land whereon the sd Richard & Mary Shakelford now doth live & is pt/o a greater tr belonging to the afsd James Shakelford adj to the plantation where the sd James Shakelford now dwelleth which land is bounded by the Horse Pen Swamp, John Waller's Quarter, sd Shakelford, John Waller Junr gent, the Main County Road, & the Spring Br, to include the sd plantation whereon the sd Richd Shakelford now liveth ... paying the rent of one ear of Indian corn on 25 Dec & the quitrents ... . Wit: Edmund Waller, Richd Phillips Junr. Ackn 5 Sep 1749 & recorded. Attest: Edmund Waller clk. (Pg 418)

5 Sep MDCCXLIX. Deed. William Golson & Susanna his wife of St. George Parish, Spotsylvania Co for £65 sold to George Blakey of same place a 500 a. tr of land in St. George Parish adj the lands of Anthony Garnett & Joseph Hawkins & is the remaining pt/o 1,000 a. of land granted by patent to Anthony Golson & the sd William Golson XXVIII Sep 1728 & is the sd William Golson's part thereof ... . Wit: Lark Chew, Larkin Johnston, Ambrose Foster, John Waggener. Ackn 5 Sep 1749 by William Golson & Susanna his wife & admitted to record. Attest: Edmund Waller clk. (Pg 419)

21 Jun 1749. Deed of Gift. John Skinner of Brunswick Parish, King George Co for divers good causes & valuable considerations have given unto Michael (Mical) Skinner of Washington Parish, Westmoreland Co a 100 a. parcel of land in St. Georges Parish on the Hasell Run bounded by James Boy, Francis Thornton, Charles Stewart, the Chaple Road & Thomas Morris ... . Wit: Richd Griffith, Anthony Griffith, William Marders. Proved 5 Sep 1749 & recorded. Attest: Edmund Waller clk. (Pg 421)

5 Sep 1749. Deed of Gift. Benjamin Woodward of Spotsylvania Co for love & effection have given to my dau Mary Woodward a Negro girl named Nan aged about 12 years with all her increase, also one feather bed & furniture, 1 ½ doz pewter plates, two pewter dishes, one large brass kittle, one tea kittle, one copper warming pan, two iron potts, one oval table, two best iron pot racks, one pair of hand irons, six silver tea spoons, tongs & strainers, one tea chest & canestore, one large looking glass & one heifer cald Rose with all her increase ... . Wit: Roger Dixon, William Strother, Anthony Strother. Proved 5 Sep 1749 & recorded. Attest: Edmund Waller clk. (Pg 422)

2 Oct 1749. Deed. Richard Coleman of Hanover Co, VA for £30 sold to John Sanders of Caroline Co, VA a 200 a. tr of land bounded by the Mine Road, Thomas West & John Bowsel ... . Wit: John Sanders Junr, Robin Sanders Junr,

John Jeter Junr. Proved 3 Oct 1749 & recorded. Attest: Edmund Waller clk. (Pg 422)

5 Jun 1749. Deed of Lease. Richard Childs of St. George Parish, Spotsylvania Co for 5 shillings leased to Nicholas Seward of same place a 150 a. tr of land (that is to say) 100 a. part thereof being purch by the sd Richard Childs of Bartholomew Wood & Charity his wife 3 Jun 1740 bounded by the land of Vincent Tapp & land which Elizabeth Tapp bought of Francis & Anthony Thornton 4 Sep 1722, the other parcel of land being 50 a. purch by the sd Richard Childs of Anthony Thornton gent 3 Nov 1741 bounded according to the deeds ... during the term of one year paying the yearly rent of one ear of Indian corn at the feast of St. Michael the Arch Angel if demanded ... . Wit: George Gray, William Cuninghame, John Gordon, Thos Foster. Ackn 3 Oct 1749 & admitted to record. Attest: Edmund Waller clk. (Pg 424)

6 Jun 1749. Deed of Release. Richard Childs of St. George Parish, Spotsylvania Co for £50 sold & released to Nicholas Seward of same place a 150 a. tr of land ... [same as above] ... . Wit: George Gray, William Cunninghame, John Gordon, Thomas Foster. Ackn 3 Oct 1749 & admitted to record. Attest: Edmund Waller clk. (Pg 426)

2 Oct 1749. Deed. Mathew Hubbard & Martha (Matha) his wife of St. Thomas Parish, Orange Co planter for £30 sold to John Adam Link of St. George Parish, Spotsylvania Co planter a 100 a. tr of land in St. George Parish bounded by Robert Stubblefield, John Smith & Wm Pruit, the sd parcel of land is pt/o a greater tr granted by patent to Henry Haines 28 Sep 1728 & by the sd Haines sold to Thomas Hubbard ... . Wit: W. Miller, Hen Brock. Ackn 7 Nov 1749 by Matthew Hubbard & admitted to record. N.B. The feme coverts acknmt recorded in fol 469 in this book. Attest: Edmund Waller clk. (Pg 428)

7 Nov 1749. Deed. George Wilcock of Spotsylvania Co & Mary his wife for £28 sold to Robert Beadles of same co a 114 a. tr of land bounded by Patterson Pulliam ... . Wit: Joseph Gale, George Shepherd. Ackn 7 Nov 1749 by George Wilcock & Mary his wife & admitted to record. Attest: Edmund Waller clk. (Pg 430)

6 Nov 1749. Deed. George Shepperd of St. George Parish, Spotsylvania Co & Elizabeth Mary Angelike his wife for £25 sold to Benjamin Holladay of same place a 60 a. tr of land whereon the sd George Shepperd now lives it being pt/o a 140 a. tr of land bounded by the East North East Run, Thomas Cartwright & the sd George Shepperd ... . Wit: Joseph Holladay, Wm Wilsher, Margett Randolph. Ackn 7 Nov 1749 by George Sheppard & Elizabeth Mary Angelike his wife & admitted to record. Attest: Edmund Waller clk. (Pg 431)

7 Nov 1749. Deed. Between Thomas Turner Junr gent & Mary his wife of Spotsylvania Co & Francis Conway gent & Sarah his wife of Caroline Co of the one part & John Allan of the town of Fredericksburg, Spotsylvania Co merchant of the other part, whereas Charles Taliaferro the elder late of Caroline Co in his life time & at the time of his death was seized in a 570 a. tr of land being at a place called Motts & being so seized on 2 Mar MDCCXXXIV made his will & is contained these clauses (viz) I give to my granddau Mary Taliaferro 200 a. of land in Spotsylvania Co at a place called Motts & one Negro garle named Milley she & her increase, Item I give to my grand dau Sarah Taliaferro 100 a. of land I now live on after my wifes decease to be left in the upper part joining upon the land that was given her by her father adj the river, I also give her the remaining pt/o that tr of land in Spotsylvania Co & place called Motts & I also give her one Negro girl called Lucy she & her increase, that soon after making the sd will the sd Charles Taliaferro died seized of the sd land & premises after whose death his granddaus Mary Taliaferro & Sarah Taliaferro entered into & was possessed of the sd land, & being so seized the sd Mary intermarried with the sd Thomas Turner & the sd Sarah intermarried with the sd Francis Conway & have sold the sd land containing 570 a. to the sd John Allan. Now this indenture wit, that the sd Thomas Turner & Mary his wife & the sd Francis Conway & Sarah his wife for £120 have sold unto the sd John Allan the afsd 570 a. of land lying on the s side of Rappahannock River at a place called Motts ... . Wit: None. Ackn 7 Nov 1749 by Thomas Turner Junr & Mary his wife & Francis Conway & Sarah his wife & admitted to record. Attest: Edmund Waller clk. (Pg 432)

21 Aug 1749. Deed. John Allan of the town of Fredericksburgh, Spotsylvania Co merchant for £140 sold to John Mitchell of the sd town merchant a parcel of land being pt/o a lot or ½ a. of land in the sd town of Fredericksburgh described in the plan of the sd town by the No. 32 according to a survey thereof made by William Waller surveyor of the sd co XVIII Mar MDCCXXXIX bounded by Caroline Street, including the houses in which Charles Valian? now lives, the land of John Lewis esqr & Lot. No. 34 ... . Wit: Chas Dick, John Gordon, Adam Stephens, James Miller, William Cuninghame, Wm Waller. Proved 7 Nov 1749 & admitted to record. Attest: Edmund Waller clk. (Pg 435)

5 Dec MDCCXLIX. Deed. George Carter of St. George Parish, Spotsylvania Co & Elizabeth his wife for £12:10 sold to John Pain of same place a 25 a. tr of land pt/o a tr whereon the sd George Carter dwelleth in the parish afsd bounded by the sd John Pain & Humphry Bell ... . Wit: Thos Duerson, Edmund Waller, Richd Phillips Junr. Ackn 5 Dec 1749 & admitted to record. Attest: Edmund Waller clk. (Pg 437)

15 Aug 1749. Deed. John Willis the younger son of that name of Col Henry Willis decd of Culpeper Co & Nanny his wife for £270 sold to Joseph Stevens of

St. Margaret Parish, Caroline Co several trs of land on Nassaponax Run the one containing 200 a. bounded by William Hollaway, Elias Downes Senr & Elias Downs (Downes) Junr, & the other tr of land containing 1465 a. is bounded by Nassaponax Cr, which two trs of land were by a deed of gift from Col Henry Willis decd given to the sd John Willis & by him sold to the sd Joseph Stevens .... Wit: Anthony Strother, Roger Dixon, Kemp Taliaferro, George Buckner, Thomas Slaughter. Proved 5 Sep 1749 & 6 Feb 1749 & admitted to record. Attest: Edmund Waller clk. (Pg 439)

19 Dec 1749. Deed. John Allan of the town of Fredericksburgh, Spotsylvania Co merchant for £150 sold to Robert Duncanson of same place merchant a parcel of land or pt/o a lot numbered 30 in the plan of the town of Fredericksburgh bounded by lot No. 32, lot No. 29 & Caroline Street, the whole tr of land containing 5,188 square feet .... Wit: William Lynn, Thomas Mackie, Jno Sutherland, Jas Fleming, Wm McWilliams Junr. Proved 6 Feb 1749 & admitted to record. Attest: Edmund Waller clk. (Pg 441)

30 Jan 1749. Deed of Lease. John Quarles of Prince William Co gent for 5 shillings leased to Charles Colson of the town of Fredericksburgh, Spotsylvania Co ordinary keeper a 278 a. tr of land bounded by Augustine Smith, Charles Taliaferro, a patent of Mott's, Capt William Hansford & Francis Thornton, which tr of land was granted to Leonard Holms by patent dated 31 Oct 1726 & was by the sd Leonard Holms sold unto John Quarles father of the afsd John Quarles party to these presents ... during the term of one year paying the rent of one ear of Indian corn at the feast of St. Michael the Arch Angel if demanded ... . Wit: M. Battaley, John Dent, John Jones, William Lynn, Thomas Mackie. Proved 6 Feb 1749 & admitted to record. Attest: Edmund Waller clk. (Pg 443)

31 Jan 1749. Deed of Release. John Quarles of Prince William Co gent for £100 sold & released to Charles Colson of the town of Fredericksburgh, Spotsylvania Co ordinary keeper a 278 a. tr of land ... [*same as above*] ... . Wit: M. Battaley, John Dent, John Jones, William Lynn, Thomas Mackie. Proved 6 Feb 1749 & admitted to record. Attest: Edmund Waller clk. (Pg 444)

23 Sep 1749. Deed. John Trusty of Spotsylvania Co for £35 sold to Zachary Lewis of same co a 108 a. tr of land which sd tr of land was by John Waller gent by deed dated 4 Jan 1734 granted to the sd John Trusty bounded by land formerly of John Wilkins now of John Wiglesworth .... Wit: William Phillips, Robert Beadles, Jno Lewis, Zachary Lewis Junr. Ackn 6 Mar 1749 & admitted to record. Attest: Edmund Waller clk. (Pg 446)

6 Mar 1749. Deed. Robert Beadles of Spotsylvania Co & Dilly his wife for £25 sold to John Trusty of same co a 50 a. tr of land which sd tr of land was by deed

dated 4 May MDCCXLVI granted by George Musick Senr to the sd Robert Beadles bounded by the Mine Road, Wyatt's line, George Musick & John Graves ... . Wit: Edmund Waller. Ackn 6 Mar 1749 by Robert Beadles & Dilly his wife & recorded. Attest: Edmund Waller clk. (Pg 448)

9 Feb 1749. Deed of Lease. Benjamin Martin of St. George Parish, Spotsylvania Co for the consideration hereafter mentioned farm lett unto Edmund Waller of the same place during the term of 10 years from 17th day this instant untill the 17th day Feb 1759 a 150 a. tr of land being pt/o a tr of land whereupon Henry Martin decd did live bounded by the Rev. James Marye, John Thornton son of Col Francis Thornton decd & Hazle Run in the parish afsd ... the sd Edmund Waller shall after the 17th day of Feb 1750 yearly pay to the sd Benjamin Martin the rent of 500 lbs of tobacco & the quitrents ... . Wit: Charles Snead, James Wiglesworth, Richd Phillips Junr. Ackn 6 Mar 1749 & admitted to record. Attest: Edmund Waller clk. (Pg 450)

5 Jan 1749. Deed. Mark Wheeler & Sarah his wife of Spotsylvania Co for £28 sold to Joseph Carter of same co a 100 a. tr of land in St. George Parish on the br of the North Fork of South River & is the same land as was conveyed to the sd Mark Wheeler by Henry Goodloe gent (since decd) by deeds of lease & release recorded 3 Jun MDCCXXXV & bounded by the sd Goodloe ... . Wit: Robt Durrett, James Younger, James Ham, Patrick Kennedy. Ackn 3 Apr 1750 by Mark Wheeler & Sarah his wife & admitted to record. The commission with the return of the feme coverts acknmt is recorded in 468 fol in this book. Attest: Edmund Waller clk. (Pg 452)

3 Feb 1749. Deed. James Jackson of Albemarle Co planter & Susanna his wife for £86 sold to Owen Thomas of Spotsylvania Co a 300 a. tr of land or woodland ground in St. George Parish bounded by a br of the River Poe, Bartlett's line, the Mine Road, Hawkins' line & William Richerson ... . Wit: Nicholas Hawkins, John Cuningham, Mumford Stevens, Isaac Scott. Proved 3 Apr 1750 & recorded. Attest: Edmund Waller clk. (Pg 453)

3 Feb 1749/50. Bond. I James Jackson of Albemarle Co am firmly bound unto Owen Thomas of Spotsylvania Co in the sum of £140 ... the condition of this obligation is such that whereas the sd James Jackson hath by an indenture [*see above*] sold unto the sd Owen Thomas a 300 a. tr of land & have promised to appear personally & Susanah his wife att the court held in Oct & there ackn the sd deed & also keep all the clauses & virtues therein express then this obligation to be void ... . Wit: Nicholas Hawkins, John Cuningham, Mumford Stevens, Isaac Scott. Proved 3 Apr 1750 & recorded. Attest: Edmund Waller clk. (Pg 455)

3 Apr 1750. Deed. John Allan & Margarett his wife of Spotsylvania Co for £14 sold to Richard Hudnall of Northumberland Co a 358 a. tr of land being that tr of land granted to the sd John Allan by Letters Pattent dated 1 Apr 1749 bounded by the Honourable Sir William Gooch barnt, a patent granted to Roger Tandy, Mr. Baylor's line, White's line, Michael Guinney decd, Corbin's line & Garnett's line .... Wit: None. Ackn 3 Apr 1750 by John Allan & Margarett his wife & admitted to record. Attest: Edmund Waller clk. (Pg 456)

1 May 1750. Deed. Henry Pendleton of King William Co, VA & Martha his wife for £27 sold to James Dyer of Caroline Co, VA a 70 a. tr of land or woodland ground in St. Georges Parish bounded by Fork Road, Pamunkey Rowlling Road, Main County Road, Zachary Lewis, Daniel Prewitt, John Shurly & Nicholas Horn, it being pt/o a 300 a. tr which the sd Pendleton bought of George Woodroofe called Woodroofs Ordinary to include the houses .... Wit: None. Ackn 1 May 1750 by Henry Pendleton & Martha his wife & admitted to record. Attest: Edmund Waller clk. (Pg 458)

30 Apr 1750. Deed of Lease. Robert True of Spotsylvania Co planter for 5 shillings leased to Edward Kelley of same co a 150 a. tr of land bounded by William Hollaway, Elias Downs & Elias Downs Junr ... during the term of one year paying the yearly rent of one pepper corn at the feast of St. Michael the Arch Angel if demanded .... Wit: Philip Vincent Vass, Robert Dudley, John Menefee. Ackn 1 May 1750 & admitted to record. Attest: Edmund Waller clk. (Pg 460)

1 May 1750. Deed of Release. Robert True of Spotsylvania Co planter & Margarett his wife for £30 sold & released to Edward Kelley of same co a 150 a. tr of land ... [same as above] .... Wit: Philip Vincent Vass, Robert Dudley, John Menefee. Ackn 1 May 1750 by Robert True & Margarett his wife & admitted to record. Attest: Edmund Waller clk. (Pg 461)

16 Jan 1749. Deed. John Holladay of St. George Parish, Spotsylvania Co & Elizabeth his wife for £46 sold to Thomas Magee of same place a 155 a. tr of land in St. Georges Parish bounded by the Main Road .... Wit: Philip Vincent Vass, Edward Herndon, Benjamin Holladay. Full & peaceable possession & seizing was given & delivered by turf & twigg. Wit: Ambrose Foster, William Gatewood, Ignathus Tureman, William Smith. Ackn 1 May 1750 by John Holladay & Elizabeth his wife & admitted to record. Attest: Edmund Waller clk. (Pg 463)

1 May 1750. Deed. Erasmus Wethers Allen of St. George Parish, Spotsylvania Co for £30 sold to John Waggener of same place a 300 a. tr of land bounded by Col Corbin & Anthony Street .... Wit: Nathaniel Allen, Thomas Allen. Ackn

1 May 1750 by Erasmus W. Allen & Sarah his wife & admitted to record.
Attest: Edmund Waller clk. (Pg 465)

28 Apr 1750. Deed. William Mash of St. Mark Parish, Culpeper Co, VA for
£20 sold to Obediah Howerton of St. George Parish, Spotsylvania Co a 300 a. tr
of land taken up by George Dowdey bounded by Lawyears Road, Joseph
Hawkins, William Stephens, Len Young, Anthony Street, Erasmus Wethers
Allen & Corbin's line ... . Wit: Erasmus Wethers Allen, James Jones, John
Faulconer. Proved 1 May 1750 & admitted to record. Attest: Edmund Waller
clk. (Pg 467)

Commission. To John Minor, Larkin Chew & William Waller gent greeting,
whereas Mark Wheeler & Sarah his wife of Spotsylvania Co by their indenture
dated 5 Jan 1749 have conveid unto Joseph Carter of sd co the fee simple estate
of 100 a. of land, & whereas the sd Sarah cannot conveniently travel to our co
court to make acknowledgment of the sd conveyance, therefore we do give unto
you or any two or more of you power to receive the acknowledgment which the
sd Sarah shall be willing to make before you & command that you do personally
go to the sd Sarah & receive her acknowledgment & examine her privately &
apart from her husband whether she doth the same freely & voluntarily &
whether she be willing that the same be recorded ... . Wit Edmund Waller clerk
of court 12 Jan 1749. 17 Jan 1749 we John Minor & Wm Waller hereby certifie
that pursuant to the within commission we personally went to Sarah the w/o the
sd Mark Wheeler & examined her privately & apart from her husband who ackn
before us that she freely & voluntarily did make & execute the indenture & that
she was willing that the same should be recorded. The within commission being
duly returned is admitted to record. Attest: Edmund Waller clk. (Pg 468)

Commission. To Thomas Chew, Taviner Beale & Henry Downs of Orange Co
gent greeting, whereas Matthew Hubbard & Martha his wife of Orange Co by
their indenture dated 2 Oct 1749 have conveyed unto John Adam Link of this co
the fee simple estate of 100 a. of land, & whereas the sd Martha cannot
conveniently travel to our co court to make acknowledgment of the sd
conveyance, therefore we do give unto you or any two or more of you power to
receive the acknowledgment which the sd Martha shall be willing to make
before you & command that you do personally go to the sd Martha & receive her
acknowledgment & examine her privately & apart from her husband whether she
doth the same freely & voluntarily & whether she be willing that the same be
recorded ... . Wit Edmund Waller clerk of court 24 Apr 1750. 24 May 1750 in
obedience to the within order Thos Chew & Henry Downs have received the
acknmt of Martha the w/o Matthew Hubbard & she desires it may be admitted to
record. The within commission being duly returned is admitted to record. N.B
The deed recorded in 428 in this book. Attest: Edmund Waller clk. (Pg 469)

4 Dec 1749. Deed of Lease. John Allan of the town of Fredericksburgh, Spotsylvania Co merchant for 5 shillings leased to Robert Todd of the Borough of Norfolk merchant a lott of land in the town of Fredericksburgh whereon the sd John Allan now lives described in the plan of the sd town by No. 52 also the remaining pt/o one other lott which remains over & above what part thereof the sd John Allan hath already sold to Charles Dick of the sd town merchant described in the plan of the sd town by No. 51 ... together with the room adj to the kitchen to be completely finished by the sd John Allan as he at first designed it & the corner cupboard in the dwelling house & the chairs in the kitchen & all the stone bott within ... during the term of one year paying the rent of one pepper corn at the feast of St. Michael the Arch Angel if demanded .... Wit: M. Battaley, William Hunter, Andr Ross, Chas Dick, Robt Duncanson, James Allan. Proved 5 Jun 1750 & admitted to record. Attest: Edmund Waller clk. (Pg 470)

5 Dec 1749. Deed of Release. John Allan of the town of Fredericksburgh, Spotsylvania Co merchant for £300 sold & released to Robert Todd of the Borough of Norfolk merchant Lot No. 52 in the town of Fredericksburgh & the remaining pt/o Lot No. 51 ... [same as above] .... Wit: M. Battaley, William Hunter, Andr Ross, Chas Dick, Robt Duncanson, James Allan. Proved 5 Jun 1750 & admitted to record. Attest: Edmund Waller clk. (Pg 470)

5 Jun 1750. Deed. Joseph Redd of St. George Parish, Spotsylvania Co carpenter & Bettey (Beth) his wife for £32:8 sold to James Redd of King & Queen Co planter a 108 a. parcel of land according to a survey lately made by Richard Tutt bounded by Col Lewis, Francis Turnley & the sd James Redd, being the pt/o the tr whereon the sd Joseph Redd & Betty his wife now dwell ... . Wit: Larkin Johnston, John Crane, John Carter. Ackn 5 Jun 1750 by Joseph Redd & Betty his wife & admitted to record. Attest: Edmund Waller clk. (Pg 472)

5 Jun 1750. Deed. Cornelius Vaughan of Caroline Co & Frances his wife for £40 sold to William Darnaby of Spotsylvania Co a 247 a. tr of land in St. George Parish bounded by Joseph Nix & Johnston's line .... Wit: Jno Battaley, W. Miller. Ackn 5 Jun 1750 by Cornelius Vaughan & Frances his wife & admitted to record. Attest: Edmund Waller clk. (Pg 475)

12 Mar 1749. Deed of Mortgage. William Crawford for £10 sold to Edmund Waller every part & parcel of my estate be it of what nature or kind soever moveable or immoveable ... & the same to remain to his own use untill such times I have paid him to his satisfaction what I am justly owing him then this writing to be void .... Wit: Richard Phillips Junr, Elizabeth Williams. Ackn 5 Jun 1750 & admitted to record. Attest: Edmund Waller clk. (Pg 477)

1 May 1750. Deed. Hancock Lee of King George Co gent & Mary his wife for £175 sold to Anthony Strother of sd co merchant two lotts or ½ acres of land in the town of Fredericksburgh on Charlotte Street know in the plan of the sd town by the numbers 35 & 36 the same being granted to the sd Hancock Lee by a deed from the feoffees or trustees for the sd town dated 1 Jul 1735 … . Wit: James Hunter, Geo Taylor, Valentine Peyton Junr. Proved 5 Jun 1750 & further proved 3 & 4 Jul 1750 & recorded. Attest: Edmund Waller clk. (Pg 477)

Commission. To Robert Jackson, Fielding Lewis & Charles Dick gent greeting, whereas Hancock Lee of King George Co & Mary his wife by their indenture dated [see above] have conveyed unto Anthony Strother of this co the fee simple estate of two lotts of land, & whereas the sd Mary cannot conveniently travel to our co court to make acknowledgment of the sd conveyance, therefore we do give unto you or any two or more of you power to receive the acknowledgment which the sd Mary shall be willing to make before you & command that you do personally go to the sd Mary & receive her acknowledgment & examine her privately & apart from her husband whether she doth the same freely & voluntarily & whether she be willing that the same be recorded … . Wit Edmund Waller clerk of court 5 Jul 1750. 1 Sep 1750 by vertue of this commission we Fielding Lewis & Chas Dick personally went to Mary the w/o Hancock Lee gent & examined her privily & apart from her sd husband & she freely & willingly doth consent that the indenture should be recorded … . The within commission being duly returned 1 Sep 1750 to the clerks office is admitted to record. Attest: Edmund Waller clk. (Pg 478)

5 Jun 1750. Deed. John Farish of Spotsylvania Co & Sarah his wife for £49:10 sold to William Waller of same co a 34 ½ a. tr of land which is pt/o a patent granted to Bernard Paine XXII Jan 1717 bounded by the River Ta, the place called the Clayhole now a Mill Dam, land the sd Farish bought of William Johnston gent & sold to the sd Waller & the Mill Land … . Wit: John Carter, John Hoskins, Richd Pollard. Ackn 3 Jul 1750 & admitted to record. N.B. The feme coverts acknmt recorded in page 509 in this book. Attest: Edmund Waller clk. (Pg 479)

4 Jul 1750. Deed. Between Archibald Mcpherson, William Hunter & James Hunter exrs of the will of John Allan late of the town of Fredericksburgh decd of the one part & John Allan of the town afsd joiner of the other part, whereas the sd John Allan by his will dated 15 Mar last proved in Spotsylvania Co Court did direct that his whole estate real & personal should be sold at publick sale after his death & whereas the lott of ground described in the plan of the sd town of Fredericksburgh by the number 64 pt/o the real estate of the sd John Allan decd was at the last Jun Fair in Fredericksburgh sold by the exrs to the sd James Allan being the highest bidder for the lott. Now this indenture wit that the sd Achd

Mcpherson, William Hunter & James Hunter exrs for £152 sold to the sd James
Allan the Lot No. 64 containing ½ a. .... Wit: Alexander Campbele, William
McWilliams Junr. Ackn 3 Jul 1750 & admitted to record. Attest: Edmund
Waller clk. (Pg 481)

6 Aug 1750. Deed. Edward Jones of Spotsylvania Co & Sarah his wife for £34
sold to Francis Meriwether of Louisa Co, VA a 69 a. tr of land which was by a
deed dated 27 Feb 1745 conveyed to the sd Edward Jones by James Shackelford
& Elizabeth his wife for £10:7 & is bounded by Edmund Waller, the Main Road,
Pamunkey Road & James Shackelford .... Memorandum Mr. Jones is to have
liberty to take away corps of his child or Paile in or put a toumbstone on the
grave. Wit: Jno Lewis, Zachary Lewis Junr. Ackn 7 Aug 1750 by Edward
Jones & admitted to record. Attest: Edmund Waller clk. (Pg 482)

2 Oct 1750. Deed. Between Joseph Redd of Spotsylvania Co carpenter & Betty
his wife of the one part & James Redd of King & Queen Co planter of the other
part, whereas Thomas Redd of King & Queen Co by his deed dated 5 Dec 1743
did sell unto the sd Joseph Redd a 377 a. tr of land bounded as in & by the sd
deed as may fully appear & whereas the sd Joseph Redd & Betty his wife by
their deed dated 5 Jun 1750 did sell unto the sd James Redd 108 a. of land pt/o
the sd tr of 377 a. bounded in & by the sd last mentioned deed is mentioned.
Now this indenture wit that the sd Joseph Redd & Betty his wife for £130 sold to
the sd James Redd the residue & remainder of the sd tr of 377 a. of land not
formerly sold by the sd Joseph Redd & Betty his wife to the sd James Redd
being 269 a. according to the bounds thereof .... Wit: Robert Huddleston, Jos
McWilliams, Alexander Guill. See a commission in the next book fol 10 & 11
for passing the womans right. Wit to receipt: Edmund Waller. Ackn 2 Oct
1750 by Joseph Redd & Betty his wife & admitted to record. Attest: Edmund
Waller clk. (Pg 484)

20 Jun 1750. Power of Attorney. I William Beverley of Blanfield, Essex Co
esqr guardian of Harry Beverley son & heir of Robert Beverly late of
Spotsylvania Co esqr decd do appoint William Waller of the sd co gent director
& manager of all the lands, slaves & other estate belonging to the sd Harry
Beverley in Orange & Caroline Cos & elsewhere within VA .... Wit: R.
Tunstall, W. Russell. Proved 2 Oct 1750 & recorded. Attest: Edmund Waller
clk. (Pg 486)

20 Jun 1750. Instructions for Col William Waller concerning Harry Beverley &
his estate. You are to use your utmost indeavour to keep Mr. Beverley at the
College till he is of age pursuant to his father's will. You may allow him for
pocket expence 10 pistoles per year & also pay the charges of keeping him at the
College. The present overseer is to have a tenth pt/o the crop for his shear.

Please to git notes for ye crops of tobacco as also for ye crop last made & sell them for goods &c for Mr. Beverley & his Negroes & plantations use & money. I shall give orders to my other attys to purch 8 or 10 Negroes for Mr. Beverley which please to settle on Octonia as you judge proper. Mr. Holt at Wmsburg has an account agt Mr. Beverley which please to pay off as also any other accounts that are already contracted. You are to maintain Mr. Beverley in such decent manner as you shall think convenient. Whatever money shall be due on balance of your account from year to year please to pay to my other attys who are John Robinson esqr, Major Richard Tunstall of King & Queen & James Mills of Tappahannock merchant. Whenever the speaker & my other attys shall have so much of his money as with what I shall have of his will make up £500 they will lay it out in Negroes & I desire they also may be settled on his land as you shall judge proper. When Mr. Beverley is of full age please to deliver up the lands, plantations, Negroes & stocks &c to him & take his receipt for them. Octonia has 14,300 a. of portabage 1250 a. the quitrents to whereof must be annually paid. Blanfield, VA 20 Jun 1750 William Beverley. Memorandum Octonia is 4600 a. Harry Beverley to pay for. Wm Waller. The within instructions from William Beverley esqr to William Waller gent being produced in court 2 Oct 1750 & admitted to record. Attest: Edmund Waller clk. (Pg 487)

20 Sep MDCCL. Deed. Thomas Duerson of Spotsylvania Co & Hannah his wife for £250 sold to Joseph Brock of sd co a 720 a. tr of land the same being conveyed to the sd Thomas Duerson by Joseph Brock decd by deed dated XXVIII Apr MDCCXXXIX bounded by the Matapony Church, a pattent of Harry Beverley decd, Larkin Chew decd, Rice Curtis Junr & Bushes Road ... . Wit: Thomas Estes, Patterson Pulliam, Ephraim Knight. Ackn 2 Oct 1750 by Thomas Duerson & Hannah his wife & admitted to record. Attest: Edmund Waller clk. (Pg 488)

2 Oct 1750. Deed. John Grayson of St. Mark Parish, Culpepper Co & Barbary his wife for £20 sold to Martin True of St. George Parish, Spotsylvania Co a 331 a. tr of land on Nassaponnax Swamp bounded by Robert Taliaferro & Lawrance Smith ... after the determination of the lease for lives already granted to James Ball of Lancaster Co gent ... . Wit: Robert Huddleston, John Elson. Ackn 2 Oct 1750 by John Grayson & Barbary his wife & admitted to record. Attest: Edmund Waller clk. (Pg 490)

20 Sep MDCCL. Deed. Joseph Brock of Spotsylvania Co for £200 sold to Thomas Duerson of sd co a 600 a. tr of land bounded by Bushes Road, Garton's corner, the River Ta & Durrett's corner ... . Wit: Thomas Estes, Patterson Pulliam, Ephraim Knight. Ackn 2 Oct 1750 & admitted to record. Attest: Edmund Waller clk. (Pg 492)

7 Sep 1750. Bond & Deed of Mortgage. I Wm Smither of Spotsylvania Co am firmly bound unto William Waller of same co in the sum of £6:5:1 & 474 ½ lbs of tobacco for the payment whereof well & truly to be made by me at or upon 1 Oct next insuring I bind myself in the penal sum of £12:10:2 & for the further securing unto the sd William Waller the payment of the sd sum I do hereby sell unto the sd William Waller the following goods & chattels, that is to say, two cows & a calf & yearling, a gun & 13 hoggs with their increase, provided that if the sd Wm Smither shall well & truly pay the sum of £6:5 a penny on 1 Oct then this bond & mortgage to be void … . Wit: Harry Beverley, Thomas McNiell, Jonathan Gibson. The following goods & chattels bought at auction 26 Sep 1750 of Wm Smither's estate, viz, a Bible, an iron pott, two sifters, a pail & piggon, a pad lock & box iron, a frying pan, two beds, two sheets, 2 ruggs & bedcords, 2 bedsteads & pillers, a cowhide, a matt. Which sd goods & affects are in possession of William Smither to be delivered to the sd Waller or order on demand. Per William Smither. Ackn 2 Oct 1750 by William Smither & admitted to record. Attest: Edmund Waller clk. (Pg 494)

23 Oct 1750. Deed of Lease. William Martin of St. George Parish, Spotsylvania Co for £53 leased to Benjamin Martin of same place a 100 ½ a. tr of land bounded by William Lindsey, Harry Beverly & the River Po … during the term of one year paying the rent of one ear of Indian corn at the feast of St. John ye Baptist if demanded … . Wit: Thomas Collins, Nathan Hawkins, Nichos Hawkins Junr, John Hutcherson, Jeremiah Smith, John Sutton, John Hawkins. Proved 6 Nov 1760 & admitted to record. Attest: Edmund Waller clk. (Pg 495)

24 Oct 1750. Deed of Release. William Martin of St. George Parish, Spotsylvania Co for £53 sold & released to Benjamin Martin of same place a 100 ½ a. tr of land … [same as above] … . Wit: Thomas Collins, Nathan Hawkins, Nichos Hawkins Junr, John Hutcherson, Jeremiah Smith. Proved 6 Nov 1750 & admitted to record. Attest: Edmund Waller clk. (Pg 496)

4 Dec 1750. Deed. John Champe of King George Co gent for £60 sold to William Waller of Spotsylvania Co gent a 200 a. tr of land whereon John Parish lately dwelt in St. George Parish bounded by Greens Br, Lawrence Battaile & Peter Mountague … . Wit: None. Ackn 4 Dec 1750 & admitted to record. Attest: Edmund Waller clk. (Pg 499)

4 Dec 1750. Deed. Abraham Rogers of St. Georges Parish, Spotsylvania Co planter & Barbary his wife for £60 sold to George Rogers of Drysdale Parish, King & Queen Co joiner a 10 a. tr of land in St. George Parish together with all the sd Abraham Rogers's right & title of in & to a water grist mill & the utencils thereto belonging called Rogers's Mill which land is bounded by Middle River

or fork of Matapony River ... . Wit: Robt Huddleston, Lancelot Warrin, Hackley Warrin. Ackn 4 Dec 1750 by Abraham Rogers & Barbary his wife & admitted to record. Attest: Edmund Waller clk. (Pg 500)

3 Dec MDCCL. Deed. George Nix of Orange Co & Elizabeth his wife for £12 sold to John Calahan of Spotsylvania Co a tr or pt/o a tr of land containing 87 ½ a. devised to the sd George Nix by the will of his father George Nix decd & is the lower pt/o 175 a. whereon the sd George Nix decd did live ... . Wit: Edmund Waller, Rd Phillips Junr, Alexander McKenny. Ackn 4 Dec 1750 by George Nix & admitted to record. Attest: Edmund Waller clk. Elizabeth Nix ackn this indenture 1 Sep 1752 & is recorded. Attest: Wm Waller clerk. (Pg 502)

28 Sep 1750. Power of Attorney. I William Sutton of Spotsylvania Co planter do hereby appoint Mary Whitehouse my well beloved friend of parish afsd to be my atty to ask, demand & require, sue for & receive all such debts, dues, duties & sums of money due or to be due to me from any person whatsoever ... . Wit: Cuthbert Artrup (Artrip), William Grayson. Proved 4 Dec 1750 & admitted to record. Attest: Edmund Waller clk. (Pg 503)

4 Dec 1750. Deed. Fielding Lewis of Spotsylvania Co & Betty his wife for £30 sold to Charles Dick of the town of Fredericksburgh, co afsd gent a parcel of land adjacent to the town of Fredericksburgh bounded by Lot No. 51 now in the possession of the sd Charles Dick, Princess Ann Street & Lot No. 52 ... . Wit: John Spotswood, Richd Tutt, Robt Armistead. Ackn 4 Dec 1750 by Fielding Lewis & admitted to record. Attest: Edmund Waller clk. (Pg 504)

Commission. To Richd Tutt, John Spotswood, Robert Jackson & William Hunter gent greeting, whereas Fielding Lewis gent of Spotsylvania Co & Betty his wife by their indenture [see above] have conveyed unto Charles Dick gent of the sd co the fee simple estate of a parcel of land, & whereas the sd Betty cannot conveniently travel to our co court to make acknowledgment of the sd conveyance, therefore we do give unto you or any two or more of you power to receive the acknowledgment which the sd Betty shall be willing to make before you & command that you do personally go to the sd Betty & receive her acknowledgment & examine her privately & apart from her husband whether she doth the same freely & voluntarily & whether she be willing that the same be recorded ... . Wit Edmund Waller clerk of court 4 Dec 1750. Pursuant to the within commission we John Spotswood & Richard Tutt did personally go to the within named Betty w/o Fielding Lewis & did examine her privily & apart from her husband & she did declare she did execute the deed freely & voluntarily & is willing the same should be recorded. The within commission being duly returned to the clerks office is admitted to record. Attest: Edmund Waller clk. (Pg 506)

4 Dec 1750. Deed. Fielding Lewis of the town of Fredericksburg, Spotsylvania Co gent & Betty his wife for £30 sold to John Mitchell of same place merchant a parcel of ground adjacent to the town of Fredericksburg bounded by Lot No. 32 upon Caroline Street now in the possession of the sd John Mitchell, Sophia Street & Lot No. 31 ... . Wit: John Spotswood, Richard Tutt, Robert Armistead. Ackn 4 Dec 1750 by Fielding Lewis gent & admitted to record. Attest: Edmund Waller clk. (Pg 507)

Commission. To Richd Tutt, John Spotswood, Robert Jackson & William Hunter, Charles Dick & Anthony Strother gent greeting, whereas Fielding Lewis gent of Spotsylvania Co & Betty his wife by their indenture [see above] have conveyed unto John Mitchell gent of the sd co the fee simple estate of a parcel of land, & whereas the sd Betty cannot conveniently travel to our co court to make acknowledgment of the sd conveyance, therefore we do give unto you or any two or more of you power to receive the acknowledgment which the sd Betty shall be willing to make before you & command that you do personally go to the sd Betty & receive her acknowledgment & examine her privately & apart from her husband whether she doth the same freely & voluntarily & whether she be willing that the same be recorded ... . Wit Edmund Waller clerk of court 4 Dec 1750. Pursuant to the within commission we John Spotswood & Richard Tutt did personally go to the within named Betty w/o Fielding Lewis & did examine her privily & apart from her husband & she did declare she did execute the deed freely & voluntarily & is willing the same should be recorded. The within commission being duly returned to the clerks office is admitted to record. Attest: Edmund Waller clk. (Pg 508)

Commission. To Larkin Chew, William Carr & Henry Willis gent greeting, whereas John Farish of Spotsylvania Co & Sarah his wife by their indenture dated 5 Jun 1750 have conveyed unto William Waller gent of the sd co the fee simple estate of a 34 ½ a. tr of land, & whereas the sd Sarah cannot conveniently travel to our co court to make acknowledgment of the sd conveyance, therefore we do give unto you or any two or more of you power to receive the acknowledgment which the sd Sarah shall be willing to make before you & command that you do personally go to the sd Sarah & receive her acknowledgment & examine her privately & apart from her husband whether she doth the same freely & voluntarily & whether she be willing that the same be recorded ... . Wit Edmund Waller clerk of court 13 Nov 1750. Pursuant to the within commission we Lark Chew, Wm Carr & Henry Willis did personally go to the within named Sarah & did examine her privily & apart from her husband & she did declare she did execute the deed freely & voluntarily & is willing the same should be recorded. The within commission being duly returned to the clerks office is admitted to record. Attest: Edmund Waller clk. (Pg 509)

29 Jan 1750. Agreement. Between Edmund Waller of Spotsylvania Co of the one part & his servant woman Elizabeth Williams now of the sd co on the other part, wit that the sd Edmund Waller for 20 shillings paid by the sd Elizabeth Williams after the date hereof & to acquit, release & discharge him the sd Edmund Waller from her freedom dues allowed her by law then the sd Edmund Waller for himself & his heirs on the afsd conditions doth by these presents forever release, acquit & discharge her from all service at this time due to him ... . Wit: Linefield Sharpe, Rd Phillips Junr. Ackn 5 Feb 1750 by Edmund Waller gent & Elizabeth Williams & is admitted to record. Attest: Edmund Waller clk. (Pg 509)

4 Feb 1750. Deed of Gift. William Bledsoe of St. George Parish, Spotsylvania Co gent for fatherly love & affection have given unto my beloved son Moses Bledsoe during his natural life & after he the sd Moses Bledsoe's decease to go to his son William Bledsoe & his heirs a 100 a. tr of land it being on the n side the Mill Br of Hunting Run all the land which I now hold on that side of the sd run, the same being by a pattent dated 12 Jul 1719 ... . Wit: Robert Coleman, Thomas Brown, John Gore. Proved 5 Feb 1750 & admitted to record. Attest: Edmund Waller clk. (Pg 510)

4 Sep 1750. Deed of Mortgage. Patrick Connelly of the town of Fredericksburg, Spotsylvania Co hatter for £28 sold to William Thomson of the town afsd one feather bed, three rugs, two counterpains, one pair of sheets, one walnut table, one walnut desk, one large chest, one safe, three pewter dishes, six plates, six knives & forks, one brass kettle, three iron pots, two frying panns, one brass mortar & pestle, two box irons, a chest of coopers ware, one walnut couch, five chairs, one powdering tub, one tea kittle, one gridd iron, four tables, one young dark bay mare, also all the goods in my possession ... provided & upon condition that if the sd Patrick Connelly do well & truly pay unto the sd William Thomson the sum of £28 upon 1 Aug next coming that these presents shall cease & be void ... . Wit: Robt Croker, Broadbent McWilliams. Ackn 5 Feb 1750 & admitted to record. Attest: Edmund Waller clk. (Pg 511)

2 Apr 1751. Deed. John Tyre of a [?] Co, within VA for £16 sold to John Williamson of Spotsylvania Co a 100 a. tr of land in St. George Parish pt/o a 400 a. tr of land granted by patent to John Smith XXVIII Sep MDCCXXVIII bounded by Ralph Williams & Popaw Run ... . Wit: Robert Huddleston, William Matthews, Andrew Caddle, Edward Land. Also wit to receipt: Wm B. Huddleston. Ackn 2 Apr 1751 & admitted to record. Attest: Edmund Waller clk. (Pg 512)

XXXI Jan 1750. Deed. Between Thomas Warrin son & heir at law to Thomas Warrin late of Spotsylvania Co decd of the one part & Lancelot Warrin son of the sd decd of the other part, wit that the sd Thomas Warrin decd in his lifetime & at the time of his death was seized in a 210 a. tr of land in St. George Parish & being so seised the sd Thomas Warrin by his will dated 13 Apr 1749 mentioned the following devises, "Imprimis, I give & bequeath to my son Hackley Warrin 95 a. of land which I formerly gave to my dau Rachel Haskew & the old orchard & the convenient timber to keep it under a fence & also a Negro girl named Dilla & all her increase, I give unto my son Lancelot Warrin all the land belonging to the plantation where I now live & also a Negro wench named Bess after me & my wifes decease." That quickly after making the will the sd Thomas Warring departed this life & thereupon the sd will was duly proved in Spotsylvania Co Court, now this indenture wit that the sd Thomas Warrin being satisfied that the sd testator intended to have devised the sd land to the sd Lancelot Warrin & his heirs forever after the death of his sd wife & she being now dead the sd Thomas Warrin to fullfill the intent of his sd father & also for 5 shillings sold unto the sd Lancelot Warrin all that afsd plantation & land containing 210 a. .... . Wit: Wm Waller, Hackley Warrin, Robert Moor, James Ham. Proved 2 Apr 1751 & admitted to record. Attest: Edmund Waller clk. (Pg 514)

13 Dec 1750. Deed. Obediah Howerton of St. Georges Parish, Spotsylvania Co for £40 sold to John Waggener of same place a 300 a. tr of land being the remainder of a tr of land taken up by George Dowdey which land is bounded by the bridge on a br of Assforemost on Lawyers Road, Joseph Hawkings, William Stephens, Lenard Young, Anthony Street, sd John Waggener & Corbin's line ... . Wit: Erasmus Wethers Allen, George Blakey, Samuel Waggener. Proved 2 Apr 1751 & recorded. Attest: Edmund Waller clk. (Pg 516)

24 Oct 1750. Deed of Mortgage. Thomas Estes of Spotsylvania Co for £40 sold to Thomas Merry of co afsd three Negro slaves named Harry, Hannah & Ben & all the increase during the term of 500 years next ensuing paying yearly during the sd term one peper corn at the feast of St. Michael the Arch Angel if demanded provided & upon condition that if the sd Thomas Estes do well & truly pay unto the sd Thomas Merry the full sum of £40 upon 15 Jun next ensuing then these presents shall cease & be void .... . Wit: John Cuningham, Charles Robins, Elizabeth Sutton. Ackn 2 Apr 1751 & admitted to record. Attest: Edmund Waller clk. (Pg 517)

2 Apr MDCCLI. Deed. Joseph Brock of Spotsylvania Co for £52 sold to Larkin Chew of same co gent a 151 a. tr of land bounded by the sd Chew & the road that leads to Mattapony Church .... . Wit: Wm Miller, Wm Waller, Wm

Williams. Ackn 2 Apr 1751 & admitted to record. Attest: Edmund Waller clk. (Pg 518)

2 Apr 1751. Deed. John Chew of Spotsylvania Co gent for £300 sold to Larkin Chew of co afsd gent a 528 a. tr of land (except a place 20' square set a part & reserved for a burying place) 193 a. pt/o the sd 528 a. being a pattent granted to the sd John Chew 4 Jun 1726, the other part thereof being 335 a. was given to the sd John Chew by his father Larkin Chew gent decd by his deeds of lease & release dated 3 & 4 Jul 1720 which 528 a. is bounded by Lawrance Battaile decd, Col John Lewis, the Beaver Dam & Marsh & the edge of the Pocoson ... . Wit: W. Miller, Joseph Steward, Jos Brock, Wm Williams, A. Foster. Proved 2 Apr 1751 & admitted to record. Attest: Edmund Waller clk. (Pg 520)

5 Mar 1750/1. Agreement. Joseph Carpenter came into court & voluntarily ackn himself to serve Doctor William Lynn or his assigns not only in the station & employment of a book keeper as mentioned in the within indenture but in any lawfull & reasonable service or labour that the sd Dr. Lynn or his assigns shall think proper to employ him in during the term of years mentioned in the within indenture in consideration of £15 paid for his purchase. This agreement being approved by the court 5 Mar 1750 is recorded. Attest: Edmund Waller clk. (Pg 522)

4 Dec MDCCL. Deed. George Woodroof of Spotsylvania Co planter & Jane his wife for £10 sold to Rice Graves of sd co planter a 100 a. tr of land bounded by Honey Ridge, Spring Br & Benjamin Woodroof ... . Wit: Robt Huddleston, John Smith, James Fox. Ackn 4 Dec 1750 by George Woodroof & Jane his wife & admitted to record. Attest: Edmund Waller clk. (Pg 523)

7 May 1751. Deed. Between Nathaniel Chapman of Stafford Co, VA merchant of the one part & Benjamin Grymes of Spotsylvania Co gent of the other part, wit that whereas the sd Natha Chapman together in partnership with John Allan of Spotsylvania Co did by a deed to them ackn by Francis Willis & the Honble John Grimes esqr gent exrs of the will of Henry Willis of Spotsylvania Co gent decd purch by way of publick sale of the estate of the sd Henry Willis all that lott of land in the town of Fredericksburgh & partly without the same being bounded by the Publick Warehouse, another parcel of ground sold by the sd John Grymes & Francis Willis to Wm Hunter, Caroline Street, Lott No. 10, Lott No. 12, Lott No. 9, Sophia Street & Lot No. 11. Now this indenture wit that whereas the sd John Allan is since dead whereupon the whole lott descends by survivourship to the sd Natha Chapman whom for the sum of £300 paid by the sd Benjamin Grymes hath sold unto the sd Benjamin Grimes the before mentioned lott ... . Wit: Peter Hedgman, Robt McLaurine, William McWilliams Junr. Natha Chapman delivered full & peaceable possession &

seizen in the land to the sd Benja Grymes. Wit: Peter Hedgman, Han Lee, Fielding Lewis, John Champe. Ackn 7 May 1751 & the livery & seizen was proved & the deed is admitted to record. Attest: Edmund Waller clk. (Pg 524)

7 May 1751. Deed. Natha Chapman of Stafford Co, VA merchant for £450 sold to Benjamin Grymes of Spotsylvania Co gent a ½ a. or lott of land in the town of Fredericksburgh described in the plan of the sd town by the figure 20 bounded by Caroline Street & George Street .... Wit: Peter Hedgman, Robt McLaurine, William McWilliams Junr. Natha Chapman delivered full & peaceable possession & seizen in the land to the sd Benjamin Grymes. Wit: Peter Hedgman, Han Lee, Andrew Crawford. Ackn 7 May 1751 by Nathaniel Chapman gent & the livery & seizen was proved & admitted to record. Attest: Edmund Waller clk. (Pg 526)

31 Jan 1750. Power of Attorney. I Samuell Kennerly of Over, Chester Co joiner eldest son & heir of Samuel Kennerly late of St. Marks Parish, Orange Co, VA joiner decd have appointed Francis Thornton of Caroline Co, Rappahanock River in VA gent my atty to ask, demand, sue for, recover & receive of & from all & every person whatsoever all sums of money which shall appear in any wise to be due & owing unto me for or in respect of any part or sheare of the personal estate of my sd late father which I may appeare to be intitled to or any legacies bequeathed to me in the will of my sd late father .... Wit: Thos Ward, William Quinney. Proved 7 May 1751 & admitted to record. Attest: Edmund Waller clk. (Pg 528)

4 Jun 1751. Deed. Between Benjamin Hubbard gent & Elizabeth Blake widow & legatee executors of the will of John Blake late of Spotsylvania Co merchant decd of the one part & John Wood of same place taylor of the other part, whereas the sd John Blake in his lifetime was seized of a 240 a. tr of land which he purch of Peter Mountague bounded by Greens Br, Thomas Merry, William Richason, John Wood & Warner's line, & being so seized on 17 May 1744 made his will & therein are contained these clauses, viz, item it is my desire that all my personal estate which my wife does not immediately want together with a Negro fellow named Toby be sold towards paying all my just debts, but if there should not be sufficient then all the residue of my estate both real & personal to be sold & the overplus to be divided between my loving wife Elizabeth & my dau Mary & the child my wife Elizabeth is now big with ... I appoint Benjamin Hubbard & my sd wife Elizabeth executors, & soon after making the sd will the sd John Blake died seized of the land & premises ... as it so happened that both the children of the sd John Blake mentioned in the will afterward died without heirs, also that the Negro & personal estate devised by the sd John Blake for the payment of his debts were not sufficient to pay the same. Now this indenture wit that the sd Benja Hubbard & Elizabeth Blake being desirous to fulfill the

will of the sd John Blake & for £45 sold to the sd John Wood a 242 a. (*sic*) tr of land bounded as afsd .... Wit: None. Ackn 4 Jun 1751 & admitted to record. Attest: Edmund Waller clk. (Pg 529)

13 May 1751. Deed. William Bell Senr of St. George Parish, Spotsylvania Co for £15 sold to Uriah Garton Junr of same place a 100 a. tr of land bounded by the River Ta, the mouth of Black Rock & Henry Brock .... Wit: Ephraim Knight, Wm Arnold, Abraham Darnal. Ackn 4 Jun 1751 & admitted to record. Attest: Edmund Waller clk. (Pg 532)

5 Jun 1751. Deed. Lancelot Warrin of Spotsylvania Co & Margaret his wife for £100 sold to William Waller of sd co gent a 210 a. tr of land whereon the sd Lancelot Warrin now dwells in St. George Parish on the s side of the Middle River of Mattapony bounded by the sd Waller, Lick Swamp, Hackley Warrin formerly Haskew's land & John Rogers, the sd land is pt/o a greater tr of land granted by patent to John Rogers & several other persons .... Wit: Richd Tutt, Geo Stubblefield, Robt Mickleborough. Note the sd Lancelot Warrin doth except out of the land hereby sold & still reserves to himself the fee simple estate in 10' square of land which is to include the graves in which his father & mother are buried & the old orchard as it is devised by his father to his brother &c. Ackn 6 Aug 1751 by Lancelot Warrin & Margaret his wife & admitted to record. Attest: Edmund Waller clk. (Pg 533)

1 Jul 1751. Deed of Lease. William Ellis & Elizabeth his wife of St. George Parish, Spotsylvania Co for 5 shillings leased to Ambrose Bullard of same place a messuage & 470 a. tr of land in St. George Parish bounded by the Hunting Run & the river side ... during the term of one year paying the rent of one ear of Indian corn on the feast of St. Michael the Arch Angel if demanded .... Wit: Jno Battaley. Ackn 6 Aug 1751 by William Ellis & Elizabeth his wife & admitted to record. Attest: Edmund Waller clk. (Pg 535)

2 Jul 1751. Deed of Release. William Ellis & Elizabeth his wife of St. George Parish, Spotsylvania Co for £100 sold & released to Ambrose Bullard of same place a 470 a. tr of land, the same being granted unto Robert Slaughter late of Essex Co by pattent dated 20 Feb 1719 & by several mesne conveyances under the sd pattent is now vested in the sd William Ellis & Elizabeth his wife ... [*same as above*] .... Wit: Jno Battaley. Ackn 6 Aug 1751 by William Ellis & Elizabeth his wife & admitted to record. Attest: Edmund Waller clk. (Pg 536)

6 Aug 1751. Deed. Richard Wyatt Royston of Petsworth Parish, Gloucester Co & Anne his wife for £350 sold to William McWilliams the younger of the town of Fredericksburgh, Spotsylvania Co merchant two lotts of land in the town of Fredericksburgh containing 1 a. described in the plan of the sd town by the

numbers 27 & 28 & whereon the Public Warehouses for receiving tobacco called Roystons Warehouses are now in the tenure & occupation of the Inspectors together with all the sd warehouses .... The execution of the commission taking the privy examination & acknmt of the sd Ann Royston is recorded in the last page of this book fol 560. Wit: None. Ackn 6 Aug 1751 by Richard Wyatt Royston & admitted to record. Attest: Edmund Waller clk. (Pg 538)

6 Mar 1751 at Glasgow in North Britain. Power of Attorney. I Robert Glen of the City of Glasgow merchant have appointed Alexander Campbell merchant in Falmouth upon Rappahanock River, VA my atty for me & in my name & to my use & benefit to uplift ingather, recover & receive by all lawfull ways & means whatsoever of & from all & sundry persons whatsoever in VA all debts, sums of money, goods, chattels, effects & others whatsoever any ways due & addebted by them to me or in their hands & keeping anyways belonging to me at the time when I last left VA .... Wit: James Allan, Gavin Roger, Wm Williamson. (Pg 540)

6 Mar 1751. These are to certify that the [above] Robert Glen merchant in the sd City appeared before me this day & signed & sealed the power of atty & that James Allan joiner in Fredericksburgh, VA & Gavin Rodger & William Williamson his servants appeared also before me & made oath that they saw the sd Robert Glen subscribe the within power of atty .... By the Honourable George Black one of the magistrates of the City of Glasgow & justices of the peace in & for the sd City. At a court held for Spotsylvania Co 3 Sep 1751 the above power of atty together with the cert was duly proved & admitted to record. Attest: Edmund Waller clk. (Pg 541)

1 Mar 1750/1. Power of Attorney. I Margaret Black alias Allan widow of the decd James Allan merchant in & late Baillie of Hamiltoun & mother of John Allan merchant in Hamiltoun eldest lawfull son of the decd James Allan thereafter of Spotsylvania Co now also decd, that whereas the sd John Allan late of Spotsylvania Co decd by his will dated 14 Mar 1749/50 did give to me the sd Margaret Black alias Allan his mother £400 to be remitted from thence as soon as the money was raised & to be remitted to Archibald Ingram merchant in Glasgow & of the sd will appointed Col William Waller Junr, Archibald McPherson, William & James Hunter, James Allan & Arch Ingram merchant in Glasgow joint exrs, & whereas I have assigned to the sd James Allan my son the just & equal ½ of the afsd legacy, now know ye that I the sd Margaret Black alias Allan have appointed Samuel Ritchie, Archibald Ritchie & John Miller on Rappahanock River, Essex Co, VA merchants my attys to ask, demand, sue for, recover & receive of & from the afsd legacy & to have use & take all lawfull ways & means in my name or otherwise for the recovery thereof .... Wit:

Gavin Roger, Wm Williamson, James Allan. Proved 3 Sep 1751 & admitted to record. Attest: Edmund Waller clk. (Pg 542)

1 Mar 1750/1. Power of Attorney. I Christian Allan dau lawfull of the decd James Allan merchant in & late Baillie of Hamiltoun & sister german of John Allan merchant in Hamiltoun eldest lawfull son of the sd decd James Allan of Spotsylvania Co now also decd that whereas the sd John Allan my sd decd brother by his bond dated 10 Mar 1733 for the causes therein specified bound & obliged him & his heirs to content & pay to me my heirs the sum of 1,000 marks Scots money being British sterling £55:11 1 penny ½
of a penny upon the term of mertimass then mixt with 200 marks money for sd liquidate expences in case of failzie together with the annuall rent of the sd principall sum confirm to 4 ½ percent from the date of the sd bond to the afsd term of payment ... as also whereas the sd John Allan late of Spotsylvania Co decd by his will dated 14 Mar 1749/50 did give & bequeath to me the sd Christian Allan his sister £400 to be remitted from thence as soon as the money was raised & to be remitted to Archibald Ingram merchant in Glasgow & of the sd will appointed Col William Waller Junr, Archibald Mcpherson, William & James Hunter, James Allan & Arch Ingram merchant in Glasgow joint executors, now know ye that the sd Christian Allan have appointed Samuel Ritchie, Archibald Ritchie & John Miller on Rappahannock River, Essex Co, VA merchants my attys to ask, demand, sue for, recover & receive of & from the executors of the sd decd John Allan the legacy & to have use & take all lawfull ways & means for the recovery thereof .... Wit: James Allan, Gavin Roger, Wm Williamson. Proved 3 Sep 1751 & admitted to record. Attest: Edmund Waller clk. (Pg 543)

1 Mar 1750/1. Power of Attorney. I Sarah Black residenter in Hamiltoun aunt of John Allan merchant in Hamiltoun eldest lawfull son of the decd James Allan merchant in & late Baillie of Hamiltoun of Spotsylvania Co now also decd that whereas the sd John Allan late of Spotsylvania Co decd by his will dated 14 Mar 1749/50 did give & bequeath to me the sd Sarah Black £20 to be remitted from thence as soon as the money was raised, now know ye that I the sd Sarah Black have appointed Samuel Ritchie, Archibald Ritchie & John Miller on Rappahannock, Essex Co, VA merchants my attys to ask, demand, sue for, recover & receive of & from Col William Waller Junr, Archibald Mcpherson, William & James Hunter, James Allan & Archibald Ingram merchant in Glasgow exrs of the decd John Allan the legacy & to have use & take all lawfull ways & means for the recover thereof .... Wit: James Allan, Gavin Roger, Wm Williamson. Proved 3 Sep 1751 & admitted to record. Attest: Edmund Waller clk. (Pg 544)

23 Mar 1750 at Aberdeen. I Jean Morison in Aberdeen North Britain lawfull
dau to the decd John Morison merchant in Stonehaven Procreate betwixt him &
Patience Wallace his spouse who was the only surviving sister of the decd David
Wallace planter on James River, VA do appoint Capt John Thomson commander
of the ship The Anne of Aberdeen my atty to ask, require, demand, sue for &
call in from Col Thomas Turner of King George Co, VA & all others whom it
may concern all & sundry my share & proportion falling to me of the personal
estate of the sd decd David Wallace as one of the nearest in kin to him & all
other debts, dues, sums of money, demands, good, chattels, personal estate &
effects whatsoever due, owing or belonging or that shall hereafter grow due,
owing or belonging to me the sd Jean Morison ... . George Trail, Alexander
Morison, Andrew Thomson. Proved 14 Mar 1750 at Aberdeen. Sworn in
presence of Alexander Robertson provost. Proved at Spotsylvania Co 3 Sep
1751 & admitted to record. Attest: Edmund Waller clk. (Pg 546)

21 May 1751. Indenture Tripartite. Between Edmund Waller pf Spotsylvania
Co gent of the first part, John Waller the elder of same co gent of the second part
& John Waller, Benjamin Waller, Mary Waller & William Edmund Waller,
children of the sd Edmund Waller of the third part, wit that for £110 by the sd
John Waller the elder to the sd Edmund Waller in hand paid the sd Edmund
Waller hath sold unto the sd John Waller the elder a tr of land & plantation
whereon the sd Edmund Waller lately lived in St. George Parish bounded
according to the known & lawfull bounds thereof & is all the land the sd
Edmund Waller holdeth by patent in the sd co ... in trust to suffer & permit the
sd Edmund Waller to hold & occupy the sd land & premises & to take the profits
thereof to his own use during his natural life without rendering any account
thereof to the sd John Waller & after the death of the sd Edmund in trust & to &
for the use & behoof of the sd John Waller, Benja Waller, William Edmund
Waller & Mary Waller the children of the sd Edmund, that is ¼ of the sd land
including the sd plantation to be allotted & assigned to the sd John Waller the
son, one other ¼ part including the plantation where William Crawford now
lives to be collected to the sd Mary Waller, & the remainder of the sd land to be
divided between the sd Benjamin & the sd William Edmund ... provided always
that nothing herein contained shall be construed to defeat the right of dower of
Mary the w/o the sd Edmund in the sd land & premises ... . Wit: Thomas
Dickinson, Zachary Lewis Junr, Benjamin Waller. Ackn 3 Sep 1751 & admitted
to record. Attest: Edmund Waller clk. (Pg 547)

3 Sep 1751. Deed. William Brock & Larkin Chew of Spotsylvania Co gent for
£4 sold to Mosley Battaley & William Waller gent churchwardens of St. George
Parish, Spotsylvania Co in trust for the sd parish a 16,384 superficial foot being
a square of 128' on each side lately laid off for a Church yard at Mattapony

including the sd Church ... . Wit: None. Ackn 3 Sep 1751 & admitted to record. Attest: Edmund Waller clk. (Pg 549)

31 Aug 1751. Deed. Between James Allan of the town of Fredericksburg, Spotsylvania Co brother & heir at law (also one of the exrs) of John Allan late of the sd town merchant decd of the one part & Charles Dick of the town afsd gent of the other part, whereas the sd John Allan in his lifetime was seized of divers lands in several cos of this Colony in the sd town & being so seized on 14 Mar 1749/50 made his will (among other things) is contained this clause (viz) Imprimis I will & desire that all my estate both real & personal shall be sold at publick sale after my decease excepting the sundry legacies hereafter mentioned, that soon after making the sd will the sd John Allan died seized of the land & premises afsd after whose death the sd James Allan with William Hunter, James Hunter & Archibald Mcpherson exrs of the sd will on 7 Jun MDCCL at a fair at Fredericksburgh at publick auction did sell the estate of the sd John Allan particularly a 5 ½ a. tr of land being the remainder of a parcel of land which the sd John Allan purch of the exrs of Henry Willis decd (for 10 a. 20 perches) out of which the sd John Allan had laid out & sold eight lotts or ½ acres & a street for the use of the purchasers which sd 5 ½ a. adj the land formerly John Royston's, Lot No. 48, Humphrey Hill gent & land formerly belonging to the sd Willis, the sd Charles Dick for £46:10 being the most that was offered or could be got for the same, now this indenture wit that James Allan for £46:10 sold to the sd Charles Dick the 5 ½ a. tr of land ... . Wit: Archibald Mcpherson, William Hunter, James Hunter, Roger Dixon, Robt Halkerson (Halkerston). Ackn 3 Sep 1751 & admitted to record. Attest: Edmund Waller clk. (Pg 550)

31 Aug 1751. Indenture Tripartite. Between Archibald Mcpherson, James Hunter & James Allan acting exrs of the will of John Allan late of the town of Fredericksburgh, Spotsylvania Co merchant decd of the one part, the sd James Allan brother & heir at law of the sd John Allan of the second part & Wm Hunter of the sd town merchant of the third part, whereas the sd John Allan by his will dated 14 Mar 1749 did will & desire that all his estate both real & personal should be sold, & whereas in pursuance of the sd will his sd estate, lands & houses were set up to publick sale to the highest bidder & were sold to divers person & the sd William Hunter became a purchaser of a 400 a. tr of land called Silverton Hill for the sum of £350:10 being the highest price that could be got for the same & whereas the sd Jas Allan brother & heir at law of the sd John Allan being intitled to the legal estate of the sd land & being willing to release all his interest & title to the sd land & premises herein after mentioned to be sold to the sd Wm Hunter that the will of his sd brother may be fulfilled, now this indenture wit that the sd Archibald Mcpherson, James Hunter, James Allan as exrs of the sd John Allan decd & the sd James Allan as brother & heir at law of the sd testator for £350:10 sold to the sd Wm Hunter the 400 a. tr of land ... .

Wit: Charles Dick, Roger Dixon, Robt Haltkerston. Ackn 3 Sep 1751 &
admitted to record. Attest: Edmund Waller clk. (Pg 552)

31 Aug 1751. Indenture Tripartite. Between Archibald Mcpherson, James
Hunter & James Allan acting exrs of the will of John Allan late of the town of
Fredericksburgh, Spotsylvania Co merchant decd of the one part, the sd James
Allan brother & heir at law of the sd John Allan of the second part & Charles
Julian of the Borough of Norfolk baker of the third part, whereas the sd John
Allan by his will dated 14 Mar 1749 did will & desire that all his estate both real
& personal should be sold, & the sd exrs being desirous to comply with the will
of the sd John Allan & the sd John being willing to release all his interest & title
that he may legally claim in & to the land to be sold, now this indenture with
that the sd Archibald Mcpherson, William Hunter, James Hunter & James Allan
for £245 sold to the sd Charles Julian a lott of land in the town of
Fredericksburgh now in the tenure & occupation of Samuel Hildrup of the sd
town being pt/o the lott denoted in the plan of the sd town by the number 30 &
all that lott except such part thereof as the sd John Allan in his lifetime by his
deed dated 19 Dec 1749 sold to Robert Duncanson ... . Wit: Charles Dick,
Robt Halkerston, Roger Dixon. Ackn 3 Sep 1751 & admitted to record. Attest:
Edmund Waller clk. (Pg 554)

7 Mar 1750. Deed of Mortgage. Andrew Crawford of the town of
Fredericksburgh for £36:16:3 ½ penny sold to Charles Dick of the sd town
merchant one servant woman named Mary York, one cow & calf, 1 black mare,
1 gray horse, a saddle & bridle & one doz of blagg bottomed chairs ... provided
that if the sd Andrew Crawford shall well & truly pay unto the sd Charles Dick
the full sum of £36:16:3 ½ penny with lawfull interest on or before the last day
Jun next insuing then this indenture shall become void ... . Wit: Jno Battaley,
Edward Herndon Junr. Proved 4 Sep 1751 & admitted to record. Attest:
Edmund Waller clk. (Pg 556)

Last day of Aug 1751. Deed. Between Benjamin Holladay (Holaday) of
Spotsylvania Co & Susannah his wife of the one part & George Shepherd of
same co of the other part, whereas the sd Benjamin Holladay had sold unto
George Shepherd a 108 a. tr of land for £19 & whereas the sd George Shepherd
departed his life before the land was conveyed to him by the sd Benjamin
Holladay having made his will dated 10 Jan 1750 & thereby devised the sd land
to his two sons George & Robt Shepherd, now this indenture wit that the sd
Benjamin Holladay & Susanna his wife in consideration of the premises & for
10 shillings have sold unto the sd George Shepherd ½ pt/o the 108 a. tr of land
devised by his father George Shepherd bounded by Joseph Peterson, Rev. James
Mary & the corner of Shepherd & Holladay ... . Wit: Zachary Lewis, John

Battaley, John Payton. Ackn 1 Oct 1751 by Benjamin Holladay & Susannah his wife & admitted to record. Attest: Edmund Waller clk. (Pg 557)

1 Oct 1751. Deed. William Collins of Southfarnam Parish, Essex Co for 5 shillings sold to James Haley of St. Thomas Parish, Orange Co a 200 a. tr of land in St. George Parish pt/o a grant formerly granted unto John Robenson adj a corner of Spotswood, Corbin's line & Lewis Conner .... Wit: Edward Collins, Lewis Collins, John Collins. I have reserve of William Golston £10:10, Lewis Collins. Ackn 1 Oct 1751 by William Collins & Elizabeth his wife & admitted to record. Attest: Edmund Waller clk. (Pg 559)

Commission. To James Baytop & Francis Tomkins of Gloucester Co greeting, whereas Richard Wiatt Royston of Petsworth Parish, Gloucester Co & Ann his wife by their indenture dated 6 Aug 1751 have conveyed unto William McWilliams of the town of Fredericksburgh merchant the fee simple estate of two lotts of land in the town of Fredericksburgh Nos. 27 & 28, & whereas the sd Anne cannot conveniently travel to our co court to make acknowledgment of the sd conveyance, therefore we do give unto you power to receive the acknowledgment which the sd Anne shall be willing to make before you & command that you do personally go to the sd Anne & receive her acknowledgment & examine her privately & apart from her husband whether she doth the same freely & voluntarily & whether she be willing that the same be recorded .... Wit Edmund Waller clerk of court 26 Sep 1751. 30 Oct 1751 at Gloucester Co, persuant to the within commission we James Baytop & Francis Tomkins did examine the sd Anne Royston apart from her husband & she declared that she doth freely & voluntarily relinquish her right of dower in the sd lotts & is willing the same may be recorded. This commission duly executed & returned & recorded. Attest: Edmund Waller clk. (Pg 560)

INDEX

Aberdeen, 189
Abney, Dannit, 69; Dannitt, 4, 5, 36;
    Dennet, 41; Dennit, 35; Mary, 36
Abney's Line, 69
Achilles Branch, 83, 129, 140
Ackillis Branch, 126
Adcock, Joseph, 52, 94, 101
Albemarle County, 172
Alexander, David, 111
Alexandria Tract, 22, 23
Allan, Christian, 188; James, 110,
    175, 177, 187, 188, 190, 191;
    John, 64, 65, 77, 78, 79, 80, 87,
    88, 92, 95, 96, 97, 98, 99, 101,
    102, 103, 110, 115, 122, 135,
    140, 149, 154, 155, 156, 157,
    167, 170, 171, 173, 175, 176,
    184, 187, 188, 190, 191;
    Margaret, 173, 187
Allan Street, 156
Allanach, James, 115
Allan's Land, 158
Allans Street, 155, 157, 161
Allcock, William, 89
Allen, Elizabeth, 114; Erasmus W.,
    174; Erasmus Weathers, 95;
    Erasmus Wethers, 95, 127, 173,
    174, 183; John, 60, 114, 140,
    161; Joseph, 134; Nathaniel, 173;
    Sarah, 174; Thomas, 89, 90, 108,
    113, 114, 127, 141, 173
Allen's Corner, 14, 142, 154
Allen's Land, 118, 129
Allen's Line, 134
Alliston, John, 23; Robert, 23
Allistone, Jacob, 22; Robert, 22
Amelia County, 64
Amelia Street, 35, 47, 60, 63, 78, 122,
    167
America, 125

Anderson, George, 3, 4; John, 46;
    Larence, 152; Lawrence, 124
Anne, The, 189
Armistead, Robert, 180, 181
Arnold, Ambrose, 145, 164;
    Benjamin, 145; Francis, 43, 66,
    93; Lydia, 149; Rachel, 43, 164;
    William, 149, 186
Arnolds Run, 128, 135, 145, 156
Artrip, Cuthbert, 180
Artrup, Cuthbert, 180
Ashen, John, 77
Asken, John, 4
Asmon, Mary, 63
Assforemast Run, 113
Assforemost, 183
Assforemost Run, 127
Atkins, James, 85, 111, 123
Atkinson, George, 89
Baker, Josias, 118, 136
Ball, James, 131, 178
Ballandine, Doctor, 79
Ballard, Ambrose, 161; Phillip, 155,
    156
Ballendine, Doctor, 98
Balware, William, 8
Barbadoes, 125
Barbar, William, 166
Barber, William, 93, 110, 129, 165
Barbour, James, 150
Barren Fields, 56
Barret, Charles, 41; Robert, 26
Barrett, Charles, 71
Bartlet, William, 5, 6, 29, 37, 50, 65,
    66, 72, 74, 75, 122, 123, 126, 155
Bartlett, Henry, 159; Samuel, 37;
    William, 37, 83, 98, 140
Bartlett's Line, 172
Baskett, Elizabeth, 144, 145; William,
    136, 144, 145

Bates, Humphry, 76
Battaile, Lawrance, 184; Lawrence, 12, 13, 93, 179; Nicholas, 40
Battaley, J., 152; John, 157, 175, 186, 191, 192; M., 10, 32, 71, 76, 149, 171, 175; Mosley, 152, 189
Bayley, Richard, 12; Robert, 6, 12
Baylor, John, 94, 95; Mr., 126, 131, 173; Richard, 165, 166; Robert, 15, 17, 43, 94, 133, 141, 154, 166
Baylor's Line, 153
Baytop, James, 192
Beadles, Dilly, 171, 172; Robert, 156, 169, 171, 172
Beale, Taverner, 150; Taviner, 174
Bean, John, 58
Beaver Dam, 184
Beaver Dam Run, 94
Beaver Marsh, 184
Beaverley, Henry, 39
Becket, John, 73
Beckett, John, 73
Beckham, Stephen, 24; William, 24
Belchaise, James, 74
Belfeild, John, 150; Mary, 150; Thomas Wright, 16, 150
Belfield, Thomas Wright, 55
Bell, Bathsheba, 149; Catherine, 149; David, 130, 148, 149; Humphry, 63, 66, 90, 91, 101, 132, 151, 159, 170; Lydia, 149; William, 70, 149, 186
Bell's Line, 46
Bells Spring, 149
Belsches, James, 53
Benger, Elliott, 24, 33, 64, 67, 85, 125, 161
Benson, Sarah, 54; Thomas, 4, 44, 54
Berry, Henry, 1
Berryman, Benjamin, 10
Beuford, James, 65
Bever Dam Swamp, 128

Beverdam Run, 9
Beverley, Ann, 13; Catharine, 134; Catherine, 12, 13, 104; Harry, 43, 86, 104, 112, 134, 154, 163, 177, 178, 179; Henry, 62, 90; Mr., 178; Robert, 13, 144, 177; William, 3, 6, 13, 69, 177, 178
Beverleys Main Road, 37
Beverlie, Robert, 121
Beverly, Ann, 12, 13; Harry, 179; Robert, 12, 13; William, 12, 13
Bigger, John, 138
Binson, Sarah, 54; Thomas, 54
Birams, 53
Biscoe, Robert, 4, 8, 9, 86
Black, George, 187; Margaret, 187; Sarah, 188; William, 143
Black Rock, 149, 186
Black Rock Swamp, 114, 149
Black Walnut Run, 6
Blackaby, John, 23, 24
Blackle, John, 123
Blake, Elizabeth, 161, 185; John, 66, 69, 90, 91, 92, 93, 102, 185, 186; Mary, 185
Blakey, George, 168, 183
Blanfield, 177, 178
Bledsoe, Moses, 182; W., 1; William, 182
Blockley, Edward, 10
Boar Run, 76
Boreman, C., 122; Charles, 129
Boswell, John, 72, 75, 106, 161
Boughan, Zachary, 161
Boutwell, John, 159
Bowker, A., 76, 154, 157; Achilles, 56, 57, 138; Achillis, 155; Bird, 56, 138; Mr., 129; Parmanas, 137; Parmenas, 76, 89, 117, 136; Ralph, 56, 138
Bowles, John, 71, 74, 76
Bowsee, John, 157

Bowsel, John, 168
Boy, James, 168
Bradburn, Isaac, 132, 146; William, 34, 45, 46, 53, 142, 159
Bradley, Richard, 114
Brammar, John, 116
Branagan's Line, 37
Branagen, William, 140
Brandagon, Phillip, 50
Brandegan, Philip, 31
Brandegon, Phillip, 109
Branham, John, 33
Braxton, G., 139, 140; George, 120
Brent, Charles, 9
Brock, Barbara, 163; Barbrey, 140; Henry, 38, 122, 123, 140, 160, 163, 169, 186; J., 118; Joseph, 32, 37, 41, 57, 61, 62, 63, 69, 70, 71, 72, 74, 75, 76, 83, 86, 100, 102, 106, 108, 114, 126, 129, 133, 140, 141, 142, 149, 158, 160, 161, 163, 164, 165, 166, 178, 183, 184; Mary, 57, 61, 72, 74, 83, 100, 114, 160, 161; Mr., 148, 160; Susannah, 161; Thomas, 163; William, 140, 161, 189
Brocks, Joseph, 70
Bronaugh, Davis, 49
Brooke, Matthew, 112; Robert, 8
Brookes, Joseph, 152
Brooks, Matthew, 77
Brown, Abraham, 66, 68, 127; Daniel, 109, 130; Daniell, 61; James, 50, 86; Robert, 46, 71; Samuel, 100, 106, 107; Thomas, 109, 148, 182
Brunswick Parish, 8, 9, 111, 168
Bryne, D., 3
Buchanan, Duncan, 5
Buckner, George, 171; John, 54, 123; Thomas, 26

Buckner's Line, 16
Buford, John, 38, 39
Bullard, Ambrose, 186
Bunting, William, 23
Burbadge, William, 111
Burk, John, 3; Mary, 3; Richard, 3
Burnett, William, 111
Burwell, Robert, 143
Bush, John, 52, 61, 76, 130
Bushes Road, 37, 62, 74, 83, 126, 140, 148, 161, 164, 178
Butler, Thomas, 37
Byram's Line, 16
Byrom, Henry, 127; Peter, 127
Byrum, Henry, 127
Cabbin Branch, 8
Caddle, Andrew, 182
Calahan, John, 180
Callaway, William, 2
Calvert, Joseph, 96, 115
Calvert County, MD, 163
Cam, Mr., 14
Camm, John, 15, 43, 90, 120, 132, 154
Campbele, Alexander, 177
Campbell, Alexander, 187
Canne, James, 123
Canney, James, 111
Cannons River, 1, 17
Carey, Patrik, 163
Caroline County (Virginia), 13, 14, 17, 18, 25, 29, 32, 35, 40, 42, 46, 47, 58, 61, 62, 66, 77, 83, 84, 88, 92, 94, 106, 111, 112, 115, 117, 122, 123, 124, 125, 127, 129, 132, 133, 135, 136, 141, 142, 145, 147, 153, 154, 157, 158, 159, 160, 168, 170, 171, 173, 175, 177, 185
Caroline Street, 26, 54, 56, 60, 63, 64, 73, 77, 78, 79, 86, 87, 91, 95, 96,

98, 119, 120, 125, 135, 143, 148, 167, 170, 171, 181, 184, 185

Carpenter, Joseph, 184

Carr, John, 138; Thomas, 29, 63, 100, 102; William, 111, 115, 138, 163, 181

Carson, Edward, 122

Carter, Charles, 9, 10, 154; Colonel, 3; Elizabeth, 52, 145, 170; George, 31, 45, 52, 72, 94, 100, 101, 104, 145, 159, 170; Henry, 94; John, 99, 104, 116, 122, 135, 162, 164, 175, 176; Joseph, 28, 29, 46, 71, 80, 151, 172, 174

Cartwright, Rachel, 144, 165; Thomas, 64, 136, 137, 144, 165, 169

Cason, Edward, 83, 84, 112, 116, 134, 135, 162; Mary, 135; Roger, 127

Casone, Edward, 162; Roger, 163

Cater, George, 145

Catlett, Thomas, 31

Cattail Fork Swamp, 141

Cattail Lick Branch, 132, 138, 141

Cattail Lick Run, 53

Cattail Run, 44, 141

Cattail Swamp Branch, 141

Cattaile Lick Branch, 148

Cavenaugh, Elizabeth, 6; Philemon, 6, 8, 42

Cayson, Roger, 127

Chambers, Abraham, 33

Champe, John, 105, 120, 143, 147, 179, 185

Chaple Road, 168

Chapman, George, 63, 74, 102, 103, 110, 118, 122, 135; John, 44; Nathaniel, 72, 73, 74, 79, 95, 96, 99, 101, 184, 185

Chapple Bridge, 118

Charles County, MD, 61

Charlotta Street, 48, 50, 54, 64, 75, 79, 87, 98, 119, 143, 150, 167

Charlotte Street, 31, 176

Chenault, Stephen, 162

Chesehixson Branch, 8

Chester County, 185

Chew, Henry, 163; Jane, 163; John, 31, 51, 52, 53, 59, 76, 81, 84, 85, 102, 103, 104, 113, 125, 130, 134, 147, 157, 160, 163, 184; Larkin, 2, 26, 28, 29, 31, 32, 34, 37, 38, 45, 50, 51, 53, 57, 61, 62, 63, 64, 65, 66, 70, 72, 74, 75, 83, 89, 92, 95, 98, 102, 106, 109, 113, 114, 115, 117, 120, 124, 133, 136, 140, 141, 146, 148, 159, 162, 163, 166, 168, 174, 178, 181, 183, 184, 189; Margaret, 76, 84, 85; Martha, 1, 153; Thomas, 1, 2, 5, 6, 28, 31, 32, 60, 76, 86, 146, 153, 162, 163, 174

Childs, Richard, 100, 127, 137, 169

Chiles, Henry, 41, 69, 124, 127, 142, 164, 165, 166; John, 35, 41, 42, 69, 70, 128; Marcy, 128, 165, 166; Mary, 165; Mercy, 41; Richard, 76

Chiles's Land, 99

Chissells Wagon Road, 155

Chissum, James, 25

Chisum, James, 20, 33, 34

Chiswells Mine Road, 88

Chiswell's Mine Road, 111

Chiswells Mine Road, 115, 138

Choice, Tully, 130

Christopher, John, 6, 16; Nicholas, 13

Clark, Ann, 42, 122, 123; John, 42, 102, 114, 122, 123; Jonathan, 28, 38, 60

Clark's Line, 146

Clayhole, 133, 176

Clayton, Philip, 109
Cleaton, Gabriel, 67
Clerk, John, 116
Clerke, Ann, 123; John, 123
Clesby Tract, 94
Cliffe, William Wombwell, 18
Clowder, Captain, 12, 118, 129
Clowder's Path, 14
Coats, Thomas, 153
Cock, Catsby, 51
Cockburn, John, 89
Cock's Line, 36
Coffey, John, 129
Coleman, Darbey, 56; Edward, 109,
    114, 133, 134; Elizabeth, 159;
    John, 143, 145; Lucretia, 133,
    134; Richard, 106, 142, 143, 144,
    145, 168; Robert, 56, 57, 92, 94,
    100, 101, 104, 108, 117, 129,
    138, 139, 142, 145, 159, 160,
    182; Robert Spilsbe, 82, 89, 90,
    109, 144; Robert Spilsby, 154;
    Samuel, 118; Sarah, 108, 138,
    139, 144, 160; Spilsbey, 142;
    Thomas, 142, 145, 154; Wiat,
    145; William, 56
Coller, John, 151
Collier, John, 7, 8, 84, 165, 166
Collins, Edward, 192; Elizabeth, 192;
    John, 192; Joseph, 82, 92, 129,
    131, 139, 140, 148; Lewis, 192;
    Thomas, 93, 139, 140, 148, 179;
    William, 131, 139, 140, 148, 192
Colman, William, 59
Colquit, John, 52, 53, 125
Colson, Charles, 126, 148, 149, 156,
    171
Colston, Charles, 156
Connelly, Patrick, 149, 182
Conner, Elizabeth, 6; John, 6; Lewis,
    139, 192; William, 2, 27, 47
Connor, William, 46, 47, 159

Conway, Francis, 170; Sarah, 170
Cook, George, 104, 105, 119, 122,
    126, 134, 150, 157; Giles, 78;
    John, 13, 14; Sarah, 122, 134;
    Thomas, 11, 148; William, 125
Copeland, Nicholas, 103
Copland, Nicholas, 103
Corban, Colonel, 95
Corbin, Colonel, 14, 55, 82, 95, 173;
    Gawin, 46, 165; Goin, 129;
    Gowin, 79; John, 164; Lettice,
    164
Corbin's Land, 139, 167
Corbin's Line, 76, 173, 174, 183, 192
Coulston, Charles, 126
County Line, 141
County Line Branch, 47
Couzens, Elizabeth, 141; Richard,
    141, 144
Couzone, Richard, 71
Coward, Benjamin, 3; Elizabeth, 3,
    14; James, 13, 14
Cowne, William, 51, 57, 90, 91
Cowper, Thomas, 89, 99, 132
Cox, James, 92
Crafard, William, 3
Crag, Taliaferro, 126, 129
Cragg, Mary, 152; Taliaferro, 129,
    148; Tallever, 164; Toliver, 152
Crags, Taliaferro, 46
Craig, Andrew, 67, 83, 97, 98, 101,
    110
Crane, John, 117, 153, 175; John
    Scandland, 80, 81
Crawford, Andrew, 185, 191;
    Thomas, 3; William, 3, 175, 189
Croker, Robert, 182
Crosthwait, William, 5, 6, 11, 55, 56
Croucher, Anne, 21; Priscilla, 21;
    William, 20, 21
Crump, Daniel, 64

Culpeper County (Virginia), 167,
174, 178
Cumings, Alexander, 64, 70
Cuningham, John, 172, 183
Cuninghame, William, 169, 170
Curtis, Ann, 74, 75; Charles, 46;
Giles, 70; John, 29, 39; Mary,
105, 106; R., 1, 28, 38, 57, 61,
62, 63, 64, 65, 66, 71, 74, 75, 93,
106; Rice, 28, 37, 38, 62, 65, 66,
68, 70, 80, 83, 84, 93, 100, 106,
159, 163, 178
Cuzens, Richard, 77
Dalton, Margrett, 162; Michael, 162;
Sarah, 162; Timothy, 46
Dalton's Land, 112, 122
Dangerfeild, William, 144
Daniel, Peter, 9, 147, 154; Reuben,
121; William, 142
Daniell, Peter, 4
Darnaby, William, 175
Darnal, Abraham, 186
Darnell, Abraham, 116, 132; David,
116; Elizabeth, 116; Isaac, 52,
72, 74, 98, 125
Davenport, Ann, 164; Anne, 42, 43;
John, 145; William, 42, 43, 145,
164
Davis, Benjamin, 157; Isaac, 132;
James, 123; John, 25, 124
Deal, 57, 58
Deatherage, William, 6
Debrise, James, 164
Deep Run, 51, 91
Delaney, Joseph, 9, 23; Mary, 9
Delanie, Joseph, 86
Delayney, Joseph, 8, 9; Mary, 9
Dent, John, 171
Devils Ditch, 126, 157, 158
Devils Ditch Swamp, 122, 150

Dick, Charles, 135, 150, 154, 156,
157, 158, 167, 170, 175, 176,
180, 181, 190, 191
Dickenson, John, 17, 18, 35; Thomas,
35, 99; William, 35
Dickinson, Edward, 45; Thomas, 189
Dillard, Elizabeth, 100; Thomas, 17,
18, 63, 84, 100, 121, 151
Dillard's Land, 151
Dismukes, James, 159
Dixon, Roger, 163, 168, 171, 190,
191
Doaelton, Themothy, 45
Dobbs, John, 74; William, 11, 12
Dobson, Richard, 165, 166
Doggett, Ann, 121; George, 43, 121
Dolton, Themoty, 46; William, 162
Dolton's Land, 162
Donaldson, Henry, 58
Dove, T., 40; Thomas, 40
Dowdall, Patrick, 56, 88, 89, 115,
119; Thomas, 56
Dowdey, George, 174, 183
Dowdy, George, 55, 82
Downes, Elias, 124, 171
Downs, Elias, 32, 41, 171, 173;
Henry, 11, 16, 59, 147, 150, 174
Drisdale Parish, 77, 105, 106, 114
Drysdale Parish, 12, 15, 44, 47, 54,
61, 62, 94, 99, 101, 106, 142,
145, 153, 179
Dudley, Robert, 122, 173
Duerson, Hannah, 140, 178; Thomas,
57, 61, 62, 63, 100, 104, 126,
132, 140, 163, 170, 178
Dun, James, 150
Duncanson, Robert, 171, 175, 191
Dunken, William, 125
Durham, Thomas, 76
Durrat, Elizabeth, 80
Durratt, Elizabeth, 80; Robert, 80

Durret, Elizabeth, 40; John, 83, 109; Robert, 39, 40

Durrett, Elizabeth, 40; John, 41, 117; Richard, 141; Robert, 38, 40, 172

Durrett's Corner, 178

Duttond, Anthony Francis, 47

Dyer, James, 173; Mary, 82; William, 82, 144, 154

Ealley, Henry, 89, 90; Mary, 90

East North East, 18, 42, 142

East North East Bridge, 35

East North East River, 10, 41, 69, 118, 128, 146, 151, 157

East North East Run, 144, 149, 158, 165, 169

Eastes, Abraham, 111

Eastham, George, 152; R., 4, 6

Eddins, Rebecca, 5; Theofelous, 6; William, 5

Eddins' Mill Run, 5

Edins, Theophilus, 6

Edmondson, Dorothy, 123; John, 144; Thomas, 54, 55, 83, 123

Edmundson, Dorothy, 123; Thomas, 123

Edwards, James, 4, 5, 69, 95, 146; John, 75, 81, 102, 115, 123

Elkwood, 3

Elles, James, 9

Elley, Henry, 89, 90, 113, 114

Elliott, James, 12

Ellis, Elizabeth, 186; Robert, 121; William, 121, 186

Ellson, John, 39

Elson, John, 100, 134, 137, 178; Thomas, 48, 49

Elstons Run, 56, 138

Emerson, William, 133

Essex County (Virginia), 3, 8, 39, 40, 47, 50, 54, 55, 67, 68, 69, 71, 75, 82, 83, 89, 90, 94, 95, 101, 121, 123, 124, 127, 133, 134, 144, 149, 154, 155, 156, 159, 164, 177, 186, 187, 188, 192

Estes, Abraham, 111, 112, 114, 151; Thomas, 30, 80, 119, 164, 178, 183

Estis, Abraham, 25, 122, 123, 151, 159

Estridge, Abraham, 16

Evans, John, 134

Fagg, Thomas, 151

Fairfax County (Virginia), 119, 125

Fall, William, 5

Fall Branch, 127

Falmouth, 3, 54, 187

Fantleroy, Apphiah, 55; Griffin, 61, 86, 87, 122, 126, 130, 150; Hannah, 55; William, 54, 55, 123

Fantleroy's Line, 16

Farish, John, 94, 101, 133, 137, 166, 176, 181; Robert, 94, 101, 119; Sarah, 133, 166, 176, 181

Farrish, Robert, 143

Faulconer, John, 164, 174

Faulkner, John, 165

Feigans Branch, 36

Feigons Branch, 52

Ferry, James, 30

Fidler, James, 11

Fieldour's Line, 158

Fields, William, 7

Finlason, John, 6

Fitzgarrell, Walter, 47

Fitzhugh, Henry, 25, 68

Flat Run, 3

Fleming, James, 171

Fleshmans Run, 6

Fork Road, 173

Forster, Doctor, 160; Thomas, 129, 138, 139

Foster, A., 50, 60, 89, 102, 109, 116, 122, 123, 130, 139, 143, 152, 160, 163; Ambrose, 162, 168,

173; Anthony, 28, 31, 32, 37, 40,
41, 42, 44, 45, 51, 57, 61, 64, 65,
66, 69, 76, 80, 92, 93, 108, 140,
148, 164; Edmund, 113, 114,
126, 130, 135, 136, 146, 148,
151, 152, 155; Isabell, 57;
Isabella, 65; John, 4, 44, 57, 64,
65, 66, 68, 80, 127; Joseph, 124;
Martha, 65, 66; Thomas, 40, 41,
126, 129, 146, 148, 169
Fox, Jacob, 138; James, 184; John,
27, 160, 167
Foy, Thomas, 14
Franklyn, Edward, 31, 45, 46, 52;
Lawrence, 68
Frazer, Frances, 10, 11; James, 10, 11
Fredericksburg(h), 3, 10, 26, 28, 31,
35, 47, 48, 49, 50, 54, 56, 58, 59,
60, 61, 63, 65, 67, 69, 71, 72, 73,
75, 77, 78, 79, 81, 86, 87, 88, 91,
92, 93, 94, 95, 96, 97, 98, 99,
101, 110, 111, 115, 118, 119,
120, 122, 125, 130, 134, 135,
140, 143, 147, 148, 149, 150,
154, 155, 156, 157, 158, 161,
167, 170, 171, 175, 176, 180,
181, 182, 184, 185, 186, 190,
191, 192
Fredericksvil Parish, 148
Freeman, Alexander, 25
Gaines, Robert, 165; William, 14
Gains, Isabell, 130; Isabella, 131;
William, 130, 131
Gale, Joseph, 169; Matthias, 50;
William, 50
Gambrill's Corner, 4
Gardner, James, 89
Garmanna Road, 153
Garnett, Anthony, 129, 168; James,
123, 154
Garnett's Line, 173
Garret, John, 159

Garris, William, 82
Garton, James, 64, 70, 81, 94; Uriah,
70, 94, 186
Garton's Corner, 178
Garton's Land, 164
Garton's Line, 114, 149, 161
Gatewood, Dudley, 85, 92, 137, 138;
Henry, 108, 137, 138; Sarah,
137, 138; William, 138, 173
Gatewood's Land, 164
Gayle, Matthew, 54, 86
George Street, 49, 61, 73, 77, 79, 88,
91, 95, 96, 120, 150, 185
Germanna, 7
Gholdston, Anthony, 130; Jane, 130
Gholeston, William, 165
Gholston, Anthony, 14, 118, 130;
Jane, 14
Gholstone, Anthony, 70, 71; Jane, 70,
71
Gibbs, James, 33, 34
Gibson, Jonathan, 16, 17, 67, 102,
179; Thomas, 76
Giffin, Thomas, 40
Gilbirt, Felix, 132
Glady Fork, 85, 138
Glady Fork Run, 31, 52, 76
Glady Run, 52, 76, 125, 138, 160,
164
Glasgow, 187, 188
Glebe Land, 163
Glen, Robert, 187
Gloucester (Gloester, Gloster) County
(Virginia), 1, 32, 60, 72, 95, 96,
97, 98, 99, 105, 111, 121, 141,
151, 154, 158, 162, 186, 192
Goard Vine Fork, 1, 17
Goldstone, Anthony, 76, 130; Jane,
130
Golson, Anthony, 82, 136, 168;
Susanna, 168; William, 168

Golston, Anthony, 55, 85, 118, 136; William, 192
Golstone, Anthony, 18, 56
Gooch, William, 61, 87, 114, 155, 163, 173
Goodloe, Diana, 117; Elizabeth, 40, 80; George, 29, 38, 39, 40, 72, 117, 160; Henry, 29, 38, 39, 40, 80, 81, 84, 85, 113, 117, 136, 141, 145, 152, 153, 157, 160, 172; Robert, 28, 29, 40, 46, 80, 117, 118, 124, 151, 152, 160
Gordon, Adam, 43, 55, 56; Archibald, 150, 157; Elisabeth, 53; Elizabeth, 51; John, 26, 38, 45, 46, 51, 53, 54, 76, 83, 110, 115, 121, 139, 169, 170; Roderick, 12
Gore, John, 182
Gouldman, Francis, 110
Graham, John, 58
Grame, George, 125; John, 18, 19, 20, 21, 22, 24, 26, 54, 115
Grasty, Mr., 137; Sharshall, 36, 39, 40, 71, 137
Gravel Run, 48
Gravelly Run, 100
Graves, John, 93, 95, 106, 124, 126, 128, 141, 151, 156, 158, 172; Rice, 184; Thomas, 51, 69, 93, 95, 135, 142, 151, 156
Gray, George, 169
Grayson, Barbary, 178; John, 57, 58, 178; Thomas, 57, 58; William, 67, 180
Great Fork, 23
Great Mountains, 2, 25
Green, Robert, 1
Greens Branch, 27, 28, 51, 66, 93, 179, 185
Gregory, Mildred, 72; Richard, 82
Gregory's Line, 131

Gresham, Mary, 110; Rachel, 110; Thomas, 77; William, 110
Griffen, John, 159
Griffith, Anthony, 168; Richard, 87, 168
Grimes, Benjamin, 184; John, 184
Grymes, Benjamin, 184, 185; John, 26, 95, 96, 97, 98, 99, 101, 184
Guaney, Michel, 52
Guill, Alexander, 177
Guinney, Michael, 173
Gustavas, Mary, 64; Peter, 30, 51, 64
Gustavase, Peter, 30
Gustavas's Line, 68, 121
Gustavus's Line, 158
Gwyn, Hugh, 1
Habendum, 12
Haines, Henry, 2, 67, 169
Haley, Ambrose, 165; James, 192; John, 46, 129, 164, 165; Mary, 164, 165
Halkerson, Robert, 190
Halkerston, Robert, 190
Haltkerston, Robert, 191
Ham, James, 172, 183
Hambleton, Luke, 148; Susanna, 148
Hambleton Parish, 113, 114
Hamilton Parish, 99
Hamiltoun, 187, 188
Hamm, Margaret, 71; Samuel, 71
Hammilton Parish, 8, 9
Hanover County (Virginia), 36, 42, 43, 69, 77, 98, 126, 128, 129, 168
Hanover Street, 56, 59, 61, 64, 67, 77, 79, 86, 88, 96, 110, 125, 147, 148, 155
Hansford, Sarah, 123; William, 39, 41, 123, 171
Harris, William, 158
Harrison, Andrew, 27; Nathaniel, 167
Hart, Margaret, 163
Hasel Run, 49, 123

Hasell Run, 36, 52, 116, 168
Haskew, Rachel, 183
Haskew's Land, 186
Hasle Run, 123
Haslee Run, 83
Haw Branch, 133, 143, 156
Hawes, Samuel, 145
Hawkings, Joseph, 183
Hawkins, Alexander, 117, 136, 137,
     146; Ann, 105; James, 117, 138,
     146; Jane, 98; John, 86, 112, 146,
     152, 159, 179; Joseph, 48, 76, 86,
     98, 112, 125, 130, 152, 165, 166,
     168, 174; Margaret, 160; Mary,
     86, 112, 114, 152; Nathan, 117,
     136, 137, 179; Nicholas, 60, 117,
     136, 137, 138, 144, 146, 153,
     160, 172, 179; Phebe, 86, 112;
     Philemon, 112, 152; Phillemon,
     86; Thomas, 105; William, 59,
     114, 159
Hawkins' Line, 172
Hawkins's Land, 32
Hayden, Thomas, 111
Haydon, Thomas, 111
Haynes, Henry, 11, 17, 18; Mary, 18
Hazel Run, 42, 127
Hazell Run, 53
Hazle Run, 172
Head, Elizabeth, 132; George, 132
Healey, Ambrose, 165; John, 165
Hedgman, Peter, 184, 185
Hencely, Kathren, 27; Martha, 27;
     Samuell, 27
Henderson, Joseph, 3; William, 15
Henrico (Henerico) County
     (Virginia), 130, 148, 149
Henslee, Benjamin, 11; William, 27
Hensley, Jane, 154; Katharine, 27;
     Martha, 27; Samuel, 28, 66, 89;
     Samuell, 27, 43; William, 43,
     154

Herndon, Edward, 4, 15, 31, 32, 34,
     36, 48, 59, 80, 90, 112, 113, 114,
     119, 123, 124, 129, 130, 143,
     157, 173, 191; Elizabeth, 124,
     129; Joseph, 154, 165, 166
Hickman, Edwin, 10, 12, 36, 69, 142
Hildrup, Samuel, 191
Hill, Alexander, 82; Elizabeth, 69, 91,
     120; Frances, 120; Humphrey,
     12, 41, 54, 120, 123, 139, 140,
     155, 157, 161, 190; Humphry,
     69, 92, 95, 99, 132, 136, 156;
     Sarah, 12; Susannah, 12;
     Thomas, 11, 12, 30, 35, 36, 46,
     51, 52, 71, 90, 91, 92, 120, 135,
     145, 156
Hillin, Nathaniel, 3
Hill's Line, 46
Hipkins, Margaret, 124; Samuel, 124,
     159, 160
Hoard, John, 40, 113
Hobby, John, 49, 87
Hobson, John, 61, 66, 67; Phebe, 104,
     159; Phebee, 100, 101
Holaday, Benjamin, 191; Susannah,
     191
Holcombs, Thomas, 46
Holladay, Angess, 118; Benjamin,
     157, 158, 169, 173, 191, 192;
     Daniel, 118, 146; Elizabeth, 158,
     159, 173; John, 34, 35, 58, 68,
     71, 118, 121, 130, 132, 146, 149,
     157, 158, 159, 161, 162, 173;
     Joseph, 118, 146, 149, 165, 169;
     Judah, 121; Judey, 121; Susanna,
     157; Susannah, 146, 157, 191,
     192; Thomas, 158; William, 121
Holladay's Corner, 142
Holladays Mill, 149, 157
Holladays Run, 142
Holladays Swamp, 30, 35, 118, 146
Holland, Nathaniel, 67, 70

Hollaway, William, 171, 173
Holliday, Daniel, 68; Elsabeth, 68;
    John, 51, 68, 71; Mr., 89;
    William, 51
Holliday's Line, 154
Hollidays Swamp, 70, 71
Hollmes, William Wilson, 43
Holloway, Robart, 63; William, 32
Holloway's Line, 41, 124
Holms, Leonard, 171
Holson, Thomas, 7
Holt, Micall, 5; Mr., 178
Home, Elizabeth, 38; G., 5, 11, 22,
    25, 26, 27, 36, 37, 50, 51, 52,
    116; George, 6, 7, 18, 19, 20, 21,
    22, 23, 24, 25, 33, 34, 35, 38, 60,
    61, 69, 154
Honey Ridge, 184
Honey Swamp, 35, 36, 89, 106, 136
Hoomes, C.W., 23; Joseph, 153
Hord, John, 99; Sarah, 99
Horn, Nicholas, 141, 142, 164, 166,
    173
Horse Pen Swamp, 168
Horsenalle, James, 67
Horsnell, James, 6
Hoskins, John, 92, 176
Houison, Thomas, 156
How, Peter, 86, 87
Howard, Alexander, 6; William, 48
Howaton, John, 82
Howel, Thomas, 167
Howell, Thomas, 167
Howerton, Obediah, 174, 183
Hubbard, Benjamin, 12, 41, 42, 90,
    91, 92, 95, 96, 97, 101, 185;
    Catherine, 100; Christian, 3;
    Janet, 100; Martha, 169, 174;
    Matha, 169; Mathew, 141, 169;
    Matthew, 174; Thomas, 2, 3, 17,
    63, 67, 100, 169
Hucherson, Robert, 28

Hucheson, William, 160
Huddleston, John, 151; Robert, 59,
    74, 84, 100, 113, 114, 121, 141,
    151, 177, 178, 180, 182, 184;
    William B., 182
Hudgens, John, 159
Hudnall, Richard, 173
Hughes, John, 136; William, 119,
    120, 130, 143, 146, 167
Hume, Alexander, 136; James, 58;
    Mary, 136
Hunney Swamp, 142
Hunny Swamp, 36
Hunter, James, 143, 176, 177, 187,
    188, 190, 191; Martha, 140, 155,
    156; William, 95, 96, 101, 130,
    140, 155, 156, 157, 161, 175,
    176, 177, 180, 181, 184, 187,
    188, 190
Hunting Run, 43, 121, 182, 186
Hutcherson, Ann, 120, 121; John,
    117, 179; Robert, 120, 121
Hutcheson, Robert, 153
Ingram, Archibald, 187, 188; Hannah,
    33; John, 19, 33, 34; Thomas, 8;
    Tobias, 8
Innis, John, 167
Iron Mine Road, 74, 126, 140
Ironmines Road, 83
Ivey Point, 13
Jackson, James, 172; Robert, 91, 92,
    98, 101, 119, 150, 160, 176, 180,
    181; Susanna, 172; Thomas, 3
James, John, 131, 137; Thomas, 142
James River, 25, 189
Jarman, Mr., 89; Thomas, 90
Jarmanah Road, 138
Jarmanna Road, 146
Jennings, John, 18
Jeter, John, 169
Johns, Mary, 110

Johnson, Benjamin, 165, 166;
William, 27
Johnston, Ann, 40, 41, 80; Anne, 113;
Captain, 85; Elizabeth, 77;
Larkin, 116, 119, 152, 168, 175;
Robert, 77, 85, 112; Stephen,
119; W., 1; William, 1, 2, 4, 27,
40, 41, 44, 45, 51, 54, 56, 57, 61,
68, 69, 72, 80, 81, 84, 85, 101,
108, 112, 113, 116, 119, 127,
133, 135, 138, 143, 151, 162,
163, 176
Johnston's Line, 146, 175
Johnstons Ordinary, 127
Johnston's Race Ground, 64
Jones, Agness, 43; Ambras, 33;
Edward, 133, 146, 177;
Elizabeth, 12, 13; James, 14, 20,
82, 98, 114, 131, 174; John, 18,
43, 154, 158, 171; Mary, 98;
Robert, 9; Sarah, 177; Suca, 124;
Thomas, 20, 21, 25, 33
Jordan, William, 5, 55, 150
Julian, Charles, 191
Kelley, Edward, 173
Kelly, W., 143
Kelsick, Richard, 86, 87
Kendell, Henry, 6
Kennedy, Patrick, 172
Kennerley, Elizabeth, 131; James,
131
Kennerly, Samuel, 185
Kent, 57, 58
King, Mary, 83, 116, 122, 134, 135;
Robert, 43, 57, 64, 65, 66, 68, 69,
83, 84, 86, 112, 116, 119, 122,
127, 134, 135, 162
King & Queen County (Virginia), 7,
8, 12, 14, 15, 18, 25, 30, 34, 36,
39, 41, 44, 47, 54, 57, 62, 69, 72,
77, 80, 84, 89, 91, 92, 94, 97, 99,
101, 105, 106, 108, 112, 114,
118, 119, 120, 122, 123, 124,
128, 129, 132, 139, 140, 143,
151, 165, 166, 167, 175, 177,
178, 179
King George County (Virginia), 4, 5,
8, 9, 10, 12, 25, 41, 44, 46, 49,
54, 56, 57, 58, 61, 71, 82, 94, 95,
97, 98, 102, 105, 110, 111, 112,
126, 128, 132, 147, 168, 176,
179, 189
King William County, VA, 4, 12, 173
Kingston Parish, 154
Kinkead, David, 7, 31
Kirtley, Francis, 16
Knight, Ephraim, 178, 186
Lamb, Alexander, 115
Lancaster County (Virginia), 43, 86,
131, 178
Land, Edward, 182
Landale, Andrew, 33, 34
Lanford, Nicholas, 7
Langford, Nicholas, 7, 8, 165, 166
Lankford, Edward, 51; Nicholas, 84,
151
Lankford's Line, 153
Latane, John, 119
Latham, John, 8, 9
Lawless, Michael, 106
Lawyears Road, 174
Lawyers Road, 183
Lea, Ann, 145; James, 100, 141;
John, 145; William, 118, 126,
129, 155, 156
Leach, John, 25
Leaden Hall Street, 40
Lease Land Wharf, 65
Lee, Hancock, 31, 119, 176; Hannah,
141, 185; James, 62, 114; Mary,
176; Mr., 79, 98; Rachel, 129;
William, 129
Levell, Edward, 54
Levill, Edward, 54

Levingston, John, 123
Lewis, Anne, 89, 102; Beery, 99;
    Betty, 180, 181; Colonel, 41,
    124, 175; Fielding, 176, 180,
    181, 185; Henry, 71, 122, 130,
    150; John, 40, 55, 89, 99, 105,
    113, 124, 170, 171, 177, 184;
    Martha, 130, 150; Mary, 102;
    Thomas, 23; Z., 10, 36, 53, 54,
    59, 67, 87, 94, 102, 134, 156;
    Zachary, 32, 36, 42, 44, 60, 70,
    71, 76, 81, 89, 95, 100, 102, 106,
    107, 142, 149, 156, 157, 158,
    163, 171, 173, 177, 189, 191;
    Zachry, 36
Lewis River, 153
Lewis's Line, 120
Lick Branch, 165, 166
Lick Swamp, 124, 186
Lightfoot, John, 23, 33
Lindsay, William, 93
Lindsey, William, 103, 117, 136, 179
Lines, Henry, 114, 149
Link, John Adam, 169, 174
Little Mountain, 21
Little Occupation Creek, 8
Livingston, George, 167; John, 154;
    Susanna, 65, 66
Login, William, 2, 112, 133
London, 40, 58, 66, 90, 91, 132, 159,
    John, 113, 127, 134
Long, Ann, 140; Blomfeild, 50;
    Bloomfeild, 115, 140, 151;
    Bloomfield, 109; Bloumfeild,
    151; John, 144; Mary, 140;
    Rubin, 151; Samuel, 29; Samuell,
    39; William, 83, 86, 117, 126,
    140, 148
Long Ordinary, 130
Louisa County (Virginia), 145, 148,
    151, 164, 177
Low Ground Swamp, 36, 142

Loyds Branch, 153
Lucas, Peter, 149
Lunenburg Parish, 5
Lunenburgh Parish, 16
Luninsburg Parish, 54
Luninsburgh Parish, 55
Lyne, Henry, 161; Mary, 61, 62
Lynes, Mary, 75; Mr., 164
Lynn, William, 120, 129, 143, 163,
    167, 171, 184
McConnicoe, William, 5
McCulloch, David, 71
McHoomes, C., 23
Mackay, William, 6
McKenny, Alexander, 180
Mackie, Thomas, 171
MackMurrin, David, 1
McLaurin, Robert, 184
McLaurine, Robert, 185
MacMurrin, David, 17
McNiell, Thomas, 179
McPherson, Archibald, 42, 103, 119,
    176, 177, 187, 188, 190, 191
McQueen, Alexander, 8
McWilliams, Broadbent, 182; Joseph,
    177; William, 48, 100, 137, 171,
    177, 184, 185, 186, 192
Madison, Ambroce, 15, 16; Elizabeth,
    15; Frances, 16; James, 15, 16;
    John, 15, 27, 47, 141
Magee, Thomas, 173
Main Branch, 76
Main County Road, 168, 173
Main Road, 6, 15, 62, 69, 130, 133,
    146, 163, 173, 177
Main Run, 99, 167
Maine River, 67
Major, Samuel, 160, 164
Mallory, Roger, 110
Malory, Roger, 110
Manard, John, 37
Marders, William, 168

Marks, John, 19; Mary, 19
Marsh, Elizabeth, 95; William, 82, 95
Marshall, William, 52, 141, 157, 158
Martain, Henry, 116
Martin, Benjamin, 39, 61, 93, 103,
    104, 119, 158, 172, 179; Henery,
    39; Henry, 32, 52, 53, 124, 125,
    172; James, 94, 101; John, 48,
    113, 143; Samuel, 156; Susanna,
    124, 125; William, 39, 117, 136,
    179
Mary, James, 191
Marye, James, 81, 119, 122, 123, 149,
    172; John, 83
Mash, William, 95, 174
Massaponax, 54
Massaponax Swamp, 123
Massaponnax Main Run, 111
Massaponnax Swamp, 111
Massapponax Run, 123
Massey, Thomas, 164
Matapony, 25
Matapony Church, 178
Matapony River, 180
Mathews, Benjamin, 84
Mattapony, 17, 27, 29, 39, 47, 48, 56,
    59, 71, 141, 186, 189
Mattapony Church, 62, 183
Mattapony River, 44, 94, 108, 126,
    141, 153, 167
Matthews, Ann, 151; Benjamin, 7,
    151; Samuel, 74; William, 182
Matthews' Land, 121
Maulden, Sarah, 6
Mauldin, Jane, 6; Richard, 6
May, Henry, 143
Mayfeild, Abraham, 31
Mayfield, Abraham, 32, 37, 50;
    Elizabeth, 50
Meander Run, 16
Megee, Thomas, 66, 151
Menefee, John, 131, 173; Mary, 131

Mennefee, John, 131; Mary, 131
Mercer, John, 9, 10; Js, 9
Meriwether, Francis, 177; Thomas,
    40
Merry, Thomas, 28, 38, 66, 72, 80,
    83, 84, 92, 93, 121, 183, 185
Micall, Francis, 6
Mickleborough, Robert, 186
Micou's Line, 114
Micow's Land, 149
Middle River, 27, 47, 56, 59, 71, 75,
    94, 101, 141, 160, 179, 186
Middlesex County (Virginia), 95, 96,
    97, 98, 99, 136, 143
Mill Branch, 182
Mill Dam, 176
Mill Land, 176
Mill Path, 85, 130
Mill Pond, 100, 149
Mill Race, 133
Mill Road, 89
Mill Run, 47, 149
Miller, Francis, 155; James, 157, 170;
    John, 29, 47, 187, 188; Simon,
    23, 159, 160; Symon, 47; W.,
    112, 135, 140, 169, 175, 184;
    William, 47, 80, 183
Mills, James, 131, 178
Mine Road, 72, 106, 110, 124, 156,
    161, 168, 172
Mine Run, 14
Mine Tract, 85
Minor, John, 29, 42, 43, 93, 107, 108,
    135, 145, 146, 147, 151, 152,
    154, 174; Thomas, 112, 113
Mitchel, John, 155
Mitchell, David, 167; John, 133, 135,
    157, 170, 181; Patrick, 157
Molton, James, 11
Moncure, John, 58

Moor, Colonel, 165; Harbin, 156;
     Robert, 151, 162, 183; Samuel,
     162
Moore, Augustine, 69, 94, 95, 112;
     Colonel, 69, 128; David, 45, 94;
     George, 69, 116, 122; Robert,
     163; Sarah, 45, 94; William, 37
Moore's Line, 11
Moreton, William, 18, 19, 20
Morison, Alexander, 189; Jean, 189;
     John, 189
Morris, Margret, 152; Thomas, 111,
     168
Morriss, Margret, 152; Thomas, 51,
     152
Morton, Elijah, 24; George, 120, 123,
     128; Jeremiah, 24; Joseph, 16,
     86, 123; William, 16, 18, 19, 20,
     21, 22, 23, 24, 25
Moseley, Edward, 8
Mosely, William, 8
Motley, Henery, 8
Motts, 170
Mott's Patent, 111, 171
Motts Run Tract, 157
Mountague, Ann, 155; Anthorit, 127;
     Clement, 155; Elizabeth, 93, 144;
     John, 74, 75, 119; Peter, 28, 38,
     45, 47, 66, 68, 80, 93, 120, 127,
     140, 144, 179, 185; Susanna,
     155; Thomas, 80
Mountain Run, 5
Mountain Run Bridge, 7
Muddy Run, 6
Mulatto, Betty, 91; Jemmy, 147; Will,
     147
Muse, Augustin, 153
Musick, Ambrose, 124; Ann, 110,
     155, 156; Ephraim, 144; George,
     89, 109, 110, 113, 114, 122, 127,
     142, 150, 155, 156, 158, 164, 172
Musick's Corner, 14

Musick's Land, 118, 129
Musick's Road, 124
MyCow, John, 62
Naked Mountain, 34
Nalle, John, 109
Nasaponix, 41, 124
Nassaponack Swamp, 86
Nassaponax, 25, 47, 50, 99
Nassaponax Creek, 171
Nassaponax Pattent, 131
Nassaponax Run, 171
Nassaponex, 131
Nassaponix, 40
Nassaponnax, 4, 124
Nassaponnax Swamp, 178
Nassaponock Swamp, 39
Neavill, Joseph, 48
Negro, Abigal, 163; Adain, 85; Alice,
     73; Amos, 73; Ampthill, 85;
     Amy, 85; Barbar, 135; Barber,
     135; Beck, 85; Ben, 64, 81, 85,
     183; Bess, 85, 183; Betty, 73, 85;
     Billy, 73, 85, 135; Blunt, 85;
     Bob, 85; Boson, 85, 138; Bridge,
     85; Bristoll, 85; Calais, 85; Cary,
     85; Castor, 85; Cato, 147; Cedar,
     85; Cesar, 147; Charles, 73, 85;
     Christian, 73; Conrie, 85; Corah,
     70; Cupid, 91; Damon, 85;
     Daniel, 147; Daniell, 85; Daphne,
     85, 147; Dick, 73, 85, 135; Dido,
     85; Dilla, 183; Dinah, 85, 118;
     Docter, 135; Doll, 85; Dover, 85;
     Duke, 85; Edie, 85; Fender, 163;
     Flora, 85; Frank, 85; George, 85;
     Grace, 73, 163; Hannah, 73, 183;
     Harry, 73, 147, 183; Hazard, 85;
     Hector, 85; Hellen, 12; Hercules,
     12; Hester, 85; Humphry, 73, 85;
     Isaac, 85; Jack, 73, 118; Jamey,
     70; Jenny, 73, 135; Jo, 73; Joan,
     73; Joe, 85; John, 70; Jolly, 85;

Jonnah, 66; Juba, 147; Judey, 135; Judie, 85; Judy, 73, 85, 147; Juno, 85, 161; Kate, 58, 70, 73; Kate Lawrel, 85; Lancaster, 91; Lawrence, 85; Leo, 85; London, 85, 91; Lucy, 73, 170; Major, 73; Manzor, 85; Marcus, 85; Maria, 91, 147; Matt, 147; Milley, 170; Mingo, 73, 85, 161; Moll, 64, 81, 147; Molly, 73; Mowyarrow, 85; Nan, 161, 168; Nanny, 73; Ned, 73, 85, 146; Nell, 73; Ness, 85; Noah, 85; Obay, 66; Oliver, 85; Pallas, 85; Paris, 85; Parish, 85; Pat, 161; Patt, 73; Patty, 85; Paulo, 85; Pedro, 85; Pender, 73; Peter, 73, 85, 147; Phil, 73; Piero, 85; Polly, 85; Pompey, 85; Pompy, 91; Potomack Tom, 73; Price, 146; Prince, 85, 147; Rachel, 73; Robin, 66, 73; Roger, 73; Rose, 70, 85; Sam, 73, 85; Sambo, 73, 85; Sarah, 73, 85, 147; Scipio, 85; Sevellah, 85; Sharper, 85; Shirbridge, 85; Simon, 85; Sorrell, 85; Stran, 85; Sue, 85; Tamerlane, 85; Toby, 147, 185; Tody, 73; Tom, 73, 85; Toney, 85; Travan, 135; True Love, 70; Truelove, 91; Venus, 73, 91; Will, 73, 85, 161; Yarrico, 85

Nelson, James, 52

Nessaponack, 29

Nessaponack Run, 29

New Land Tract, 163

New Mine Bank Road, 122, 150

Newpost, VA, 125

Nicholas, John, 150

Nix, Elizabeth, 180; George, 48, 49, 54, 137, 180; Joseph, 175

Norfolk, 175, 191

Norman, Isaac, 3

North America, 125

North Britain, 187, 189

North Carolina, 163

North Fork, 29, 86, 112, 136, 153, 157, 165, 166, 172

North Fork Branch, 38

North Fork Swamp, 152

North Hampton County, NC, 117

North River, 9

Northanna, 4, 12, 30, 42, 71, 76, 86, 95, 112, 151

Northanna River, 10, 25, 87

Northfolk, 145

Northumberland County (Virginia), 61, 86, 87, 130, 173

Nussaponock Swamp, 8

Ny River, 40, 99, 124

Octonia, 178

Octuana, 25

Octuna Land, 2

Orange County (Virginia), 31, 43, 45, 46, 48, 49, 56, 59, 60, 64, 65, 66, 91, 100, 102, 103, 109, 111, 114, 116, 120, 121, 126, 130, 141, 147, 148, 150, 151, 152, 153, 156, 160, 162, 164, 165, 169, 174, 177, 180, 185, 192

Otterdam Swamp, 48

Over, 185

Over Wharton Parish, 126

Owen, Augustine, 38, 39, 136, 152

Pagan, John, 64, 67

Page, Man, 57

Pagett, Edmund, 3, 31

Pain, Frances, 141; John, 132, 141, 159, 170

Paine, Barnet, 59, 60, 101; Barnett, 56; Bernard, 101, 176; Bernat, 101; Bernerd, 101; John, 77; William, 59, 60

Pains Swamp, 119

Pamunkey River, 44, 82, 113, 127, 128, 134, 144
Pamunkey Road, 146, 177
Pamunkey Rowlling Road, 173
Pamunky River, 76
Pannel, Sarah, 32; William, 32, 33
Pappan Run, 151
Pappau Run, 84
Pappaw Run, 7, 11
Parish, John, 179
Parker, Alexander, 144
Parkes, John, 32; Margaret, 32
Parks, John, 32, 109
Parmunkey River, 104
Parrish, Joel, 121, 158, 164; John, 47, 50, 70, 88, 89, 93, 115, 116, 135, 138, 139, 143, 148, 149, 150
Parrish's Land, 157
Pattey, John, 18, 19, 20, 22, 24; Thomas, 20, 22, 34
Patty, John, 22; Thomas, 33
Paupen Swamp, 145
Payton, John, 192
Pen, George, 2, 60; John, 60; Joseph, 61, 62, 72, 75, 85, 92, 106
Pendleton, E., 94; Edmund, 100; H., 121, 126; Henry, 95, 99, 106, 109, 115, 121, 133, 173; J., 157; James, 109; Martha, 173
Penn, George, 16, 153; John, 153; Moses, 153
Pen's Line, 146
Perkins, Elisha, 16; Margery, 16
Permunkey River, 165
Peterson, Joseph, 64, 142, 151, 158, 165, 191
Petsworth Parish, 111, 186, 192
Pettey, Christopher, 21; John, 22; Katharine, 21; Thomas, 22
Petty, John, 22; Rebecca, 22; Thomas, 21
Peyton, Valentine, 176

Phillips, Catharine, 5; David, 13; Katherine, 151, 152; Richard, 4, 5, 10, 15, 93, 95, 127, 133, 148, 151, 152, 157, 159, 168, 170, 172, 175, 180, 182; William, 2, 3, 13, 171
Pickering, Richard, 55, 56
Picket, William, 115
Pidgeon River, 82
Pigg, Ann, 42; Charles, 101; Charles F., 27; Charles Filkes, 118; Charles Filks, 56, 57, 59, 85, 101, 102, 115, 118, 119; Edward, 27, 42, 47, 56, 59, 77, 85, 114, 116, 163; Henry, 27, 47; Jane, 118; Mr., 85; Paul, 160; Sarah, 102, 115, 116, 118
Pike Run, 94, 109, 148
Piney Branch, 51
Pitcher, Thomas, 24
Plentifull, 14, 104, 134
Plentifull Run, 89
Po River, 31, 39, 51, 57, 65, 66, 68, 80, 92, 112, 117, 122, 127, 136, 139, 148, 162, 163, 167, 179
Pocoson, 184
Poe, Samuel, 94
Poe River, 172
Poison Field, 100, 153
Pollard, Richard, 176; William, 98, 130
Pool, George, 50
Poole, Elizabeth, 50; George, 50
Popaw Run, 182
Poplar Swamp, 20
Porteus, James, 9, 42, 78
Potter, Myles, 42; William, 134
Powell, Benjamin, 13, 14
Power, William, 85
Poyson Field, 1, 102, 124, 143
Poyson Fields, 32
Prestwood, Thomas, 130

Prewett, William, 132, 133, 166
Prewit, William, 94, 133
Prewitt, Daniel, 173
Price, Edward, 54, 83, 123
Prince, John, 134
Prince William County (Virginia), 8,
    9, 16, 17, 64, 67, 68, 76, 99, 113,
    114, 171
Princess Ann(e) Street, 26, 35, 47, 48,
    59, 67, 72, 75, 78, 79, 81, 88, 92,
    98, 101, 110, 111, 118, 143, 147,
    150, 167, 180
Pritchett, Ann, 146; James, 146;
    Thomas, 112
Prockter, George, 36, 37, 49, 51, 52;
    John, 36, 37, 49, 51, 52, 116;
    Margaret, 49; Sarah, 51, 52;
    William, 116
Procter, George, 38, 83; John, 132
Prosser's Line, 143
Pruess, William, 15
Pruet, William, 2, 63
Pruett, William, 2
Pruit, Daniel, 7, 8, 151; William, 67,
    100, 169
Public Warehouses, 187
Publick Branch, 116
Publick Warehouse, 184
Publick Warehouses, 95
Pulliam, Benjamin, 161; Elizabeth,
    128, 161, 162; Joseph, 161;
    Patterson, 118, 128, 130, 169,
    178; Pattison, 161, 162; Thomas,
    13, 34, 35, 118, 146
Punch Branch, 165, 166
Purvise's Line, 1
Pye Island, 23
Quakers Run, 13
Quarles, John, 18, 29, 171; Roger, 4,
    5, 17
Quarrell, John, 47
Quinney, William, 185

Raccoon Branch, 33
Raccoon Swamp, 26, 99
Rains, Henry, 143, 164; Mr., 137
Rallings, James, 55, 56, 165
Ramsey, Daniel, 80
Randall, Nicholas, 110, 122, 150
Randell, John, 34
Randolph, Beverley, 154; Margaret,
    124; Margett, 169; Nicholas, 110,
    124
Rapadam River, 20
Rapidanne River, 18, 21, 22, 23, 24,
    32, 33, 34
Rappahannock River, 6, 9, 16, 23, 36,
    40, 49, 50, 57, 67, 102, 105, 150,
    170, 188
Rappahanock River, 4, 23, 185, 187
Rappidanne River, 19
Rawlins, James, 87
Rawllings, James, 165, 166
Ray, John, 153; Joseph, 142
Read, Adam, 54, 143; John, 3;
    William, 115
Reaves, Henry, 127
Red, James, 124; John, 11; Joseph,
    124; Mary, 11; Thomas, 41, 124
Redd, Beth, 175; Bettey, 175; Betty,
    177; James, 124, 175, 177; John,
    11; Joseph, 99, 124, 162, 175,
    177; Mary, 11; Thomas, 177
Reeves, George, 67, 68; Henry, 42;
    Joseph, 68; Kerenhappuck, 134;
    Thomas, 68, 95
Reeves' Line, 16
Reid, Adam, 143; William, 67, 83,
    115, 120
Reins, Henry, 48
Reynolds, Joseph, 134
Rhodes, Anthony, 12, 25
Rice, Henry, 45, 46; Margeret, 46;
    William, 7, 8

Richards, Philemon, 63; Phillemon, 62; William Bird, 132
Richardson, Sarah, 38; William, 38
Richason, William, 28, 60, 185
Richerson, William, 28, 38, 60, 93, 119, 121, 138, 172
Richmond County (Virginia), 5, 16, 54, 55, 143, 150
Rieves, Henry, 53
Ritchie, Archibald, 187, 188; Samuel, 156, 187, 188
Robenson, John, 192
Roberts, Joseph, 58, 122, 131, 132, 150, 158; Susanna, 131; Susannah, 132
Robert's Land, 157
Robertson, Alexander, 189
Robins, Charles, 183
Robinson, Benjamin, 31, 163; Colonel, 117, 126, 148, 153; Duncan, 8; John, 45, 63, 92, 94, 101, 139, 140, 145, 167, 178; Major, 50; Thomas, 30, 41, 44; W., 28, 29, 69, 85, 148, 161; William, 81, 84, 94, 102, 107, 108, 151
Robinson River, 4, 13
Robinson Run, 46, 129, 142, 145, 164, 165
Robinsons Branch, 28
Robinson's Line, 46, 132, 141
Robinsons Run, 44, 94
Robinsons Swamp, 46, 71
Rockey Branch, 34
Rodger, Gavin, 187
Roger, Gavin, 187, 188
Rogers, Abraham, 27, 47, 59, 111, 112, 114, 159, 179, 180; Barbary, 111, 112, 159, 179, 180; Barbra, 111; Frances, 77; George, 179; Henery, 64, 65; Henry, 66; John, 27, 47, 71, 77, 141, 186; Peter, 27, 47, 56, 77, 159; William, 159
Rogers' Mill, 27, 179
Rolfe, William, 129
Rootes, Philip, 97, 111
Roots, Phillip, 157
Rootts, Phillip, 157
Rose, Robert, 155
Ross, Andrew, 175; Robert, 85
Rosse, Andrew, 51
Rove, John, 120
Rowzees Neck, 8
Roy, David, 101; Elizabeth, 83; James, 8, 9, 25, 83, 123; Mungo, 159; Thomas, 111
Royston, Ann, 187, 192; Anne, 186; John, 36, 54, 123, 140, 155, 157, 190; Richard Wiatt, 192; Richard Wyatt, 186, 187
Royston's Line, 16
Roystons Warehouses, 187
Rucker, John, 5, 6, 49, 150; William, 5, 6
Rush, Amey, 4; Benjamin, 4; Mary, 13; William, 4, 13
Russel, Joseph, 154
Russell, Petter, 6; W., 1, 110, 161, 177; William, 3
St. Ann Parish, 3, 159
St. Anne Parish, 54, 55, 83, 154
St. Anns Parish, 8, 95, 127
St. Drisdale Parish, 72
St. George Parish, 1, 2, 3, 4, 6, 7, 11, 12, 14, 15, 18, 25, 26, 27, 28, 29, 30, 31, 32, 34, 36, 37, 38, 39, 40, 41, 42, 43, 44, 45, 46, 48, 49, 51, 52, 53, 55, 56, 57, 58, 59, 60, 61, 62, 63, 64, 66, 67, 68, 69, 71, 72, 74, 76, 77, 80, 82, 83, 84, 85, 86, 87, 89, 90, 91, 92, 93, 94, 95, 98, 99, 100, 101, 103, 104, 105, 106, 108, 109, 110, 111, 112, 113,

114, 115, 116, 117, 118, 119,
120, 121, 122, 123, 124, 125,
126, 127, 128, 129, 130, 131,
132, 133, 134, 136, 137, 138,
139, 140, 141, 144, 145, 146,
147, 151, 152, 153, 154, 155,
156, 157, 158, 159, 160, 163,
164, 165, 168, 169, 172, 173,
175, 178, 179, 182, 183, 186,
189, 192
St. Johns Parish, 4, 25, 56, 95, 127,
128
St. Margarets (Margret, Margrits,
etc.) Parish, 12, 18, 25, 35, 42,
46, 58, 77, 117, 122, 123, 124,
128, 142, 153, 157, 158, 159, 171
St. Maries Parish, 17, 40
St. Mark Parish, 3, 5, 6, 11, 15, 16,
17, 19, 20, 22, 24, 31, 32, 33, 34,
49, 59, 60, 100, 120, 174, 178
St. Marks Parish, 1, 2, 4, 6, 8, 12, 13,
18, 25, 45, 46, 48, 109, 126, 185
St. Martin Parish, 42
St. Martins Parish, 77, 145
St. Marys Parish, 29, 83
St. Pauls Parish, 36
St. Peter Parish, 116
St. Stephen Parish, 34, 112
St. Stephens Parish, 25, 56, 57, 61,
69, 80, 89, 94, 101, 114, 118,
119, 122, 123, 128
St. Stevens Parish, 62
St. Thomas' Parish, 153
St. Thomas Parish, 111, 114, 130,
147, 148, 165, 169, 192
Sale, Anthony, 127; Cornelius, 127;
James, 127
Sallomon, William, 83
Salman, Thomas, 126
Salmon, Mary, 68; Thomas, 57, 68,
148; William, 68
Salt Pond, 37, 163

Samm, James, 159
Samms, Anne, 138; James, 34, 53,
138, 141, 148; Mary, 132, 138,
148; William, 132, 138, 148
Sams, Anne, 138; James, 138;
William, 138, 141
Samuell, James, 55
Sandage, William, 131
Sanders, Catey, 85, 86, 108; Hugh,
76, 85, 86, 92, 93, 108, 127, 129,
154, 164; John, 168; John Winill,
77; John Wynill, 117, 124;
Katey, 92; Mary, 106; Nathanal,
117; Nathanel, 117; Nathaniel,
57, 61, 76, 85, 92, 117; Philip,
105, 106, 126, 140; Phillip, 72,
83; Robin, 168; Thomas, 85, 126
Sander's Line, 75
Sandidge, Ann, 136; Anne, 136;
William, 64, 136
Sandige, Ann, 155; Anne, 156;
William, 25, 128, 142, 155, 157
Sandys, Cuthbert, 122
Sartin, Anna, 105, 119; John, 105,
110, 119, 124, 126, 157; Mary,
30; Thomas, 30, 64, 105, 119
Sartin's Line, 158
Sartin's Patent, 136
Saunders, Hugh, 138
Scott, Alexander, 149, 156; Anthony,
3; Isaac, 172; Thomas, 150, 159
Sculthorpe, Anthony, 23
Seales, Aniclina, 80
Searcy, William, 133, 145
Seartin, Thomas, 68
Searton, Thomas, 68
Seaton, George, 118, 127, 149; Mr.,
69
Seayres, Robert, 115
Semmes, Ignatius, 58

Sertain, Anna, 105; John, 105, 122; Mary, 68; Thomas, 51, 68, 121, 122, 158
Seward, Nicholas, 163, 169
Sexton, John, 3
Seyres, John, 123
Shackelford, Elizabeth, 146; James, 146
Shackleford, James, 102
Shakelford, Elizabeth, 177; James, 168, 177; Mary, 168; Richard, 168
Sharp, Edward, 6; Elias, 36, 37, 48, 49, 52; Margaret, 49; Richard, 6; Stephen, 8, 86, 131
Sharpe, Elias, 49; Lincefeild, 111; Linefield, 111, 182
Shelton, Thomas, 122, 150
Shepherd, George, 169, 191; Robert, 191
Sheppard, George, 64, 144, 165
Shepperd, Elizabeth Mary Angelike, 169
Ship, Elizabeth, 111, 115; Margret, 141; Richard, 88, 115; Thomas, 39, 88, 111, 115
Shipp, Richard, 88, 144; Thomas, 39, 88
Shurley, John, 132, 133; Thomas, 121
Shurly, John, 173
Silverton Hill, 190
Simms, Peter, 58; Rebecca, 19; Thomas, 19, 20
Simpson, John, 167
Sims, Thomas, 18, 19, 20, 21, 22, 24
Sisson, Bryan, 33, 34
Skinker, Samuel, 105
Skinner, John, 168; Mical, 168; Michael, 168
Slaughter, Francis, 1; Mary, 44; Robert, 1, 13, 14, 43, 44, 121,

186; Thomas, 16, 17, 25, 43, 44, 119, 147, 171
Sleet, James, 11
Smethers, William, 117
Smith, Augustine, 1, 3, 16, 17, 25, 39, 54, 60, 102, 111, 123, 127, 153, 171; Charles, 32, 86; Christopher, 30, 71, 128; Elias, 20, 24, 25; Elizabeth, 15, 86, 112, 152; Francis, 40, 56, 60, 138, 146; George, 86, 112, 114; Jeremiah, 179; John, 2, 11, 12, 15, 17, 63, 67, 68, 74, 84, 94, 100, 133, 151, 169, 182, 184; Lawrance, 131, 178; Lawrence, 8, 86, 147; Margaret, 12, 63, 94; Maurice, 120, 132; Mr., 71; Oswald, 151, 152; Phebe, 152; Samuel, 43, 154; Thomas, 16, 17, 67, 68; Thomas Ballard, 10, 15, 133; William, 10, 11, 12, 24, 51, 129, 133, 151, 173
Smither, Robert, 124; William, 47, 124, 179
Smith's Line, 36, 88, 115, 142, 151
Snal, John, 51, 66; Philadelphia, 66
Snale, John, 28, 64
Snales Bridge, 28
Snales Road, 62
Snall, John, 51, 65, 127
Snall Bridge, 62
Snead, Charles, 172
Sneles, John, 80
Snell, John, 27, 28, 57, 64, 65, 68
Sollemon, William, 80
Solman, Thomas, 126
Solmon, Thomas, 64; William, 127
Solomon, William, 65
Sophia Street, 26, 49, 50, 61, 78, 79, 87, 91, 95, 97, 98, 150, 167, 181, 184
South Branch, 111

South Farnham Parish, 67, 68
South Fork, 153, 165, 166
South Po, 139
South River, 15, 17, 29, 94, 153, 165, 166, 172
Southfarnham Parish, 133, 134, 154, 192
Spallding, John, 153
Sparkes, Henery, 39, 48, 49
Sparks, Henry, 165; James, 154; Thomas, 46
Spencehead, Alexander, 124, 125
Spencer, William, 43, 76
Spoe, Charles, 33, 34
Spooner, John, 163
Spotswood, Alexander, 16, 18, 19, 20, 21, 22, 23, 24, 25, 32, 33, 34, 42, 85, 167; Butler, 85; Colonel, 103, 153; John, 180, 181
Spotswood's Corner, 192
Spotswood's Land, 139
Spotsylvania Tract, 18, 19, 20, 21, 22, 24, 32, 34
Spring Branch, 33, 133, 135, 138, 143, 168, 184
Stafford County (Virginia), 9, 10, 36, 37, 39, 73, 95, 100, 126, 137, 184, 185
Staige, Reverend Mr., 77, 96
Staines, Thomas, 9
Stapp, Joseph, 3
Stears, Abel, 138, 148; Richard, 148
Stephens, Adam, 170; William, 82, 174, 183
Stevans, James, 141; Jeremiah, 141
Stevens, Alice, 131; Charles, 14, 58; James, 34, 62, 100, 108, 131, 148, 165; Jeremiah, 100, 108, 148; Joseph, 69, 116, 170, 171; Mary, 100, 108; Mumford, 172; William, 50
Stevenson, William, 58

Stevens's Corner, 138
Steward, John, 49; Joseph, 126, 184
Stewart, Charles, 6, 7, 168; James, 31, 37
Stodghill, Daniel, 16
Stone, Eusebins, 153
Stonehaven, 189
Stonehouse, 78
Stoney Branch, 149
Stoney Lick Run, 160
Stony Run, 85, 116, 119, 151, 163
Strange, Casar, 115
Street, Anthony, 95, 173, 183
Strother, Anthony, 4, 9, 36, 40, 67, 118, 134, 158, 168, 171, 176, 181; James, 49; Joseph, 105; William, 49, 51, 168
Strutton Major Parish, 92, 139
Stuart, Robert, 11
Stubbelfield, John, 17, 18
Stubblefeild, Catharine, 134; Catherine, 104; George, 104, 114, 123, 124, 133, 134; Robert, 7, 17, 121, 151
Stubblefield, Ann, 166; Anne, 7, 8; George, 100, 186; John, 52; John J., 11; Richard, 153; Robert, 2, 8, 29, 67, 84, 151, 153, 165, 166, 169; Thomas, 90, 159
Stubelfield, John, 18
Stureman, Ignatious, 44, 108
Sutherland, John, 171
Sutten, John, 48
Sutton, Amey, 53, 141; Elizabeth, 183; John, 103, 111, 117, 179; William, 180
Ta River, 41, 61, 94, 116, 130, 133, 149, 151, 176, 178, 186
Tabb, Vincent, 48
Talbert, John, 2, 53, 62, 67, 100, 141, 148; Margaret, 67; Margret, 141
Talbert's Line, 148

Talburt, John, 141; Margret, 141
Taliaferro, Charles, 16, 17, 147, 157,
    170, 171; Francis, 43, 44, 57,
    147, 163; J., 31; James, 10, 35;
    John, 26, 28, 38, 42, 47, 51, 54,
    63, 66, 67, 73, 75, 81, 87, 88, 97,
    98, 120; Keamp, 17; Kemp, 171;
    Mary, 170; Richard, 147; Robert,
    131, 147, 178
Taliferro, John, 47
Talliaferro, John, 28; William, 156
Tandy, Roger, 15, 16, 18, 82, 154,
    173; Sarah, 82
Tapp, Christian, 48, 49; Elizabeth, 48,
    76, 169; Vincent, 39, 76, 169;
    William, 39, 48, 49
Tappahannock, 178
Tappahanock, 156
Tay River, 42, 122, 123
Tayloe, John, 143
Taylor, Colonel, 131; Erasmus, 15;
    George, 15, 111, 150, 176;
    James, 30, 35, 64, 68, 69, 70, 71,
    105, 112, 119, 121, 122, 128,
    131, 132, 144, 154, 158, 165,
    166; John, 35, 128; Martisha,
    128, 132; Thomas, 22; William,
    89; Zacharias, 16; Zachary, 2, 5,
    12, 13, 14
Temple, Captain, 135; Hannah, 128;
    Joseph, 128, 132, 145; William,
    128
Tennant, Dorothy, 115; John, 35
Tennent, John, 42, 47, 72, 111
Terrey, James, 51
Terry, James, 51, 68, 121; Margaret,
    51
Terrys Run, 76, 86, 112, 130
Tery, James, 158
Terys Run, 152
Thacker, Chisly Corbin, 47

Thomas, Joseph, 14, 15, 25, 30, 38,
    68, 71, 81; Joshua, 48, 54, 76,
    119, 126; Mr., 71; Oen, 138;
    Owen, 93, 138, 139, 144, 146,
    159, 172; Robert, 60; Rowland,
    30, 71, 76, 87, 154; Sarah, 71, 81
Thompson, John, 156
Thomson, Andrew, 189; John, 161,
    189; William, 149, 182
Thornton, Anthony, 36, 39, 40, 48,
    76, 100, 131, 132, 137, 169;
    Antony, 36; Elizabeth, 105;
    Frances, 73; Francis, 1, 4, 8, 10,
    16, 17, 25, 36, 40, 43, 44, 47, 48,
    53, 66, 67, 72, 73, 76, 77, 78, 79,
    80, 81, 86, 87, 88, 95, 97, 98,
    105, 111, 116, 123, 125, 127,
    131, 132, 137, 147, 168, 169,
    171, 172, 185; John, 40, 71, 95,
    96, 97, 98, 99, 101, 110, 115,
    125, 130, 135, 172; Luke, 22, 33,
    34; Mary, 48; Rowland, 40;
    Thomas, 96; Wenifred, 39;
    William, 40, 54, 123; Winifred,
    48, 137; Winnifred, 39
Thruston, Captain, 116; John, 162;
    Sarah, 162
Thurston, Ann, 141, 142; John, 141,
    142
Tilly, Lazarus, 11, 45
Tirrey, James, 51
Todd, Mark, 12; Richard, 118, 119,
    143, 154; Robert, 175; Thomas,
    12, 118, 119, 143; William, 118,
    143, 159
Tolbert's Line, 138
Tolefferro, John, 28
Tomkins, Francis, 192; Thomas, 71
Tompkins, Christopher, 142; Giles,
    142
Trail, George, 189
Trew, Martin, 54

Trible, George, 83, 164
True, John, 32; Margaret, 173;
    Martin, 32, 52, 53, 125, 164, 178;
    Robert, 173
Trustee, Elizabeth, 155; John, 26, 99;
    William, 155
Trusty, John, 44, 171; Mr., 142
Tub Lick Branch, 116
Tunstall, R., 177; Richard, 178
Tureman, Ignatious, 57, 106, 138;
    Ignatus, 173
Turman, Ignatious, 72, 92, 126;
    Ignatius, 57, 61, 85, 109, 129
Turner, Catharine, 76; Catherine, 87;
    Harry, 61; James, 3; Katherine,
    87; Kerehappuck, 3; Mary, 170;
    Robert, 2, 9, 13, 25, 30, 36, 39,
    44, 71, 76, 87; T., 31, 147, 150;
    Thomas, 57, 58, 71, 150, 160,
    170, 189
Turnley, Francis, 86, 175
Tutt, Richard, 38, 96, 115, 119, 132,
    147, 175, 180, 181, 186
Tyler, Francis, 134
Tyre, John, 11, 63, 100, 182; William,
    11, 12
Tyre's Corner, 84
Tyre's Line, 151
Urbanna, 143
Valian, Charles, 170
Vass, Philip Vincent, 69, 93, 106,
    149, 173
Vaughan, Cornelius, 44, 175;
    Frances, 175; Martin, 44
Vawter, B., 8
Venable, Joseph, 154
Vennable, Joseph, 154
Vicaris Island, 40
Waggener, John, 168, 173, 183;
    Samuel, 183
Waggon Road, 146
Waggoner, James, 134; Samuel, 133

Walden, John, 51
Walding, William, 86
Walker, John, 74, 109, 140; Richard,
    37; Thomas, 150
Walker's Line, 148, 163
Wallace, David, 189; Patience, 189
Waller, Agnes, 102; B., 29;
    Benjamin, 29, 99, 189; Edmond,
    44, 145; Edmund, 26, 30, 35, 44,
    51, 52, 53, 56, 59, 60, 61, 63, 64,
    65, 67, 68, 74, 75, 81, 82, 83, 87,
    88, 89, 92, 93, 94, 95, 98, 99,
    104, 105, 106, 107, 108, 109,
    110, 111, 112, 113, 114, 115,
    116, 117, 118, 119, 120, 121,
    122, 123, 124, 125, 126, 127,
    128, 129, 131, 132, 133, 134,
    135, 136, 137, 138, 139, 140,
    142, 143, 144, 145, 146, 147,
    148, 149, 150, 151, 152, 153,
    154, 155, 156, 157, 158, 159,
    160, 161, 162, 163, 164, 165,
    166, 167, 168, 169, 171, 172,
    174, 175, 177, 178, 180, 181,
    182, 184, 186, 187, 188, 189,
    190, 191, 192; John, 1, 2, 3, 4, 5,
    6, 7, 8, 10, 11, 12, 13, 14, 15, 16,
    17, 18, 19, 20, 22, 23, 24, 25, 26,
    27, 28, 29, 30, 31, 32, 35, 36, 37,
    38, 39, 40, 41, 42, 43, 44, 45, 46,
    47, 48, 49, 50, 51, 52, 53, 54, 55,
    56, 57, 58, 59, 60, 61, 62, 63, 64,
    65, 66, 67, 68, 69, 70, 71, 72, 73,
    74, 75, 76, 77, 78, 79, 80, 81, 83,
    84, 85, 86, 87, 88, 89, 90, 92, 93,
    94, 95, 96, 97, 99, 100, 101, 102,
    103, 104, 105, 107, 108, 110,
    111, 119, 132, 142, 145, 146,
    147, 150, 151, 152, 166, 168,
    171, 189; Mary, 32, 89, 106, 107,
    108, 124, 126, 144, 156, 159,
    189; Pr, 26; Thomas, 4, 5;

William, 2, 4, 5, 10, 11, 12, 15, 25, 26, 28, 29, 30, 31, 32, 34, 35, 36, 39, 40, 41, 42, 44, 45, 49, 51, 53, 54, 71, 76, 82, 94, 96, 118, 124, 132, 133, 134, 135, 137, 141, 142, 157, 162, 163, 164, 166, 167, 170, 174, 176, 177, 178, 179, 181, 183, 186, 187, 188, 189; William Edmund, 189

Wallis, Humphrey, 165; Humphry, 166, 167

Ward, John, 42; Thomas, 185

Ware, Edward, 59, 94, 109, 113, 127; Lucy, 127

Warner, Augustine, 25

Warner's Line, 28, 45, 60, 93, 119, 143, 144, 146, 185

Warner's Pattent, 13

Warren, John, 77, 101, 124; Samuel, 77, 119; Thomas, 77, 124; William, 77

Warrin, Hackley, 180, 183, 186; Lancelot, 180, 183, 186; Margaret, 186; Thomas, 183

Washington, Ann, 125; August, 72, 73; Augustine, 97, 98, 110; John, 72; Lawrance, 125; Lawrence, 64, 119

Washington Parish, 168

Wasnonson Creek, 8

Watts, Arth, 57; David, 11; Thomas, 122

Waugh, Joseph, 23

Waugh's Branch, 23

Weaver, Peter, 13

Webb, John C., 165; John Crittenden, 166; John Crittendon, 165; William, 165

Webber, Henry, 41, 69

Welch, John, 126

Wells, Frances, 109; George, 165; John, 62, 63, 109

West, Catherine, 126; Francis, 82; Thomas, 72, 82, 83, 84, 88, 89, 106, 126, 140, 168

West Indies, 125

West Side Branch, 141

Westmoreland County, 168

Wetherall, John, 110

Wharton, Michael, 128; Samuel, 74; William, 74

Whealer, Mark, 29

Wheeler, John, 152; Mark, 29, 152, 160, 172, 174; Sarah, 172, 174

White, Chilion, 126; James, 126; Jeremiah, 144, 157, 166; John, 126; Mary, 157; Sarah, 126; Thomas, 126, 151, 155, 156

White Chappell Parish, 131

Whitehaven, 50, 86, 87

Whitehouse, Mary, 180

White's Line, 173

Wiat, Edward, 142, 145, 158; Francis, 158; Sukey, 164; Thomas, 142, 164; William, 142, 158

Wiatt, Ann, 141; Edward, 141, 142; Francis, 141, 142; Thomas, 141, 142; William, 141, 142

Wiglesworth, James, 172; John, 45, 53, 54, 83, 89, 99, 106, 107, 119, 136, 146, 158, 171; Mary, 99

Wilcock, George, 169; Mary, 169

Wilcocks, George, 162

Wilderness Run, 42

Wilkins, John, 26, 44, 53, 54, 99, 171; Mary, 54

Willcocks, George, 162

Willcox, George, 64

William Street, 26, 49, 78, 118, 143, 150

Williams, David, 2, 16; Elizabeth, 151, 175, 182; Francis, 15; James, 96; Jannet, 121; Jennet, 121; John, 84, 121, 151; Mary, 2,

111; Ralph, 7, 11, 63, 84, 121, 151, 182; Robert, 111; William, 67, 84, 91, 92, 143, 151, 184

Williamsburg, 163, 178

Williamsburgh, 99, 115, 161

Williamson, Elizabeth, 129; Henry, 133; John, 182; Robert, 46, 129; William, 187, 188

Willis, Francis, 87, 88, 95, 96, 97, 98, 99, 101, 184; Henry, 26, 31, 35, 36, 39, 42, 46, 48, 49, 50, 51, 53, 55, 56, 59, 60, 61, 64, 65, 66, 67, 69, 70, 72, 73, 74, 77, 78, 79, 81, 87, 88, 95, 96, 97, 98, 99, 101, 102, 103, 110, 111, 125, 130, 140, 150, 155, 157, 167, 170, 171, 181, 184, 190; Humphrey, 165; John, 78, 87, 141, 150, 167, 170, 171; Lewis, 70, 73, 78, 79; Mildred, 72, 73, 78, 79, 87, 125, 167; Nanny, 167, 170; Ralph, 74

Willson, George, 135; John, 5, 6, 16, 144

Wilsher, William, 169

Wilshire, Jack, 70; Lucy, 70

Wilson, George, 133

Winslow, Benjamin, 71, 75, 101, 127, 144, 149; Susannah, 149

Wisdom, Thomas, 165

Wise, Kezia, 68

Wolf Pit Branch, 29

Wolf Swamp, 30, 76, 87

Wood, Bartholomew, 76, 169; Charity, 39, 76, 169; Isabel, 18; John, 28, 29, 38, 58, 66, 93, 121, 185, 186; Thomas, 78, 79, 80, 88, 95, 96, 97, 98, 99, 101, 110; William, 18

Woodford, Anne, 147; William, 64, 147

Woodrof, David, 35

Woodroof, Anne, 35; Benjamin, 133, 135, 184; George, 42, 43, 87, 133, 156, 164, 165, 184; Jane, 42, 43, 133, 156, 164, 165, 184; William, 133

Woodroofe, Ann, 142; Benjamin, 135, 143, 145, 164; George, 15, 133, 135, 142, 143, 145, 173; Jane, 133, 135; Mary, 145; William, 133

Woodroofs Ordinary, 173

Woodward, Benjamin, 160, 161, 168; Mary, 168; W., 156

Woolf Swamp, 71

Woolfolk, Joseph, 35, 36, 69; Richard, 165, 166

Woolfolk's Line, 142

Woolfork, Joseph, 58

Woollfolk, Joseph, 35

Word, John, 98

Wright, Alexander, 135, 154, 158

Wyat, Edward, 151

Wyat's Line, 131, 155, 156, 157

Wyatt, Francis, 154; Sukey, 164; Thomas, 164; William, 154, 164, 165, 166

Wyatt's Line, 124, 158, 172

Wythe, George, 157

Yancy, Lewis Davis, 6

York, John, 27, 47, 77; Mary, 191

Young, Lenard, 174, 183; Leonard, 134

Younger, James, 166, 172

Zachary, John, 13, 14

Zachry, David, 14; James, 164; Thomas, 14

Heritage Books by Mary Marshall Brewer:

Abstracts of Administrations of Montgomery County, Pennsylvania, 1822–1850

Abstracts of Land Records of King George County, Virginia, 1752–1783

Abstracts of Land Records of Richmond County, Virginia, 1692–1704

Abstracts of the Wills of Montgomery County, Pennsylvania, 1824–1850

Early Union County, New Jersey Church Records, 1750–1800

Essex County, Virginia Land Records, 1752–1761

Essex County, Virginia Land Records, 1761–1772

Essex County, Virginia Land Records, 1772–1786

Kent County, Delaware Guardian Accounts: Aaron to Carty, 1752–1849

Kent County, Delaware Guardian Accounts: Caton to Edinfield, 1753–1849

Kent County, Delaware Guardian Accounts: Edmondson to Hopkins, 1744–1855

Kent County, Delaware Guardian Accounts: Houston to McBride, 1739–1856

Kent County, Delaware Guardian Accounts: McBride to Savin, 1739–1851

Kent County, Delaware Guardian Accounts: Savin to Truax, 1754–1852

Kent County, Delaware Guardian Accounts: Truitt to Young, 1755–1849

Kent County, Delaware Land Records, Volume 2: 1702–1722

Kent County, Delaware Land Records, Volume 3: 1723–1734

Kent County, Delaware Land Records, Volume 4: 1735–1743

Kent County, Delaware Land Records, Volume 5: 1742–1749

Kent County, Delaware Land Records, Volume 6: 1749–1756

Kent County, Delaware Land Records, Volume 7: 1756–1764

PDF: Kent County, Delaware Land Records, Volume 7: 1756–1764

Kent County, Delaware Land Records, Volume 8: 1764–1768

Kent County, Delaware Land Records, 1776–1783

Kent County, Delaware Land Records, 1782–1785

Kent County, Delaware Land Records, 1785–1789

Kent County, Delaware Land Records, 1788–1792

King George County, Virginia Court Orders, 1721–1724

King George County, Virginia Court Orders, 1724–1728

King George County, Virginia Court Orders, 1728–1731

King George County, Virginia Court Orders, 1731–1736

King George County, Virginia Court Orders, 1736–1740

King George County, Virginia Court Orders, 1740–1746

King George County, Virginia Court Orders, 1746–1751

King George County, Virginia Court Orders, 1751–1754

King George County, Virginia Court Orders, 1754–1756

Land Records of Sussex County, Delaware, 1681–1725

PDF: Land Records of Sussex County, Delaware, 1681–1725

Land Records of Sussex County, Delaware, 1753–1763

Land Records of Sussex County, Delaware, 1763–1769

*Land Records of Sussex County, Delaware: Various Dates:
1693–1698, 1715–1717, 1782–1792, 1802–1805*

Land Records of York County, Pennsylvania, Libers A and B, 1746–1764

Land Records of York County, Pennsylvania, Libers C and D, 1764–1771

Land Records of York County, Pennsylvania, Libers E and F, 1771–1775

Land Records of York County, Pennsylvania, Libers G and H, 1775–1793

New Castle County, Delaware Wills, 1800–1813

Northumberland County, Virginia: Deeds, Wills, Inventories, etc., 1737–1743

Northumberland County, Virginia: Deeds, Wills, Inventories, etc., 1743–1749

Probate Records of Kent County, Delaware, Volume 1: 1801–1812

Probate Records of Kent County, Delaware, Volume 2: 1812–1822

Probate Records of Kent County, Delaware, Volume 3: 1822–1833

Quaker Records of Cedar Creek Monthly Meeting: Virginia, 1739–1793

Spotsylvania County, Virginia Deed Books, 1722–1734

Spotsylvania County, Virginia Deed Books, 1734–1751

York County, Virginia Deeds, Orders, Wills, Etc., 1698–1700

York County, Virginia Deeds, Orders, Wills, Etc., 1700–1702

York County, Virginia Deeds, Orders, Wills, Etc., 1705–1706

York County, Virginia Deeds, Orders, Wills, Etc., 1714–1716

York County, Virginia Deeds, Orders, Wills, Etc., 1716–1718

York County, Virginia Deeds, Orders, Wills, Etc., 1718–1720

York County, Virginia Deeds, Orders, Wills, Etc., 1728–1732

York County, Virginia Land Records: 1694–1713

York County, Virginia Land Records: 1713–1729

York County, Virginia Land Records: 1729–1763

York County, Virginia Land Records: 1763–1777

York County, Virginia Wills, Inventories and Court Orders, 1702–1704

York County, Virginia Wills, Inventories and Court Orders, 1732–1737

York County, Virginia Wills, Inventories and Court Orders, 1737–1740

York County, Virginia Wills, Inventories and Court Orders, 1740–1743

York County, Virginia Wills, Inventories and Court Orders, 1743–1746

York County, Virginia Wills, Inventories and Court Orders, 1745–1759